Springer Series in Neuropsychology

Harry A. Whitaker, Series Editor

Springer Series in Neuropsychology

Harry A. Whitaker, Series Editor

Phonological Processes and Brain Mechanisms
H.A. Whitaker (Ed.)

Contemporary Reviews in Neuropsychology
H.A. Whitaker (Ed.)

Neuropsychological Studies of Nonfocal Brain Damage: Dementia and Trauma
H.A. Whitaker (Ed.)

Linguistic Analyses of Aphasic Language
W.U. Dressler and J.A. Stark (Eds.)

Synesthesia: A Union of the Senses
R.E. Cytowic

Discourse Ability and Brain Damage: Theoretical and Empirical Perspectives
Y. Joanette and H.H. Brownell (Eds.)

Morphology, Phonology, and Aphasia
J.-L. Nespoulous and P. Villiard (Eds.)

Cognitive Microgenesis: A Neuropsychological Perspective
R.E. Hanlon (Ed.)

Neuropsychology and the Law
J. Dywan, R.D. Kaplan, and F.J. Pirozzolo (Eds.)

Jane Dywan Ronald D. Kaplan
Francis J. Pirozzolo
Editors

Neuropsychology and the Law

With 11 Illustrations

Springer-Verlag
New York Berlin Heidelberg London
Paris Tokyo Hong Kong Barcelona

Jane Dywan, Ph.D.
Department of Psychology
Brock University
St. Catharines, Ontario
Canada L2S 3A1
and
Department of Psychiatry
Faculty of Health Sciences
McMaster University
Hamilton, Ontario
Canada L8N 3Z5

Ronald D. Kaplan, Ph.D.
Head, Psychology Services
McMaster University Medical Center
Chedoke-McMaster Hospitals
and
Department of Psychiatry
Faculty of Health Sciences
McMaster University
Hamilton, Ontario
Canada L8N 3Z5

Francis J. Pirozzolo
Department of Neurology
Baylor College of Medicine
Houston, TX 77030, USA

Neuropsychology and the law/Jane Dywan, Ronald D. Kaplan, Francis Pirozzolo, editors.
p. cm.—(Springer series in neuropsychology)
Includes bibliographical references.
ISBN-13: 978-1-4612-7798-9 e-ISBN-13: 978-1-4612-3106-6
DOI: 10.1007/978-1-4612-3106-6
1. Forensic neuropsychology. 2. Clinical neuropsychology.
I. Dywan, Jane. II. Kaplan, Ronald D. III. Pirozzolo, Francis J.
IV. Series.
[DNLM: 1. Head Injuries—diagnosis. 2. Jurisprudence.
3. Neurologic Examination. 4. Neuropsychological Tests. WL 141
N4937]
RA1147.5.N48 1991
614'.1—dc20
DNLM/DLC
for Library of Congress 91-4618

Printed on acid-free paper.

Softcover reprint of the hardcover 1st edition 1991

Typeset by Best-set Typesetter Ltd., Hong Kong.

9 8 7 6 5 4 3 2 1

ISBN-13: 978-1-4612-7798-9

Contents

Contributors

MAUREEN DENNIS, PH.D. Department of Psychology, The Hospital for Sick Children, Toronto, Ontario M5G 1X8, Canada

BRYAN D. FANTIE Neuropsychology Laboratory, Psychology Department, The American University, Washington, DC 20016, and Laboratory of Psychology and Psychopathology, National Institute of Mental Health, Bethesda, MD 20892, USA

DIANA FISHBEIN, PH.D. Department of Criminal Justice, University of Baltimore, Baltimore, MD 21201 and Department of Health and Human Services, National Institute on Drug Abuse, Addiction Research Center, Baltimore, MD 21224, USA

JANICE L. FUNK, PH.D. The Health Law Program, School of Public Health, Science Center, University of Texas Health Center, Houston, TX 77030, USA

JAMES B. GILLESPIE, JR., J.D. Licensed Practicing Attorney, Wilmington, NC 28401, USA

RAQUEL E. GUR, M.D., PH.D. Brain Behavior Laboratory and the Neuropsychiatry Program, Departments of Psychiatry and Neurology, University of Pennsylvania, Philadelphia, PA 19104, USA

RUBEN C. GUR, PH.D. Brain Behavior Laboratory and the Neuropsychiatry Program, Departments of Psychiatry and Neurology, University of Pennsylvania, Philadelphia, PA 19104, USA

BRYAN KOLB Psychology Department, University of Lethbridge, Lethbridge, Alberta, T1K 3M4, Canada

GABE J. MALETTA, PH.D., M.D. Director, Geriatric Research, Education and Clinical Center, V.A. Medical Center, Minneapolis, MN, and Departments of Psychiatry and Neurology, University of Minnesota Medical School, Minneapolis, MN 55455, USA

CATHERINE A. MATEER, PH.D. Good Samaritan Hospital, Puyallup, WA 98372, USA

ANTONIO E. PUENTE, PH.D. Department of Psychology, University of North Carolina at Wilmington, Wilmington, NC 28403, USA

JANET SMITH SHEPHERD, PH.D. Psychology Service, V.A. Medical Center, Iowa City, IA 52240, USA

ROBERT W. THATCHER, PH.D. Research Scientist, Severna Park, MD 21146, USA

NILS R. VARNEY, PH.D. Psychology Service, V.A. Medical Center, Iowa City, IA 52240, USA

ALISON MARY WEBER, PH.D. Presbyterian Brain Injury Programs, Presbyterian Hospital, Oklahoma City, OK 73104, USA

Introduction

We have had a number of interesting cases come to our attention over the years. The following are illustrative of some of the issues that can emerge at the interface between neuropsychology and the law. The first involved a patient suffering from a debilitating fear of heights. The fear seemed a reasonable consequence of the fact that he had been a passenger on a plane that crashed while attempting take off. Given that many of the passengers and crew died or were seriously injured, this man was quite fortunate. In fact, he could be said to have lived a charmed life. It had been just a year since he had been involved in an industrial accident in which he could have easily died. He came away from that accident with injuries to his legs and a concussion. That accident had also involved him falling from a considerable height so that there was some discussion among clinic staff about how well the patient's circumstances and symptoms fit the diagnostic category of "posttraumatic stress disorder."

Supportive psychotherapy was used as an aid in dealing with his recurring memories of the plane crash and systematic desensitization was quite successful in reducing the most disruptive consequences of his fear of heights. However, during the course of treatment, it became apparent that there were a number of problems that had not been addressed. For example, he had trouble controlling his emotions which proved very disruptive to family relationships. To his great consternation, he could no longer build or repair things around the house or fix his car. This was highly unusual since his friends had grown to rely to his mechanical skill and would call on him regularly for help with such tasks. Although music had always been a source of great enjoyment, he now found it to be a source of irritation. He felt lost and frustrated hanging around the house each day but seemed unable to negotiate a return to work. Amongst the clinic staff, there was talk of an instantiation of illness behaviour and knowing nods about pending litigation.

Neuropsychological evaluation was undertaken many months after the original referral, primarily due to the problems the patient seemed to be having with his memory. He would find dates and times written on pieces of paper in his pokcet and would phone the clinic to see if perhaps the dates and times referred to appointments that had been set up for him. The results of the assessment revealed a pattern of deficits common in those who have suffered traumatic brain injury.

A diagnosis of brain injury was not accepted during litigation hearings because the patient had not reported a loss of consciousness as a consequence of the airline disaster. The opinion of a neurologist and a psychiatrist was that permanent brain damage was not possible if there had been no loss of consciousness. The previous work-related accident was not seen as relevant because the debilitating cognitive symptoms were not evident until after the plane crash. The possibility of the cumulative nature of neural insult was not considered. The financial settlement finally awarded provided a clear indication of the court's low regard for disorders considered to be "neurotic". Thus, after having been in the work force from the age of 14, this middle aged man, with an excellent work record, had lost this home, suffered severe familial disruption and remained unemployed.

Cognitive rehabilitiation was not considered until very late in his course of treatment. There were few facilities providing such services, there was little reliable evidence that such approaches would be effective, and the patient could certainly not afford them even if they had been available. This case is typical of the ever growing number of individuals who suffer neurological damage and who are, for the most part, not adequately served by either the health care or the legal system. This case also raises the question of whether unconsciousness and amnesia are necessary conditions for brain dysfunction to occur. The larger question is whether one can always expect a tight relationship between such "predictor variables" and severity of deficits.

In another instance, a prominent middle aged gentleman was tried for hiring a man to kill his wife. He pleaded not guilty. It was subsequently revealed that the defendant had suffered a right hemisphere stroke, after which he had shown considerable evidence of a deterioration in judgement and in impulse control. However, the defendent in this case argued that there was nothing wrong with his cognitive functioning. The defendent denied any part in his wife's murder. He also denied that there was anything wrong with his ability to monitor his own cognitive and affective responses. The failure to appreciate one's own neurological deficits is not at all unusual in the clinical setting. It occurs frequently enough to be given a name—anosognosia. Nonetheless, this gentleman refused to allow his attorney to plead insanity. The defendent was clearly not insane. But what was he? Where did he fit within our legal and clinical definitions of competence? How does one argue for diminished responsibility when individuals exhibiting anosognosia insist that they are well and fully competent before the law?

This particular individual was found guilty and sentenced to prison with little consideration of the neurological sequelae of the stroke or the issue of what precisely would constitute an appropriate setting for his incarceration. In some U.S. jurisdictions he could have been executed. Since that time, he has remained in prison, developing rather incredible schemes for breaking out.

Another case demonstrates both the utility of current neuroscientific perspectives on sleep and the necessity of innovative categories in law. An Ontario court recently accepted the defense of "noninsane automatism" for a man who murdered his mother-in-law while sleepwalking. The sleepwalker could not be said to have an illness, nor a disease of mind or brain. Sleep was considered to be a natural phenomenon and while asleep the notion of conscious reflection is not a reasonable consideration.

Some Recurrent Themes

Many other cases could be presented in this context, each providing interesting problems from a neuropsychological and legal perspective: toxic torts, least restrictive alternatives in terms of competency in old age, and so on. As the behavioural neurosciences develop, there is a growing appreciation of the many ways the central nervous system can be disrupted. As well, problems associated with cognitive impairment are coming up more frequently. The rapid evacuation of head injured accident victims and the increase in specialized trauma centers has dramatically increased the survival rate of those who have sustained serious head injury. The increasing proportion of impaired elderly individuals in our population also make issues of competency with respect to financial and professional responsibility more frequently encountered. There is a growing awareness of the relatively high burden of neurocognitive impairment in the criminal population and the necessity of presenting this information to the court when considering the issue of intent in committing criminal acts and in sentencing. The careful analyses of dysfunctional behaviour reveal important distinctions that do not fit easily within traditional legal criteria. Thus, courts are coming to rely more heavily on the testimony of expert witnesses, many of whom represent the rapidly developing field of neuropsychology.

For this relationship to work well, it becomes important to know which kinds of questions should most usefully be asked by the courts and answered by the expert witness. There are standards developing within the field of neuropsychology that define what one should expect from a neuropsychological assessment. Nonetheless, individual differences, preexisting factors, and lack of well documented followup studies make prognoses difficult. The inconsistencies that can emerge between various measures can be seen as casting doubt on the validity of the data used as evidence. Further, we have insufficient knowledge as to the patterns of test performance most difficult or least likely to be deliberately produced through frank malingering, poor motivation and effort. Coping with clients motivated to induce us to believe they are impaired presents a clinical-scientific challenge that is only slowly being addressed. While such difficulties call for the cautious interpretation of data, equal caution is required so as not to jeopardize the legitimate claims of individuals whose welfare is often dependent on the results of the legal proceedings in which they become involved.

Who is our Audience?

This book is directed to those in the mental health and legal professions who are interested in the theoretical and practical problems that arise when the adequacy of neuropsychological function has a bearing on the outcome of legal decisions. The legal system has a long history of dealing with competency when a person's sanity or general mental capacity is questioned. It has developed concepts, definitions, and rules to guide the decision-making process. British law as early as the 14th century made the distinction between "idiocy" and "lunacy" and outlined separate provisions for how the estates of those so classified were to be maintained and for the rights of their heirs. A review of the historical development of the legal definitions of competence from a British, Canadian and American perspective makes for interesting reading and is available in the Weisstub report on mental competency (Ontario Ministry of Community and Social Services, 1990).

It is relatively recent that researchers in the neurological and behavioural sciences have focussed on issues of competence through the systematic study of brain-behaviour relationships. The data from research and clinical work are making evident the myriad ways in which cognitive processes can be disrupted as a result of neurological dysfunction due to damage, disease, or developmental abnormality. A more complete understanding of these disorders may require changes in the way that competence is defined before the law and the way it is assessed.

There have been recent attempts to bring order to the resolution of issues of competence both in the United States (see, for example, the American Bar Association's *Criminal Justice Mental Health Standards*, 1989) and Canada (see, for example, the Ontario Ministry of Social Services' *Enquiry on Mental Competency: Final Report*, 1990). Although mental health professionals were called upon in a consultatory role, these documents, quite rightly, take the legal perspective as their primary focus. The present volume explores some of the same territory, but from the neuropsychological perspective.

Our goal, however, was not to provide a "how to" book on forensic neuropsychological assessment. Developing skills appropriate to a sensitive neuropsychological examination requires adequate training and supervised experience. Developing the skills to plan the assessment and interpret the data requires a solid knowledge of brain-behaviour relationships in normal as well as impaired populations. Moreover, the optimal choice with respect to tests may change as research expands the number and sensitivity of our measures. Nonetheless, as the authors discuss their work, the principles with respect to what constitutes a thorough and competent assessment emerge.

Each author has added an important topic. These topics range from the nature of neuropsychological assessment to the development of technologically sophisticated computer imaging and electrophysiological measures to current efforts in cognitive rehabiliation. There are also chapters in which authors discuss issues that arise when working with special populations, such as children and older adults, or special problems, such as those involved in workers' compensation litigation.

The authors speak to the problems they have encountered, the models they have developed to deal with these problems and the issues that they see to be still in need of resolution. It is hoped that their conceptualizations will be of interest to neuropsychologists, neurologists, and psychiatrists who are faced with similar problems. We quite expect there will be some disagreement about some of the views expressed here. There are those who are of the strong opinion that neuropsychologists should have very limited influence in the legal forum. We believe, however, that discussion spawned by a multiplicity of views is important for the advancement of the field and should be encouraged. On a more practical note, we hope that physicians, lawyers, judges, health care administrators and other professionals involved in issues of client competence or disability will get a better understanding of neuropsychology with respect to what it offers, what they should expect when they seek consultation, and the kinds of questions that can most productively be asked. We see the dialogue between neuropsychology and the law as having just begun and believe that as it develops, both disciplines will have gained from their interaction with one another.

JANE DYWAN
RONALD KAPLAN
FRANCIS PIROZZOLO

References

Ontario Ministry of Community and Social Services (1990). *Enquiry on Mental competency: The final report*. Toronto: Ontario Publication Centre.

American Bar Association (1989). *ABA criminal justice mental health standards*. Washington, D.C.: American Bar Association Criminal Justice Standards Committee.

1 Neuropsychology and Its Applications to the Legal Forum

FRANCIS J. PIROZZOLO, JANICE FUNK, and JANE DYWAN

Everything should be made as simple as possible, but not simpler.

Albert Einstein

Basic mental competence is not only a requirement for regular daily functioning in society, it is a necessary prerequisite for participation within the legal system. The issue of competence arises in all aspects of legal proceedings. Individuals must be competent to execute wills, vote, marry, testify in court, or stand trail. Each of these competencies may be considered separately by the judicial system. Persons may be declared to be competent within a specific area and noncompetent within another. Thus, a person may be able to comprehend the nature and extent of his or her property and the consequences of making a will, while being unable to execute the living skills required for adequate management of their daily financial affairs. Competency, therefore, must be considered not only on a case-by-case basis, but also as separate domains within a single individual.

The question of legal competence occurs most often in connection with the question of competency to stand trial. The requirement that an accused individual must be competent in order to participate in the criminal process dates back to British common law and was codified by the 17th century (Melton, Petrilla, Poythress & Slobogen, 1987). Early English law required that a defendant enter a plea. When a defendant failed to comply with this requirement it became necessary to establish whether he was "mute by malice" or "mute by visitation of God." By the 18th century, the legal concept of competence had advanced to the point where any aspect of the criminal process, arraignment, trial, or punishment could be discontinued if the defendant were found to be "mad" (Roesch & Golding, 1980).

The common law standards for competence to stand trial were defined as: (a) the ability to cooperate with an attorney in order to assist in one's defense, (b) an understanding of the charges and the nature of procedures brought against him, and (c) comprehension of the consequences of those procedures. In the United States, the modern standards for the formal evaluation of competence to stand trial were established by the Supreme Court in Dusky v. United States (1960): "It is not enough for the district judge to find that the defendant is oriented to time and place and has some recollection of events, but that the test must be that he has sufficient present ability to consult with his lawyer with a reasonable degree of rational understanding and whether he has a rational as well as factual understanding of the proceedings against him" (p. 402). Unfortunately, the court in this two paragraph ruling did not establish what it considered acceptable procedures for meeting these criteria. Considerable subsequent discussion has focused on the definition of "reasonable degree of rational understanding," including how and when it is to be evaluated and by whom.

Mental Illness Versus Incompetency

The somewhat flexible and open-ended nature of the Dusky ruling and the lack of subsequent judicial clarification regarding its interpretation has led to a situation in which the evaluation of competence has come to be functionally synonymous with the presence or absence of mental illness or mental defect. The equation of psychosis with competence often has been challenged (Higgins v. McGraph, 1951), and various federal statutes make it clear that judgment of competency to stand trial is not to be totally synonymous with mental illness, that is, one defendant may be competent to stand trial, although mentally ill, while another may be incompetent to stand trial without the presence of mental illness. Nonetheless, confusion regarding this issue is common. Recent research data indicate that "the gross diagnostic categories of psychosis and mental retardation account for 83% of the determinations that the defendant was incompetent" (Roesch & Golding, 1980, p. 19).

The findings of Dusky were later expanded when Pate v. Robinson (1966) addressed the issue of who may question the competency of the defendant and when during the trial proceedings this question may be raised. The U.S. Supreme Court held that the question of competence *must* be raised if either the defense or prosecution raises a "bona fide doubt" regarding the accused's ability to comprehend the proceedings, or if the court itself finds substantial reason to doubt the defendant's capacity to understand and participate in his trial.

Competence Versus Responsibility

The question of a defendant's competence to stand trial is separate from the determination of criminal responsibility. The former addresses a person's mental and cognitive ability to understand the procedures and processes of his trial whereas the latter is concerned with the individual's state of mind during the commission of the crime that is the focus of the trial. The M'Naughten rule, established in England in the 1840s, remains the most prominent and popular judgement regarding responsibility for criminal actions. The M'Naughten rule maintains that "to establish a defense on the ground of insanity, it must clearly be proved that at the time of the committing of the act, the party accused was laboring under such a defective reason from disease of the mind as not to know the nature and quality of the act he was doing; or if he did know it, that he did not know what he was doing was wrong." Commonly known as the insanity defense, the M'Naughten rule is the primary statute for the establishment of criminal responsibility in slightly fewer than half of the states (Tancredi, 1975). In an additional 15 states, the M'Naughten rule is augmented by the "irresistible-impulse test," which states that an offender may know right from wrong, but because of an irresistible impulse be driven to commit a criminal act. (See Blau, [1984] for a complete description of each state's statutes.)

In the landmark case of Dallas Williams v. United States (1962), the court found that, although mental disease might be present, it is not always sufficient to release the accused from responsibility for his acts. Eleven psychiatrists testified that Williams showed evidence of psychiatric disturbance. Of the 11, 9 declared that he was a "psychopath," "only six characterized his condition as a mental disease or defect and of these six only three could say that the killings were the product of that disorder" (Williams v. US). It was the conclusion of the court that since out of 11 psychiatrists, only 3 could state that the crimes were a direct result of mental disease, the diagnosis of psychopathic personality was, in and of itself, insufficient to remove the adjudication of this issue from the pervue of the jury. The original verdict against the defendant was upheld. Thus, when the existence of a mental disease or defect is not deemed significant enough to render the accused unfit to stand trial, the jury may take the existence of such a mental condition into account during the weighing of the evidence, but it is not a prima facie reason for acquittal.

Additional alternatives to the insanity defense have been proposed to ameliorate the concept that a mentally ill individual must receive total exoneration of the responsibility for a criminal act. The concept of "guilty but mentally ill" seeks to establish a format whereby a defendant may be tried, but the jury may, if it desires, take the defendant's mental state at the time of the crime into consideration.

Sadly, despite considerable discussion regarding the distinctions between competence and responsibility, many professionals in both law and the behavioral sciences continue to confuse these two standards by indiscriminately applying the mental health criteria for mental illness to issues concerning competence to stand trial. In each instance "mental health professionals, and psychiatrists in particular, continue to exhibit a marked tendency to equate psychosis with responsibility and/or competency in spite of the fact that this is not in accord with either legal standard" (Rosche & Golding, 1980, p. 16). Although statutes and case law continue to evolve, there remains considerable uncertainty at all levels of the legal system regarding the medical and legal criteria for the establishment of mental competency and criminal responsibility (Smith, 1983).

The determination of competence takes up considerable court time even in noncriminal proceedings. The adjudication of appropriate settlement when an individual's competence has been affected because of an accident or injury requires a careful determination of the degree and nature of the deficits incurred and the degree of disability the deficits will engender.

In United States v. Jenkins (1962) the U.S. Court of Appeals for the District of Columbia ruled on whether a psychologist, as opposed to a psychiatrist, has the legal right to express an opinion regarding the existence of mental disease and mental defect. Both the American Psychological Association (APA) and the American Psychiatric Association were asked to file briefs on this issue. The American Psychological Association's Statement of Interest of Amicus Curiae discussed the credentials, qualifications, and training of psychologists, the organization of the APA, and the practice of psychology as a learned profession. It was ruled that the testimony of a psychologist is admissible on questions of brain disease and mental defect. An individual psychologist's acceptability as an expert witness depends, however, on "the nature and extent of his knowledge and not on the title of psychologist itself" (US v. Jenkins, 1962). Thus, some psychologists may not qualify to testify on issues of mental disease or defect because their training and expertise lie in areas such as statistical analysis or human factors research, which are unrelated to issues of mental health. US v. Jenkins stated that the determination of a psychologist's competence will be left to the discretion of the trial court, subject to review.

Currently, there is considerable controversy regarding the capacity of neuropsychologists to give expert testimony to the triers of fact in the nation's court system. Most vocal in their opinion of the "dubious status" of neuropsychiatrists (as well as psychologists) to give expert opinions are Ziskin and Faust, who have stated that psychological evidence "does not meet reasonable criteria of admissibility and should not be admitted in a court of law, or if admitted should be given little or no weight" (Ziskin &

Faust, 1988, p. 1). Ziskin and Faust base their conclusion on the issue of whether the behavioral sciences can, in fact, meet the criteria for a science.

In this chapter we attempt to show that psychology in general, and neuropsychology in particular, unquestionably meet the criteria for a science. We further propose that the neuropsychologist who can apply current, state-of-the-art neuropsychological research and clinical methods and who can clearly elucidate both their usefulness and their limitations in individual cases, can be a significant addition to court proceedings when knowledge of brain/behavior relationships is necessary for the adjudication of legal issues.

The Scientific Basis of Neuropsychology

Science as a Process/Cycle

In the past 50 years, science has shifted from an arcane academic pursuit to a phenomenon that reaches daily into the lives of many people. Not a day goes by that a new scientific finding is not reported on, or an old scientific issue debated in *The New York Times*. This has resulted in a situation in which many Americans are familiar with the products of science, without necessarily understanding the process.

The term "science" refers both to the procedures used to obtain scientific knowledge and to the body of knowledge that is established via those methods. This dual usage of the term illustrates one of the most basic facts about science and the scientific method, that is, that science is an iterative process. It evolves through a methodological process of trial and error through which gradual approximations toward a solution are obtained. Thus, science is best understood as a self-correcting, changing process, not as a static, accumulated body of knowledge.

Criteria for the Establishment of Scientific Data

What constitutes the process of science and does neuropsychological research and clinical practice adhere to it?

The process of scientific research often begins with the realization that currently available knowledge is insufficient to explain certain phenomena. Modifications to currently held working hypotheses are generated to account for the unexplained observations. Methods of testing the implications of the modified hypotheses are then developed and the results of these tests are analyzed for their closeness-of-fit with the original hypotheses. These methods must meet certain criteria. The scientific method requires that one:

1. ask well-formulated, unambiguous questions
2. develop testable hypotheses capable of being invalidated
3. design techniques to test the hypotheses
4. test the techniques for reliability and validity
5. perform the tests and interpret the results
6. evaluate the results
7. determine the conditions where the results hold and where they do not hold
8. state the new problems raised by the research (Bunge, 1967).

Neuropsychological research systematically employs all of the above operations, although certainly with varying degrees of success.

Much of the current confusion regarding the status of neuropsychology as a science stems from the fact that neuropsychologists may often disagree with one another regarding the diagnosis or treatment of a patient. This is sometimes characterized in courtroom situations as "the battle of the experts." Critics of neuropsychological research have suggested that this lack of professional consensus is atypical of the hard sciences, such as chemistry and physics, and renders the results of a neuropsychological assessment too speculative and conjectural for admission in a court of law (Ziskin & Faust, 1988).

This is a misperception of the nature of science. Lack of "consensus" appears at all times in all sciences. This disagreement should be viewed as healthy and indicative of the progress of science. Disagreement between scientists is not evidence of the invalidity of science as the following anecdote by Thomas Kuhn illustrates:

> An investigator who hoped to learn something about what scientists took the atomic theory to be asked a distinguished physicist and an eminent chemist whether a single atom of helium was or was not a molecule. Both answered without hesitation, but their answers were not the same. For the chemist, the atom of helium was a molecule because it behaved like one with respect to the kinetic theory of gases. For the physicist, on the other hand, the helium atom was not a molecule because it displayed no molecular spectrum. Presumably both men were talking of the same particle, but were viewing it through their own research training and practice. Their experience in problem solving told them what a molecule must be. Undoubtedly their experiences had had much in common, but they did not, in this case, tell the two specialists the same thing. (Kuhn, 1970, pp. 50–51)

According to Ziskin and Faust, disagreement on such a basic definition removes this inquiry from the realm of science. Kuhn and other historians of science (Feyerabend, 1965; Popper, 1959) suggest the opposite. They state that such disagreements lie at the very heart of the scientific method. Scientific progress cannot be made without competition between theories and the crises and instabilities that are subsequently created. Further, if a scientific theory is to receive a full confrontation against the facts, if its adequacy is to be truly tested comprehensively, then "a whole set of partly overlapping but *mutually inconsistent* [emphasis added] theories must be entertained; for otherwise relevant facts will be suppressed." We can never "prove" a theory or causal hypothesis. The highest status that even an advanced scientific theory can achieve is that of "not yet disconfirmed" (Cooke & Campbell, 1979). "Harmony among practitioners" (Ziskin & Faust, 1988, p. 715) is not a requirement for a field to be considered an "advanced" science. Indeed, it may be a hindrance.

Ziskin and Faust further assert that psychologists and psychiatrists cannot maintain themselves as scientific experts because selected research findings (e.g., Helzer, 1981) suggest that lay persons can classify psychiatric conditions as reliably as psychiatrists. They do not emphasize, however, that in many of these studies the lay technician received considerable training in structured interview procedures. Ziskin and Faust suggest that these findings jeopardize the asumption that psychology is based on a strong science when, in fact, the opposite conclusion is warranted. That reliable diagnoses can be produced by individuals with a moderate amount of training indicates that the system of classification for psychological and psychiatric diseases is reasonably accurate and congruent with readily observable phenomena. Current research (Matarazzo, 1983) indicates that reliable diagnostic categories can be delineated by gathering the appropriate data (e.g., using a structured interview procedure) and applying a standardized set of algorithms to the data. The results of the Matarazzo study indicated that all the raters examined, whether professional or lay-trained, achieved kappa values ranging between .77 and .52. The fact that lay persons can successfully apply these algorithms when trained to do so, argues *for* the validity of this system, not against it.

Although it is interesting that a series of decision rules will allow lay person and expert alike to achieve similar levels of accuracy in diagnosis, it is important to draw the reader's attention to the fact that the evaluation of decision making as undertaken in such studies in no way comes close to current standards of practice. It is typical that studies of diagnostic accuracy involve sending selected practitioners a set of scores based on a variety of measures and asking them to make some determinations about the nature of the damage or disease process that would have lead to such a set of scores. In some cases (e.g., Goldstein, Deysach & Kleinkneckt, 1973) the scores are not based on tests that have been designed to assess neuropsychological impairment (e.g., the WAIS and MMPI) or tests that have long since been abandoned by most neuropsychologists because of their lack of specificity with respect to differentiating neuropsychological syndromes (e.g., the Bender-Gestalt). It is also important to note that there was nothing to indicate that the "practitioners" in question had ever received any training in neuropsychology. Despite these shortcomings, the Goldstein et al. study continues to be used by Faust and his colleagues as evidence for the inaccuracy of clinical judgment in neuropsychology (e.g., Faust, Hart & Guilmette, 1988; Wedding & Faust, 1989).

In another study, Faust, Guilmette, Hart, Arkes, Fishburne & Davey (1988) attempted to recruit practitioners who claimed to have some training in neuropsychology and used test scores from the Halstead-Reitan Neuropsychological Test Battery. However, these researchers were no more sophisticated in what they required their practitioners to do, that is, form diagnostic judgments solely on the basis of a disembodied set of scores. From these test scores, the practitioner was asked to determine whether the protocol was abnormal, whether it may have been the result of psychiatric as opposed to cortical disturbance, if the disorder were progressive, and the areas of the cortex involved. The practitioner was also asked to make a diagnosis and specify whether further medical assessment would be appropriate.

It was heartening to note that of the 600 practitioners who were originally approached, a majority (60%) refused to play such a game. To us, the most astonishing aspect of this study was that 40% actually responded and attempted to diagnose patients they had never seen. Moreover, they attempted to do this outside the context of a full clinical evaluation (i.e., an evaluation that takes into account the history of the presenting problem, the patient's current status, information from medical examinations, interview with a family member, etc.). These practitioners were even asked to determine whether the disorder represented was static or progressive on the basis of one snapshot in time—a logical as well as a practical absurdity.

It is not at all surprising that, under such circumstances, diagnostic accuracy would be low. It is also not surprising that it would be difficult, under such circumstances, for a practitioner to distinguish between lists of scores based on real patients and those of individuals faking disease and disorder. Competent neuropsychological assessment involves far more than scanning a set of test scores (see, e.g., Dennis, 1991; Dywan, Maletta & Pirozzolo, 1991; Puente & Gillespie, 1991; Varney & Shepherd 1991). Ziskin and Faust have based their critique on studies in which psychologists are asked to make diagnoses in a way that we believe does not meet the criteria of normal, ethical practice in the field and then use such data to discredit the profession.

The Nature of Science and the Needs of the Court

Although neuropsychology has its roots in basic science, applications of neuropsychological research are currently used in the clinical diagnosis and treatment of medical diseases, and in family and social situations where appropriate understanding of patients' abilities can help alleviate many of the problems associated with central nervous system disorders. Thus, motivation in neuropsychological research often shifts between clinical need and scientific theory testing.

This may explain some of the purported ambiguity currently surrounding the issue of neuropsychology's scientific status. Most neuropsychologists receive both clinical and research training and are sometimes daily required to shift between the two. Certain types of neuropsychological investigation may be entirely relevant for application to clinical need without necessarily advancing our understanding of brain–behavior relationships. Conversely, neuropsychological research that is valuable for deciding between two scientific theories may have little practical clinical application. These two perspectives often become confused in the forensic area. Critics of psychological testimony often deprecate the use of clinical methods as unscientific. What they fail to realize is that basic research in neuropsychology has as its goal the discovery of general scientific principles through an analysis of group differences. It is the clinical method, based on relevant research and established neurological/neuropsychological principles, that is most appropriate for describing individual patients, their current status, and their future needs.

Statistical analysis of any phenomenon gives information regarding the *probabilities* that the hyotheses under scientific investigation are correct. Because of the inherent variation within a studied group, the knowledge acquired from group data cannot be applied to a given individual without some error. Thus, the results of even the most well-controlled studies yield information that may be scientifically valid, but will not be completely predictive of every individual member of the group. This is analogous to current methods of predicting the weather. A meteorologist's statement that there is a 30% chance of rain on a given day is based on a statistical analysis of 100 days where the atmospheric conditions were identical to the given day; on 30 of those days it rained. Whether it will actually rain tomorrow remains unknown. Similarly, a neuropsychologist can know that of 100 patients with severe head trauma leading to coma, 30 never recovered. The neuropsychologist can offer important information regarding the *probability* of individual recovery, but cannot predict with absolute certainty the outcome of an individual case.

It should be clear from the preceding discussion that the nature of science and the needs of the court system frequently are at odds. The judicial process requires proof where science is based on disproof. It requires fact where science provides theories and models. It requires certainty where science provides only statements of probability and estimates of error. In fact, error and its measurement is at the very heart of the scientific process. Scientific knowledge, as we know it, cannot move forward without it. If the judicial system wishes to use the findings of science in its proceedings, it must understand and accept that there is a marked difference between probative stands and scientific confidence limits.

The Psychometric Methods of Neuropsychology

It is important to note that *clinical method*, as it has developed in the field of neuropsychology, does not depend on intuition and unaided judgment. Neuropsychologists make use of psychometric evaluation as an important source of data in clinical decision making. Considerable confusion exists, however, regarding the concepts of reliability, validity, and stability so that the forensic neuropsychologist often may be required to explain psychometric theory in a manner that a judge and/or jury can understand the use in their findings. This can be a challenging task because standard English words and concepts are used to refer to very specific statistical concepts.

Reliability

Reliability is an indication of the consistency and stability of a test. It is an expression of the test's ability to produce the same score for an individual consistently over time and with as little error as possible. Any factor that affects the amount of error in a test will adversely affect the test's reliability. Empirical assessment of reliability, however, focuses primarily on analyses of the items of the test. Split-half and alternate-form reliability are two procedures whose purpose it is to evaluate the amount of intercorrelation between the test items. Interrater reliability assesses the consistency between two scorers. The stability of a test over time is conceptually very different from reliability and will be discussed separately.

The accuracy of a test can be affected when individual test items measure different constructs. For example, if a test purporting to measure calculational ability contains several items that require the memorization of mathematical formulae, an individual's score could be lowered because of poor memory skills, even if his calculation skills are superior. This situation would obscure the relationship between this person's true ability to calculate arithmetical problems (his hypothetical calculation ability) and his ability to calculate as measured by this test (his observed score). The test will be less accurate because it is incidentally testing the subject's memory skills as well as his ability to perform mathematical calculations. Restricting the domain of test items to a specific area and increasing the number of "pure" items so that poorly worded and ambiguous items have less influence on the total score will increase the reliability of the test.

Thus, a major indication of a test's reliability is reflected in the internal consistency of the items of a test. This can be expressed as the relationship between an individual's obtained score and his hypothetical true score. It should be noted that an individual's true score can never be measured because, as discussed earlier, all measurements contain error. This relationship between true score or ability (T) and measured score (X) is called the index of reliability and can be expressed by the correlation coefficient r_{xt}. The higher the consistency of the items, the higher the correlation between the true score and the measured score, and thus, the reliability of the test.

The most common methods used to report test reliability are coefficient alpha, sometimes known as Cronbach's alpha (Cronbach, 1951), and the Kuder-Richardson 20 (K-R 20) (Kuder & Richardson, 1937). Both of these formulas produce reliability coefficients that express estimates of the average correlation of items within a test. The K-R 20 is used when the answers to the questions are scored as a dichotomous right or wrong, whereas coefficient alpha is used for multiple-choice items or Likert-scale type items where responses to labels such as "always" "usually," "sometimes," or "never" are assigned rank-ordered numerical scores. It should be noted that these estimates of test reliability, when obtained in any particular study, are not related to the number of people in the study but are instead related to the number of items on the test (Nunnally, 1978). That is to say, reliability is improved by lengthening the test rather than adding additional persons to the study.

A relevant issue regarding the use and interpretation of these estimates of reliability is whether the criterion to be measured by the test is itself homogeneous. Although consistency within tests is preferable because it allows relatively straightforward interpretation of the test results, a single, homogeneous test, where all of the test items measure the same thing, may not be an adequate predictor of a highly heterogeneous variable. In this situation a heterogeneity of test items would not necessarily reflect measurement error, and utilization of the reliability coefficients listed above may not be appropriate for the calculation of reliability in such tests. This problem can be addressed by creating a battery of relatively homogeneous tests each measuring a different aspect of the heterogeneous variable. Traditional IQ tests such as the WAIS-R and WISC-R are probably the best known examples of this approach (Anastasi, 1982).

A second form of reliability should be calculated when the test items are not answered directly by the individual being tested, but are scored by an observer. When this occurs, it is necessary to establish that the test items themselves are consistent as well as establish that the different observers are consistent in their method of scoring. This estimate of scorer consistency is called interrater reliability and can be calculated simply by having a sample of tests scored independently by the two or more observers and correlating the obtained scores. The correlation coefficient obtained will be a measure of interrater reliability. When the data are categorical in nature, a measure of interrater reliability can be calculated using kappa statistics (Cohen, 1960). Kappa is an intraclass correlation coefficient that corrects for possible chance agreement between the raters that would possibly inflate the index of reliability. Kappa can be computed in both weighted and unweighted forms (see Fleiss, 1981). General parameters for the interpretation of kappa suggest that a kappa above .75 indicates excellent agreement between raters, a kappa between .75 and .40 indicates fair to good agreement, and kappa below .40 indicates poor interrater agreement (Landis & Koch, 1977).

The characteristics of the group upon which the reliability coefficient is computed is an additional factor influencing the assessment of test reliability. If the group is too homogeneous with regard to the variable in question, the calculation of reliability will be artificially low, as the restricted range of the sample lowers the ability of the items to discriminate within the sample. If the group shows considerable variability, the estimation of reliability will be higher. In general, calculation of reliability should be based on a representative sample of individuals drawn from the group for which the use of the test is intended.

Stability

Jensen (1980) has argued that the stability of a test is different from its reliability, as described above. The stability of a test refers to the constancy of test scores over time and has sometimes been referred to as test–retest reliability (Anastasi, 1982; Jensen, 1980). The stability of a test is measured by correlating the test scores obtained at one administration of test with scores obtained at another administration separated in time. The time interval used may vary, and should be appropriate to the variable in question. Thus, a test of long-term memory might require readministration at intervals of months, or possibly years, in a normal sample. Alternately, assessment of stability on a measure of short-term memory for patients with cognitive defects might require weekly administrations.

It is possible for a test to have a high reliability, that is be internally consistent, and have low stability. Conversely, it is possible for the scores of a test to be very stable across time, while the test itself may have low reliability. In neither situation is use of the test necessarily invalid. For example, a reliable test designed to be a sensitive measure of mood will likely be unstable, appropriately reflecting the natural variations in a subject's moods over time. This is an especially relevant and contentious issue in forensic cases. Such a test would be highly reliable (the questions pertain only to affective states), unstable (scores will be different at each administration), and valid, if used to measure mood and not cognitive ability. Conversely, it is possible for a test to have zero reliability and perfect stability. An example of this would be subjects' responses to a demographic questionnaire. There is no intercorrelation among the items (each question is from a different domain), but individuals answer the items identically at each administration (Jensen, 1980).

Thus, it is the *use* of the test that indicates whether either high reliability or high stability or both are necessary for valid test interpretation. Prediction of the future status of a patient will require a measure with high stability (so that a low score currently will probably mean a low score in the future), but high reliability may be unnecessary. If the goal of assessment is to measure a single, enduring trait, both high reliability and stability will be necessary.

An important point regarding the interpretation of stability coefficients is made by Jensen (1980). He notes that high stability does not necessarily represent a high degree in the constancy of the measurement itself, but represents instead "the degree of constancy in the person's relative standing among others on the same test" (Jensen, 1980, p. 277), obviously another vital point in an expert's testimony. If all subjects' scores changed by the same amount over time, the stability coefficient would equal 1.0. Factors that lower test reliability will also lower test stability. The stability coefficient is usually smaller than the square root of the reliabilities of the test calculated for the two administrations.

Validity

Validity is an assessment of whether a test measures what it was intended to measure and can be established only within the structure of a particular theoretical framework. This, naturally, involves the issue of the test's appropriate use. A test developed for the assessment of intelligence may be valid for the prediction of scholastic achievement, but invalid if used to estimate personality. Consequently, a test cannot be said to have "high" or "low" validity in the abstract; validity is always linked to the purpose for which the test is used (Anastasi, 1982). Although a test may be valid for a number of purposes, each of these uses must be evaluated separately.

Standards have been set for these concepts, and the commonly held notion of the "seat of the pants" psychological assessment or reasoning is unjustified and/or the result of faulty practice. The American Psychological Association's manual *Standards for Educational and Psychological Tests* (APA, 1974) states that "questions of validity are questions of what may properly be inferred from a test score . . . It is important to note that validity itself is inferred, not measured . . . (and) is something that is *judged* adequate, or marginal, or unsatisfactory" (p. 25). Thus, validity is important to establish because of the causal inferences that are inherent in psychological test interpretation.

The components necessary to render a judgment of valid test use always require empirical evaluation. Validity is assessed by comparing the results of the test in question with a criterion representing the appropriate domain of use for the measure. The three most common domains of use for psychological tests are: (a) to establish a statistical relationship between two or more variables, (b) to sample a specific area of content, and (c) to measure psychological traits (Nunnally, 1978). Historically, discussions of psychometric test evaluation procedures have divided validity into several "types" (i.e., face validity, content validity, construct validity, criterion validity, etc.) (Anastasi, 1982). These various types of validity correspond in general to the domain of use for the measure being validated. For example, the establishment of a relationship between two variables requires an evaluation of predictive validity, the demonstration of content sampling requires content validity, and the establishment of traits and other psychological phenomena requires the assessment of construct validity. However, in recent discussions, Messick (1980) and others (Dunnett & Borman, 1979; Guion, 1980) have taken issue with this fractionization of the general concept of validity. They have suggested that when establishing validity "different kinds of inferences from test scores require different types of *evidence*, not different types of validity . . . By focusing on the nature of the evidence [for the judgment of validity] in relation to the nature of the inferences drawn from test scores, we come to view validity as a general imperative in measurement" (Messick, 1980, p. 1014).

Messick (1980) suggests that this overspecification of validity has lead to confusion. Different aspects of validity have variously been labeled criterion-related validity, discriminant validity, trait validity, factorial validity, structural validity, or population validity. There is a risk that test users may focus on one limited aspect of validity without considering the basic constructs underlying inferences that will be made based on the test scores. As we have mentioned above, all scientific theory is based on abstract explanatory constructs, which are then verified through observation. Guion (1977) suggests that because prediction and content issues are inherently related to the underlying constructs of a theory, "all validity is at its base some form of construct validity" (p. 410). Thus, whereas other forms of validity are important for judging the appropriateness of a test for specific types of use, all tests should attempt to establish construct validity.

Construct Validity

Construct validity is the extent to which a test score can be interpreted as representing the theoretical trait, ability, or abstract construct that the test purports to measure. It is an index of the "believability" of the test, and thus has great interest to triers of fact. Like validity in general, estimations of construct validity are arrived at through a variety of methods in a number of domains. For example, if there is a high correlation between the score of the test in question and an existing test, a logical judgment can be made that these tests measure the same construct. If measures achieve consistently high associations and show similar changes over time or identical response to treatment, a common underlying construct may be presumed (Messick, 1980). Constructs additionally may be established by contrasting them against variables that are hypothesized to be opposite, or unrelated to the construct in question. This subtype of construct validity is referred to as discriminate validity. Low correlations between variables are desirable for determining discriminant validity. The empirical calculation of validity is more complex than the calculations required for the computations of reliability and stability. A detailed description of the specific methods of calculation and interpretation of the formulas that provide evidence for the establishment of validity can be found in Jensen (1980).

In addition to purely empirical issues regarding the evaluation of appropriate test use, Messick (1980) emphasizes the importance of judging test adequacy with respect to two domains: test adequacy, through an analysis of construct validity, and test appropriateness, through an appraisal of the social consequences of test use. He makes the important distinction between judging test adequacy on an evidential basis, that is, construct validity, as well as on a consequential basis, that is, the potential social impact of test use. "Since validity is an evaluation of evidence, a judgment rather than an entity, . . . validity has always been an ethical imperative in testing" (Messick, 1980, p. 1020). Thus, positive judgment of the evidential adequacy of a psychological measure is necessary, but not sufficient, for an evaluation of the consequential or ethical uses of those measures. This dual approach to the evaluation of validity issues reflects many issues salient to the judicial system, where the results of psychological test interpretation impact human lives. An appreciation of the society's stake in what psychologists often regard as issues of science can serve to bridge the gap between lawyer and psychologist.

The Neuropsychological Assessment

Damage to the brain is frequently accompanied by behavioral impairment. A neuropsychological assessment is a comprehensive evaluation of brain function, emphasizing the identification and measurement of psychological deficits. Neuropsychological assessment is usually requested to assist a neuropsychologist, physician, or other health care professional in reaching a diagnosis or in developing treatment plans for patients with disorders of brain function. This goal is accomplished by observing the patient's ability to perform various tasks on a group of tests designed to evaluate systematically the functioning of the human brain. Numerous tests for the assessment of both the normal and impaired brain have been developed over the years (e.g., Kolb & Whishaw, 1990; Lezak, 1983).

Although the establishment of causal relationships between observed behaviors and neural substrates has been one of the basic goals of neuropsychological research, early research efforts had difficulty establishing a straightforward causal relationship between brain structure and higher order cognitive functioning. Traditional psychological tests (as opposed to neuropsychological measures) proved to be unsuitable measures for assessment of "brain damage" (Walsh, 1978). Tests such as the Bender-Gestalt Test (Bender, 1938) were based on a unitary model of brain damage and were shown to lack specificity; their "miss" rates of false positives and false negatives were too high for reliable diagnosis. The poor specificity of early psychological tests in detecting brain damage lead researchers to question the unitary model of brain function. The concept of functional systems was advanced over the unitary model to provide a theoretical structure that was more congruent with observed behavior.

The concept of functional systems describes the relationship between a complex psychological function and its neurological substrate. This major advance in neuropsychological theory was developed in part by Luria (1973). Luria recognized that "mental functions, as complex functional systems cannot be localized in narrow zones of the cortex or in isolated cell groups, but must be organized in systems of concertedly working zones, each of which performs its role in complex functional system (sic) . . ." (p. 31). This systems approach to cerebral organization has proved to be theoretically more productive than the strict localizationalist model. In a functional system, damage to any part may disrupt psychological processes, whereas "damage to different parts of a system impress a different character on the complex of symptoms and signs which result from brain damage" (Walsh, 1978, p. 21). The concept of functional systems has advanced neuropsychology beyond a strict localizationist position redefining the concept of localization to include multiple brain sites working in concert.

The concept of complex functional systems describes the relationship between behavior and its possible neurological substrate, but a neuropsychological *syndrome* describes a constellation of specific neuropsychological signs and symptoms that suggest the presence of damage or the existence of a disease process. Syndrome analysis requires the careful evaluation of patterns of spared function as well as patterns of deficits. These patterns of relative strength and weakness in the patient's performance are then matched to corresponding diagnostic categories. Developments in the field of psychometric assessment in conjunction with a broader appreciation of psychometric theory have lead to more precise measurement of the ways in which a patient's performance may vary from expected norms. The utility of such data, however, depends on a sophisticated knowledge of the many ways in which brain dysfunction can influence behavior. The clinician must be aware of what patterns to look for and recognize the implications of the patterns seen. Fortunately or unfortunately, the choice of neuropsychologist can be more important than the choice of neuropsychological tests.

Fixed Battery Versus Eclectic or Flexible Methods

Although the delineation of complex functional systems represents an advance in the scientific theory of neuropsychology, it has not provided any assistance in formulating the best methods to assess these systems. Neuropsychologists typically use either a fixed or flexible approach when choosing the tests that make up the objective part of a neuropsychological assessment. In choosing these tests, they must decide how heavily they wish to rely on a highly standardized, fixed, or actuarial approach. A fixed battery refers to one that is applied in a standardized fashion to all patients irrespective of the condition of the patient or the question to be addressed. The "process" approach is more flexible in nature, and tests are selected for each individual case with regard to a number of patient variables. Each of these methods has advantages and disadvantages, both for the neuropsychologist and for the lawyer who may be using the results of a neuropsychological report in a forensic case. There is no clear choice of method even with regard to assessment for forensic purposes, although our opinion is that flexible methods used in standardized ways provide the greatest and most accurate information. In any case, an understanding of these approaches to neuropsychological measurement can assist both the clinical neuropsychologist and lawyer in making informed choices. The advantages and disadvantages of each method are discussed below as they pertain to forensic issues.

The Fixed Battery

Fixed batteries of neuropsychological tests have been championed by a number of researchers over the years (Halstead, 1947; Reitan & Davidson, 1974; Russell, Neuringer & Goldstein, 1970). The best known and most widely used battery is the Halstead-Reitan (Reitan & Davidson, 1974). The Halstead-Reitan consists of seven measures and requires between 6 and 8 hours to administer. Test items are scored either right or wrong and summed into an index of impairment, which ranges from 1.0 to 0.

One of the strongest arguments for the use of fixed batteries is the ease of comparison with previously collected data. Additionally, research into the definition and etiology of disease can be facilitated when issues of test interpretation are not compounded across different types of tests. Thus, most research protocols require standardization at least for the duration of the project. In a forensic setting, the fixed battery approach usually can withstand a more rigorous cross examination regarding data supporting the reliability and validity for the tests that comprise the battery. Fixed batteries are generally administered in a standardized manner, which maximizes the replicability of the test results. Such standardization also may be more readily explained to a lay population such as a jury. There is ample evidence, however, to suggest that certain batteries lack the psychometric properties and standardization data (e.g., The Luria-Nebraska) to assess adequately the broad range of behaviors that are of concern in the clinical setting.

There are also major disadvantages to the fixed battery method. First and most important, the fixed battery method cannot be modified to meet the individual needs of the patient nor is it easily modified on the basis of new developments in the field. Thus, the battery is limited to measuring only those variables represented by the specific tests in the battery and impairment that might be detected by other tests is not examined. A weakness, for example, of the Halstead method would be the poverty of memory measures. A second problem is the impairment index. Summing across tests reflects a notion of "organicity" that has long since been abandoned in the scientific literature. These problems necessarily impose limitations on the type and nature of the information available from a fixed battery of tests. Third, an overreliance on the scores themselves could lead the clinician to ignore data regarding *how* the individual patient reaches a solution to a test problem. Very often the specific strategy used by the patient to solve a problem can provide more insight into the patient's adaptive or maladaptive cognitive functioning than the simple knowledge of a correct or incorrect response. We have often reminded our students of the comment made by Disraeli who said, "Do you want the truth or do you want numbers."

The Process Approach

Stemming from its theoretical orientation, (e.g., Kaplan, 1988), the process model is

> based on a desire to understand the qualitative nature of the behavior assessed by clinical psychometric instruments, a desire to reconcile descriptive richness with reliability and quantitative evidence of validity, and a desire to relate the behavior assessed to the conceptual framework of experimental neuropsychology. (Milberg, Hebben & Kaplan, 1986, p. 65)

The process approach does not abandon the use of well validated and standardized measures that are given and scored in a standardized way. However, there are many reasons why an individual may do poorly on any of our psychometric tests and the reason that the individual does poorly may be of more interest to the court than any particular test score on its own. This is especially true in neurologically impaired populations for whom interface problems, that is, various forms of sensory or motor deficit, make standardized administration of tests or standardized interpretation of test results problematic.

It is important to note that the process approach differs from a purely clinical approach in that descriptions of the quality of the patient's responses to test stimuli often can be quantified and subjected to statistical analyses. Unlike its detractors would have us believe, the test administrator is not really free to cavalierly change test procedures. The testing of clinical limits should be done in an "operationally defined, repeatable, and quantifiable" manner. Attempts are always made to modify the administration procedures so that they do not interfere with the standard administration and scoring of the test.

The process approach has a number of advantages when compared to the fixed battery method of neuropsychological assessment. First, this method allows for sensitive, detailed observation of individual responses to test questions that can lead to a more accurate picture of the patient's neuropsychological functioning. Second, the interpretation of the test results can be based more fully on the patient's history and cultural and linguistic idiosyncrasies. This is important as the patient's premorbid physical and mental status, education, and cultural heritage can all affect cognitive style and strategies. Third, the increased accuracy of the neuropsychological profile is more responsive to clinical questions regarding issues such as diagnosis, surgical intervention, and rehabilitation of lost functioning. Finally, the exceptional detail provided during the assessment may permit the explication of additional specific factors from multifactorial tests; providing data that would be overlooked by the standardized scoring procedures.

The disadvantages of the process approach spring precisely from the very aspects of the approach that give the method its power. The flexibility of the method, the ability to tailor each assessment to the exact needs of each patient means that sometimes it can be difficult to compare the results of assessments across patients. This can limit the types of research that can be based on data gathered by this method and the calculation of certain types of reliability measures.

In summary, the fixed battery method and the process approach to neuropsychological assessment each address some of the inherent limitations of neuropsychological measurement. The fixed battery method holds as many variables as possible constant and maximizes replicability and reliability of procedures and the generalization of test results over large patient and research groups. It may not detect important aspects of an individual case and its neuropsychological features and cannot reflect current scientific progress within the field. The process approach optimizes the amount of sensitive data gathered regarding each individual patient's cognitive ability but may increase the difficulty of generalizing the test results across groups and establishing reliability and validity. Most clinical neuropsychologists use a mixture of the two methods.

Summary and Conclusions

The goal of this chapter has been to articulate the position that neuropsychology is an active, evolving discipline at the interface between biological and social science, which readily uses scientific methodology. Nonetheless, it is acknowledged that neuropsychology is a young science with many competing theories and paradigms. Unlike the natural sciences, society finds the issues that psychology and neuropsychology investigates (i.e., questions regarding human behavior) so relevant it frequently requests answers to questions that have yet to be scientifically addressed, or a single answer where two or more hypotheses are currently competing. This situation has lead to criticism regarding the appropriateness of using the results of psychological and neuropsychological tests to assist in the evaluation of legal questions.

There are two possible actions that society can take in response to this situation. One is to deny the current level of scientific progress in psychology and neuropsychology because it cannot provide ultimate solutions to difficult social problems, the second is that society can understand and accept the inherently recursive nature of the social sciences and allow its professionals to apply currently available knowledge in an optimal manner.

> In the context of testing, a particularly powerful and general form of counterproposal is to weigh the potential consequences of the proposed test use against the potential social consequences of *not* testing at all. (Messick, 1980, p. 1020)

What would be the justification for not using any of neuropsychology's research findings regarding the brain? Would justice truly be better served by denying the neuropsychologist's current knowledge of brain and behavior to the triers of fact in the nation's courts?

We believe that such a rigid position would be unproductive and is unwarranted. It is hoped that a greater understanding of both the strengths and limitations of the basic scientific method will assist the legal system in using the products of psychological and neuropsychological research. The judicial system should not assume that the current state of neuropsychological research and practice, because it is not complete, is of no use in the evaluation of current social questions regarding brain–behavior relationships. Fowler and Matarazzo have stated that:

> Clearly, expert witness testimony should not be used to make assertions beyond the limits of the expert's knowledge and ability. But to argue for a cautious approach to the use of expert witness testimony cannot be equated with arguing for the elimination of experts in the courtroom. (Fowler & Matarazzo, 1988, p. 1143)

The practice of forensic neuropsychology is enjoying an unprecedented popularity. The interplay of social need and scientific inquiry, as seen through the workings of the judicial process, has stimulated neuropsychological research. As the court system addresses various specific social issues related to the nature of brain–behavior relationships, it draws attention to some of the limitations of neuropsychological test interpretation and leads to additional scientific debate regarding the theories and assumptions hypothesized to underlie neuropsychology. Such interplay ultimately will strengthen both science and law. In the following chapters we address some of the important questions and research needs that are relevant to forensic neuropsychology.

The numerous scientific, clinical, practical, and ethical issues raised in this volume have been a growing concern of neuropsychologists and other scientists for the past decade (e.g., Pirozzolo, 1989). Implicit in the exercise of psychological practice is the psychologist's commitment to the principles espoused in The American Psychological Association's "Ethical Principles of Psychologists" (1981). Adherence to these principles, as well as those described in the APA Standards for Psychological and Educational Testing, along with a willingness to incorporate scientific advances in the field, will ensure that the scientific integrity of neuropsychology will be maintained and continue to exert an important influence on the myriad aspects of competency whether in the clinic or the courtroom.

References

American Psychological Association (1981). Ethical principles of psychologists. *American Psychologist 36*, 633–638.

American Psychological Association, American Educational Research Association, & National Council On Measurement In Eduation. (1974). *Standards for eduational and psychological tests*. Washington D.C.: American Psychological Association.

Anastasi, A. (1982). *Psychological tesing* (5th ed.). New York: Macmillan.

Bender, L. (1938). A visual motor gestalt test and its clinical use. *American Orthopsychiatric Association. Research Monographs, 3.*

Blau, T. (1984). *The psychologist as expert witness*. New York: John Wiley and Sons.

Bunge, M. (1967). *Scientific research I: The search for a system*. New York: Springer-Verlag.

Cohen, J. (1960). A coefficient for agreement for nominal scales. *Educational Psychological Measurement, 20*, 37–46.

Cooke, T.D., & Campbell, D.T. (1979). *Quasi-experimentation: Design and analysis issues for field settings*. Boston: Houghton Mifflin.

Cronbach, L.J. (1951). Coefficient alpha and the internal structure of tests. *Psychometricka, 16*, 297–334.

Dennis, M. (1991). Assessing the neuropsychological abilities of children and adolescents for personal injury litigation. In J. Dywan, R. Kaplan, & F. Pirozzolo (Eds.), *Neuropsychology and the law*. New York: Springer-Verlag.

Dunnett, M.D., & Borman, W.C. (1979). Personnel selection and classification systems. In M.R. Rosenzweig & L.W. Porter (eds.). Annual review of psychology (Vol. 30). Palo Alto, California: Annual Reviews.

Dusky v. United States, 362 U.S. 402 (1960).
Dywan, J., Maletta, G., & Pirozzolo, F. (1991). The assessment of competency in the older adult. In J. Dywan, R. Kaplan, & F. Pirozzolo (Eds.), *Neuropsychology and the law*. New York: Springer-Verlag, 93–134.
Faust, D., Guilmette, T.J., Hart, K., Arkes, H.R., Fishburne, F.J., & Davey, L. (1988). Neuropsychologists' training, experience, and judgment accuracy. *Archives of Clinical Neuropsychology*, *3*, 145–163.
Faust, D., Hart, K., & Guilmette, T.J. (1988). Pediatric malingering: The capacity of children to fake believable deficits on neuropsychological testing. *Journal of Consulting and Clinical Psychology*, *56* (4), 78–582.
Feyerabend, P. (1965). Problems of Empiricism. In Colodny, R. (Ed.), *Beyond the edge of certainty*. Englewood Cliffs, NJ: Prentice Hall.
Fleiss, J. (1981). *Statistical methods for rates and proportions* (2nd ed.). New York: John Wiley and Sons.
Fowler, R.D., Matarazzo, J.D. (1988). Psychologists and psychiatrists as expert witnesses. *Science*, *241*, 1143–1144.
Goldstein, S.G., Deysach, R.E., & Kleinkneckt, R.A. (1973). Effect of experience and amount of information on identification of cerebral impairment. *Journal of Consulting and Clinical Psychology*, *41*, 30–34.
Guion, R.M. (1980). On trinitarian doctrines of validity. *Professional Psychology*, *11*, 385–398.
Guion, R.M. (1977). Content validity: Three years of talk—What's the action? Public Personell Management, *6*, 407–414.
Halstead, W.C. (1947). *Brain and intelligence*. Chicago: University of Chicago Press.
Helzer, J.E. (1981). The use of a structured psychiatric interview for routine psychiatric evaluations. *The Journal of Nervous and Mental Disease*, *169*, 45–49.
Higgins v. McGraph, 98 F. Supp. 670 (1951).
Jensen, A.R. (1980). *Bias in mental testing*. New York: Free Press.
Kaplan, E. (1988). A process approach to neuropsychological assessment. In T. Boll & B.K. Bryant (Eds.), *Clinical neuropsychology and brain function: Research, measurement and practice*. Washington, DC: American Psychological Association.
Kolb, B. & Whishaw, I.A. (1990). *Fundamentals of human neuropsychology*, 3rd ed. New York: W.H. Freeman and Co.
Kuder, G.F., & Richardson, M.W. (1937). The theory of estimation of test reliability. *Psychometricka*, *2*, 151–160.
Kuhn, T.S. (1970). *The structure of scientific revolutions* (2nd ed.). Chicago: The University of Chicago Press.
Landis, J.R., & Koch, G.G. (1977). The measurement of observer agreement for categorical data. *Biometrics*, *33*, 671–679.
Lezak, M.D. (1983). *Neuropsychological assessment* (2nd ed.). New York: Oxford Press.
Luria, A.R. (1973). *Fundamentals of neuropsychology*. Moscow: MGU Press.
Matarazzo, J.D. (1983). The reliability of psychiatric and psychological diagnosis. *Clinical Psychology Review*, *3*, 103–145.
Melton, G., Petrila, J., Poythress, N.G., & Slobogen, C. (1987). *Psychological evaluations for the courts*. New York: Guilford Press.

Messick, S. (1980). Test validity and the ethics of assessment. *American Psychologist, 35* (11), 1012–1027.
Milberg, W.P., Hebben, N., & Kaplan, E. (1986). The Boston process approach to neuropsychological assessment. In I. Grant & K. Adams (Eds.), *Neuropsychological assessment of neuropsychiatric disorders*. New York: Oxford University Press.
Nunnally, J. (1978). *Psychometric Testing* (2nd ed.). New York: McGraw Hill.
Pate v. Robinson 383, U.S. 375 (1966).
Pirozzolo, F.J. (1989). *New developments in neuropsychological evaluation*. Philadelphia: WB Saunders.
Popper, K. (1959). *The logic of scientific discovery*. London: Hutchinson.
Puente, A.E., & Gillespie, J.B. (1991). Worker's compensation and clinical neuropsychological assessment. In J. Dywan, R. Kaplan, & F. Pirozzolo (Eds.), *Neuropsychology and the Law*. New York: Springer-Verlag.
Reitan, R.M., & Davidson, L.A. (1974). *Clinical neuropsychology: Current status and applications*. New York: Hemisphere.
Roesch, R., & Golding, S. (1980). *Competency to stand trial*. Urbana: University of Illinois Press.
Russell, E.L., Neuringer, C., & Goldstein, G. (1970). *Assessment of brain damage: A neuropsychological approach*. New York: John Wiley and Sons.
Smith, J. (1983). *Forensic psychiatry: A programmed study guide*. Potomac, MD: Communication in Print.
Tancredi, L., Lieb, J., & Slaby, A.E. (1975). *Legal issues in psychiatric care*. New York: Harper & Row.
United States v. Jenkins, 307 F. 2d 637 (1962).
Varney, N.R., & Shepherd, J.S. (1991). Minor head injury and the post-concussive syndrome. (pp. 24–38). In J. Dywan, R. Kaplan, & F. Pirozzolo (Eds)., *Neuropsychology and the law*. New York: Springer-Verlag.
Walsh, K.W. (1978). *Neuropsychology: A clinical approach*. New York: Churchill Livingstone.
Wedding, D., & Faust, D. (1989). Clinical judgment and decision making in neuropsychology. *Archives of Clinical Neuropsychology*, *4*, 233–265.
Williams v. United States, 250 F. 2d 19 (D.C. Cir. 1962).
Ziskin, J., & Faust, D. (1988). *Coping with psychiatric and psychological testimony* (Vols 1–3). Marina del Rey, CA: Law and Psychology Press.

2
Minor Head Injury and the Post-Concussive Syndrome

NILS R. VARNEY and JANET SMITH SHEPHERD

It is not surprising that head injury should have substantial relevance to the law. Each year in the United States there are two million head injuries in motor vehicle accidents alone, with a new injury occurring about every 16 seconds. The annual direct and indirect costs of head injury total 25 billion dollars and accidental head injuries result in 35,000 lost man *years* of productive labor. Since most head injuries that occur in motor vehicle accidents are the result of negligence, lawsuits are common.

The term "minor head injury" has no standard definition, but for the sake of argument, let's take the most restricted definition: a head injury is "minor" if the patient's combined loss of consciousness and post-traumatic amnesia last less than 15 minutes, his computed tomography (CT) scan, magnetic resonance image (MRI), and electroencephalogram (EEG) are all normal, and there is no period of postinjury hospitalization for neurological reasons. This definition certainly rules out anything that could be remotely viewed as a medical emergency, or even a cause for concern on the part of the patient. At the same time, however, those forces that cause one's head to only "crack the windshield" and leave the patient "dazed" for only a few seconds can cause abrasions of orbital frontal cortex and the mesial temporal lobe. As a result of these injuries alone, a seemingly trivial "minor" head injury can have catastrophic neuropsychiatric sequelae. Thus, because a head injury is medically minor does not mean that it is neuropsychologically trivial as well.

The term "post-concussive syndrome" is a rather unfortunate term, at least as it is used by many neurologists and neuropsychologists. For many, the term denotes a disorder in which an apparently minor head injury is followed by a variety of vague or neurasthenic complaints voiced by a patient with pending litigation. The common wisdom is that these symptoms are brought on by the stress of being involved in an accident and the prospect of remuneration through litigation. Unfortunately, many of these complaints (Tables 2.1 & 2.2) are symptoms of major depressive disorder (MDD) or complex partial seizures (CPSz).

TABLE 2.1. Symptoms of major depressive disorder shared with post-concussive syndrome.

Dysphoria
Anergia
Insomnia
Crying spells
Memory difficulty
Physical aches and pains (i.e., enhanced pain sensitivity)
Poor appetite
Low sex drive
Irritability
Loss of interest
Social withdrawal
Poor concentration

TABLE 2.2. Symptoms of complex partial seizures shared with post-concussive syndrome[a].

Paresthesias
Anesthesias
Headache
Photophobia
Nausea
Abrupt mood shift
Memory gaps
Episodic confusion
Episodic irritability
Episodic anxiety
Episodic tinnitis
Occasional speech difficulty
Jamais vu
Déjà vu
"Odd" abdominal sensations
Episodic suicidal inclinations
Olfactory hallucinations and other paranormal sensations
Intrusive thoughts about the accident

[a] List not comprehensive for symptoms of complex partial seizures.

For more information about the relationship between partial seizure symptoms and depression, please consult Springer, Varney, Garvey and Roberts (1991). For more information about the psychological-like presentation of partial seizures in both normals and the head injured, consult Roberts, Varney, Hulbert et al. (1990).

There is an additional matter to be considered with regard to the etiology of post-concussive syndrome. This disorder has been described precisely and consistently for the past two hundred years (e.g., Benton, 1989). It seems peculiar to dismiss it on an individual basis as "functional" when its presentation is consistent. No other reaction to environmental stressors is so consistent (not even post-traumatic stress disorder in combat veterans). It would seem more logical to assume that the disorder has an organic cause that is not readily demonstrable with current medical technology such as the MRI.

Obviously, the various psychological pressures that come about as a result of litigation are complex. It would seem reasonable to conclude that even among patients with clear and obvious physical disabilities, the stress of a lawsuit requiring as long as five years to resolve can cause personality changes of an unattractive nature. If patients, as is common, are the subject of multiple psychological and psychiatric examinations, the results of which are sometimes pejorative, they are likely to become quite defensive or strident. It is worth noting in this regard that two papers by Mendelson (1982, 1984) indicate that the vast majority of litigants with head, back, or neck injuries who claim disability without substantial medicotechnical verification remain unemployed two years after their lawsuits have been settled. As Mendelson put it in the title of one paper, they are "not cured by the verdict."

The Importance of Interviewing Collaterals

Whether one is examining a head injury patient for clinical or forensic reasons, it is critically important to include a private and confidential interview with at least one relative or coworker as part of the examination. There are a number of sound reasons for doing this:

1. Patients with memory trouble or frontal lobe injuries are not reliable historians. Patients with frontal lobe injuries in particular are inclined to underreport symptoms or claim to be in perfect psychological health.
2. The examination setting is highly structured and, for most of a neuropsychological exam, the patient is being told what to do. So long as patients are cooperative, they have little opportunity to display the psychosocial deficits that are the hallmark of the disability.
3. From an evidentiary perspective, the purpose of testing is, ultimately, to predict how well patients are able to function vocationally and socially so that the economic impact of their injury is fully grasped. A collateral interview is, therefore, a convenient form of external validation for one's predictions based on testing.
4. In many cases, head injury creates changes in character, mood, or mental status that are not readily apparent to examiners but are obvious to persons familiar with the patient premorbidly. For example, a patient whose word finding performance falls between the 90th and 40th percentiles is still well within normal limits but is substantially impaired relative to premorbid status.

5. There are certain areas in which a psychologist cannot obtain accurate information by personal observation. Short of having patients live with you in your home for a few days, it is very difficult to assess their performance in activities of daily living except by consulting close relatives or household members. Information can be obtained about daily habits, sexual behavior, interactions with children, and so on.
6. Collateral interviews may save the clinician from embarrassing surprises. For example, patients might fail to remark that they have been arrested five times for drunk driving since their injury.

One disadvantage of relying on collateral information is that spouses, family members, or friends are not trained observers and the information they provide is subjective at best. However, for the purposes of diagnosing frontal lobe injury via disturbances in activities of daily living, the collateral interview is the only source of data.

There are two common arguments offered against using such data. The first is that the opinions and observations of relatives are biased to some degree in favor of the patient. This is sometimes true, but the result is that relatives underreport disagreeable symptoms to avoid embarrassing the patient or the family. The second argument is that such information is hearsay. This is a legal argument so it would be important to establish a "foundation" for the practice by indicating that this is necessary for a more complete and accurate examination and is a standard practice in such examinations (cf. Lezak, 1983).

Some Special Considerations Regarding Assessment of Children

Determining the degree of functional disability in a head-injured child presents some special problems in forensic exams. One objective of such assessments, which is often overlooked, is to determine not only the degree of existing disability but also to project how this will impact on the ability to function as an adult. Moreover, it must be remembered that good recovery on tests and good performance in school do not guarantee that the child will be free of serious impairment(s) as an adult.

There are two important factors to be considered here. First, frontal lobe damage, particularly orbital frontal damage, may not be readily apparent on testing or in activities of daily living in a small or even school-aged child. Children, being immature, are less dependent on "frontal lobe functions" than are adults. For example, most major decisions are made for them and their daily activities are structured by adults (even play is supervised). It would be absurd to expect even a mature and well behaved child of 10 to live independently, raise children, or hold a steady job. Indeed, few parents would feel comfortable leaving a child of

10 unattended for more than a few hours. Thus, younger children with frontal damage would have little opportunity to manifest their deficits until later life offers challenges in which intact frontal lobe functioning is essential (by analogy, one can not tell if a child with a left parietal lesion is going to be alexic until he has been in school for a few months).

The second consideration is far less complex. After puberty, there are a number of central nervous system changes that result in a substantial lowering of seizure thresholds. A head injury in 1984 can create conditions that do not lead to a seizure disorder until 1988, when the child has passed puberty. Thus, the conditions for post-traumatic seizures were created by the head injury in 1984, but lay dormant until 1988. The problems with assessment of neuropsychological deficit in children and the issues involved in prognosis are dealt with in some detail in the chapter by Dennis in this volume.

Frontal Lobe Tests

There are a number of tests available that assess or claim to assess "frontal lobe functioning." The validity and clinical utility of these tests have been established, for the most part, using case material of patients with imageable lesions in the lateral frontal lobe (e.g., stroke and tumor). The mild head injury patient is much more likely to have damage to orbital frontal cortex, and if this damage were imageable, the injury would not be regarded as mild. The question can be raised, therefore, "How useful are these tests in assessing orbital frontal injury?"

To investigate this question, Martzke, Cooper and Varney (1988) assembled a group of 20 patients with mild head injury who met the following entry criteria: (a) all were partially or totally anosmic, (b) all had WAIS Full Scale IQ scores of at least 100, (c) all had been chronically unemployed or had highly unstable work histories for at least 2 years after their injury, (d) none had significant physical injuries as a result of the accident that caused their head injury, and (e) each was described by a relative as having at least half the symptoms of orbital frontal injury (see Table 2.3). In other words, the patients' behavior and work histories since their injuries were consistent with impaired orbital frontal functioning. Each of these patients was given a battery of five "frontal lobe tests": the Wisconsin Card Sorting Test, Porteus Mazes, Controlled Oral Word Association, the Picture Arrangement subtest from the WAIS, and the Tinker Toy Test (cf. Lezak, 1983).

Although it is arguable that all the patients involved showed gross frontal lobe deficits in activities of daily living, more than half of the patients performed within the normal range on each of the tests. Porteus Mazes and Picture Arrangement proved particularly insensitive (with only 20% of the patients falling below the norm) whereas the best indicator,

TABLE 2.3. Orbital frontal symptoms difficult to detect in an office visit.

Absentmindedness
Mental inertia
Indecisiveness
Immaturity
Nonspontaneity
Poor planning
Poor anticipation
Poor insight
Poor empathy
Poor judgment
Impolitic social "skills"
Unreliability
Disorganization
Fiscal impulsivity
Inadequate parenting
Vocational unreliability
Low motivation
Inflexibility
Dependence

the Tinker Toy Test, showed only 40% of the patients performing below normal controls. The Tinker Toy Test and Controlled Oral Word Association scores, taken to be the best combination, showed 55% of patients falling below the normal range. When all five test scores were considered, there were still 40% of the patients who performed within normal limits. It would appear safe to conclude on this basis that there is no single test or combination of tests sensitive enough to predict functional deficits even in a patient population clearly exhibiting frontal lobe syndrome.

Although no single test is diagnostic of frontal lobe functioning, the Tinker Toy Test has been found to have some predictive value with regard to future employment. Specifically, Bayless, Varney and Roberts (1989) have studied a group of patients with supposedly mild head injury at a point two years after being given medical clearance to return to work. The first group of 25 patients had returned to work successfully. Another group contained 25 patients who had been employed for less than 25% of the time after their release to return to work. A group of 25 normal controls was also tested. All were given the Tinker Toy Test with a modified scoring system that emphasized complexity rather than number of pieces employed.

The Bayless et al. (1989) results were straightforward. Only one head-injured person who had successfully returned to work scored below the normal range on the test. However, 13 of the patients who had been unsuccessful in reintegrating back into their jobs scored below the normal range. Thus, failure on the Tinker Toy Test implies that the affected patient, even with a mild head injury, is likely to be vocationally disabled. It must be noted, however, that one can be vocationally disabled and still perform well with Tinker Toys.

As a piece of evidence to be used in court, one's first reaction to this might be that the use of Tinker Toys trivializes the many more sophisticated aspects of neuropsychological assessment. In response to this, two arguments may be put forward. First, the Bayless et al. (1989) data suggest that it works better than any other test. Second, it has a good deal of face validity and the results are readily comprehensible to the lay person. That is, since the expression "Any five-year-old could do it" applies to the Tinker Toy Test, failure is particularly graphic in demonstrating how profoundly impaired the patient is.

Anosmia and Parosmia

The term anosmia refers to loss of the senses of smell and taste as a result of damage to the olfactory nerves. The term parosmia refers to gross distortion in senses of smell and taste as a result, once again, of damage to the olfactory nerves. Anosmia and/or parosmia are common sequelae of closed head injury, particularly if the blow to the head is frontal or occipital (Zusho, 1982). Since the olfactory nerves are located within the rhinal fissures in the orbital frontal cortex, it is common for post-traumatic anosmia to be associated with contusions or abrasions of orbital frontal cortex (cf. Jennett & Teasdale, 1981). Indeed, it would be difficult to damage the olfactory nerves via trauma without also damaging the surrounding central nervous system tissue.

Assessment to determine whether a patient has anosmia/parosmia can be as sophisticated or as simple as the clinical situation demands. The primary concern, particularly in forensic exams, is to avoid false positive results. That is, it is important to be absolutely sure that if someone fails the test, he is truly anosmic. As stimulus material, familiar, "loud" smells are best, such as peanut butter or oil of peppermint. The procedure is to hold the jar under the patient's nose while his eyes are closed. Since taste is also impaired in true anosmics, it is a good idea to inquire of relatives whether the suspected anosmic overseasons food. When smell is absent or very weak and taste is also very weak, it is safe to conclude that the patient is anosmic. If the patient reacts violently to the olfactory stimulus claiming that it smells like fish bait, fecal matter, or other offensive odor, he is probably parosmic.

Of what significance are these findings? The answer is that damage to orbital frontal cortex, while being an injury of minor medical import (as in not "life threatening"), still has castastrophic psychosocial consequences for the patient (cf. Varney, 1988). A list of common descriptors for patients with severe or total anosmia is shown in Table 2.3.

From a medicolegal perspective, there are a number of significant observations to be made with regard to the anosmic/orbital frontal damaged patient.

1. Their vocational outcome is poor. Among patients with total or near total anosmia (n = 40), 93% are unable to maintain consistent employment. Among partial anosmics (n = 24), 54% are apparently unemployable (Varney, 1988).
2. Anosmics often perform well on tests of abstract reasoning, memory, language, and so forth, while actually being quite functionally impaired. The data cited above were based on anosmic patients with average scores on tests of intelligence and memory. That is, they were unemployable for reasons other than being uninformed or forgetful. The most common complaints (noted by relatives) were absent-mindedness, poor planning and anticipation, indecisiveness, perplexity, unreliable quality of work output, inability to learn from errors or instruction, and an inability to get along with coworkers, particularly supervisors.
3. The key problem for most patients is that they have difficulty with spontaneous mentation and decision making. This leads to frequent errors of omission in their jobs. It is also noteworthy in this regard that a patient engaged in psychological testing is not required to make many decisions by himself. Rather, he follows instructions for the entire session. As a result, he has little or no opportunity to demonstrate his deficits.
4. Anosmics are not reliable historians. Indeed, frontal lobe patients rarely complain; at least they rarely complain about what is actually wrong with them. It is important, as we have noted, to interview a relative or other person who was familiar with the patient both before and after the accident. Quite frankly, the diagnostic work-up of any patient suspected of having a traumatic brain injury cannot be complete without such an interview (cf. Lezak, 1983, for a lengthy discussion of this issue).

Dichotic Listening

A rather large number of studies have demonstrated the clinical utility of dichotic listening for words as a means of detecting structural lesions that disrupt the transmission of verbal information from the left ear to the right hemisphere and then, via the corpus callosum, back to the left hemisphere. Vascular or neoplastic lesions of the corpus callosum often result in a substantial or total suppression of dichotic performance in the left ear. Even in the normal population, there is a slight right ear advantage, presumably because of the shorter distance of transmission required for right ear stimuli to reach the left hemisphere.

The clinical significance of dichotic word listening has been clearly established with regard to space occupying lesions, but its relevance to disturbances in white matter functioning has only recently been investigated. Findings reported by Roberts, Varney, Paulson, and Richardson (1990) and by Gorman, Roberts, Varney and Hines (1990) are particularly interesting in this regard. In their first study, Roberts et al. (1990) tested dichotic word listening on 24 patients with presumed partial complex seizures before and after treatment with anticonvulsants. These patients initially performed quite poorly, either in the left ear or bilaterally. With treatment, all showed substantial improvement. In 58% of cases, performance improved from below the 5th percentile in one or both ears to above the 10th percentile in each ear.

Roberts et al.'s (1990) data would appear to demonstrate that dichotic word listening can be used as an index of seizure activity as well as a measure of the structural integrity of fibers of passage. It would appear that in the untreated condition, seizure activity interfered with the patients' ability to perform the task and that with treatment, their performance improved. A simple attentional deficit is unlikely because improvement in dichotic listening was poorly correlated with improvement in Digit Symbol ($r = .23$) or Controlled Oral Word Association ($r = .28$). Thus, the seizures probably interfered with the actual transmission of the stimulus material over subcortical white matter pathways.

In a separate study Gorman, Roberts, Varney and Hines (1990) looked at the relative sensitivity of dichotic listening in comparison to the standard 16-lead EEG. Patients ($n = 350$) were selected based on manifest behavioral evidence of partial complex seizures. There were 18 patients who exhibited abnormal EEGs while performing normally in dichotic listening. By contrast, there were 158 patients who performed poorly in dichotic listening while producing normal EEGs. As can be seen, dichotic listening was by far the more sensitive diagnostic tool.

These findings regarding dichotic listening have more than academic significance. It has been demonstrated repeatedly that the surface electrode EEG is inadequate for demonstrating the presence of many types of seizures, particularly complex partial seizures (cf. Neppe & Tucker, 1988 for an extensive review in this regard). At the same time, there has been nothing but the EEG to demonstrate "objectively" that a patient has a seizure disorder for forensic purposes. The dichotic word listening paradigm would seem at least partly to fill this gap. It should also be mentioned that the procedure used is not particularly cumbersome or expensive. The 10 practice items and 50 test items take no more than 15 minutes to administer, and this can be done with a portable cassette tape playing device. Thus, this clinically valuable information can be obtained with a relatively small investment of time and money.

The Minnesota Multiphasic Personality Inventory

The MMPI is not a first rank neuropsychological assessment tool, yet the results of MMPIs frequently appear in court-related records. They are given, if for no other reason, to provide as comprehensive an exam as possible. Unfortunately, the results are sometimes quite abnormal and raise questions about the patient's veracity or premorbid mental health.

A particularly important factor to be considered in evaluating an MMPI from a head-injured patient is whether the patient suffers from partial complex seizures. These may not as yet have been diagnosed correctly because patients with partial complex seizures mistakenly report, in large proportion, to psychiatrists (cf. Neppe & Tucker, 1988). Tucker, Price, Johnson and McAllister (1986) and Neppe and Tucker (1988) have also pointed out that partial complex seizure patients run a high risk of being misdiagnosed as having a conversion reaction, schizophrenia, or affective disorder because of the multiple peculiar symptoms associated with this type of seizure disorder (e.g., intrusive thoughts, a variety of sensory illusions, abrupt shifts in mood, automatisms, unexplained somatic sensations).

The basic problem is illustrated in Figure 2.1 (from Roberts, Paulsen, Marchman & Varney, 1988). This is the mean MMPI obtained from 40 patients with supposedly mild head injuries who produced abnormal EEGs which, along with clinical considerations, led to a diagnosis of partial complex seizures *and* successful treatment with anticonvulsants. It should be clear that the profile is grossly abnormal. Such a profile from a non-head-injured person would suggest schizophrenia with somatic delusions, generalized distress, or malingering. However, when obtained

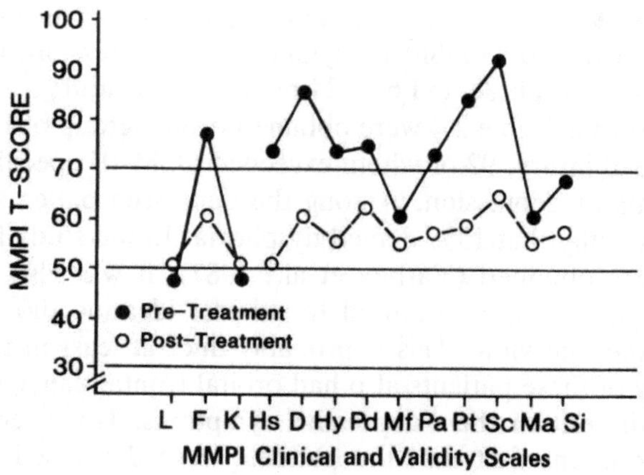

FIGURE 2.1. Mean MMPI profiles of patients with apparent partial seizures before and after treatment with anticonvulsants.

from a seizure patient, the profile is valid and is a reasonable illustration of the patient's real symptoms so that the conventional psychological or psychiatric interpretations would be completely incorrect.

It is interesting to note that each of the individual profiles used to produce the mean MMPI in Figure 2.1 was obtained from a psychiatric patient who had never seen a neurologist. Indeed, their head injuries were viewed as being so trivial at the time that neither they nor their physicians saw the head injury as having any relevance to their subsequent psychiatric complaints (mostly depression). Thus, the case material shown in Figure 2.1 is hardly rare or exotic. The problem is that the patients were misclassified, often by themselves.

Psychodiagnostic Assessment

While the world of psychodiagnostic evaluation includes hundreds of possible disorders, the world of "purely" psychological/psychiatric disorders that are common sequelae of minor head injury is decidedly more limited. Depression is its only member. About 77% of persons who suffer closed head injury are depressed within 2 years of their injury (versus 32% with traumatic back injury). About half of these do not show depressive symptoms to a significant degree until at least 6 months after their injury (Varney, Martzke & Roberts, 1987). If these figures seem rather high, they are closely similar to those reported on patients with stroke (68%), and once again, stroke patients often show delayed or gradual onset of depressive symptoms (Robinson, Starr & Price, 1984). Mania is rare except in persons with a family history of bipolar affective disorder. Schizophrenia can be exacerbated by a head injury, but schizophrenia brought on by a head injury is uncommon (Lishman, 1986). It is recommended, therefore, that any person with a head injury be questioned with regard to DSM-III symptoms of depression, both in the immediate postacute phase and 6 to 24 months after injury.

Findings shown in Table 2.4 were obtained from a group of 120 patients with closed head injury, 92 of whom exceeded DSM-III specifications for diagnosis of major depression. Among the depressed patients, it is particularly noteworthy that 15% denied dysphoria. In the study from which these data were obtained (Varney et al., 1987), it was also noted that many of the patients who admitted to suicidal ideation did not appear depressed in the interview. This is probably due, at least in part, to the fact that many of these patients also had orbital frontal damage and were curiously indifferent to their depressive symptoms. However, this does not detract from the fact that the patients were depressed. Rather, it underscores the importance of asking about depressive symptoms rather than simply trusting in clinical judgment or the patient's willingness to spontaneously report symptoms of depression.

TABLE 2.4. Frequency of depressive symptoms in head injury patients.

Poor memory/concentration	96% (88/92)
Anergia	96% (88/92)
Low libido	91% (84/92)
Indifference	90% (83/92)
Irritability	87% (80/92)
Insomnia	87% (80/92)
Dysphoria	85% (78/92)
Anorexia	77% (71/92)
Crying spells	67% (62/92)
Suicidal ideation	51% (47/92)
Social withdrawal	37% (34/92)
Family history of MDD	21% (19/92)

In trial situations, it is often argued that an individual's major depression might simply have come about spontaneously, regardless of the accident. It is probably fair to say that this is the less parsimonious argument. If three-quarters of a group become depressed within 2 years post head injury, it is quite logical to argue that the injury is the most likely contributing cause of their depression. From a medicoeconomic viewpoint, this is important to the patient since lifetime psychiatric expenses may be high and are not well covered in most health insurance programs.

Conclusion

Mild head injury cases differ qualitatively from serious head injuries in both the role of the neuropsychologist and in the most appropriate methods of evaluation. Dealing with a severely head-injured patient is similar, in many ways, to assessing a patient who has suffered a stroke or has an identifiable tumor or other lesion. In these cases, the neuropsychologist can rely on supportive data from imaging techniques that predict at least partly the nature of quantifiable deficits on neuropsychological deficits apparent in testing (e.g., amnesia, aphasia). It is, in a manner of speaking, a more orderly and highly objective assessment procedure than what is often necessary with the mild head injury patient. Here, the first question is whether there is brain damage of any sort because there is no radiodiagnostic or electroencephalographic "back-up" to aid in diagnosing damage. (Although microshearing and abrasions to the inferior aspect of the brain commonly occur in closed head injury, usually they are not demonstrable through CT, MRI, or EEG.) Moreover, these types of injuries are more likely to produce behavioral disorders of a less quantifiable, more neuropsychiatric nature, such as complex partial seizures or an orbital frontal lobe syndrome.

In a curious sense, there is a distressingly greater degree of ambiguity in the assessment of a mild head injury. Neuropsychologists must become more like detectives and by default often may find themselves primary diagnosticians. Nevertheless, the indecisiveness of a frontal patient or the formication paresthesias of a patient with partial seizures are significant clues that should not be devalued simply because they are behavioral data and not found on "objective" testing.

End Notes

One would hope that a clinician who is planning to appear as an expert witness in a head injury case would be already familiar with the basics of neuropsychological assessment, functional neuroanatomy, the strengths and weaknesses of DSM-III, phenomena such as microshearing and complex partial seizures, and the limitations of diagnostic tools such as EEG and MRI. Clinicians who are not comfortable with these topics would probably be in error in describing themselves as experts. For this reason, some of the more basic features of forensic assessment of the patient with mild head injury has not been covered in this chapter. The following is a list of readings that the authors consider essential for anyone who wishes to familiarize himself with the relevant issues. Some recent references that have proven particularly valuable in advancing the understanding of those involved in cases of minor head injury are presented below.

1. Binder, L.M. (1986). Persisting symptoms after mild head injury. *Journal of Clinical and Experimental Neuropsychology*, *8*, 323–346.
   This provides a comprehensive review of studies that demonstrate that loss of consciousness is not essential as a sign that a head injury has been of significant severity. This is important because many neurologists, psychiatrists, and neuropsychologists maintain that without loss of consciousness, there can be no brain injury of importance.
2. Mendelson, G. (1984). Follow-up studies of personal injury litigants. *International Journal of Law and Psychiatry*, *7*, 179–188.
   This is one of the few studies to determine the frequency with which patients complained of symptoms once their lawsuits were settled. The results demonstrate that a clear majority of personal injury litigants remain "ill" 5 years after settlement and thus were not simply "in it for the money." It also serves to debunk the "common wisdom" that symptoms will resolve if lawsuits are dropped.
3. Neppe, V.M., & Tucker, G.J. (1988). Modern perspectives on epilepsy in relation to psychiatry. *Hospital and Community Psychiatry*, *39*, 262–271.
   This is a highly useful reference. Not only does it do an excellent job of discussing the why and how of seizure patients presenting with psychiatric/psychological symptoms, but explodes many long-held preconceptions about the nature of complex partial seizures. It also has a good review on the limitations of EEG in the diagnosis of any type of seizure disorder.

4. Lezak, M. (1978). Living with the characterologically altered brain injured patient. *Journal of Clinical Psychiatry*, *39*, 592–598.
   This provides a disturbing view of what families experience when a parent suffers a head injury. The type of information contained, although not "objective test data," is of critical importance in any expert testimony, particularly in the area of psychosocial disability for the patient and loss of consortium for the spouse and children.
5. Lieb, J.P., Walsh, G.O., Babb, T.L., Walter, R.D., & Crandall, P.H. (1976). A comparison of EEG seizure patterns recorded with surface and depth electrodes in patients with temporal lobe epilepsy. *Epilepsia*, *17*, 137–160.
   Wieser, H.G., Hailermariam, S., Regard, M., & Landis, T. (1985). Unilateral limbic epileptic status activity. *Epilepsia*, *26*, 19–29.
   Devinsky, O., Kelley, K., Porter, R.J., & Theordore, W.H. (1988). Clinical and electroencephalographic features of simple partial seizures. *Neurology*, *38*, 1347–1352.
   These articles put to rest that EEG is a reliable means of demonstrating that a seizure is *not* present. The Lieb et al. article is particularly extraordinary in that it offers simultaneous depth and surface recording in relation to patients' experiential symptoms. Surface EEG loses badly (1/10) against depth electrodes, whose readings are closely synchronous with patient experiential reports.

Acknowledgement. Preparation of this manuscript was supported by funds from the Department of Veterans Affairs.

References

Bayless, J.D., Varney, N.R., & Roberts, R.J. (1989). Tinker toy test performance and vocational outcome in patients with closed head injuries. *Journal of Clinical and Experimental Neuropsychology*, *11*, 913–917.

Benton, A.L. (1989). Historical notes on the postconcussion syndrome. In H.S. Levin, H.M. Eisenberg, & A.L. Benton (Eds.), *Mild head injury* (pp. 3–7). New York: Oxford University Press.

Binder, L.M. (1986). Persisting symptoms after mild head injury. *Journal of Clinical and Experimental Neuropsychology*, *8*, 323–346.

Devinsky, O., Kelley, K., Porter, R.J., & Theodore, W.H. (1988). Clinical and electroencephalographic features of simple partial seizures. *Neurology*, *38*, 1347–1352.

Gorman, L.L., Roberts, R.J., Varney, N.R., & Hines, M.E. (1990). Dichotic listening is more sensitive than standard EEG to cerebral dysfunction in patients with multiple seizure symptoms. *Journal of Clinical and Experimental Neuropsychology*, *12*, 76. (Abstract).

Jennett, B., & Teasdale, G. (1981). *Management of closed head injuries*. New York: F.A. Davis.

Lezak, M.D. (1978). Living with the characterologically altered brain injured patient. *Journal of Clinical Psychiatry*, *39*, 592–598.

Lezak, M.D. (1982). The problem of assessing executive functions. *International Journal of Psychology*, *17*, 281–297.

Lezak, M.D. (1983). *Neuropsychological assessment.* (2nd ed.). New York: Oxford University Press.

Lieb, J.P., Walsh, G.O., Babb, T.L., Walter, R.D., & Crandall, P.H. (1976). A comparison of EEG seizure patterns recorded with surface and depth electrodes in patients with temporal lobe epilepsy. *Epilepsia*, *17*, 137–160.

Lishman, W.A. (1978). *Organic psychiatry: The Psychological consequences of Cerebral disorder*. Philadelphia: Blackwell Scientific.

Martzke, J.S., Cooper, W.E., & Varney, N.R. (1988). Neuropsychological assessment of orbital frontal deficits: A report of recent attempts at test development and validation. *Journal of Clinical and Experimental Neuropsychology*, *10*, 54. (Abstract).

Mendelson, G. (1982). Not "cured by a verdict": Effect of legal settlement on compensation claimants. *The Medical Journal of Australia*, *2*, 132–134.

Mendelson, G. (1984). Follow-up studies of personal injury litigants. *International Journal of Law and Psychiatry*, *7*, 179–188.

Neppe, V.M., & Tucker, G.J. (1988). Modern perspectives on epilepsy in relation to psychiatry: Classification and evaluation. *Hospital and Community Psychiatry*, *39*, 262–271.

Roberts, R.J., Paulsen, J.S., Marchman, J.N., & Varney, N.R. (1988). MMPI profites of patients who endores multiple partial seizure symptoms. *Neuropsychology*, *2*, 183–198.

Roberts, R.J., Varney, N.R., Hulbert, J., Paulsen, J., Richardson, E., Springer, J., Shepherd, J., Swan, C., LeGrand, J., Harvey, J., Struchen, M., & Hines, M. (1990). The neuropathology of everyday life: The frequency of partial seizure symptoms among normals. *Neuropsychology*, *4*, 65–85.

Roberts, R.J., Varney, N.R., Paulsen, J.S., & Richardson, E.D. Dichotic listening and complex partial seizures. *Journal of Clinical and Experimental Neuropsychology*, in press.

Robinson, R.G., Starr, L.B., & Price, T.R. (1984). A two year longitudinal study of mood disorders following stroke. *British Journal of Psychiatry*, *144*, 256–262.

Springer, J., Varney, N., Garvey, M., & Roberts, R. (1991). Dichotic listening in dysphoric neuropsychiatric patients who endorse multiple seizure-like symptoms. *Journal of Nervous and Mental Disease*, (in press).

Tucker, G.J., Price, T.R.P., Johnson, V.B., & McAllister, T. (1986). Phenomenology of temporal lobe dysfunction: A link to atypical psychosis—a series of cases. *Journal of Nervous and Mental Disease*, *174*, 348–356.

Varney, N.R. (1988). Prognostic significance of anosmia in patients with closed-head trauma. *Journal of Clinical and Experimental Neuropsychology*, *10*, 250–254.

Varney, N.R., Martzke, J., & Roberts, R.J. (1987). Major depression in patients with closed head injury. *Neuropsychology*, *1*, 7–9.

Wieser, H.G., Hailermariam, S., Regard, M., & Landis, T. (1985). Unilateral limbic epileptic status activity: Stereo EEG, behavioral, and cognitive data. *Epilepsia*, *26*, 19–29.

Zusho, H. (1982). Posttraumatic anosmia. *Archives of Otolaryngology*, *108*, 90–92.

3
Workers' Compensation and Clinical Neuropsychological Assessment

ANTONIO E. PUENTE and JAMES B. GILLESPIE, JR.

Despite the common perception that the practice of psychology has focused almost exclusively on the delivery of clinical services to clinical populations, psychology does have a lengthy history of involvement with the legal process (Asch, 1984). More recently psychology and forensic concerns have broadened to include a wide variety of issues including assessment of work disability from a psychological perspective (Volle, 1975).

Specific concerns have arisen over the past few years in the application of the rapidly developing field of clinical neuropsychology to the legal setting (e.g., Dorken, 1979). Because of the intrinsic nature of the etiology of brain dysfunction (e.g., head trauma), a significant and increasing number of these types of cases have legal implications. For example, Puente (1987) recently reported that 41% of all applications for Social Security assistance each year (or close to 150,000 individuals) have organic brain syndromes or related disorders. This chapter will focus on the application of clinical neuropsychology, especially assessment issues, to one source of support covering work-related disabilities, namely, workers' compensation.

Workers' Compensation and Neuropsychological Information

Defining Workers' Compensation

According to Merrikin, Overcast, and Sales (1982), the origin of present-day worker's compensation could be traced to the late 19th and early 20th century when employers were legally responsible for the welfare of their employees. Nevertheless, worker's compensation issues and laws are quite different from common law test recovery (Mussoff, 1981) as well as from government-regulated insurance programs such as Social Security disability. Social Security programs support the workers if total disability is present whereas workers' compensation assists in providing partial assistance based on the amount of deficit relative to the original earning capacity. The major focus of workers' compensation is to assist the injured worker to return to gainful employment.

The first modern law protecting the worker was established in 1911. At present all states in the United States have a workers' compensation law. However, as Merrikin et al. (1982) suggest, the laws have been oriented toward physical injury. These authors indicate that either the cause or the effect could be either physical or mental resulting in four different hypothetical categories of injuries: physical–physical, physical–mental, mental–mental, and mental–physical. Of these, the latter three have been of greatest interest and application to psychologists.

The possibility of mental variables causing physical disorders or physical variables causing nervous disorders has been well accepted for some time (Larson, 1970). However, in numerous states mental injuries have not been favorably considered (Schwartz, 1987). Most jurisdictions prefer objectively measurable deficits and focus on causation (often more so than on the residual level of dysfunction). Presumably, this is why mental disorders have not been well accepted in compensation cases.

The Relevance of Objective Data

The issue of measurable deficits is of great concern to both referral sources as well as to insurance companies in large part because of intrinsic difficulties in assessing the validity of "psychological" symptoms and, in turn, of subjective symptoms. However, the question of validity according to Larson (1970) is linked intrinsically to the question of malingering. Specifically, "the issue comes down to the presence of responsible conscious volition on the part of the patient to invent, protract, misinterpret, or exaggerate his complaint." This situation is exacerbated by two potentially contradicatory assumptions of the medical and legal professions. According to Mussoff (1981), the medical and health professions find it more acceptable to label a healthy person sick than the opposite. In contrast, the legal profession operates on the assumption that it is better to acquit a guilty person than to convict an innocent one. Thus, these contradictory positions provide the foundation for the perception of malingering. Considering the subjectivity of most psychological or mental symptoms, it should come as no surprise to note that malingering is perceived to be such a critical issue in compensation cases. (Malingering is reviewed later in this chapter.)

To avoid the issue of potential malingering, the health care professional needs to rely primarily on objective data (Satz, 1988) that can be supported by clinical and behavioral observations. Thus, a composite picture is developed using a variety of information. It is important to note that the role of neuropsychology is not to decide disability or compensation but to provide data to increase the likelihood of the most accurate administrative judgment possible. Medical experts have generally heeded the warning to avoid becoming involved with the adjudicative process (Ziporyn, 1983). Neuropsychology should similarly realize its limitations with regard to adjudication.

Legal Prospective

There are many areas in which the expertise of a neuropsychologist could be of great advantage to the Court, to the attorneys and others who are trying to make sense out of people's seemingly unreasonable behavior, and often to the parties themselves who do not understand what is happening to them.

The most highly publicized and, thus, the most visible area of neuropsychology (as it relates to the legal field) is in the area of personal injury. Numerous cases throughout the country have demonstrated the value of psychologists and neuropsychologists in presenting and portraying severe damage done to an injured party by events that have left little in the way of physical residual scars (Waldman, 1987). As neuropsychology has progressed from the mid-1970s through the 1980s it is increasingly apparent that injured parties suffer as greatly from the harm done to their higher cognitive skills as to the more grossly defined injuries traditionally dealt with in court. The victim of an automobile accident whose leg is severed at the knee and who must forego playing baseball or jogging is a sympathetic figure, and one who typically brings judgment from juries against the wrongdoer with substantial compensation awarded. Far more sympathetic, however, would be a victim of the same accident who is knocked unconscious for several hours, but who recovers with no permanent scar or visible motor dysfunction. As time passes that individual's home life deteriorates, his relationship with a spouse ends in divorce, personality dysfunction keeps him from promotion or terminates employment altogether, and retraining is difficult because he cannot seem to "remember" or "learn." It then falls to the neuropsychologist and attorney, working together, to link the trauma to this seemingly amorphous residue of dysfunction.

A second major legal area for neuropsychology is disability in the workplace. As the population grows older and as technology changes, it is less likely that an injured employee who in the past might have been retained by a beneficent company in an "inspector" position will be held on and given a secure nominal position until he can retire at 65. Injured workers are increasingly being turned back into the job market by terminations, plant closings, and technological advancement. As these workers realize that they cannot obtain employment because of previous injuries or residual impairments, they are turning to the workers' compensation programs of the state and federal governments for compensation for their actual incapacity. Further, they are calling on the safety net of Social Security to provide disability benefits for them and their families. Again the neuropsychologist, working with the lawyer, is a vital link in assessment and the determination of disability.

Role of Clinical Neuropsychology in Workers' Compensation

There is little question that a considerable amount of money can hinge on the outcome of a workers' compensation case: financially, some clients can potentially benefit (or lose) hundreds of thousands of dollars—essentially, their anticipated future earning capacity minus their residual capacity. From a different perspective, such outcomes affect the insurance carrier losses. Further, the company purchasing such insurance may be faced with higher rates. Thus, the future of both individuals and organizations are intrinsically bound to be both directly and indirectly affected. Possibly because of these high stakes, compensation cases often deteriorate into highly antagonistic encounters.

Medical experts have carved a comprehensive niche in the world of disability evaluation. To date, the following organizations have been formed to address disability issues specifically in medical cases: American Disability Evaluation Research Institute, National Association of Disability Evaluating Physicians, American Academy of Compensation Medicine, the American Academy of Occupational Medicine, and the American Occupational Medicine Association. There are, however, no organized groups similar to these in psychology (Puente, 1989). Considering that historically most clinical neuropsychologists have focused on assessment issues (e.g. Seretny, Dean, Gray & Hartlage, 1986) and that a large percentage of referrals have legal and work-related implications, this situation is indeed perplexing.

Statistics are not readily available for workers' compensation because of state government rules and because private insurance companies usually administer these programs. However, according to Bowe (1980), approximately 15% of the population of the United States experiences physical and/or mental disability. Furthermore, the U.S. Bureau of the Census (1983) reported that work-related disability (which would be covered by workers' compensation) ranges between 3% (16–25 years of age) and 24% (55–64 years of age).

Clinical Neuropsychological Assessment Issues

The clinical neuropsychological evaluation can be critical to a workers' compensation case whenever the injury involves the brain. More preparation and effort are involved in these medico-legal evaluations than in standard clinical psychological evaluations. Moreover, workers' compensation cases are oriented toward and involve issues that distinguish them from other legal cases. The following aspects of these evaluations, referral, evaluation, and court presentation, will be specifically addressed.

Referral

Clients may be referred from one or more sources, sometimes placing the neuropsychologist in a potentially adversarial position. An evaluation may be requested by an attorney or legal representative of the client to support the claimant's position. The referral question is typically concerned with determining what percentage of impairment exists. A focus on strengths and an interest in potentially confounding factors is rarely encouraged by this type of referral source. The neuropsychologist is quickly placed in an adversarial position since most clients do not request legal advice or representation until a negative situation has developed, that is, when an undersirable offer has been made to the client by the insurance carrier.

Another source of referrals is workers' compensation insurance companies or their representatives. Although these referrals may be prompted by the recommendation of the primary treating or consulting physician, they are usually generated by the insurance carrier because of doubts about the validity of the patient's complaints. In contrast to patient-initiated referrals, those from insurers tend to focus on the clarification of functional strengths rather than on deficits of the client.

Less "antagonistic" referrals can come from physicians or other health care professionals or attorneys who are more interested in the welfare of the client. Thus, the goals of referral source reflect the motivation for the evaluation so that in all cases, the specific purpose of the referral needs to be clarified at the outset. However, although it is important to clarify the goal of the referring agent, the task of the clinical neuropsychologist should remain the same: to provide accurate scientific data about the patient's neurobehavioral functioning at the time of the evaluation. For the neuropsychologist to take an adversarial role negatively affects the welfare of the client as well as the discipline of neuropsychology. Such positions should be considered unethical.

Persons outside of the legal field probably misunderstand this aspect of the expert witness as much as any other area of law. Some experts usually testify on behalf of plaintiffs, whereas others testify more often on behalf of defendants (or on behalf of the state in criminal proceedings, or in defense of doctors in malpractice actions, etc.); however, experts should never present evidence without fully and independently arriving at their own conclusions. It is important to recognize that attorneys do shop around for expert witnesses. With this in mind, neuropsychologists who become involved with a patient who may have, based on the outcome of the evaluation, a claim for compensation, are to establish the objectivity of the process and make the report and the ultimate assessment as professional and objective as possible to avoid the appearance of being only a hired gun for one side or the other.

Pragmatic Issues

Most referral sources have little appreciation of the time and expense involved in a comprehensive neuropsychological evaluation. This is especially true in most compensation cases that include record review, testing and scoring time, dictation, discussion with attorneys, depositions, and court appearances. It is important to provide an estimate of the time needed to review records and complete the evaluation with the less predictable time factors involving such issues as court appearances to be decided on at a later date. Another time issue involves the time taken to schedule the client to complete the evaluation and submit a final report. This issue should be discussed before initiating the evaluation since court dates may affect the procedure.

Just as critical as time is the issue of payment. As stated earlier, workers' compensation cases can have a significant impact on the financial status of both the individual and the employer and this financial concern carries over into the evaluation process. To minimize potential ethical complications it is advisable to provide initial cost estimates with conditions for later adjustments clearly set forth.

A final pragmatic issue revolves around interested third parties. These could include defense attorneys, insurance companies, and even other health care professionals. These relationships should be clarified from the outset.. Clear channels of communication, with emphasis on written communication and specific roles for all parties, must be clarified. This may be difficult with issues of payment of services since in most cases insurance companies fall into one of two categories: health or compensation. To maintain objectivity, neuropsychologists should consider themselves to be consultants in these cases, delegating primary care to other health care professionals. For example, evaluating neuropsychologists should refer the client to another professional for therapy in order to maintain the objectivity of the initial evaluation.

Evaluation

Educating the patient is a preliminary step often ignored in any evaluation process, especially in compensation evaluations where the possibility of malingering, as well as lack of knowledge, makes the gathering of useful data a difficult task. The patient, and possibly the family, should be provided with a brief introduction to the field of clinical neuropsychology. Emphasis should be placed on the evaluation and procedures as well as their relationship to the legal questions.

When patients enter the legal sphere they may have already undergone significant testing, evaluation, and treatment by professionals in medicine, psychiatry, psychology, and neuropsychology and will arrive at the office of the lawyer with reams of documentation; alternatively they may come to the attorney's office with a smattering of medical data but presenting with physical and emotional problems that render them disabled, without knowing the reason for their dysfunction. The first of these circumstances provides an easy entry into the legal-neuropsychological realm. The treating professionals at that point usually have communicated among themselves, arrived at a reasonably clear picture of what has happened to the patient as well as what the manifestation and functional limitations of the injury or disease are, and thus can reasonably predict the implications for the client. The attorney's function in such a situation is to become fully conversant with all of the types of treatment, the expertise that has gone into the patient's evaluation, and to place that medical history—with the conclusions of the treating professionals—in the context of the appropriate legal setting.

Unfortunately, all too frequently the presenting client does not come in with a full evaluation by a neuropsychologist in combination with the more traditional fields of neurology, psychiatry, psychology, or neurosurgery. The typical client approaching an attorney brings a problem ("I can't work because . . . ," "I was hit on the head when I fell at the supermarket and now I can't remember . . . ," "After the car accident I just can't control myself and now I am in trouble for hitting a policeman . . ."). If the client has had any psychological workup before seeing the attorney, it will likely have been discounted by the more conventional areas of medicine or will have been done to screen for possible psychological problems—not to detect neuropsychological dysfunction. In those circumstances, the attorney representing the client should recognize and evaluate the full medical and psychological history of the client, as well as be conversant with the tests and evaluations already performed, the limitations of those evaluations, and understand what additional evaluations are needed to document injury and correlate it to dysfunction. At the same time, the attorney must establish a nexus or causality between the dysfunction and the legal issue(s) at stake.

From a neuropsychologist's perspective, an evaluation should not be initiated until sufficient information is available. It is not unusual for a client to be accompanied by few or no prior records. Since neuropsychologists rarely are the first health professional to evaluate a client, records are usually available and should be consulted. These records are critical to the full appreciation of the many variables impinging on the client's current level of functioning. Although not as common, but just as disruptive is the situation in which too much information is sent or the records are not coherently organized. When this occurs, records must be organized chronologically, according to discipline (e.g. neurology, neurosurgery, etc.) and according to tests or findings. Themes or patterns should be developed and hypotheses about deficits and strengths considered. This preliminary investigation allows for the development of a purposeful and directive interview, testing, and general evaluation.

Of particular importance in workers' compensation cases are work histories and related premorbid data. This information often can be obtained from job descriptions, annual evaluations, and coworker interviews. Additional data can be obtained from the Armed Services as well as school or university records. As one might anticipate, such records are often difficult to locate. However, this type of information is critical to the development of an accurate and comprehensive picture of the client's premorbid level of functioning.

A word of caution regarding record keeping: records used in evaluation or entered as testimony can be legally requested by the courts. If taken to the stand during testimony, records certainly will be reviewed. Although some forensic experts suggest that notes and evaluation materials should not be reviewed by others, the possibility of review does exist. Thus, careful record keeping is a must. The problems that arise from illegibly written notes, incompletely filled out test forms, and poorly or incompletely recorded test responses can be avoided.

As with any other neuropsychological evaluation, the interview is the foundation for clinical data gathering. Excellent interview formats or protocols can be found elsewhere and will not be dealt with here. However, variations are applicable. For example, interviews should be completed not only with the client and significant others, but (if possible) with coworkers and employers (e.g. immediate supervisor). Additionally, several evaluations may help in addressing issues of validity. Similarities should be noted and discrepancies should be further explored.

Regarding test batteries, industrial commissions have not expressed a preference for flexible or standardized approaches. The merits and shortcomings of each approach have been presented in several chapters of Incagnoli, Goldstein, and Golden's (1986) *Clinical Application of Neuropsychological Test Batteries*. The type of problem and the issue in question may help determine the approach. Tailoring the evaluation both to the complaints or the residual effects of the trauma as well as to the specific vocational tasks may be helpful. Work potential may be similarly considered by using appropriate tests. While this approach implies the merits of a flexible or nonstandardized approach, testimony based on standardized criteria is less susceptible to attack.

One method to deal with this issue is to use tests accepted by other governmental agencies such as the Social Security Administration. Well accepted tests such as the WAIS-R, Halstead-Reitan, and Luria-Nebraska Neuropsychological Batteries should form the foundation for compensation evaluation. If nonstandardized, experimental, or new assessment strategies or tests are used, these can be anchored to the basic tests (e.g. WAIS-R), both in terms of the logic or rationale for doing the test and with respect to enhancing or expanding the original data. If one prefers nonstandardized or more flexible approaches, care must be taken to explain carefully the rationale for test selection and to limit the inferences about the obtained data.

Care should also be taken to deal with such standard testing issues as the use of a technician. Although considered an acceptable and common practice by such groups such as Division 40 (Clinical Neuropsychology) of the American Psychological Association, and by many neuropsychologists (e.g., Seretny et al., 1986), attorneys question the credibility of test results not directly obtained by the neuropsychologist. The credibility of the technician and the lack of direct observation are presented as confounds by opposing attorneys. Some of these problems can be avoided with proper testimony of the neuropsychologist in regard to training and use of the technician. Variables such as fatigue, time of day of testing, and medications take on an important role in determining the residual functional capacity of the worker. Thus, careful pretest planning may not only increase the scientific validity of the results but also reduce complications in later deposition or testimony.

Malingering

In any compensation case, the issue of secondary gain becomes a primary concern and thus needs to be addressed. Malingering may be defined as "the fabrication or gross exaggeration of physical and/or psychological symptoms" (Rogers, 1985). This exaggeration may include, but not be limited to, the presentation of new symptoms that could be related to the trauma (e.g. personality changes in mild head injury), exaggeration of symptoms already present, or fabrication of clinical symptoms unrelated to the trauma in question. All pose serious difficulties to the clinician. This is especially the case since the symptoms of mild head injury often present as psychiatric problems (Binder, 1986; Kelly, 1980; Miller, 1961) and the potential for secondary gain (e.g. financial settlement) is often present (Derebery & Tullis, 1983; Johnson, 1987).

According to Rogers (1985), malingerers can easily fake unusual symptoms as well as general degree of impairment. What is most difficult to fake is subtle (or less understood) negative and combined symptoms. In an interview situation, malingering of mental illness tends to produce unusual attitudes toward the clinician (Resnick, 1984). This includes unusual presentation and a willingness to discuss symptoms. The focus is typically on form rather than content. With regard to organic symptoms, malingers may also tend to overpresent their "problem." Malingerers exaggerate organic symptoms even when compared to patients actually suffering from diffuse brain damage. Other issues considered by Rogers includes deliberateness and carefulness as evidenced by stalling and hedging. This may be reflected in slower response times, repetition of questions, and tendency to provide complex responses to simple questions. Finally, consistency is a key factor in determining valid symptoms. Thus, brief interviews conducted over several days rather than a single, lengthy interview may provide measures of self-report reliability.

With regard to testing, the neuropsychologist can focus both on direct and indirect measures of faking. For example, Gynther (1961) indicated that the F and K scales of the MMPI may be useful for the detection of faking. The F scale is rarely endorsed by psychiatric patients whereas the K scale may provide a barometer of symptom presentation. More recently, Osborne, Collegan, and Offord (1986) have provided support for the use of the F-K value (raw score) as a robust dissimulation index. According to Heaton, Smith, Lehman, and Vogt (1978), a score of $\geq +5$ could be considered useful for detecting faking bad even in those with neurological impairment.

Benton and Spreen (1961) indicated that faking was evident on the Visual Memory Test using quantitative measures alone (i.e. malingerers did worse than brain-damaged patients). Faking can also be detected by observing patterns of responses rather than simple quantitative analyses of the responses to the Halstead-Reitan Neuropsychological Battery (Heaton et al., 1978). Similar findings have been noted with the Luria-Nebraska Neuropsychological Battery. Mensch and Woods (1986) reported that items on the Motor, Rhythm, and Tactile (the first three clinical scales) were faked most often by those who wished to present themselves as impaired.

The evaluation of the validity of memory impairments can also be addressed using the method developed by Pankratz and colleagues. Using the Symptom Validity Test, Binder and Pankratz (1987) assessed the probability of faking bad by presenting 100 (or more) trials of a simple visual or auditory memory discrimination task. Malingerers will most likely exhibit significantly more errors than would be expected by chance.

Although such clues may lead to a suspicion of malingering, there is no clear and easy way to detect fabrication or exaggeration of symptoms. Even if an individual produces an atypical pattern of scores, one cannot assume on this basis alone that they are faking. Careful review of records, extensive and multiple interviews, and a pattern analysis of structured and unstructured instruments must all be considered in making such determinations.

Interpretation of Results

By far the greatest error in workers' compensation cases, and probably in most neuropsychological evaluations, is the tendency to make unwarranted inferences or to ignore information that is incongruent with the general conclusions that have been reached. Overinterpretation or oversimplification may be encouraged by pressure within the legal system for certainty, but they pose clear problems on both scientific and ethical grounds. For pragmatic reasons as well, it is preferable to arrive at a tentative conclusion and to address inconsistencies than have to defend invalid inferences when facing a knowledgeable cross-examining attorney or a competent neuropsychologist hired by the opposing counsel to review and critique the evaluation and report. Even if the substance of the report is correct, it may not be accepted once credibility has been lost.

Criticism can also arise when neuropsychologists attempt to address dysfunction from an anatomical perspective. This criticism is not valid. Neuropsychologists inevitably do have to address the relationship between the presenting symptoms and the alleged accident. The question is whether the observed symptoms are most probably caused by the injury in question. If the injury is related in *any* way to the symptoms, then the data should be considered useful and credible. This includes the issues of confounding variables. Indeed, a head injury could exacerbate the residual effects of other damage. If *any* change in the behavior is noted and the change could reasonably be attributed to the injury, then it should be considered by the Industrial Commission.

Report

Reports for workers' compensation cases differ somewhat from standard clinical reports. Beyond the usual identifying information, reason of referral, evaluation procedure, history, clinical findings, test results, summary, and conclusion, there should also be an especially comprehensive report on premorbid functioning. As well, a clear description of current abilities as well as residual dysfunction must be provided, especially as these pertain to work-related activities. For example, if the individual's position requires attending for brief periods of time to alternating auditory stimuli, one could relate the findings of the Paced Auditory Serial Task to the requirements of the vocational task. Unfortunately, there has been little research to date that relates neuropsychological test scores to performance on vocational tasks. Indeed, the absence of such data is seen as a major weakness with respect to the predictive validity of neuropsychological assessment. Nonetheless, the deficits found must be related to prior and future employment. This is often best achieved by examining this issue with a vocational expert who may be better able to equate neuropsychological deficits to job performance. With respect to the issue of employability, it is important to consider not only the most appropriate type of employment for which the client is now suited but also the availability of such employment and the likelihood of the client being hired in a competitive job market. Economists may also be involved to determine more accurately specific dollar figures with respect to total lost earning capacity coupled with anticipated costs for future medical and psychological care. Psychological treatment and rehabilitative potential and approaches can also be considered.

The neuropsychology report prepared for workers' compensation cases needs careful preparation to ensure that the required detail is presented in an organized and succinct fashion. Regardless of the length, the neuropsychologist should carefully scrutinize their written presentation and possibly have the data reviewed by others, such as another neuropsychologist, before its submission.

The segment that most differentiates the workers' compensation report from others is that of the "rating." This is a percentage of impairment based on guidelines published periodically by the American Medical Association and sometimes by the state industrial agencies. As seen in Table 3.1, a composite percentage with rehabilitation potential is presented. As unempirical as such an approach might be, this percentage rating may be the most critical aspect of a neuropsychological report in workers'

TABLE 3.1. American Medical Association guidelines for the evaluation of psychiatric impairment

	Class and percentage of impairment				
	1 0–5%	2 10–20%	3 25–50%	4 55–75%	5 over 75%
Mental status					
Intelligence	Normal or better	Mildly retarded	Moderately mildly retarded	Moderately severely retarded	Severely retarded
Thinking	No deficit	Slight deficit	Moderate deficit	Moderately severe deficit	Severe deficit
Perception	No deficit	Slight deficit	Moderate deficit	Moderately severe deficit	Severe deficit
Judgment	No deficit	Slight deficit	Moderate deficit	Moderately severe deficit	Severe deficit
Affect	Normal	Slight problem	Moderate problem	Moderately severe	Severe problem
Behavior	Normal	Slight problem	Moderate problem	Moderately severe problem	Severe problem
Activities of daily living					
Ability	Self-sufficient	Needs minor help	Needs regular help	Needs major help	Quite helpless
Rehabilitation or treatment potential					
Potential	Excellent	Good	Good for partial restoration	Condition static	Condition will worsen

compensation cases. Surprisingly, however, it is also this portion of the report that is least contested. In the final analyses, the outcome of the compensation hearing hinges on the actual rating. As Table 1 indicates, a specific rating is provided for each type of problem/behavior. In addition, the potential for rehabilitation is also assessed. These ratings are then compounded into a composite or overall rating. It is this rating that is used by the Commission to establish final compensation for the worker.

Accompanying the report may be an introductory letter briefly explaining such issues as purpose, procedure, and overall results of the evaluation that can be incorporated into the report itself. Attached to the letter should be a detailed (and easily understood) billing statement. This statement will also be reviewed by others and may become part of the case record.

Court-Related Issues

Preparation

The key to any forensic case presentation or court appearance is preparation. The first person to prepare for a court appearance or court-related appearance, such as a deposition, is the author of the report. Editorial scrutiny similar to that of a journal review of an experimental manuscript is needed. A preliminary consultation, with a review of potential questions with the attorney, should help in clarifying the issues. The client should be advised of potential procedures and complications.

Statement or Affidavit

Some attorneys prefer a signed written statement that may clarify the issue at hand. Although not extensively used in neuropsychological cases of workers' compensation, legal representatives may prefer to draft questions to be answered. Response can be by affidavit, letter, or other format.

Deposition

A deposition is an examination conducted by one or both attorneys in the presence of a court reporter. This may be preliminary to later, in-court testimony or may be in lieu of testimony. As with any form of data presentation, extreme care should be taken to correctly present the issues or the intended inferences or conclusions.

Court Appearance

Although some neuropsychologists prefer not to appear in court, the likelihood of such an appearance in a workers' compensation case is relatively high. The first test in any legal proceeding involving the testimony of a neuropsychologist is going to be whether the testimony itself, or the person offering the testimony, is competent to sit on the witness stand and talk about the client. Competence is a term of legal art and is an all-or-nothing decision, generally made by the judge or whoever will decide the case. If a witness is ruled incompetent the testimony will not be heard by the jury and will be excluded in its entirety.

Throughout legal history there have been an impressive number of persons who were deemed incompetent to testify, including spouses, infidels, and felons. Those absolute bars to testimony have generally been stricken from the rules of evidence of the states, various commissions, and the federal courts. The term competency, now as it is more generally used, is an issue of relevance in regard to the qualification of the individual who is going to testify, or the admissibility of the underlying tests on which opinions are to be given.

To prevent the exclusion of the test results, the neuropsychologist and counsel should work carefully to research the validity and reliability of the particular tests and methods. They must ensure that the methods used are generally accepted in the scientific community or professional community out of which the expert is testifying, and that the person who administered the specific test or performed the analysis had the appropriate background qualifications. With the qualifications of the expert and tests established, the foundation is laid. It is then appropriate to discuss the test results and clinical analysis as part of the professional opinion of the neuropsychologist. Care should be taken, however, to make certain that the elements for validity of conclusions are presented in direct examination of the expert, so that the results are not successfully objected to as incompetent, thereby undermining the foundation on which the neuropsychologist's ultimate opinion rests.

One of the issues that has arisen in the areas of psychology and neuropsychology is the competency to give a "medical opinion" as to a mental disorder or dysfunction. In these cases it is important to note that "medical" can include psychological. Total disqualification—complete exclusion—on the basis of competence was earlier ruled on by the federal courts when the Court of Appeals for the District of Columbia noted that "The general rule is that anyone who is shown to have special knowledge and skill in diagnosing and treating human ailments is qualified to testify as an expert, if his learning and training show that he is qualified to give an opinion on a particular question and issue "(Jenkins v. United States, 1962).

A neuropsychologist can expect virtually every question addressed to him to obtain the expert testimony in the courtroom to meet with objection from counsel for the other side. The objections will be to the effect that a neuropsychologist, while possibly an expert of sorts, is not a competent person to render a medical opinion. Although the weight of authority is in favor of allowing neuropsychologists to testify and give expert opinion, litigants regularly will find judges at the trial court level who will rule adversely unless carefully instructed. Judges are obviously not health care professionals and, thus, they often lack expertise in numerous health-related areas, especially in new and emerging subdisciplines. Judges need to be educated as to how neuropsychologists may aid in the adjudication process. It is thus critical, if neuropsychologists are not to have their ultimate opinion ruled incompetent during direct examination, to set out fully and completely how the client was interviewed, what considerations were taken in coming to a decision, and how the opinion was derived, relating it with specificity to the expert's field of neuropsychology. This could include extensive explanation of the field of clinical neuropsychology, the training and expertise of the neuropsychologist as well as of the evaluation procedures. Specifically, information about data gathering, types of tests, and limitations or confounds would be appropriate.

The Expert's Opinion

Historically courts have been reluctant to allow an expert's opinions as to what may be considered the "ultimate facts" be decided. This is because the perceived prejudicial impact of an expert's opinion on the jury outweighs any assistance it might otherwise give to the trier of fact. Courts historically do not want to allow experts to come into a courtroom and decide the case for the jury. Someone recognized and qualified as an expert is entitled to give opinions from the witness stand and have those opinions accepted as facts, whereas a nonexpert can only testify as to what he has personally observed and may not offer opinions. Thus, by the recognition of a neuropsychologist as an expert, the Court is giving permission for them to draw inferences from facts—including tests, clinical evaluations, and third party communications (which would be labeled hearsay if presented by a nonexpert witness)—therefore achieving such recognition is a major tactical victory.

The modern definition of expert varies considerably. Supported by hundreds of appellate decisions, an expert is now considered an individual who is better qualified than the jury to draw appropriate inferences from a factual situation based on skill, education, background, training, or simple observational capacity. As discussed earlier, judges at the trial level continue to be reluctant to allow expert status of a witness. On a frequent basis either the witness' entire testimony, or the testimony or opinions regarding specific issues, will be denied competency by a judge who will rule that the jury is equally as well able to determine an issue as the testifying witness. When challenged for competency as an expert witness at the outset, or when an opinion is challenged, it is critical that the attorney establish a clear foundation of education, training, experience, and expertise higher than any that could be reasonably expected to exist in the jury. Whether a witness qualifies as an expert is a question of fact and is considered to be within the exclusive province of the trial judge. The significance of this cannot be over emphasized from a litigant's point of view: If the trial judge rules the witness incompetent at hearing, the ruling will likely be sustained on appeal and the entire testimony of the neuropsychologist—or perhaps a crucial opinion—may be excluded.

Establishing Relevance and Credibility

Two terms that the neuropsychologist may hear in a courtroom, with overlapping meanings, are "relevance" and "credibility." These mean similar things in a legal proceeding, but they do have different consequences. For a working definition the term relevance can be considered to answer the question, "If this fact is introduced, does it have any bearing on what is to be decided by the Judge or the jury?". Credibility answers the question, "If this fact is introduced, does it support the testimony of the expert?". For the litigating attorney the differentiation of relevance and credibility is significant, since the court, whether it be a judge, hearing officer, or other, is required to assess every question and answer as to its applicability or relevance to the proceedings. Thus, an objection by a party as to relevance of testimony of a neuropsychologist puts at issue whether the testimony will be heard. Credibility of the evidence, that is, whether the fact to be placed into evidence supports the opinion of the expert, is for the jury or fact finder to determine but the testimony itself is not barred.

Assume a case of an injured worker who has received a blow to the head: a testing instrument documents severe brain damage evidencing itself in some basic cognitive dysfunction. When the neuropsychologist is placed on the witness stand the first objection will be to his competency as an expert; the second will be to his competency to describe the test results in to the hearing testimony; the third objection will be to the competency of the neuropsychologist to render an opinion; the next will be to the relevance of the testimony to prove anything of legal significance to the case; the next objection will be to the relevance of the tests to the dysfunction and disability exhibited by the claimant; and (assuming all other objections are overruled and the testimony is allowed) the final objection will be that the credibility of the entire testimony is so low as to be inadmissible or to undercut it to such an extent as to be unbelievable. Stated another way, the final objection is that assuming all of the evidence was appropriate to be heard by the jury, they should not believe that the information actually meas what the neuropsychologist said it meant.

It is helpful to understand that the testimony of a neuropsychologist, like the testimony of physicians and other professionals who deal with an injured, disabled, or damaged human being, does not in and of itself "prove" a case for the client. To visualize this, imagine two islands in a body of water, separated by an inlet, one island being the client, the other island the legal goal that is being sought by the client, whether it is recovery of money, disability benefits, revocation of a contract or will, nullification of a divorce, and so forth. The neuropsychologist as well as the other professionals is essentially called on to define the condition of the first island, the patient. They have to chart its contour, determine whether there has been an injury, determine how severe that injury is, and determine if anything can be done to repair the injury, make it well, or put the island back to its original condition.

On the second island, complete with all of the goals sought in the legal proceeding, is an amalgamation of problems patients say they are having, difficulties they have doing their job, getting work, relating to other people, learning, or understanding things about themselves. The function of the neuropsychologist is to construct a bridge from one island to the next, categorize those difficulties that are being experienced by the patient and identify for the legal system which of the functional restrictions are related to the damage. A second aspect of the linking of patients to the symptoms and subjective problems is the opinion, as an expert, as to whether the actual dysfunction is reasonably to be expected in individuals given the degree of pathology evident in their evaluation. It is not the role of the expert to testify as to whether the patient *was* hit on the head, nor how much force was exerted in the blow, nor how long he was unconscious. The proof of those issues is for the attorney and client to establish. The role of the neuropsychologist, in litigation, is to identify for the attorney the major operative factors, accept and assume the testimony as offered by the client and developed at trial, and then to define, for the judge and a jury, the extent or degree to which the client has been damaged by the trauma received.

A neuropsychologist is, therefore, required to construct a bridge of understanding for the court from the damaged client to the disabilities experienced. It is reasonable to assume that not all symptoms displayed by a brain-damaged individual will correlate directly to the findings, and it is equally true that most people who are evaluated come to their accident, injury, or period of incapacity already ladened with a lifetime of events that have contributed to their overall condition. The neuropsychologist is called on as an expert to differentiate those limitations that seem, with a reasonable degree of probability, to be related to the trauma.

The issues of degree of impairment, compensability, inability to work, or future prognosis and expected course of the condition are all areas in which it may be appropriate for the neuropsychologist to render an informed, expert opinion. These are also areas in which opposing counsel will object strenuously on the basis of competency, relevance, and credibility. For example, a blow to the head that might restrict short-term memory and the learning of new material may be related to a patient's inability to succeed in a retraining environment at work. The bridge having been established from the trauma to the reported symptoms can then be used to define the damage clearly, with statements of possible treatment, further decline in condition, and effect on life situations not yet experienced by the patient.

The role of the neuropsychologist has ended when damage is fully defined. It is the lawyer's function to argue the proof to the judge and jury and to provide the materials from which the neuropsychologist can construct the bridge. While the patient, third-party observations, and circumstantial evidence can provide the raw material, it lies within the particular realm of the neuropsychologist to shape and define the boundaries of the dysfunction. The attorney then can work with professional opinions offered as to the degree of injury and can place them in their proper legal context. Assuming all evidence is allowed to get to the fact finder (whether that be judge or jury), the final question is whether the definition of the "first island," the construction of the bridge, and the elaboration of the difficulties to the patient, of the "second island," are sufficient to allow for compensation or recompense.

Content of Testimony

Most neuropsychologists are closely allied with the medical profession, many are involved in academics, and most have had a significant relationship with the practices of psychiatry and clinical psychology. None of these professions is given to making definitive statements about patients, and, like medical students, most neuropsychologists are nurtured in the belief that what they present as an opinion is best propounded in the conditional: may have caused, might have caused, could have been caused, will probably be, and so forth. The legal system, on the other hand, looks for definitives and punishes those who do not express themselves in absolute terms. Neuropsychologists will often be called on to testify in situations in which they will be given a fairly free rein to describe their methodology. It is imperative that the expert witness know what questions counsel can and cannot ask and the direction these questions can take. The basic rule is that a witness called by a client's lawyer can be asked only questions that do not suggest a correct answer. Thus, when plaintiff's counsel asks a neuropsychologist "When did you first see the client and what did you do?" the field is open. There is very little the attorney should do other than keep the testimony running in the proper direction. It is appropriate for the neuropsychologist to testify about all of their observations of the patient, to testify about all of the testing methodologies used to detect brain damage, and to give an opinion as to the relationship between the clinical evaluation and permanent damage as well as any permanent damage and incapacity or disability of the patient.

In most jurisdictions, it is proper at the end of the expert's testimony for counsel to present a question based on either an actual set of facts or a set of hypothetical statements. Older laws required an expert witness to offer an opinion only in response to a hypothetical propounded (now assume the following facts, a 35-year-old male with a ninth grade education . . .), which gave a bizarre aspect to courtroom proceedings. The expert often testified for days about a specific patient, only to conclude testimony with response to a "hypothetical" set of facts. The more modern rule, in effect in most jurisdictions, is to pose the question as to whether experts have, to a reasonable degree of certainty within their field of expertise, an opinion as to diagnosis, damage, impairment, or whatever. Although the terminology varies from jurisdiction to jurisdiction, neuropsychologists should be aware that the response to a hypothetical question or a question concerning the actual patient—or even a spontaneous statement that gives an opinion—should express an opinion to a reasonable degree of certainly or high degree of probability consistent with the field of expertise. Conditional words such as "may," "might," or "it is possible . . . ," which may sound fine in conversation or in the course of testifying, stand out when the testimony is reduced to writing and an appeals court is looking for error. Whereas the academic and even the medical professions allow for probabilistic models, the judicial system is harsh to the point of punitiveness for what is perceived as uncertainty. The last thing a neuropsychologist wishes to hear, listening to the jury summation by opposing counsel, are words quoted back: "And you heard their own witness say that the blow to the head *may* have caused his memory problems. Even their own expert did not *know* the blow caused any injury, he was only guessing."

Conclusions and Legal Proceedings

From the position of the counsel for a client for whom a neuropsychologist is testifying, there are three major and distinct stages in the course of the neuropsychological/legal relationship. They are:

1. evaluation to determine if the client has brain damage
2. assessment of the damage to determine causation and extent
3. if damage is present and causation and extent identified, what affect do they have on the client's functional capabilities?

With a proper initial consultation the first question, the presence of brain damage, should be answered so that the claim can either proceed or be dropped. This could include clear neuroradiological findings or patterns of behavioral dysfunction highly similar to patterns observed in specific syndromes (e.g. post-concussive syndrome). If the matter proceeds, the attorney knows that he is going to be called on to prove legal causation of the injury as well as the relationship between the injury and the full extent of the impairments.

The rule used by courts to define just how far an expert can go in testifying is that the expert may express an opinion to whatever extent and to whatever degree his expertise will allow him to do so, but he should not "invade the province" of the jury as the ultimate determiner of fact. Just how close a judge will allow the expert neuropsychologist to go in concluding the "ultimate" facts in a case depends on how well the judge understands the science of neuropsychology, how well the initial factual background is laid before the neuropsychologist's testimony, and how well the neuropsychologist conveyed his professionalism to the court. As happens over and over again, in cases in which physicians testify, by the time the "opinions" of experts has ceased, there is nothing left for the jury to do but decide a dollar amount: the experts will have completely defined the two islands, of injury and damage, constructed a bridge of causation, and predicted the future course of the patient. Such completeness should be the testimonial goal of the neuropsychologist and counsel for the injured party. By the conclusion of the testimony the judge and jury should be convinced of the validity of the practice of neuropsychology as a distinct area of the expertise and should be comfortable with the conclusions that can be reasonably drawn from a competent professional in the field.

The Relevance of Neuropsychological Data

The question of the validity of symptoms has made it difficult for psychologists to become involved in compensation cases. This problem is magnified in the field of clinical neuropsychology. While the efficacy of clinical neuropsychological assessment of the delineation of a higher order deficit is well documented and generally accepted by both psychological and medical professions, it has received less than enthusiastic acceptance from significant segments of the legal profession (e.g. judges) and even weaker reception from insurance and compensation companies.

An excellent example of the situation is the Horne v. Goodson (Marvin L. Goodson Logging Co. v. Edward Horne) case in which both chapter authors were involved, Antonio E. Puente as clinical neuropsychologist and James B. Gillespie as attorney. In this case, Edward Horne was injured at his job in a lumber camp when a 2,000-pound pine tree/log fell 14 feet onto his head, driving him several inches into the ground and injuring several of his teeth and vertebrae. Initial emergency room evaluations did not reveal specific brain injury, but Mr. Horne's wife requested additional medical assistance since her husband had begun to act "very differently." A cursory examination long after the accident by a neurosurgeon, a skull x ray, and a noncontrast CT scan (approximately 1 year post-injury) did not reveal the existence of "brain damage." The patient was discharged from the neurosurgeon's care with a suggestion to take aspirin to relieve his pain.

Eventually Mr. Horne's case was brought to the attention of Mr. Gillespie, who referred the client to Antonio Puente. An exhaustive clinical neuropsychological examination was performed in the manner described above. This entailed extensive review of records, interviews with several family members, and a multi-session neuropsychological evaluation spanning a period of several months. A comprehensive report was submitted to counsel.

On March 6, 1985, the Industrial Commission of North Carolina ruled in favor of the employer and compensation carrier stating that the testimony provided by the clinical neuropsychologist was neither relevant nor credible. Neither the evaluation, the findings, nor the qualifications of the neuropsychologist were accepted. Instead, the neurosurgeon's testimony was accepted by the court because a medical background was considered necessary to comment on a complaint of an "organic" nature.

The North Carolina Psychological Association (including Ann Majestic, Attorney, Sally Cameron, Executive Director, and Landy Anderton, Legislative Affairs Committee Chairperson) and the American Psychological Association (Bryant Welch, Director of the Practice Directorate, Anne Marie O'Keefe, and Donald Bersoff, Counselors at law) submitted a most comprehensive amicus brief to the North Carolina Court of Appeals in 1986. Based on a new and more comprehensive review of the case, the higher court reversed the lower court decision with respect to the issue of competency of psychologists to render testimony under the Workers' Compensation Act. The determination of credibility was left to the discretion of the lower courts. The neuropsychological evidence was then considered but rejected, this time on the grounds of credibility. On August 25, 1989, Lawrence Shuping, Deputy Commissioner, ruled that Mr. Horne "has not suffered any type of disabling permanent brain injury with associated adverse physical and/or behavioral manifestation."

The tragedy of this ruling is that it prevents Mr. Horne from collecting disability pension for job-related injuries. Thus, despite the marked changes in personality and cognition noted since the accident by Mr. Horne's wife and family and documented through a comprehensive neuropsychological evaluation, Mr. Horne returned to his job with the logging company. He was subsequently involved in an accident while operating his logging truck. The accident resulted in the death of two young girls.

The legal tradition has nurtured the view that it is better to err on the side of a false negative decision. This is wise in most forensic situations whereby the cost of false positive decision could cost innocent persons their freedom, or in some states, their lives. This may not be an appropriate model, however, in decisions regarding the neuropsychological consequences of brain damage where the "costs" of a false positive are far less serious than the risks of pressing cognitively impaired individuals back into positions that have the potential of putting them and others at risk.

Summary

There is a requirement that representatives from both professions learn enough about each other's respective disciplines so as to facilitate the just settlement of legal decisions regarding the loss or diminution of cognitive function. In the legal system a client comes to an attorney with a specific goal; the attorney gathers information to obtain the desired result for the client; the goal is obtained or not obtained; and the attorney/client relationship is severed. The focus in litigation is therefore apt to be quite different from the focus in a treatment system (or even an evaluation process), which has as its ultimate goal the long-term rendering of health care to a patient.

As a consequence, the testing, evaluation, and measurement of difficulty in the brain-damaged individual by the psychologist is traditionally going to be treatment oriented; the motivation of the legal system is to arrive at specific answers, tie them to legal criteria, resolve the legal issue, and dispose of the case with finality. These conflicting orientations of the two systems involved are often at the bottom of misunderstandings that may take place between neuropsychologist and attorney, even when there is the best attempts at communication and understanding.

With the increasing interrelationship between neuropsychology and the law, it is vital that the neuropsychologist understand clearly the legal framework in which the patient is placed, the goals sought by the attorney, and the type of evidence that needs to be obtained to address the legal issues. It may be relatively easy to determine the presence of brain damage in order to make a diagnosis and to make recommendations for treatment on probation of a minor criminal offense. On the other hand, it is substantially more difficult to provide the full analysis—including the functional restrictions and limitations in the employment sector—of individuals who come to their injury often encumbered by a lifetime of experiences that render them more or less vulnerable to the injury for which they are claiming compensation.

Once the basic examination process is complete, it is not improper, and, in fact, is crucial, that the neuropsychologist work closely with the lawyer in developing and presenting the evidence necessary to substantiate the findings. Just as the expert must clearly understand what is being asked in a legal sense in terms of an opinion and the conclusions to be drawn from the opinion, so counsel needs to be apprised of what information to ask for from the neuropsychologist to establish a basis for the subsequent expert testimony.

The educational process is fourfold. First, neuropsychologists must be prepared to defend their qualifications, especially those pertaining to their training and experience in assessing neuropsychological disorders. Second, neuropsychologists must provide information about clinical neuropsychology as a discipline and the evaluations performed. Third, the neuropsychologist must provide a thorough description of the client, the accident, and the residuals of that accident. This must include an explanation of the degree to which historical, clinical, and psychometric analyses explain both premorbid, confounding factors as well as residual deficits.

After the neuropsychologist has made a determination in the case, the goal is to present it in an understandable way to those who will see the information and make decisions; that is to achieve the goal that is being sought by the attorney and client. Just as the attorney cannot remain silent as to the purpose of the evaluations, the goals sought by the patient, or the methods or form that will be used to achieve those goals, neither should the neuropsychologist leave the attorney in the dark as to how his opinion was reached, what formed the basis of that opinion, and what challenges may be raised to those opinions. At all times, the attorney and the neuropsychologist must work together as a professional team, whose goal is the determination of whether there is objective evidence of dysfunction that can reasonably be attributable to brain damage.

Although a team effort is required, it is essential that the neuropsychologist arrive at an independent decision as to the nature and consequences of the injury in question. An unbiased approach and presentation are critical to effective communication of neuropsychological data to the court. To do otherwise would endanger potentially valuable information, the welfare of the client, and the worth of the discipline.

References

American Medical Association. (1984). *Guides to the Evaluation of Permanent Improvement*. Washington, DC: Author.

Asch, A. (1984). The experience of disability. *American Psychologist, 39*, 529–536.

Benton, A.L., & Spreen, O. (1961). Visual memory test: The simulation of mental incapacity. *Archives of Clinical Psychiatry*, *4*, 79–83.

Binder, L.M. (1986). Persisting symptoms after mild head injury: A review of the postconcussive syndrome. *Journal of Clinical and Experimental Neuropsychology*, *8*, 323–346.

Binder, L.M., & Pankratz, L. (1987). Neuropsychological evidence of a factitious memory complaint. *Journal of Clinical and Experimental Neuropsychology*, *9*, 167–171.

Bowe, F. (1980). *Rehabilitating America*. New York: Harper and Row.

Derebery, V.J., & Tullis, W.H. (1983). Delayed recovery in the patient with a work compensable injury. *Journal of Occupational Medicine*, *25*, 829–835.

Dorken, H. (1979). Worker's compensation: Opening up a major market for psychological practice. *Professional Psychology*, *10*, 834–840.
Marvin L. Goodson Logging Co. v. Edward Horne, N.C. App. 3-6-85.
Gynther, M. (1961). The clinical utility of invalid MMPI F scores. *Journal of Consulting Psychology*, *25*, 540–542.
Heaton, R.K., Smith, H.H., Lehman, R.A.W., & Vogt, A.T. (1978). Prospects for faking believable deficits in neuropsychological testing. *Journal of Consulting and Clinical Psychology*, *25*, 486–491.
Incagnoli, T., Goldstein, G., & Golden, C.J. (1986). *Clinical application of neuropsychological test batteries*. New York: Plenum.
Jenkins v. United States, 307 F.2d 637, 643 (D.C. Cir. 1962).
Johnson, R. (1987). Return to work after severe head injury. *Internal Disability Studies*, *9*, 49–54.
Kelly, M. (1980). The post-traumatic syndrome. *Journal of the Royal Society of Medicine*, *74*, 243–245.
Larson, A. (1970). Mental and nervous injury in workmen's compensation. *Vanderbilt Law Review*, *23*, 1243–1263.
Mensch, A.J., & Woods, D.J. (1986). Patterns of feigning brain damage on the Luria-Nebraska Neuropsychological Battery. *International Journal of Clinical Neuropsychology*, *8*, 59–63.
Merrikin, K.J., Overcast, T.D., & Sales, B.D. (1982). Worker's compensation law and the compensability of mental injuries. *Health Psychology*, *1*, 373–387.
Miller, I.I. (1961). Accident neurosis. *British Medical Journal*, *April 1, 1961*, 919–928.
Mussoff, J.C. (1981). Determining the compensability of mental disabilities under worker's compensation. *Southern California Review*, *55*, 193–253.
Osborne, D., Collegan, R.C., & Offord, K.D. (1986). Normative tables for the F-K Index of the MMPI based on a contemporary normal sample. *Journal of Clinical Psychology*, *42*, 593–595.
Puente, A. (1987). Social Security Disability and clinical neuropsychological assessment. *The Clinical Neuropsychologist*, *1*, 353–363.
Puente, A. (1989). Historical perspectives in the development of clinical neuropsychology as a professional specialty. In C.R. Reynolds and E. Feltcher-Jantzen (Eds), *Handbook of child clinical neuropsychology*. New York: Plenum.
Resnick, P. (1984). The detection of malingered mental illness. *Behavioral Sciences and the Law*, *2*, 21–38.
Rogers, R. (1985). Assessment of malingering within a forensic context. In D.N. Weisstub (Ed.), *Law and mental health: International perspectives* (pp. 209–237) Riverside, NJ: Pergamon Press.
Satz, P. (1988). Neuropsychological testimony: Some emerging concerns. *The Clinical Neuropsychologist*, *2*, 89–100.
Schwartz, M.L. (1987). Limitations on neuropsychological testimony by the Florida appellate decisions: Action, reaction, and counteraction. *The Clinical Neuropsychologist*, *1*, 51–60.
Seretny, M.L., Dean, R.S., Gray, J.W., & Hartlage, L.C. (1986). The practice of clinical neuropsychology in the United States. *Archives of Clinical Neuropsychology*, *1*, 5–12.
United States Bureau of the Census. (1983). *Labor force status and other characteristics of persons with a work disability: 1982*. (Current Population

Reports Series P-23, No 127). Washington, DC: US Government Printing Office.

Volle, F.O. (1975). *Mental evaluation of the disability claimant*. Springfield, IL: Charles C Thomas.

Waldman, S. (1987). Representing your patients: Legal aspects of post concussive syndrome cases. *Texas Medicine*, *83*, 55–61.

Ziporyn, T. (1983). Disability evaluation a fledging science. *Journal of the American Medical Association*, *250*, 873–880.

4
Assessing the Neuropsychological Abilities of Children and Adolescents for Personal Injury Litigation

MAUREEN DENNIS

Children and adolescents often become involved in personal injury litigation (*The Profoundly Injured Child*, 1986). Increasingly, neuropsychologists are engaged in this process to provide opinions for triers of fact that will assist them in their task of determining appropriate compensation in childhood personal injury cases. The burgeoning involvement of neuropsychologists in litigation (e.g., Golden & Strider, 1986; Shapiro, 1984), especially that involving minors, has revealed gaps in our knowledge of how to perform forensic assessments that reflect advances in the neuropsychological testing of children and adolescents and, at the same time, meet the requirements of triers of fact in personal injury litigation.

In personal injury litigation, neuropsychological analysis of cognitive capacities and disabilities provides evidence bearing on three questions: Whether a loss or diminution of cognitive function has been sustained, that is, the existence of neuropsychological impairment; whether a demonstrated loss or diminution of cognitive function is transient, temporary or permanent, and of a form amenable to treatment, that is, the potential for recovery and rehabilitation; and the likely antecedents, coexisting factors, or causes of any demonstrated loss or diminution of cognitive function. While some aspects of the neuropsychologist's involvement in personal injury litigation are similar for younger and older clients, other issues differ according to the client's age.

Assessment of brain-injured children and adolescents for legal purposes requires knowledge of developmental tests, issues, and inferences. Sometimes this knowledge is lacking. Nearly two-thirds of self-designated neuropsychologists routinely assess children, despite the specialized training and experience required for this population (Adams, 1988). Children are

---

This chapter was originally published in *The Clinical Neuropsychologist*, 1989, *3* (3), 203–229. It has been reprinted here with the kind permission of Swets & Zeitlinger bv, Heereweg 347, 216 CA Lisse, The Netherlands.

less likely than adults to have their difficulties brought to the attention of neuropsychologists (Boll, 1983). And in assuming that hypothetical head-injured children will have little or no cognitive deficit (Hart & Faust, 1988), clinicians may fail to perform an adequate neuropsychological assessment of cognitive function in actual head-injured children.

This chapter outlines the range of childhood personal injury litigations in which neuropsychologists are typically involved, and then discusses each of three types of neuropsychological information (concerned, respectively, with evidence, remediation, and cause of observed cognitive profiles) in children and adolescents.

Neuropsychologists and Personal Injury Litigation

Personal Injury Litigation

The term "tort" is etymologically related to the Norman word for "wrong." Tort law concerns civil wrongs not arising from contracts (Prosser, 1971). Mental or cognitive damages are causes of action in personal injury suits falling within the parameters of the tort liability system (Weissman, 1985). Many cases in which neuropsychological opinion is solicited fall under the tort liability system, although it is not clear whether tort law is the ideal mechanism for resolving personal injuries such as childhood head trauma.

One purpose of the tort (although not the sole purpose; see Canadian Law Reform Commission papers) is to arrange correction or compensation, to ensure a set of principles whereby a plaintiff can be fairly compensated from a liable defendant. Under tort law, injured parties are entitled to compensation for harms *intentionally inflicted* by a defendant on a plaintiff; *inflicted negligently* through a lack of reasonable or ordinary care; or inflicted on the plaintiff *without intention or negligence* on the part of the defendant (Gregory, Kalven & Epstein, 1977; Norton, 1981).

Personal injury actions may be categorized according to the basic facts of the situation (Blau, 1984a, 1984b). Common patterns of fact in personal injury litigation involving children include: personal injury from vehicles or transportation situations, such as head injury and coma arising from a motor vehicle accident; injuries occurring on premises, such as post-traumatic seizures after a fall in a day care center; contractor and construction cases, such as those involving improperly installed playground equipment; medical malpractice, such as failure to follow a prescribed asthma ventilation routine resulting in respiratory and cardiac arrest and prolonged coma; sports and athletic suits, such as those involving skull fractures in hockey games; and personal injury cases involving family responsibilities and actions. Less common are "toxic" torts involving exposure to and injury by a variety of pollutants, chemicals, or radiation sources; and special personal injury actions, including prenatal injuries or preconception cases involving harmful or mutigenic substances. An increasing trend in litigation, sometimes involving minors, is the product liability suit in which one or more plaintiffs bring action for harm done by virtue of defective design or manufacture of a drug or device.

Proximate, Preexisting, and Coexisting Events

When cognitive factors are advanced as damages in a legal action, a relationship must first be identified and then established between legally relevant events such as the personal injury and the events surrounding it on the one hand, and any profile of cognitive disorders on the other. To address this relationship in personal injury suits involving children and adolescents, three classes of events should be distinguished: Events proximally related to the tortious injury (e.g., prolonged coma immediately arising from cardiac arrest); preexisting events or neuropsychological problems (e.g., a long-standing learning disability), and coexisting events (e.g., a second head injury occurring subsequently to a first, the topic of a personal injury action). The proximately related event is legally relevant in the personal injury action, although any injury may serve to exacerbate a preexisting problem.

Standards of Proof in Neuropsychology and Law

The burden of proof refers to the obligation of a party to substantiate an allegation, to convince triers of fact about the truth of a claim. Probative standards in law are a means of determining "truth value." Different probative standards exist for criminal and civil law. In civil cases, of which tort law is a subcategory, proof involves a preponderance of evidence (in contrast to criminal cases, which require proof beyond a reasonable doubt). In personal injury litigation, it is necessary to determine whether a tortious injury played a substantial role in producing cognitive disorder at a level of proof where the preponderance of evidence standard is met (Weissman, 1985).

There are divergent probative standards in neuropsychology and law for what constitutes a preponderance of evidence. Specifically, probative levels (in law) differ from significance levels and confidence limits (in psychology and neuropsychology).

Probative levels, significance levels, and confidence limits each use probabilistic reasoning. However, probative standards pertain to the individual, and confidence limits pertain to group data and to inferences drawn from such data (Weissman, 1985). For the neuropsychologist, significance characteristically involves the probability of a statistical statement (e.g., estimates of Type I error in drawing a conclusion as being 1 in 100 or 5 in 100 instances). For the lawyer, the issue is whether the preponderance of evidence ("more likely than not") standard has been met; in psychological terms, this question asks whether there are confidence limits with probability greater than .51 that a tortious event (e.g., head injury causing prolonged coma) constituted a substantial factor in bringing about an effect (e.g., impaired memory). The explication of statistical probabilities and decision making may be made before written reports, depositions, or testimony.

This is not to deny that the neuropsychologist also forms an overall opinion that involves preponderance of evidence, or neuropsychological certainty. This opinion, which typically will be expressed in formal report and/or in courtroom testimony, is based on the neuropsychologist's knowledge, background, training, experience, and education.

Information likelihoods and professional opinion may be distinguished within a framework of Bayesian decision theory (Wagenaar, 1988). Less formally for discussions of neuropsychological data in personal injury cases, it is useful to separate the preponderance of evidence criterion in law, the probability of a statistical statement in the evaluation of test scores, and overall clinical opinion or neuropsychological certainty. Both neuropsychology and law deal in personal injury cases with ideographic data involving one particular child or adolescent, even when the disciplines have somewhat different frames of reference for proof or significance. The neuropsychologist uses data based on the assessment of an individual within a frame of reference at least partially grounded in normative group data.

Postdicting Preinjury Status and Skills

A particular feature of personal injury suits involving children is that the data from assessment of the individual child (perhaps supplemented by independently verifiable sources or by serial neuropsychological assessments) must often be used by the neuropsychologist to "postdict" the child's cognitive capacities before the tortious injury. Postdicting preinjury levels of functioning involves questions of cognitive developmental stability, for which a critical distinction is that between developmental functions and individual differences.

Continuity-Discontinuity in Developmental Functions, Stability-Instability in Individual Differences

A skill can change with age, or one skill can replace, supplement, or grow out of another in the course of development. This is the developmental function for a given skill (Wohlwill, 1973), which can take a variety of forms, not all straight-line or linear. Developmental functions of whatever form refer to changes in scores across age for an individual or group (McCall, 1979). But change and continuity can also pertain to individual differences. By correlating scores at two ages, the relative rank ordering of individual subjects on a given attribute can be related to the relative rank ordering of those individuals on the same or another attribute assessed at a subsequent age. The two types of changes are independent: Emmerich (1964) used the terms *continuity-discontinuity* to refer to the status of the developmental function and *stability-instability* to identify the relative consistency of individual differences across age.

In personal injury questions involving children—for example, the effects of a childhood head injury on later intellectual development—the two types of developmental effects must be kept separate. If intelligence were demonstrated to be age-appropriate at two different points in time post-injury, then the continuity of its developmental function would be normal. Another instance of a normal developmental function would be the demonstration that the child passes through the same series of developmental stages as age peers. At the same time, however, the stability of the individual's intellectual functioning could be quite different at the same two time points if, for instance, a first assessment revealed a 50% drop in intelligence relative to premorbid levels and a second did not. The important point is that developmental continuity and developmental stability involve different reference comparisons.

When speaking of developmental changes, it must be made clear whether continuity or stability is being invoked. Developmental issues are especially difficult to disentangle when one opinion claims normality on the basis of developmental continuity and a second opinion asserts abnormality on the basis of developmental instability.

Issues in Personal Injury Claims

Issues in the resolution of personal injury claims involve a series of contingent questions (Prosser, 1971): Did a particular event actually occur? Did the plaintiff sustain a loss? Was this loss caused or substantially aggravated by the event? If the answer to all three questions is affirmative, then two other questions arise: What are the consequences of the loss to the plaintiff? Is the defendant responsible for the event?

Neuropsychological expertise is relevant to some but not all of these questions, and particularly the following (Weissman, 1984): The extent to which the personal injury constituted a substantial factor in causing a new cognitive loss or impairment in the child or in aggravating or accelerating a preexisting disorder; whether a cognitive loss would have occurred at all but for the personal injury; the relative contributions to the cognitive disorder of proximate, preexisting, and coexisting factors; the extent to which a preexisting disorder in its natural progression or evolutionary course would have resulted in the demonstrated cognitive disorders, in the absence of the personal injury.

The Neuropsychologist's Role

In personal injury cases involving children, one feature of the neuropsychologist's role is to assist triers of fact in determining whether the claimed cognitive impairments were caused proximally by the incident in question, and where this is so, to define the range and severity of their consequences for current and future educational, vocational, and adaptive functioning. As always, the neuropsychologist assumes a positive and protective role in the interest of the client that extends to protection of records, referral for needed care as well as a host of other usual considerations afforded every client.

Sometimes, neuropsychological test results in personal injury cases are presented as criterion variables, that is, as presumptive evidence of brain dysfunction. More usually, the neuropsychologist evaluates the consequences of documented brain trauma for cognitive functioning, that is, whether impaired cognition can be demonstrated and whether the causative mechanisms of cognitive deficits are likely to be found in the personal injury or in some other factor in the developmental history. In this view, in which neuropsychological tests are predictor variables, the question is not whether demonstrable brain tissue injury has occurred, but rather, whether such brain damage as can be documented has likely resulted in loss or diminution of cognitive capacities.

Medical evidence of brain tissue injury in childhood personal injury cases comes from investigative procedures like x rays or computed tomography (CT) scans of the brain. Particularly in cases of mild head injury, some procedures may produce negative results in the acute period of the injury that are incorrectly assumed to remain negative throughout the course of the disorder.

Evidence of brain tissue injury increases with technological advances in brain imaging. The most common types of head injuries, and those producing significant psychological-behavioral disruption, are ones resulting from acceleration/deceleration or rotation of the head without entailing a blow. The structural brain damage induced by forces of shearing, tension, and compression (which in animals include degeneration of axons and their terminal arborizations in locations including reticular nuclei, vestibular nuclei, and dorsal regions of the medulla [Adams, Graham & Gennarelli, 1981]) are not obvious even on routine microscopic inspection, but require careful electron microscopic identification. Shearing causes microscopic lesions in the human brain, which may be missed on the standard 10-mm CT scan cuts, but which may be identified by more sophisticated forms of brain imaging. Regardless of the evidence for structural brain damage, the neuropsychologist remains the best source as to whether any such injury has had an impact on function or behavior.

Evidence, Remediation, and Causes of Injury

Neuropsychologists may provide an opinion in a number of evidentiary aspects of personal injury litigation involving the causes, outcomes, and consequences of alleged injuries or losses. The three main evidentiary aspects for a neuropsychologist involved in evaluating a personal injury are the following: the evidence for existence of an injury, the potential for remediation of an injury, and the causes of an injury.

Neuropsychological assessment may bear on decisions as to the existence of a loss or disturbance of brain function. The plaintiff's attorney usually will attempt to convince triers of fact that a loss (e.g., of intelligence) has been sustained. The neuropsychologist provides documentation of the nature and extent of the alleged loss of cognitive function. The neuropsychologist may be asked to provide triers of fact with information relevant to a just and fair remedy, that is, to give an opinion as to the degree to which the brain-injured child might recover, the future capacity to function, and the potential for cognitive rehabilitation. Part of the opinion may involve a judgment about any gap between the child's potential for education and employment as a result of the injuries suffered in comparison with the potential had the injury not occurred. The neuropsychologist may also assist in determining the probable source or causal factors of the documented cognitive diminution or loss.

Existence of Neuropsychological Impairments

This section reviews some procedures involved in the forensic neuropsychological assessment of children. These range from clinical examination and interview techniques to the administration and scoring of cognitive tests. As in any assessment, the testee's cooperation and motivation should be encouraged and maximized.

A detailed evaluation of cognitive functions is central to a forensic neuropsychological assessment of children and adolescents. The current approach describes a particular set of tests, not prescriptively, but as exemplars of intelligence, language, memory, and attention as these cognitive functions are currently understood in mainstream clinical, experimental, and cognitive psychology.

Goals of a Neuropsychological Assessment of Children

Neuropsychological testing, a form of statistical decision making about behavior in a test situation, also involves an inference about the possible brain bases of the observed test behavior (Dennis, 1979, 1987). Decision making involves several steps: establishing the level of test performances; describing the skill configuration or pattern constituting cognitive functions like intelligence, language, memory, or attention; and making hypotheses about the processing impairments that underscore a set of test performances. An assessment requires a set of rules for guiding decision making about level, pattern, and process of cognitive skills.

A neuropsychological assessment relies on the use of psychological tests. The value of such tests is that they allow focused observations to be made under standard conditions in ways that reduce subjective bias, so that different children can be compared, or the same child can be compared at different times, in a quantitative manner along various dimensions of neuropsychological functioning (Dennis, 1979).

The neuropsychological tests chosen, of course, should be age-appropriate, culturally fair (Bersoff, 1983), and selected from among those finding general acceptance with neuropsychologists. Under the 1923 Frye rule (Blau, 1984b), the proponent of evidence must demonstrate that the procedure is generally accepted in the relevant scientific community. The Frye rule is not fixed and absolute, however; it has been limited and modified, and, in addition, special rules of admissibility exist for novel scientific evidence (Horne, 1987). Neuropsychological tests or statistical treatments not in general use at one point may later find acceptance and applicability. Initially used in a single study or small group of studies, a neuropsychological test may increase its reliability and validity as a net of confirmatory studies is added. And any reliable and valid test, regardless of its level of acceptance, may contribute to formulating a neuropsychological opinion.

Test scores should be interpreted as estimates of performance under a given set of circumstances rather than as absolute characteristics of the testee or as necessarily permanent or applicable to all circumstances. The need is always to give triers of fact careful, qualified, and generalizable explanations of test results so that they can view them with clarity and understanding.

Structured Questionnaire Interviews with Parent and Child

Considerable information relevant to providing an informed neuropsychological opinion can be gleaned from clinical interviews with the parent(s) and the child. Interviews should be conducted in a relaxed and open-ended manner so that the concerns of each interviewee can emerge, but they should also be structured sufficiently to ensure that all relevant functional domains are explored. The goals of these interviews are to determine the child's preinjury status, the events surrounding the injury, the range and nature of problems experienced since the injury, and the current phenomenological status of the interviewee vis-a-vis the effects of the injury.

The interview should include questions about family (family structure, age and educational attainments of other family members), pregnancy, birth, and delivery (complications of pregnancy, birth, postdelivery status), developmental milestones (age of smiling, crawling, walking, speaking propositional words and sentences, identifying letters, reading single words), school history (progression through classes, remedial work, repeating grades, behavior in class, school problems), and medical history (childhood diseases, complications, hospitalizations; major systemic and brain infections, immunization reactions, other head injuries).

The clinical interview often involves reconstruction of the injury, perhaps in conjunction with medical records providing information about sequelae such as loss of consciousness, brain bleeds, bleeding from the ears, focal brain contusion, coma, basal skull fracture, or seizures as well as about treatments like intubation, resuscitation, ventilation, elevation of skull fracture, or debridement of wounds. Some neuropsychologists prefer to conduct clinical interviews without making reference to medical data, and to study the records at a later time.

The clinical interview should include an attempt to redentigrate the child's memories surrounding the accident. This is often difficult to do, and results may be confounded by parental or professional reconstruction of the period surrounding the injury; nevertheless, some attempt at establishing the child's first clear memory before the injury and the first clear memory after the injury should be made. Usually, children have spoken to their parents during the hospitalization about what they did or did not remember and parents have sometimes been able to judge from their child's behavior whether memory gaps existed.

The clinical interview should also include a comprehensive checklist of immediate postinjury and current symptoms, ranging from questions about smell, taste, and basic sensory functions through motor functions and sensory discrimination skills, to higher cognitive functions like language, memory, attention, and personality. Care must be taken in devising interview protocols so as to tap such complaints while limiting the influence of response sets (i.e., overreporting or underreporting of problems).

The parents and child should be given an opportunity to outline their main subjective concerns since the injury. Some of these concerns will be overt and physical, whereas others may entail changes in personality, temperament, and behavior. It is important to allow subjective complaints to emerge in order of perceived importance, because the most pressing family concerns may not be the most medically obvious ones.

Traumatic brain injury in children and adolescents has an enormous effect on the family (D.A. Martin, 1988); the presence of increased distractibility, irritability, lowered frustration tolerance, forgetfulness, and apathy after brain injury often generates considerable family stress (Boll, 1983). In many jurisdictions, family members of the injured person are entitled to bring suit for damages because of the effect the injury has had on them; in such instances, a court will need to know the impact the injury has had on family functioning. The clinical interview should attempt to assess some dimensions of this impact, not only because it is an indirect effect of brain injury, but also because family functioning is one of the moderator variables that determines how successfuly a brain-injured child or adolescent will adjust to the cognitive sequelae of brain injury (Ewing-Cobbs & Fletcher, 1987).

Neuropsychological Status Examination

A clinical status examination of the child or adolescent involved in personal injury litigation should survey basic neurodevelopmental skills (such as fine motor control, writing, and drawing; complex repetitive unimanual and bimanual hand movements; unilateral and bilateral tactile sensory functions; visual tracking, proprioceptive control, and eye–hand coordination; reproduction of rhythms and the gross motor skills involved in standing, balance, tandem walk, and skipping). Most clinical status examinations, whether formally structured or based on accumulated clinical experience or both, draw from pediatric neurological examinations and neurodevelopmental scales. Whichever tasks are selected for the examination should provide an opportunity to sample, in an organized and orderly manner, the child's maturity of motor development, skill in controlling large and small muscles, motor planning and sequencing, sense of rate and rhythm; spatial organization, visual and auditory perceptual skills, balance, proprioception, cerebellar-vestibular function, and attentional abilities (e.g., Mutti, Sterling & Spalding, 1978).

Intelligence

It would be beyond the scope of this chapter to discuss all of the issues involved in the administration and interpretation of intelligence tests for children as part of a neuropsychological assessment; these issues have been addressed in a variety of sources (e.g., Dennis, 1987; Kaufman, 1979; Rourke & Adams, 1984). For personal injury litigation, what is important are the processes of statistical decision making and clinical inference.

In recent years, the formal aspects of decision making with standard intelligence tests have become better understood. This trend can best be illustrated by describing some new approaches to the most widely used individual child intelligence test, the Wechsler Intelligence Scale for Children-Revised (WISC-R). Statistical decision making for the WISC-R has been expanded in a variety of ways. In addition to earlier procedures for deciding whether differences within and between parts of a test are abnormal (i.e., so large as to occur infrequently in a population of normal children), reliable (larger than the variability arising from errors of test measurement), or erratically patterned (e.g., Field, 1960; Rhodes, 1975), several new procedures have been developed.

The Tardor Interpretation Scoring System for the WISC-R (Vitelli & Goldblatt, 1979) summarizes the WISC-R based on accepted statistical interpretation, without entering into clinical, educational, behavioral, or other inferences. Statements in the Tardor report are based on scaled score equivalents of raw scores, reliability coefficients of the tests, IQ scores, the intercorrelation of the tests by age level, and the differences between scaled scores required for statistical significance. The aim of the system is to allow the clinician to take all these factors into account simultaneously in a consistent and standardized manner when scoring the test and describing the test results.

Decision making has also been formalized as a series of interpretive strategies with corresponding remedial implications. Profile handbooks (e.g., Nicholson & Alcorn, 1980) provide worksheets that systematically examine a number of hypothesized factors influencing test performance. Addressing both predictive and remedial issues with the framework of the psychometric properties of the intelligence test, such systems greatly increase the coherence with which the clinician can link a defective pattern of test performance to particular remedial suggestions.

Recent user manuals for the WISC-R (e.g., Kaufman, 1979) stress the logic of decision making rather than either purely quantitative or remedial issues. They encourage the tester to use simple psychometric guidelines and then go beyond the statistics to formulate hypotheses about the child's strengths and weaknesses.

These various new approaches to the WISC-R combine clinical skills with statistical decision making. A decision about whether any two WISC-R subtest scores differ from each other, for instance, requires evaluation of the test error associated with each subtest in the context of clinical and case history information. Although these programs and algorithms cannot and do not substitute for the neuropsychologists's judgment, they are time-saving adjuncts to clinical decision making: they quantify the statistical issues associated with test performance and sharpen the clinical questions raised by test performance. Some understanding of these programs and algorithms is critical to the application of intelligence tests to the assessment of children and adolescents involved in personal injury litigation.

Language

After traumatic brain injury, children and adolescents are at risk for language disorders (e.g., Ewing-Cobbs, Levin, Eisenberg & Fletcher,

1987). Language assessment of children involved in personal injury suits should be directed toward two principal questions, one involving the developmental level of oral and written language skills, the other concerned with the pragmatic or functional use and understanding of language in everyday situations. Additionally, for those children demonstrating specific disabilities within the language domain, more specialized, age-referenced or norm-referenced tests of language functions like auditory discrimination (Goldman, Fristoe & Woodcock, 1974c), word finding (Wiegel-Crump & Dennis, 1986), or understanding of grammar (Dennis & Kohn, 1985) may be administered.

Clinical Language

The level of the child's use and understanding of oral and written language functions (such as articulating the sounds and blends of English, understanding single words and spoken commands, producing names for common objects, formulating sentences, verbal fluency, repeating sentences, reading and writing single words and sentences) should first be tested, using some type of childhood aphasia test or adult aphasia test with norms for children (e.g., Spreen & Gaddes, 1969).

Social-Contextual Language

To be fully competent in language, one must not only master the form and content of language, but also be able to use and understand language appropriately in a variety of social, conversational, and interpersonal contexts. Language competence can be said to exist when language form, language content, and its social, discourse, and conversational usage are all appropriate to the individual's level of development.

The Test of Language Competence (Wiig & Secord, 1989) provides standardized measures of language competence for children over the age of 6 years. The test evaluates delays in the emergence of linguistic competence and problems in the use of semantic, syntactic, and pragmatic language strategies. Each of four subtests taps a particular domain of discourse study: the identification of sentence ambiguity that could have been encountered in a specific topical-situational context; memory for one or more intervening event chains or scripts connected by their cooccurrence in the same event or time span; speech acts that express the speaker's intent; and figurative or nonliteral expressions used in discourse and conversations.

Much of language requires an appreciation of its social or pragmatic contexts, and this ability is disrupted by brain trauma. Milton, Prutting, and Binder (1984) described inappropriate regulation of discourse between speakers and listeners in some head-injured adults, and Holland (1982) has observed that such adults talk better than they communicate. The pragmatic and social-contextual use and understanding of language, as measured by the Test of Language Competence, is disrupted after traumatic brain injury in young adults and adolescents (Wiig Alexander & Secord, 1988) as well as in children and adolescents (Dennis & Barnes, 1990). Such data highlight the importance of a language assessment for brain-injured children and adolescents involved in personal injury litigation that includes a specific evaluation of pragmatic and social-contextual language functions.

Memory

In adults, the especially vulnerable cognitive skills after closed-head injury are those involving memory (Levin, Benton & Grossman, 1982). This statement is no less true of children and adolescents: nearly one-half of a sample of children who have sustained head injury show memory disorders in the 6-month period after the insult (Levin, Eisenberg, Wiig & Kobayashi, 1982). A comprehensive examination of memory functions in the child involved in personal injury litigation is therefore important.

The assessment of memory might involve three components. The first is an evaluation of the clinical level of memory functioning, the second is a functional analysis of the various dimensions of memory skill, and the third is a probing of everyday memory functioning.

Clinical Level of Memory

It is useful to have a clinical measure of memory functioning in children and adolescents that provides a quotient, comparable to the Wechsler Memory quotient used with older individuals, to define the characteristic amnesia pattern of memory function disproportionately lower than intelligence. Few procedures are available for a global clinical assessment of memory in children younger than 10 years, although some of the memory scales from tests such as the McCarthy Scales of Children's Abilities (McCarthy, 1972) may be used. For children over 10 years of age, the Denman Neuropsychology Memory Scale (Denman, 1984) provides Verbal and Non-Verbal Memory quotients, analogous to IQ quotients, derived from tasks requiring the immediate and delayed recall of a variety of language, visual-spatial, and musical material.

Functional Analysis of Memory

Of more practical importance to determining the consequences of a brain injury for memory functioning is the assessment of how the memory system operates in children and adolescents after damage to the brain. Such an assessment must be theoretically motivated in the sense that it will reflect a particular view about the internal organization of the memory system. Some such assessment systems are currently being outlined for adults (e.g., Delis, 1989), but there exists no theoretically coherent model for the assessment of memory in children and adolescents. The following constitutes a preliminary discussion of some domains of memory function that need to be assessed in children and adolescents involved in personal injury litigation.

The memory test procedures used to tap these domains of memory function must be assembled from a variety of sources: published tests (e.g., Goldman, Fristoe & Woodcock 1974a; Webster, 1981), clinical research test procedures with norms for pediatric populations (e.g., Siegel, 1988), and the developmental cognitive-experimental literature. Regardless of the panel of tests selected to assess memory function, it is important that the validity of each come to be established in relation to the prediction of discrete memory dysfunction caused by brain injury.

For information to be processed by the memory system, some initial registration of what is heard or seen must occur. Different registers may exist for each sensory modality (e.g., an echoic register for the auditory modality, an iconic register for the visual modality). Tests of memory span, such as the digits forwards section of the Digit Span subtest on the WISC-R or the immediate recall of letter strings in the Learning Efficiency Test (Webster, 1981), provide a measure of the initial registration of information.

After information is registered, it must be held and manipulated as well as being combined with other information. Age-referenced tests of working capacity, such as those used by Case, Kurland, and Goldberg (1982) and Siegel (1988), measure the simultaneous holding and processing of incoming information and the retrieval of older information.

The bulk of the assessment of memory concerns stored information and how successfully or unsuccessfully the child or adolescent can access it. Stored memory involves several different processes. The procedural memory system acquires and retains motor or cognitive habits (riding a bicycle, playing the piano) through repeated exposure to a specific activity constrained by rules. The functioning of the procedural memory system (at least in older individuals—no normative data are currently available for children) is measured through tests of the retention of context-specific routines, such as mirror drawing, mirror reading, rotor pursuit tasks, and puzzles like the Tower of Toronto (Saint-Cyr, Taylor & Lang, 1988). Declarative memory involves the recall or retrieval of facts (which can be words, pictures, events, or personal encounters). The products of this system are what is usually meant in common parlance by the word memory. Declarative memory may be tapped through tests that require either implicit knowledge or explicit, consciously articulated, information. Implicit memory is demonstrated when previous experiences facilitate performance on a task that does not require conscious or intentional recollection of those experiences (Schacter, 1987). Perceptual priming and word-stem completion tasks (e.g., Cermak, Blackford, O'Connor & Bleich, 1988) provide measures of implicit memory in older individuals; at present, no normative information on such tasks is available for children and adolescents. Declarative memory also encompasses two forms of explicit memory: semantic memory, concerned with knowledge of the world, or organized information about words, pictures, and vocabulary, and episodic memory, concerned with how past events in an individual's experience are temporally dated, with when and how particular episodes were experienced. Age-referenced or grade-referenced tests requiring the child to retrieve remotely stored lexical items in response to semantic, phonological, or visual cues (e.g., Wiegel-Crump & Dennis, 1986), or to recall the gist of heard stories after a delay (e.g., Mandler & Johnson, 1977) provide an assessment of semantic memory. Judgments of prior experiential occurrence regardless of the content of what was experienced provide measures of episodic memory.

Everyday Memory

Information about whether any memory deficits demonstrable on neuropsychological tests are also apparent in everyday situations adds to the consistency of any picture of cognitive impairment on formal testing. The Everyday Memory Scale (Sunderland, Harris & Cleave, 1984) assesses the impact of memory problems on everyday functioning, at least for the adolescent population, and provides reference data for male and female head-injured adults. Comparison may be made between the older child's self-perception about memory and the parents' perception of the same domain, thus allowing some clinical comments to be made about the client's degree of insight into any memory problems demonstrated on neuropsychological tests. Reference data for male and female brain-injured adults are available.

Attention

Immediate attention refers to the ability to orient to a task. Sustained attention or vigilance is the ability to maintain attention over time. Selective attention, or freedom from distraction, is the ability to focus on selected parts of the information that is stimulating the sensory system while at the same time ignoring the remainder; it is concerned with performance in selecting among inputs in a context where there is conflict between signals (Posner, 1988). The ability to attend selectively is especially important in a learning situation like a classroom, where many types of noise occur; here, the child or adolescent must be able to disengage attention from irrelevant classroom sounds to focus on learning.

It has long been known that attention becomes volatile after head injury in adulthood and that remediation of attentional deficits is difficult (e.g., Wood, 1988). After head injury in children, too, attention is impaired (e.g., Chadwick, Rutter, Shaffer & Shrout, 1981). Tests of attention, therefore, are an important part of the neuropsychological assessment of children and adolescents involved in personal injury litigation. The Children's Paced Auditory Serial Addition Task (Johnson, Roethig-Johnson & Middleton, 1988) provides a technique for testing the capacity and rate of information processing in children of different ages. The Gordon Diagnostic System (Gordon, 1987) includes a vigilance task that measures the ability of children and adolescents to maintain attention without tangible reinforcement. Auditory selective attention may also be assessed by tests (Goldman, Fristoe & Woodcock, 1974b) that measure an individual's ability to attend to a listening task in the presence of competing noise that is systematically varied in intensity and type: steady-state noise like an air conditioner or fan, intermittent "cafeteria" noise such as would come from several people conversing at the same time, and a distracting voice telling a story.

Consequences of Neuropsychological Impairments

Neuropsychological impairments have profound and widespread effects on future education and future employability. Should they persist into adulthood as a mental disability, they will have additionally a significant effect on the individual's legal rights and obligations (Robertson, 1987).

Future Education

Posttraumatic neuropsychological deficits have an impact on the ability of the child and adolescent to function in the classroom situation. The following example illustrates how disorders of cognitive function might impact on the ongoing attainment of educational skills.

An 11-year-old boy is returning to school after clinical recovery from brain trauma. His low-average to average intelligence would imply the basic potential to master core academic attainments at a rate approximating his age. The ability to use intelligence effectively, however, is likely to be hampered by language, memory, and attentional difficulties. Speech and language were normal in several areas, although he exhibited word-finding problems and difficulties with sentence memory as well as problems in using language in a contextually and conversationally appropriate manner. Learning based heavily on language and verbal processes will be difficult for him, and his verbally based social interactions will be deficient. His memory was lower than expected on the basis of either age or intelligence, and he had shown various mnemonic difficulties: an inability to encode what he heard effectively so that he could later recall it; difficulties with working memory and with retrieval of episodic information, particularly information presented in the auditory mode. Problems in the recall of information, particularly heard information, are likely to create difficulties in the successful learning of new material in the classroom, especially material based on language. Although he will generally understand what he hears, he will tend to recall significantly less than he understands, particularly when he is required to impose order or meaningfulness on what he attempts to remember; in consequence, he will depend on to-be-learned material being presented to him in well-organized or meaningful form, and he is also likely to need assistance in organizing so as to permit later recall. Selective attentional skills were lower than would be expected on the basis of his age, which means that he will be more distracted from hearing and listening tasks in the classroom than age mates, that his attention may fluctuate considerably with variations in his study environments, and he may be unable to study in a sustained manner or for long periods of time.

Part of evaluating the impact of a traumatic brain injury on educational function is to outline some required remedial approaches, using neuropsychological assessment profiles as a base. Providing an individualized remedial program with specific classroom materials, of course, is not the task of the neuropsychologist specializing in assessment. Such a program needs to be planned by remedial education specialists, working in conjunction with individuals knowledgeable about the entitlement of traumatically injured children to special educational services (see R. Martin, 1988, for a discussion).

Future Employability

A vocational evaluation assists in the projection of future employability by determining the effect of the brain injury on a person's ability to work and earn a living (Lees-Haley, 1987). Earnings regression analysis is a technical method for demonstrating a child's lost earnings by measuring psychological characteristics that can be correlated with earning power; it projects future earnings based on statistical correlations between observable personal characteristics and income (Lees-Haley, 1986).

Vocational evaluations and earnings regression analyses are more difficult in very young brain-damaged children, who have no record of earning, no identifiable occupation with which to make peer group comparisons, and no available jobs on which to analyze employability (Les-Haley, 1986). For older children and adolescents, however, some of the functional neuropsychological impairments that will serve to limit future employability may be more readily identified. Physical limitations may provide some constraints on employability; cognitive and psychosocial or behavioral difficulties would likely constitute another type of constraint.

Nine of 10 jobs require the physical capacity for reaching, handling, fingering, and feeling. Such physical skills usually improve with time since trauma, but often the child or adolescent continues to have residual fine motor problems or deficits in balance and coordination. Sensory loss or dysfunction in hearing or vision is not uncommon. A proportion of individuals with trauma are at risk for posttraumatic epilepsy. Persisting physical difficulties constitute limiting factors on future employability.

Deficits in language, memory, and selective attention are also likely to limit employment options. They make any educational attainments more labored or more difficult, and, in addition, they would be likely to prevent the individual functioning reliably and effectively in the workplace. Even modest memory losses may translate into major difficulties in holding a job. Altered personality and emotional state, as well as decreased social awareness and ability to plan, all affect employability, and persisting problems in these areas may prevent employment in supervisory or management jobs that require interpersonal skills.

Projections about future employability in head-injured children and adolescents involve a different time frame from that in adults. Children with mild brain injury, for example, may not experience any vocational limitation for many years but then suffer substantial economic losses over a lifetime (Lees-Haley, 1987).

Causes of Neuropsychological Impairments

Neuropsychological and Other Reasoning About Cause

Establishing a possible association between brain injury and a subsequent profile of neuropsychological deficit begins with ideas about causation. Cause is a somewhat volatile concept in law (see, for e.g., Rothstein, 1987; Thomson, 1987), and analyses of causal judgment making in psychology are relatively recent (e.g., Einhorn & Hogarth, 1986).

The disciplines of medicine, law, and neuropsychology may all be involved in personal injury suits. Experts in these field are likely to differ in how they reason about cause (Loutzenhiser & Amsel, 1988).

The medical definition of causation (Zulch, 1969) in head injury is based on "natural" correlations and involves deductions about the physical effect of an external factor, such as trauma, on the brain. Medical causation often involves intermediate functional mechanisms that bring about the effect (e.g., head injury causes the effect, papilledema, by raising intracranial pressure). Causal reasoning in a medical context, then, would be something like: "Event C causes event E because mechanism M connects event C to E." Psychologists are trained to subsume a unique causal relation under a generalization (Loutzenhiser & Amsel, 1988). Causal reasoning for a psychologist, then, would involve something more like the following: "Event C causes event E because C-type events have been shown to cause E-type events." Neuropsychologists probably apply both medical and psychological forms of causal reasoning.

Lawyers are trained with a framework for causal reasoning that is different again, and they often apply a "but for" rule when reasoning about causation (Loutzenhiser & Amsel, 1988): "Event C causes event E because E would not have occurred *but for* the occurrence of C."

Of course, each of the professions cited uses all of these logical forms, and, in addition, various nuances of pleadings may require lawyers to deviate from expected logical forms. It is not suggested that neuropsychologists should attempt to master the forms of argument in a discipline like law; rather, what is important is that differing approaches to establishing cause be recognized during interdisciplinary discussions of the content of a personal injury case where the issue is whether brain injury caused later-emerging cognitive deficits.

Evaluating the Causes of Neuropsychological Deficit

Any profile of performance on neuropsychological tests reflects the operation of a range of factors. The parameters of a traumatic brain injury represent one set of biological factors that may cause, exacerbate, or contribute to the observed profile. But there also exists a set of moderator variables (social, environmental, and motivational factors) that influence whether cognitive impairments will disrupt home and school functioning (Ewing-Cobbs & Fletcher, 1987). In evaluating the origins of observed neuropsychological deficits, each of these factors must be considered.

For the practical purpose of formulating a neuropsychological opinion, the question of cause reduces to three questions: Were there any neuropsychological deficits predating the accident? Was the accident or its sequelae severe enough to have likely resulted in a significant loss of neuropsychological functions? Are any neuropsychological difficulties observed in the child or adolescent similar to those reported to arise from similar injury sustained during childhood and adolescence?

Postdiction of Preaccident Functioning

This refers to evaluation of the level of preaccident function. This task is often difficult in children because of a lack of academic and employment history; however, various types of information are pertinent: developmental histories, school and medical records, and the developmental and educational history of parents and siblings.

With younger children, a useful technique is to request the parents to complete a developmental questionnaire as they recall the child to have functioned before the injury, thus indicating the child's preinjury developmental level. This permits the neuropsychologist to identify those domains of functioning that have not progressed since the accident, those that have slowed, and those in which skills have regressed (e.g., when the child knew the alphabet at the time of injury, but subsequently lost that knowledge).

With older children and adolescents, an academic history is available, providing a formal measure of preaccident functioning. Also, cognitive tests with national norms may have been administered in school. Even when IQ scores are available, however, preaccident and postaccident data need to be interpreted with reference to base-rate and test-retest reliability issues (of the kind discussed for adults by Matarazzo and Herman, 1984).

Preexisting and Coexisting Factors

Brain trauma may occur in a context of preexisting or coexisting factors. These may be biological, such as a congenital brain malformation, a previous head injury, or a history of encephalitic or meningitic brain infection; or they may involve functional deficits, such as language or reading problems.

Social and cultural factors that predate or coexist with brain injury can influence cognitive function and, hence, the interpretation of neuropsychological test profiles. Assessment of siblings close in age to the traumatically brain-injured child or adolescent can be useful in establishing the role of factors such as a mixed or bilingual family background, significant cultural deprivation, or a family history of specific sex-linked reading disability.

Proportionality between Brain Trauma and Neuropsychological Effects

It is increasingly apparent from neuropsychological research that a young age confers no immunity from the effects of a traumatic brain injury, and that children may be at least as vulnerable as adults to cognitive deficits later in life (Levin, Eisenberg et al., 1982). Brain injury may also result in secondary cognitive deficits that exacerbate a preexisting problem, such as a reading disability, or speed up the natural course of some other disorder.

One question of importance about these neuropsychological sequelae in personal injury litigation concerns their proportionality to the injury (*The Profoundly Injured Child*, 1986). In children and adolescents considered as a group, more severe brain injuries are associated with more severe neuropsychological sequelae. For a particular child or adolescent, it is important to decide whether brain trauma produced some, all, or none of the sequelae that have been reported to be prognostic of later, persisting, neuropsychological problems in groups of children and adolescents. To judge the proportionality between the observed cognitive impairments and the presumed causal brain injury, it is useful to quantify the severity of the child's brain injury. Severity concerns principally the following: duration of coma, extent of posttraumatic amnesia, neuropathological changes, brain and skull damage, and delayed brain effects.

Two measures of severity associated with later neuropsychological impairments are duration of coma (an altered state of consciousness combined with a reduced capacity for arousal, Vannucci & Young, 1980) and extent of posttraumatic amnesia (a loss of memory characterized by confusion and an inability to consolidate information about ongoing events). Head injuries are usually deemed to be severe when either or both of the following has occurred: a coma lasting more than 1 day or a posttraumatic amnesia of more than several days' duration.

Some scales of overall injury severity (e.g., Mayer, Matlak, Johnson & Walker, 1980) include a system like the Glascow Coma Scale (GCS) designed to code severity of coma. Severe coma, defined by a GCS score of 8 or less on Hospital admission, corresponds to a lack of eye opening, a failure to respond to commands, and an inability to verbalize in a propositional manner.

Head injuries involving loss of consciousness are usually followed by amnesia for events surrounding the injury (Russell, 1971), including disrupted recall for events before the injury (retrograde amnesia) and/or postinjury events (anterograde amnesia). The assessment of posttraumatic amnesia is often complicated. It involves a variable constellation of behavioral disturbances including disordered attention, agitation, lethargy, inappropriate and disinhibited behavior, confusion, and incoherent speech. Also, retrospective estimates of the duration of posttraumatic amnesia may reflect both the duration of coma and a period of anterograde amnesia without differentiating these components. In an attempt to separate the various factors involved in the retrospective estimate of posttraumatic amnesia, scales have been developed to evaluate posttraumatic amnesia from the time the patient is able to obey commands. The Galveston Orientation and Amnesia Test (GOAT; Levin, O'Donnell & Grossman, 1979), now has a children's version, the COAT, or Children's Orientation and Amnesia Test (COAT, Ewing-Cobbs, Levin, Fletcher, Miner & Eisenberg, 1989). The COAT includes items pertaining to orientation to person, place, and circumstance as well as to a detailed description of the first postinjury memory and the last event recalled before the injury.

There exist three main forms of neuropathological changes after brain trauma (Alexander, 1987; Zulch, 1969): diffuse axonal injury, focal cortical contusion, and hypoxic-ischemic injury. Diffuse axonal injury refers to mild or widespread axonal shearing or disruption, usually in the cerebral hemispheres, corpus callosum, and midbrain. Focal cortical contusion involves local abrasions of the brain surface as a result of coup injury, contracoup injury, or both. Hypoxic-ischemic injury is indicated by clinical features of increased intracranial pressure and/or infarction. Brain damage may also occur in the form of intracranial, extradural, or subdural hematomas, or space-occupying collections of blood; or as subarachnoid or intraventricular hemorrhages, bleeds into the cerebral ventricles or the subarachnoid space.

Delayed effects of traumatic brain injury may also occur, and these include (Levin, Benton & Grossman, 1982) cerebral ventricular enlargement, supratentorial or infratentorial atrophic changes, and posttraumatic epilepsy, arising from areas of brain parenchyma adjacent to scars, cysts, abscesses, chronic hematomas, and other pathological changes. The particular set of delayed brain effects operative for children and adolescents are somewhat different from those in adults (Levin, Benton & Grossman, 1982).

Tables of Risk Factors

A variety of factors concerned with traumatic brain injury, such as duration of coma and level of cognitive functioning, have been shown to be predictive, albeit weakly, of later neuropsychological problems. But the effect of these factors has only been assessed in isolation. In evaluating proportionality between later neuropsychological impairment and brain trauma in a particular child or adolescent (e.g., between severe problems in memory and attention and a closed-head injury involving an initial 1-week coma and 3-week posttraumatic amnesia, focal neurological signs, posttraumatic epilepsy, and delayed brain atrophy), it would be of value to have available actuarial tables that quantify the outcome of this particular type of childhood closed-head injury for these cognitive functions.

What forensic neuropsychological assessments require is a series of studies on traumatically brain-injured children and adolescents that evaluate the additive, cumulative, and concerted effect of medical, social, and academic factors on posttrauma cognitive functioning. The preliminary effect of such studies would be the creation of tables of predictive medical variables that are comparable to those being developed for intelligence in brain-damaged children (Dennis 1985a, 1985b). If replicated across samples, actuarial prediction tables could be developed. The research needed to produce such actuarial information should be high on the agenda of individuals interested in forensic psychology (Grisso, 1987); certainly, such actuarial tables would be of enormous assistance to clinicians interpreting neuropsychological test data for personal injury actions.

Issues Unique to Children

Many of the issues arising when cognitive functioning is entered as evidence in personal injury litigation are common to children, adolescents, and adults. Some issues, however, are different.

A Heuristic for the Effects of Brain Damage in Children

The possible effects of brain injury in children are actually more wide-ranging than those in adults (Dennis, 1988). In adults, many skills are crystallized; in children, skills can either be emerging, partially developed, or already mastered. Before describing the cognitive consequences of traumatic brain damage in children, one must first consider the range of its possible effects. Dennis (1988) has described a heuristic depicting how brain damage at various points in skill evolution influences skill function (Table 4.1).

The legal issues relevant to the delayed cognitive effects of traumatic brain injury have long been discussed for adults (e.g., Blackmun, 1969), but only recently for children and adolescents (*The Profoundly Injured Child*, 1986). Yet it is probably for these latter groups that the most complex forensic issues are likely to arise. The Dennis heuristic emphasizes that the extent of functional impairment after brain damage in infancy or childhood cannot be assessed for some considerable time after the onset of the damage—not, in fact, until that point in development when the function would normally have developed. Clearly, we cannot judge the intactness of a skill without making reference to the elapsed time since the onset of traumatic brain injury. The model also forces us to consider future, as-yet-unacquired, or later developing skills as well as skills functional or semifunctional at the time of brain damage. The model thus underscores the fact that brain injury in children may some-

TABLE 4.1. Degree of skill maturation

Emerging Skill (not yet functional or in preliminary stages of acquisition)
Developing Skill (partially acquired or semifunctional)
Established Skill (fully acquired or crystallized)
Aspects of skill function:
Onset (the point in development when skill begins to be expressed)
Delay (a deferral in the expected time of skill onset)
Order (temporal emergence relative to other skills)
Garble (a jumble in the expected order of skill emergence)
Rate (the speed of skill development)
Lag (a slowed progression through the projected skill course)
Strategy (the tactics used to put skill into effect)
Detour (an atypical manoeuvre for normal skill endstate)
Mastery (the final level of skill attained)
Shortfall (a skill mastery less than projected)
Control (the ability to use or effect skill when needed)
Symptom (loss of the ability to use skill when required)
Upkeep (long-term skill maintenance and deployment)
Deficit (loss of long-term skill maintenance)

times have more long-lasting and more widespread potential consequences than later brain injury.

Ability to Meet Increasing Classroom Demands

In children, just as in adults, time usually improves neuropsychological deficits. In the child or adolescent with brain trauma, however, the classroom involves a set of cognitive demands that may prove increasingly difficult to meet.

Progress through school involves the ability to recall increasing amounts of information. These demands peak in the higher school grades. When the ability to attend, to learn new information, and to recall old information are deficient, children may experience more difficulty, rather than less, as they move into the higher school grades. A 20% loss of declarative memory may make little discernible difference in Grade 1, where a low information level is presented with great redundancy; whereas the same level of memory deficit may devastate performance in a Grade 8 classroom. Cognitive skills may not deteriorate after brain injury, but escalating cognitive demands become harder to meet.

Recovery Rate for Old Functions and Acquisition Rate for New Functions

Recovery of cognitive functions is typically incomplete for at least 12 to 24 months postinjury, or even longer (Mandelberg & Brooks, 1975). Prognostic comments about neuropsychological functions in brain-injured children, adolescents, and adults should therefore be guarded within the first 2 years postinjury.

Developmental factors compound the recovery process in children even further. One effect of an injury to the developing brain may be to slow or truncate the acquisition process for a particular skill (see Dennis, Hendrick, Hoffman & Humphreys [1987] for a discussion of slowed acquisition rate for certain language skills after developmental anomalies of the brain). Two sources might exist for memory deficits 1 year post-trauma in a brain-injured child. One is an incomplete restitution of memory functions existing at the time of injury, a mechanism that also exists in the adult. The other is acquisition of new memory skills at a retarded rate, so that only 6 months' worth of new memory skills might have been acquired, in contrast to the full year's worth age peers have developed.

The requirement to hold conclusions about cognitive recovery until after the full recovery period is even more cogent with children than with adults. After head injury, the child has not only to recover what was lost but grope toward new cognitive acquisitions, so the status of a range of neuropsychological functions needs to be monitored carefully for several years postinjury.

Conclusion

It must be borne in mind in any dialogue between neuropsychology and law that many concepts—causation, proof, probative value, and the like—are used differently in the two disciplines. Nonetheless, neuropsychological examination of children involved in personal injury actions can provide important information about a brain-based cognitive impairment; specifically, about its dimensions, its potential for remediation, and its probable causes. Certain forms of statistical and actuarial data treatment used in neuropsychology (e.g., predicting future function from present profile of cognitive skill) are highly germane to many core issues in personal injury suits. Neuropsychological assessment information is useful in personal injury actions involving children and adolescents when neuropsychologists apply statistical decision making and inferencing to test profiles so as to provide triers of fact with informed clinical opinions about previous, present, and future cognitive development.

Acknowledgments. Preparation of this article was supported by personal and project awards to the author from the Ontario Mental Health Foundation. Productive ideas about cognitive testing have been developed through discussions with my colleagues: for discourse and contextual language, Dr. Maureen Lovett; for memory, Drs. Marcia Barnes, Jeannie Ridgley, and Brenda Spiegler (the women from NGRAM). I thank the two TCN reviewers for their thoughtful evaluation of the submitted manuscript. I am grateful to Crawford M. MacIntyre, Q.C. for his comments on the legal aspects of personal injury litigation with children. Residual ambiguity and fuzziness in the chapter I managed by myself.

References

Adams, G.H., Graham, D.I., & Gennarelli, T.A. (1981). Acceleration induced head injury in the monkey: The model, its mechanical and physiological correlates. *Acta Neuropathologica*, *7*, 226–28.

Adams, K.M. (1988). Neuropsychology is not just in the eye of the provider. *Professional Psychology: Research and Practice*, *19*, 488–489.

Alexander, M.P. (1987). The role of neurobehavioral syndromes in the rehabilitation and outcome of closed head injury. In H.S. Levin, J. Grafman, & H.M. Eisenberg (Eds.), *Neurobehavioral recovery from head injury* (pp. 191–205). New York: Oxford University Press.

Bersoff, D.N. (1983). Regarding psychologists testily: The legal regulation of psychological assessment. In C.J. Scheirer & B.L. Hammonds (Eds.), *Psy-*

chology and the law (pp. 41–88). The Master Lecture Series Vol. 2. Washington, DC: American Psychological Association.

Blackmun, H.A. (1969). Legal problems attendant upon the late effects of head injuries. In A.E. Walker, W.F. Caveness & M. Critchley (Eds.), *The late effects of head injury* (pp. 439–446). Springfield, IL: Charles C. Thomas.

Blau, T.H. (1984a). Psychological tests in the courtroom. *Professional Psychology: Research and Practice*, *15*, 176–186.

Blau, T.H. (1984b). *The psychologist as expert witness*. New York: John Wiley & Sons.

Boll, T.J. (1983). Minor head injury in children—Out of sight but not out of mind. *Journal of Clinical Child Psychology*, *12*, 74–80.

Case, R., Kurland, D.M., & Goldberg, J. (1982). Operational efficiency of short-term memory span. *Journal of Experimental Child Psychology*, *33*, 386–404.

Cermak, L.S., Blackford, S.P., O'Connor, M., & Bleich, R.P. (1988). The implicit memory ability of a patient with amnesia due to encephalitis. *Brain and Cognition*, *7*, 145–156.

Chadwick, O., Rutter, M., Shaffer, D., & Shrout, P.E. (1981). A prospective study of children with head injuries. II. Specific cognitive deficits. *Journal of Clinical Neuropsychology*, *3*, 101–120.

Delis, D.C. (1989). Neuropsychological assessment of learning and memory. In F. Boller & J. Grafman (Ed.), *Handbook of neuropsychology*. Amsterdam: Elsevier.

Denman, S.B. (1984). *Denman Neuropsychology Memory Scale*. Charleston, SC: Denman.

Dennis, M. (1979). Neuropsychological assessment. In J. Noshpitz, I. Berlin, J. Call, R. Cohen, S. Harrison, & L. Stone (Eds.), *Basic handbook of child psychiatry* (pp. 574–583). New York: Basic Books.

Dennis, M. (1985a). Intelligence after early brain injury. I: Predicting IQ scores from medical history variables. *Journal of Clinical and Experimental Neuropsychology*, *7*, 526–554.

Dennis, M. (1985b). Intelligence after early brain injury. II: IQ scores of subjects classified on the basis of medical history variables. *Journal of Clinical and Experimental Neuropsychology*, *7*, 555–576.

Dennis, M. (1987). Advances in neuropsychological assessment. In J. Noshpitz, I. Berlin, J. Call, R. Cohen, S. Harrison, & L. Stone (Eds.), *Basic handbook of child psychiatry,* Vol. 5 (pp. 164–169). New York: Basic Books.

Dennis, M. (1988). Language and the young damaged brain. *Master lecture series: Clinical neuropsychology and brain function: Research, measurement, and practice* (pp. 89–123). Washington, DC: American Psychological Association.

Dennis, M., & Barnes, M.A. (1990). Knowing the meaning, getting the point, bridging the gap, and carrying the message: Aspects of discourse following closed head injury in childhood and adolescence. *Brain and Language*, *39*, 428–446.

Dennis, M., Hendrick, E.B., Hoffman, H.J., & Humphreys, R.P. (1987). The language of hydrocephalic children and adolescents. *Journal of Clinical and Experimental Neuropsychology*, *9*, 593–621.

Dennis, M., & Kohn, B. (1985). The Active-Passive Test: An age-referenced clinical test of syntactic discrimination. *Developmental Neuropsychology*, *1*, 113–137.

Einhorn, H.J., & Hogarth, R.M. (1986). Judging probable cause. *Psychological Bulletin*, *99*, 3–19.

Emmerich, W. (1964). Continuity and stability in early social development. *Child Development*, *35*, 311–332.

Ewing-Cobbs, L., & Fletcher, J.M. (1987). Neuropsychological assessment of head injury in children. *Journal of Learning Disabilities*, *20*, 526–535.

Ewing-Cobbs, L., Levin, H.S., Eisenberg, H.M., & Fletcher, J.M. (1987). Language functions following closed head injury in children and adolescents. *Journal of Clinical and Experimental Neuropsychology*, *9*, 575–592.

Ewing-Cobbs, L., Levin, H.S., Fletcher, J.M., Miner, M.E., & Eisenberg, H.M. (1989). Posttraumatic amnesia in children: Assessment and outcome. *Journal of Clinical and Experimental Neuropsychology*, *11*, 58.

Field, J.G. (1960). Two types of tables for use with Wechsler's intelligence scales. *Journal of Clinical Psychology*, *16*, 3–7.

Golden, C.J., & Strider, M.A., eds. (1986). *Forensic neuropsychology*. New York: Plenum.

Goldman, R., Fristoe, M., & Woodcock, R.W. (1974a). *GFW Auditory memory tests*. Circle Pines, MN: American Guidance Service.

Goldman, R., Fristoe, M., & Woodcock, R.W. (1974b). *GFW Auditory selective attention test*. Circle Pines, MN: American Guidance Service.

Goldman, R., Fristoe, M., & Woodcock, R.W. (1974c). *GFW Diagnostic auditory discrimination test*. Circle Pines, MN: American Guidance Service.

Gordon, M. (1987). *Gordon diagnostic system*. Odessa, FL: Psychological Assessment Resources.

Gregory, C.O., Kalven, H., & Epstein, R.A. (1977). *Cases and materials on torts*, 3rd ed. Boston: Little, Brown.

Grisso, T. (1987). The economic and scientific future of forensic psychological assessment. *American Psychologist*, *42*, 831–839.

Hart, K., & Faust, D. (1988). Prediction of the effects of mild head injury: A message about the Kennard Principle. *Journal of Clinical Psychology*, *44*, 780–782.

Holland, A.L. (1982). When is aphasia aphasia? The problem of closed head injury. In R.H. Brookshire (Ed.), *Clinical aphasiology. Conference proceedings* (pp. 345–349). Minneapolis, MN: BRK Publishers.

Horne, M.M. (1987). Novel scientific evidence: Does Frye require that general acceptance within the scientific community be established by disinterested scientists? *University of Detroit Law Review*, *65*, 147–162.

Johnson, D.A., Roethig-Johnston, K., & Middleton, J. (1988). Development and evaluation of an attentional test for head injured children-1. information processing capacity in a normal sample. *Journal of Child Psychology and Psychiatry*, *29*, 199–208.

Kaufman, A.S. (1979). *Intelligent testing with the WISC-R*. New York: John Wiley & Sons.

Lees-Haley, P. (1986, February). Earnings regression analysis. Proving a child's lost earnings. *Trial*, 37–38.

Lees-Haley, P. (1987, November). Mild brain injury. Proving lost earnings. *Trial*, 83–86.

Levin, H.S., Benton, A.L., & Grossman, R.G. (1982). *Neurobehavioral consequences of closed head injury*. New York: Oxford University Press.

Levin, H.S., Eisenberg, H.M., Wiig, E.R., & Kobayashi, K. (1982). Memory and intellectual ability after head injury in children and adolescents. *Neurosurgery, 11*, 668–673.

Levin, H.S., O'Donnell, V.M., & Grossman, R.G. (1979). The Galveston Orientation and Amnesia Test: A practical scale to assess cognition after head injury. *Journal of Nervous and Mental Disorders, 167*, 675–684.

Loutzenhiser, L., & Amsel, E. (1988). Causal reasoning among professionals: Comparing lawyers and psychologists. *Canadian Psychology, 29*, Abstract 478.

Mandelberg, I.A., & Brooks, D.N. (1975). Cognitive recovery after severe head injury. I. Serial testing on the WAIS. *Journal of Neurology, Neurosurgery, & Psychiatry, 38*, 1121–1126.

Mandler, J.M., & Johnson, N.S. (1977). Remembrance of things parsed: Story structure and recall. *Cognitive Psychology, 9*, 111–151.

Martin, D.A. (1988). Children and adolescents with traumatic brain injury: Impact on the family. *Journal of Learning Disabilities, 21*, 464–470.

Martin, R. (1988). Legal challenges in educating traumatic brain injured students. *Journal of Learning Disabilities, 21*, 471–485.

Matarazzo, J.D., & Herman, D.O. (1984). Base rate data for the WAIS-R: Test-retest stability and VIQ-PIQ differences. *Journal of Clinical Neuropsychology, 6*, 351–366.

Mayer, T., Matlak, M.E., Johnson, D.G., & Walker, M.L. (1980). The Modified Injury Severity Scale in pediatric multiple trauma patients. *Journal of Pediatric Surgery, 15*, 719–726.

McCarthy, D. (1972). *McCarthy Scales of Children's Abilities*. New York: The Psychological Corporation.

Milton, S.B., Prutting, C.A., & Binder, G.M. (1984). Appraisal of communicative competence in head injured adults. In R.H. Brookshire (Ed.), *Clinical aphasiology. Conference proceedings* (pp. 114–123). Minneapolis, MN: BRK Publishers.

Mutti, M., Sterling, H.M., & Spalding, N.V. (1978). *QNST. Quick Neurological Screening Test. Revised ed. Novato*, CA: Academic Therapy Publications.

Nicholson, C.L., & Alcorn, C.L. (1980). *Educational application of the WISC-R: A handbook of interpretive strategies and remedial recommendations*. Los Angeles: Western Psychological Services.

Norton, J.E. (1981). *The anatomy of a personal injury law suit*, 2nd ed. Washington, DC: Association of Trial Lawyers of America.

Posner, M.I. (1988). Structures and functions of selective attention. In T. Boll & B.K. Bryant (Eds.), *Clinical neuropsychology and brain function: Research, measurement, and practice* (pp. 169–202). Washington, DC: American Psychological Association.

The profoundly injured child (1986). Washington, DC: Association of Trial Lawyers of America.

Prosser, W.L. (1971). *Handbook of the law of torts*. St. Paul, MN: West Publishing Company.

Rhodes, F. (1975). *Manual for the Rhodes WISC-R scatter profile*. San Diego: Educational and Industrial Testing Service.

Robertson, G.B. (1987). *Mental disability and the law in Canada*. Toronto: Carswell.

Rothstein, P.F. (1987). Causation in torts, crimes and moral philosophy: A reply to Professor Thomson. *The Georgetown Law Journal, 76*, 151–167.

Rourke, B.P., & Adams, K.M. (1984). Quantitative approaches to the neuropsychological assessment of children. In R. Tarter & G. Goldstein (Eds.), *The neuropsychology of childhood.* (pp. 79–108). New York: Plenum Press.

Russell, W.R., (1971). *The traumatic amnesias.* New York: Oxford University Press.

Saint-Cyr, J.A., Taylor, A.E., & Lang, A.E. (1988). Procedural learning and neostriatal dysfunction in man. *Brain, 111*, 941–959.

Schacter, D.L. (1987). Implicit memory: History and current status. *Journal of Experimental Psychology: Learning, Memory, and Cognition, 13*, 501–518.

Shapiro, D.L. (1984). *Psychological evaluation and expert testimony: A practical guide to forensic work.* New York: Van Nostrand Reinhold Co.

Siegel, L.S. (1988). Evidence that IQ scores are irrelevant to the definition and analysis of reading disability. *Canadian Journal of Psychology, 42*, 201–215.

Spreen, O., & Gaddes, W.H. (1969). Developmental norms for 15 neuropsychological tests, age 6 to 15. *Cortex, 5*, 171–191.

Sunderland, A., Harris, J.E., & Cleave, J. (1984). Memory failures in everyday life following severe head injury. *Journal of Clinical Neuropsychology, 6*, 127–142.

Thomson, J.J. (1987). The decline of cause. *The Georgetown Law Journal, 6*, 137–150.

Vannucci, R.C., & Young, R.S.K. (1980). Coma in childhood. *Practice of Pediatrics, 9*, 1–24.

Vitelli, R.J., & Goldblatt, R.B. (1979). *Tardor interpretative scoring system for the WISC-R.* Manchester, CT: Tardor Corporation.

Wagenaar, W.A. (1988). The proper seat. A Bayesian discussion of the position of expert witnesses. *Law and Human Behavior, 12*, 499–510.

Webster, R.E. (1981). *Learning Efficiency Test.* Novato, CA: Academic Therapy Publications.

Weissman, H.N. (1984). Psychological assessment and psycholegal formulations in psychiatric traumatology. *Psychiatric Annals, 14*, 517–529.

Weissman, H.N. (1985). Psycholegal standards and the role of psychological assessment in personal injury litigation. *Behavioral Sciences and the Law, 3*, 135–147.

Wiegel-Crump, C.A., & Dennis, M. (1986). Development of word finding. *Brain and Language, 27*, 1–23.

Wiig, E.H., Alexander, E.W., & Secord, W. (1988). Linguistic competence and level of cognitive functioning in adults with traumatic closed head injury. In H.A. Whitaker (Ed.), *Neuropsychological studies of non-focal brain damage: Dementia and trauma* (pp. 186–201). New York: Springer-Verlag.

Wiig, E.H., & Secord, W. (1989). *Test of Language Competence* Expanded ed. San Antonio, TX: Psychological Corporation.

Wohlwill, J. (1973). *The study of behavioral development.* New York: Academic Press.

Wood, R.L. (1988). Attention disorders in brain injury rehabilitation. *Journal of Learning Disabilities, 21*, 327–332.

Zulch, K-J. (1969). Medical causation. In A.E. Walker, W.F. Caveness, & M. Critchley (Eds.), *The late effects of head injury* (pp. 453–472). Springfield, IL: Charles C Thomas.

5 The Assessment of Competency in the Older Adult

JANE DYWAN, GABE J. MALETTA, and
FRANCIS J. PIROZZOLO

Although an individual's competence can come into question at any stage during the life cycle, each stage brings with it certain developmental tasks and vulnerabilities that can change the nature of the questions and the implications of the answers. In this chapter we attempt to outline the issues that are likely to arise with respect to competence during late adulthood. We review some of the basic physiological changes that comprise normal aging and the disorders that can occur with increasing probability in the later years. The primary focus, however, is on how these changes can affect cognitive and emotional processes in ways that would undermine the ability of individuals to act in their own best interest or in the best interest of others. We also review some of the issues that arise in assessing the competence of older adults given that the results of such assessments could affect the status of the individual before the law.

Decisions about competency are usually covered by some provincial or state body. In Ontario the Mental Incompetency Act (1980) defines a mentally incompetent person as one in whom there is such a condition of arrested or incomplete development of mind, whether arising from inherent causes or induced by disease or injury, or who is suffering from such a disorder of the mind that he requires care, supervision, and control for his protection and the protection of his property. There is another provision that provides for the application of the management and administration provisions of the Mental Incompetency Act for a person who "through mental infirmity arising from disease, age or other casue . . . is incapable of managing his affairs." Such statutes do not establish the criteria by which a person ought not to be considered competent, nor does it allow for cases in which competence may have been variably or partially diminished.

The issue of whether or not elderly persons were competent at the time they made their will has provided considerable courtroom intrigue as well as the grist for innumerable novelists and playwrights. Although the disposition of wills is a frequently contested issue, there are a number of other questions that arise with some frequency in older populations. For example, the question may arise as to whether elderly persons have maintained adequate comprehension, communicative ability, or judgment to manage their own business or financial affairs. Signing contracts, keeping financial records, and using a credit card could have devastating consequences when attentional capacity, memory, and problem-solving abilities are seriously compromised.

Health care decisions provide another context in which the cognitive competency of individuals can raise concern. In order to decide about a course of treatment or nursing home placement, individuals must be able to comprehend the nature of the choice to be made and the implications of that choice. Not only do older people tend to be more cautious than younger people in dealing with the health care system (Woodward & Wallston, 1987), but the apathy that can accompany serious depressive disorder, the rigidity that can accompany cognitive decline, or the suspicion that can accompany paraphrenia or the dementias often raise serious concerns about whether some individuals are able to make truly informed decisions.

Potential difficulty surrounds the determination of whether an elderly person is competent to carry on activities that may endanger others as well as themselves. Driving is a prime example of such an activity but it is clear that other activities such as operating machinery could raise concerns. Because of the serious implications for lifestyle and self-esteem, such decisions are particularly difficult to make. Similarly, as mandatory retirement becomes an outmoded policy, the assessment of competence in the older worker will increase in importance. In jobs that involve public safety such as air traffic control, piloting an aircraft, or driving a bus, the issues are similar to those that arise with respect to driving. There are, however, a number of jobs for which the assessment of competence is even less straightforward. Speed and accuracy are important on a production line but they are not necessarily the primary factors modifying the performance of a teacher or a draftsperson. It is interesting to note that as the personal power of an individual rises, that is, as the number of individuals over which one has authority grows, the less likely it is that competence can be monitored by others. Junior members of a law office, interns in a medical school, or junior ministers in a government office are unlikely to question openly the competence of those in charge. One cannot help but wonder about the competence of an aged and unwell president or military leader when the decisions that they make seem increasingly arbitrary. Such leaders could continue to make decisions on the basis of distorted perceptions and reasoning skills or they could become passive figureheads for some political faction within the country.

The interplay between legal and neuropsychological issues arise as well when considering diminished responsibility for criminal actions, the weight to give the testimony of an elderly eyewitness, or the appropriate compensation due to an accident or injury that has further impaired an already vulnerable or compromised nervous system. In the latter situation, the problem of proportioning deficits can often arise, that is, there is often much discussion about how much of the deficit is caused by the injury and how much is caused by normal decline.

From a neuropsychological perspective, changes in adaptive functioning are due to a large extent to the physiological changes that serve as indicators of the aging process. Loss of functional capacity is perhaps best translated into the concept of homeostasis, that is, the diminution over time in the ability of an organism, or one of its parts, to adapt successfully to its environment. This is manifested as a gradual diminution in the capacity of the organism to withstand the stresses and strains to which it is constantly subjected, eventually culminating in death. Implied is an integral relationship between structure and function, that is, normal maintenance of the one presupposes normal maintenance of the other over time. Understanding the nature of these changes helps to structure our understanding of normative as well as atypical patterns of decline.

Normal Aging

The Aging Nervous System

The Peripheral Nervous System

In the peripheral nervous system (PNS), it is well known that a general decrease in sensory acuity occurs with aging (Maletta & Pirozzolo, 1980). This includes the modalities of touch, taste, smell, the awareness of temperature change, vibration, pain, and proprioception. There is a gradual decrease in visual acuity, dark adaptation, and depth perception as well as in the ability to discriminate among colors (especially between blue and green). Visual defects (including blindness) occur in 4% of individuals in their 60s and in 15% of those in their 80s. Specific auditory problems of the aged, for example, presbycusis, are manifested in a decreased acuity for high-frequency sounds and an inability to modulate sounds of differing amplitudes as well as a decrease in the ability to discriminate among different sounds. This seems to be more prevalent in older men than women. Hearing defects occur in 5% of those in their 60s and in 25% of those in their 80s (Maletta & Pirozzolo, 1980).

Functional changes are known to occur at the level of peripheral sensory receptors, with a decrease in their number and an increase in the threshold level of stimulation necessary for activation (Hamill & Buell, 1981). Also, functional changes occur in the afferent (toward) and efferent (away from) pathways in the brain with aging, as evidenced by a small decrease in nerve conduction velocity, primarily in the efferent direction. However, changes in the nervous system at the sensory receptor and the afferent and efferent pathways account for only about 4% to 5% of the overall decrease in reaction time seen in experiments on aging individuals. Most of the functional changes occur within the brain itself, that is, within the central nervous system (Lons, 1985; Maletta & Pirozzolo, 1980; Vernadakis, 1985). Irrespective of the source or the sensory modality, these changes result in a slowing in the assimilation and processing of information. Given the same exposure level to sensory stimuli, less information is extracted from the environment, leaving the older person with less information available on which to base subsequent cognitive operations (e.g., Fozard, 1990).

The Central Nervous System

The cental nervous system (CNS) consists of the brain and spinal cord. In the CNS various domains of intellectual functioning are related grossly to specific morphologic locations in the cerebral cortex. For example, sensory, motor, visual, auditory, and olfactory functions are located in specific "primary" areas, whereas language and cognitive functions reside in more morphologically broad "association" areas of cerebral cortex. Specific cognitive activities like verbal fluency and ability to shift conceptual set are frontal cerebral cortical functions, whereas comprehension, calculation, construction, and repetition are considered posterior cortical functions. Recent memory is related in part to the hippocampus and amygdala. Therefore, the brain-behavior relationship suggests that damage to specific brain locations would result in loss of particular cognitive functions.

The brain is metabolically a very active organ, comprising only about 2% of total body weight, but at any given time using approximately 20% of the oxygen and 65% of the glucose in circulation (Dastur, 1985). Also, brain blood flow, at the rate of about 1 liter/minute, is disproportionately great by weight. During the course of normal aging, the brain is subjected to substantial morphologic and biochemical changes (Brizzee, 1981; Brody, 1980; Terry, 1988; Timiras & Venadakis, 1972).

For example, cerebral blood flow decreases with age, from approximately 65 ml/min/100 mg tissue at age 25 years to 51 ml/min/100 mg tissue at age 70 years. It is thought that this decrease is not primary but rather secondary to a shrinkage of neurons in certain brain areas, leading to gradual cerebral atrophy with a concomitant decreased blood flow requirement (e.g., Metter, 1988). Not much is known about changes in the blood-brain barrier, except that no major pathology has been documented in normal human aging.

Structurally, the brain undergoes a slowly accelerating shrinkage with aging, losing 7% to 12% of its maximum weight in the course of an 80 to 90 year life (from about 1390 gm at ages 20–29 years to about 1250 gm at ages 70–79 years). In the cerebral cortex a narrowing of the gyri is seen, along with deeper and wider sulci and increased ventricular size, especially in the 8th and 9th decades. Both gray and white matter are involved, but these losses are at different rates, depending on the regions studied. The spinal cord also atrophies with normal aging, as does the cerebellum, with both gray and white matter involved. The deeper structures, for example, the basal ganglia and thalamus, undergo cell loss and there is a thickening and increased opacity of the membrane encasing the brain. The functional importance of these gross CNS changes may not be significant. What is more important is the considerable reorganization of brain cytoarchitecture involving both neuronal and glial elements (Hamill & Buell, 1982, Terry & Hansen, 1988; Vernadakis, 1985).

Many argue that the major cause of the decrease in brain weight with aging is the loss of neurons in the brain in a somewhat linear fashion throughout adult life (e.g., Brody, 1955; Katzman & Terry, 1983). However, there is new evidence (Terry & Hansen, 1988) suggesting that in normal, healthy older adults there is no dramatic change in the total number of neurons. Although the cell count for large neurons decreases by about 40%, the count for small neurons increases by about 22% and the glia, or connective fiber, appears to increase by about 50%. It is therefore hypothesized that the large neurons are not lost but that they have shrunk and account for the apparent increase in small neurons. Thus, it may be more appropriate to refer to a shrinkage as opposed to a loss of large neurons and the previously mentioned reorganization of the cytoarchitecture.

These data are based on exceptionally healthy individuals and may vary with the integrity of the cerebrovascular system. In cases of dementia, the shrinkage of large neurons can be up to 22% greater than in healthy age-matched controls. Moreover, this change in the neuron structure is not a general phenomenon throughout the entire brain, but is limited to certain areas. The cerebral cortex seems most affected, especially after age 50 years, particularly in the frontal, superior temporal, precentral, and occipital regions. There are also significant changes in the cerebellum, the hippocampus, the locus coeruleus, putamen, and substantia nigra. In contrast, the medulla, pons, and hypothalamus show little neuronal loss with aging. The relationship between these changes in neuronal counts and functional capacity of the central nervous system (CNS) is not clear but it is the case that the areas described as showing the greatest cellular change are also the areas implicated in well established age-related behavioral changes, for example, movement (cerebellum) and memory (hippocampus).

Neurons in the cerebral cortex in aging humans show a progressive loss of the branchlike dendrites and dendritic spines, which play a critical role in synaptic communication. These losses occur primarily in layers 2 through 5 of the multilayered cortex and certainly cause an overall decrease in the number of synaptic connections leading to an interruption in intracortical circuitry and increased likelihood of functional impairment. However, despite this observation there also seems to be a potential for dendritic "plasticity." In some cortical areas of the normal aged brain, there is actually slow but continued growth seen of the terminal dendritic branches. This dendritic growth suggests that there may be two populations of cortical neurons. One population, which may be dying, shows the age-related atrophy of the dendritic field. The second population is not only surviving, but expresses continued plasticity of the CNS by actually expanding its dendritic field with age. There is little evidence of these surviving and growing neurons in elderly individuals with senile dementia of the Alzheimer's type (SDAT) (e.g., Buell & Coleman, 1981; Flood, Buell, DeFiore, Horwitz, & Coleman, 1985), providing one indication of the dissociation between normal and pathological aging.

Other morphologic changes seen in the normal aging brain include lipofuscin, neurofibrillary tangles, and senile plaques. Lipofuscin refers to a yellow pigment deposited in neurons that begins to accumulate early and continues consistently throughout life. It eventually involves most neurons in the brain. It is seen as a biological marker of aging but its functional significance remains unknown (Kemper, 1984).

Neurofibrillary tangles (NTs) refer to paired helical filaments within the cell body. They are prominently visible in the normal aging brain and are found especially in the frontal, temporal, and hippocampal cortex (Terry, 1978). By age 80 years, virtually all humans have evidence of tangles in their neurons. Patients with Alzheimer's disease can be identified at autopsy by the vastly numerous NTs seen by the neuropathologist in the hippocampus and in areas of the cerebral cortex. High concentrations of NTs are seen in a number of neuropathological conditions (e.g., post-encephalitic Parkinson's disease, aging adults with Down syndrome, Guam-Parkinson's dementia, subacute sclerosing panencephalitis [Dawson's disease], and dementia pugilistica, known as "punch-drunk syndrome"). NTs are seen only in humans and are believed to represent a nonspecific neurological response to physical or chemical trauma (e.g., Selkoe, 1988).

Unlike NTs, senile plaques (SPs) are found in the extracellular spaces in monkey and dog as well as in human brains, and they are specific to normal aging, Alzheimer's Disease, early and late onset, and to the brains of older Down syndrome patients. Plaques are found only in gray matter, not myelinated areas of the brain, and are composed of a central amyloid core surrounded by degenerated synapses and other debris. There appears to be a direct relationship between the concentration of senile plaques and neurofibrillary tangles found in certain cortical areas and the severity of cognitive dysfunction, although it is important to note that they can be found, to a lesser degree, in the brains of many cognitively normal elderly (Selkoe, 1988).

Biochemical Changes

There are, as well, a number of biochemical changes in the aging nervous system (Lons, 1985; Maletta & Pirozzolo, 1980; Selkoe & Kosik, 1984). These can involve proteins, lipids, nucleic acids, and water/electrolytes. As an example, proteins are important in the brain not only structurally, but also because they provide crucial enzymatic activities. The activity of these enzymes, both synthesizing and hydrolytic, are necessary for optimum functioning of the multiple neurotransmitters active in the CNS. Across the lifespan there are alterations in the total amount of protein in the brain. In a 1-year-old child, there is about 7%, which increases to 12% from age 20 to 65 years and from 75 years on it decreases again to about 7%.

Synaptic Changes

Structurally, the progressive loss of dendrites and dendritic spines, as previously described, is responsible for an overall decrease in the number of synaptic connections with aging. Chemically, synaptic changes with aging are also exemplified by the observed decline in activity of many of the enzymes responsible for the synthesis and hydrolysis of some CNS neurotransmitters (Selkoe, 1982). For example, brain levels of the neurotransmitters dopamine and norepinephrine show a significant decline with aging.

It is also well established that there is a decrease in some brain areas in choline acetyltransferase (ChAT) and acetylcholinesterase (AChE), the synthesizing and hydrolyzing enzymes of acetylcholine, respectively, in patients with Alzheimer's disease (Terry & Davies, 1980). There is, however, currently no evidence for changes in activity of these enzymes in older individuals without clinical disease. Acetylcholine, along with the neurotransmitter serotonin, shows small decreases in content in brains of aging individuals. Attempts to relate changes in concentration of neurotransmitters as well as changes in their metabolites and their corresponding enzyme activities with CNS functional activity is currently a rich area of research interest (Carlsson, 1985).

Behavioral Change

Associated with the morphologic and biochemical changes in the aging nervous system are a variety of behavioral changes that also occur; these may be observed and measured clinically. Often, one of the first questions asked is whether intelligence declines as a function of age.

Intelligence

Early studies of aging and cognition compared intelligence quotients (IQ scores) of individuals of different ages. Researchers found that older people did less well than the young but they did not control for cohort effects, education, health, and a myriad of differences other than age that accounted for some of the variance in test performance. Eventually it became clear that for most people, verbal skills remained relatively intact but there was a decline in visuospatial performance that appeared to be fairly stable and could be observed in a wide variety of testing situations. This decline in Performance IQ relative to Verbal IQ is known as the Classic Aging Effect (see, e.g., Albert & Heaton, 1988).

It was felt that the verbal subtests tapped well established knowledge systems or "crystallized intelligence" whereas the performance subtests tapped the ability to adapt to novel task demands and was described as "fluid intelligence." Fluid intelligence was seen as more dependent on the viability of the CNS and as a result would be more affected by age (Horn & Cattell, 1967). Some authors have concluded on the basis of such data that the right hemisphere, which subserves visuospatial abilities, is more susceptible to the effects of aging (e.g., Lapidot, 1983). However, careful analysis of task demands combined with neurophysiological evidence suggests that, if there is differential decline, it would not be in the right hemisphere but rather in the frontal lobes (Hochanadel & Kaplan, 1984; Mittenberg, Seidenberg, O'Leary & DiGiulio, 1989). The frontal lobes are considered important in attentional, integrative, and monitoring functions (e.g., Stuss & Benson, 1986).

Newer formulations of intelligence based on both biological and sociocultural perspectives indicate that there are multiple intelligences (Gardner, 1983). Traditional IQ tests are woefully inadequate with respect to quantifying them and there is not likely any single dichotomy, whether it be Verbal/Performance, Crystallized/Fluid, or Right/Left Hemisphere that could adequately describe the full range of processes involved in normal cognitive activity or its demise.

A more fruitful approach is to study more specific aspects of information processing and ralate these on the one hand to CNS function and on the other to higher level skills. From this perspective, one would be less likely to question whether intelligence or competence declines with age, but would rather try to determine more specifically what the mechanisms are that might account for any observed decline.

Neurocognitive Processes

The most basic of processes that can undergo age-related change is arousal. There is some debate as to whether as individuals age they become over or underaroused (Woodruff-Pak, 1988, chap. 8). A number of physiological indices suggest that aging is associated with a lower level of arousal but at the same time, the older individual is likely to become hyperaroused when activated and has a harder time bringing that arousal back to baseline. These alterations in arousal, if severe enough, could affect performance on cognitive tasks as well as in everyday life circumstances in which control of arousal levels would be essential to adequate task performance.

Closely related to arousal are attentional processes. No matter what happens to the brain, attention is likely to be disrupted to some degree. Age-related CNS changes are no exception. There are, however, a number of ways of thinking about attention (e.g., selective, sustained, divided) and these can be differentially affected by the aging process (McDowd & Birren, 1990). With respect to selective attention, that is, the ability of focus on a goal-relevant target, it seems that older adults perform as well as young adults if the targets are easily discriminable (e.g., Nebes & Madden, 1983). However, as discriminability of the target decreases, the performance of older adults on selective attention tasks declines (Plude & Hoyer, 1985). With respect to the ability to sustain attention, there is considerable evidence that older adults do more poorly than young adults on vigilance tasks. However, their performance does not decline more quickly than the performance of young people as a function of how long they keep at the task (McDowd & Birren, 1990).

Dual task performance is usually considered an area in which older adults are most vulnerable: dividing one's attention between two tasks simultaneously is a common requirement of many tasks in everyday life. Recent evidence suggests that if one controls for any age-related differences in subjects' ability to perform each task, then older adults are as able to divide their attention between the two tasks as the young. It is only when the two target tasks reach higher levels of complexity that the older adults have a significantly more difficult time than the young dividing their attention between them. Thus, under some circumstances older adults are as able as the young to monitor two tasks at the same time (e.g., Somberg & Salthouse, 1982). However, as the individual tasks increase in complexity, age-related decrements in divided attention increase (McDowd & Craik, 1988).

Information processing speed shows a fairly consistent decline with age and seems to be best explained by its dependence on the integrity of the CNS (Cerella, 1990). Nonetheless, predicting individual task performance on the basis of age would still remain hazardous. When it comes to task performance, the effects of aging differ as a function of the bodily system involved, the individual, and the task (Spirduso & MacRae, 1990). Complexity of the task is usually associated with increased age-related deficits but skill and physical fitness in real life tasks are often enough to reduce the effects of aging for many healthy people.

When most people think of age-related changes in cognition they think of memory. Memory is a term that refers to multiple processes and can be measured in many ways. One must attend to the stimulus, encode it, store the information in some way, and retrieve it. When memory is impaired it may be the result of dysfunction in any or all of these processes. Most people worry about their memory by the time they reach middle age but in most cases the problems they are experiencing are not pathognomonic and are referred to as benign senescent forgetfulness (Kral, 1978). This type of memory loss is evident on laboratory measures of recall in healthy normative samples by the time they are 50 years old (Albert, Duffy & Naeser, 1987). As well, the level of memory complaint is often more related to level of anxiety or depression rather than to standardized measures of dysfunction (e.g., Larrabee & Levin, 1986).

The determination of the degree of memory loss associated with age is strongly related to the manner in which memory is measured. If one asks a subject to recall information, age-related differences will be much more apparent than if one simply observes the effects of previous experience on subsequent task performance. Such measures of implicit memory are much less likely to show differential decline as a function of age (e.g., Light & Singh, 1987).

The organization and monitoring of one's own cognitive processes can also have an effect on patterns of memory change. Older adults are more likely than the young to have problems remembering the source of information that they do, in fact, recall, a problem that can lead to what appear to be errors of judgment. Dywan and Jacoby (1990) have shown that older people are more likely than the young to judge nonfamous names as famous if some of the nonfamous names had been presented immediately before the fame judgment task. The older adults tend to mistake the source of familiarity that attends the previously presented nonfamous names. This occurs even though the older subjects are generally better than the young at the basic task of discriminating famous from nonfamous names.

Not only does memory performance vary as a function of how it is measured, it also varies as a function of individual differences in education and lifestyle. Craik, Byrd, and Swanson (1987) have shown that groups of elderly individuals who differ markedly on socioeconomic and lifestyle variables differ as well with respect to how much their memory performance differs from that of a young sample. They also demonstrated that environmental support in the form of cuing maximized performance when used at the initial encoding stage or at retrieval with the maximum benefit occurring with cuing at both phases of the task. Thus, even though some aspects of memory are less efficient as individuals age, monitoring, organization, and reminders can reduce the degree of dysfunction.

Language and linguistic functioning seem to be the least affected by age. When decrements are found in expressive language they can often be traced to word finding difficulties and a decline in verbal fluency. These age-based differences, however, are usually not statistically significant in laboratory assessments until healthy subjects are in their seventies (Albert, Heller & Milberg, 1988). With respect to comprehension, it seems that age effects are most apparent as the memory component of the task becomes more substantial (Light, 1990). Thus, when older adults are faced with large amounts of material or extraneous or exceptionally complex information, they may show some comprehension difficulty but this does not mean that there is any alteration in basic linguistic competence.

Nonetheless, as mentioned earlier, there is clear evidence that auditory acuity and auditory perception are affected by changes in both peripheral and central sensory processing systems (e.g., Fozard, 1990). Thus, tones within the speech range may be more difficult to discern, especially with background noise. As well, the interstimulus interval necessary for the discrimination of discrete sounds increases so that the speed with which information is presented becomes problematic for older adults much sooner than for the young. Context becomes increasingly important to the older individual as an aid to speech comprehension (Wingfield, Poon, Lombardi & Lowe, 1985) and in many real world settings older adults may have to rely on getting the gist rather than the specifics of spoken language. These interface problems can affect functional language comprehension even in the absence of linguistic deficits, per se.

Older adults tend quite consistently to perform more poorly than younger adults on visuospatial and visuoperceptual tasks (Benton, Eslinger & Damasio, 1981). They tend to be slower and less efficient in mental rotation abilities (Cerella, Poon & Fozard, 1981). They are also less accurate and efficient in a number of nontimed drawing and construction tasks (Farver & Farver, 1982). Researchers have argued that the deficits are due to the fact that many of the tasks used in the assessment of visuospatial abilities are novel, or that they tend to be unrelated to real world activities so that the longer one is out of school, the less practiced one would be with such tasks (Denny, 1982). Practice does improve performance and will reduce the difference between young and old but it will not eliminate it (e.g., Denney, 1990). The results of a recent study (Salthouse, Babcock, Skovronek, Mitchell & Palmon, 1990) have indicated that a decline in performance on spatial visualization tasks is evident in cross-sectional samples across the adult lifespan. When addressing the role of experience, Salthouse et al. found that older architects performed better than age-matched controls who were unselected with respect to profession. However, when compared with younger architects, the same age-related pattern of decline was evident even though the older architects had spent their lives gaining extensive spatial visualization experience. Moreover, the age effects occurred for measures of accuracy even when uncontaminated by speed.

Interface problems owing to central and peripheral sensory processing will have some influence on measurable deficits in visuospatial performance as they would in most measures of neuropsychological functioning. These would be less of an issue, however, in the quiet, well structured laboratory setting than in the real world where extraneous attentional demands more frequently come into play. On the other hand, the real world setting allows more readily for the facilitating effects of task-specific experience. It is important to note that there is no evidence that the older architects in the Salthouse et al. study were in any way less competent or less productive than their younger counterparts.

Finally, there are some cognitive processes that are harder to define and measure because they cut across domains. Some refer to them as metacognitive skills and they are linked to such abilities as abstraction, hypothesis generating, problem solving, and monitoring. In general, older adults do more poorly on such tasks (Salthouse, 1985a). As an example, in a recent study, Albert, Wolfe, and Lafleche (1990) have demonstrated age-related decline in measures of abstraction ability using a verbal proverb interpretation task and a nonverbal test of concept formation. Age-related decline in abstraction was not a function of general IQ or memory but did seem to be related to verbal fluency. Albert et al. propose that the decline in this set of abilities may be related to the decline that occurs physiologically in the prefrontal cortex, an area of the brain that has been associated with some aspects of attentional control, the higher order integration of information, and cognitive flexibility. Others (e.g., Hertzog, 1989; Salthouse, 1985b) have proposed that a decline in complex problem solving or "fluid intelligence" may be due to the well documented slowing in information processing described earlier.

Such links between task performance and their underlying neural structures often are not examined in normative samples. Data from our laboratory show that individual differences among older adults in complex problem solving as measured by the Wisconsin Card Sorting Test (Heaton, 1981) could not be explained by electrophysiological measures of response speed (P300 latency). We found that P300 latency was related to Digit Span, which is usually considered to be a measure of attention and short-term memory and to subjects' performance on the Benton Facial Recognition Test (Benton, 1983), a measure of complex visual pattern matching. Variability in the problem-solving task could be best accounted for by an index of subjects' health based on conditions, such as hypertension, that relate to cerebrovascular health (Dywan, Segalowitz & Unsal, 1990; Segalowitz, Dywan & Unsal, 1990). These data indicate that there is not likely to be a single factor that can account for normal change. Different functions are subserved by different neurophysiological systems and are subject to different patterns of decline.

In summary, it is important to note that a measurable deficit in one or more information processing systems on its own does not necessarily lead to a decline in a person's competency with respect to any particular real world task (Salthouse, 1990). First, with respect to any particular function, for example, attention, there may be a considerable range that may be sufficient in order to carry out the task in question. Until the function falls below some threshold, overt behavior may not be especially affected.

As well, most real world tasks depend on a number of neurocognitive processes, such as attention, memory, organizational skill, and so on. This is why it is difficult to deduce the underlying cause of behavioral impairment without resorting to more precise measures of the various functions involved. Nonetheless, when a decline occurs in one aspect of information processing, the individual may still be able to perform the task by relying more heavily on other processes, that is, increasing organization can make up for a decline in attention or memory. The benefits of experience, a reduction in the number of activities in which one is involved, and increased reliance on available environmental and social supports all play a part in modifying the direct relationship between age-related changes in neurocognitive function and levels of competence as seen in daily life.

The relationships between neurocognitive processes and aging in the preceding section were all based on group data and, as such, may not represent adequately the performance of any particular individual. The range in performance among older adults is usually greater than for any other age groups. Normative data can define areas of vulnerability but it is important that the issue of competence for a specific individual never be decided on the basis of group means.

It is important as well to view age-related cognitive change from a developmental perspective. One can chart cognitive development in children by measuring ever increasing levels of performance on various psychomotor and cognitive tasks. However, as development progresses, competence becomes intrinsically intertwined with particular propensities and experiences. In giving an older adult some measure of general cognitive efficiency, one can usually detect the beginning of physiologically based, age-related decline. However, one would have failed to measure the specialized skills that the older person has developed over their lifetime. It is quite likely that the pianist Arthur Rubenstein, the painter Pablo Picasso, and a competent but otherwise unexceptional high school teacher would have produced neuropsychological profiles that would be indistinguishable from one another. It is clear, however, that the typical cognitive assessment would have missed the distinct competencies of these three individuals.

Diseases and Disorders

Superimposed on this natural aging process, there are a number of disorders such as Alzheimer's and Pick's disease that occur specifically in older people and others, such as stroke, that can occur at any time but occur with greater likelihood in old age. Physiological disorders that can have an indirect effect on the CNS include such conditions as hypertension, chronic obstructive lung disease, and heart attack. There are others, as well, that are considered less often with respect to their possible impact on cognitive function, such as the metastases that can occur in the CNS because of malignant growths, the effects of chemotherapy, and the iatrogenic effects of overmedication (e.g., Hall, 1980; Jefferson & Marshall, 1981; Strub & Black, 1981).

Dementia

Dementia may be defined as a clinical symptom complex in an alert patient marked by an acquired, gradual, persistent, and generalized deterioration of intellectual (and behavioral) function. Over time, this deterioration may be progressive, static, or remitting. The deteriorating intellectual and behavioral criteria include memory, abstract thinking, judgment, impulse control, and personality change. It follows, of course, that dementia seriously interferes with social and occupational functioning.

It was not long ago that if neurological dysfunction was suspected in the etiology of behavioral disturbance, the patient was diagnosed as "organic." Further clarification was rarely sought. Things have changed dramatically in that there is now great effort being put forth to differentiate the dementias on the basis of their neurophysiological underpinnings and their behavioral manifestations. It is becoming clear that, although dementias may look very much alike in the end stages, they may have different etiologies and behavioral manifestations. These differences are important if we are ever to understand, treat, and possibly prevent these devastating disorders.

Primary Dementia

The most common cause of dementia is Alzheimer's disease. It is considered a primary dementia because it is related directly to a deterioration of brain tissue. The deterioration is, in some ways, an extreme version of the neurophysiological decline seen in normal aging but there are some signs specific to Alzheimer's disease as well (e.g., Buell & Coleman, 1981; Terry & Hanson, 1988). In Alzheimer's disease, morphological studies indicate the early destruction of the locus coeruleus and the nucleus basalis of Meynert while neurochemical studies show evidence for denervation of noradrenergic tracks as well as the loss of cholinergic and serotonergic fibers (Bowen, Palmer, Francis, Procter & Lowe, 1988). The primary symptom in early Alzheimer's disease is impaired memory function with either visuospatial deficits or language impairment serving as the next in a series of cumulative losses.

The neuropathology of Alzheimer's disease differs from that of Pick's disease, another primary dementia that results in severe cognitive deterioration but with somewhat different behavioral manifestation and course.

Structurally, the brains of patients with Pick's disease are characterized by severe atrophy of the frontal and temporal lobes. Histopathological studies indicate dense intracellular structures called Pick bodies, which enlarge the cells in which they occur, giving the impression of inflated neurons. These Pick bodies do not occur in normal aging. Changes in personality characterize the early stages of Pick's disease with language disturbance often the first of a series of cognitive losses (Cummings & Benson, 1983).

Parkinson's disease is often referred to as a subcortical dementia. Idiopathic Parkinson's disease involves degenerative changes in the basal ganglia, nucleus basalis of Meynart, and the locus coeruleus. However, the most characteristic sign is the destruction of the substantia nigra in the basal ganglia and the loss of the neurotransmitter dopamine. These changes produce the rigidity, tremor, and shuffling gait that serve as early signs of Parkinson's disease (Cummings & Benson, 1983). Although the percentage of patients who suffer a frank dementia varies, it is generally accepted that it is more prevalent among Parkinson's patients than in the general population (Boller, Mizutani, Roessmann & Gambetti, 1980). Although some of the most severe dementias seen in Parkinson's patients may be caused by the individual simultaneously suffering from Alzheimer's disease or multi-infarct dementia, there are a number of studies that have documented particular patterns of memory loss (e.g., Heindel, Salmon, Shults, Walicke & Butters, 1989) and other deficits (e.g., Taylor, Saint-Cyr & Lang, 1987) that fall short of dementia but nonetheless interfere with optimal cognitive function.

Huntington's disease is a hereditary condition that also results in severe motor impairment, but of a different kind from Parkinson's, because a different part of the brain is affected. Atrophy occurs primarily in the caudate nucleus and the putamen of the basal nuclei. Rather than suffer the rigidity seen in Parkinson's disease, patients with Huntington's disease are unable to inhibit movement, giving rise to the continual and disorganized movement associated with the disease (Cummings & Benson, 1983). The onset of the disease is tragically early (35–42 years) and the behavioral symptomatology is also quite different (e.g., Josiassen, Curry, Roemer, DeBease & Mancall, 1982) and can, in fact, prove difficult with respect to the determiniation of competence because of the long, slow decline with no clear indication as to when individuals would actually begin to have difficulty managing their own affairs. Competence to engage in demanding occupations may be hampered initially beause the individual is faced with problems of attention, organization, and personality alterations that may have their source in neurophysiologically based dysinhibition as well as the reactive depression that would accompany diagnosis.

There are other forms of primary dementia but the point we wish to make is that each has a distinct neurophysiological basis, behavioral manifestation, and course. Careful evaluation of the patterns of cognitive decline as well as history and physiological test results are all important in arriving at an appropriate diagnosis. Diagnosis is essential with respect to prognosis and treatment but diagnosis on its own does not speak to the individual's current level of competency. For this, there is no option but careful evaluation.

Vascular Disease

Although cerebrovascular health has been implicated in some loss of cognitive efficiency, hypertension and arteriosclerosis on their own do not produce a dementia. However, the multiple small strokes that can occur as a consequence of these systemic conditions can (Cummings & Benson, 1983). The manifestations of cognitive dysfunction are dependent on the size, location, and number of cerebral infarcts. Thus, dysfunction ranges from a general cognitive decline caused by multiple small infarctions scattered throughout the brain to the more focal dysfunctions such as aphasia that can occur with a single large infarction in the language area of the left hemisphere.

Individual differences in brain organization, in the nature of the infarct, the health of remaining tissue, and the particular psychological strengths and weaknesses of the patient all prevent any facile extrapolations about subsequent deficits and disability. After stroke, it is essential to evaluate systematically residual strengths and weaknesses, particularly when patients may have to resume activities that might place them or others at risk or when they will resume positions of authority.

With respect to issues of competency, it is essential to be particularly vigilant about the more subtle deficits associated with stroke. Such damage does not lead to the obvious language disturbance often associated with left hemisphere lesions but, nonetheless, may result in serious losses in spatial ability, visual memory, planning, judgment, and cognitive flexibility. Potentially dangerous as well is the fact that such lesions can leave individuals with little appreciation of their deficits, a condition referred to as anosognosia (McGlynn & Schacter, 1989), and they may therefore assume they can continue to function in positions where critical judgment and cognitive flexibility are essential. Also, without proper assessment they may not be provided with appropriate rehabilitation or financial support through insurance benefits.

More comprehensive reviews of the dementias may be found elsewhere (e.g., Bayles & Kaszniak, 1987; Cummings & Benson, 1983; Maletta, 1988). There are, however, three major points that must be considered regarding dementia in an elderly person: (a) all unusual behavior in the elderly is not necessarily dementia; therefore, the differential diagnosis is important since it follows that the subsequent specific treatment modes will substantially differ, (b) if the unusual behavior is due to a dementia, the dementia may be due to a wide variety of organic causes, both intracranial and extracranial, (c) following the biopsychosocial model of medicine, dementia must be considered as a multidimensional problem—not simply a medical one, but one that involves physiological, socioeconomic, cultural, and psychological parameters as well.

Mental Illness

Mental illness is often referred to as a "functional" disorder in the context of the functional/organic distinction. This distinction is not clear-cut. Functional usually implies a lack of physiological involvement and reversibility. However, as we learn more about mental illness we find that whether or not serious mental disorder is environmentally triggered, it is subserved and maintained by manifest alterations to the biochemical activity of the CNS. Moreover, treatment most often has a biochemical component (for further discussion of the functional/organic distinction see Kaplan, chap. 10, this volume).

Determining the true prevalence of psychiatric disorders among the elderly is difficult, in part because of an increased tolerance by society of deviant behavior in older people, and a reluctance to identify disturbed behavior in the elderly as a "psychiatric problem." Even so, there is a well documented increase in the prevalence of psychiatric disorders in the United States for individuals 65 years and older (Crook et al., 1986). The explanation for these high numbers is not known, but both physiological and environmental factors probably play a role. The increase in adverse environmental stresses for the elderly, frequently manifested as multiple, unplanned losses, contributes to this increased prevalence of mental illness. Additionally, it is likely that the age-related degenerative changes in the nervous system reduce the adaptive capacity of the older adult and increase the prevalence of psychiatric disorders.

Psychoses of Late Onset

Schizophrenia

Schizophrenia is primarily a chronic disorder in the elderly and is better defined as a syndrome rather than as a single disease entity. Most older schizophrenics develop the problem in their early years and carry it into old age, with few having the initial onset of illness late in life. In fact, the position of DSM-III in this matter was that first-time schizophrenia did not begin after the age of 45 years (American Psychiatric Association, 1980). Recent evidence clearly refutes that position (Gold, 1984; Rabins, Panker & Thomas, 1984; Volanka, 1985) and DSM-IIIR (American Psychiatric Association, 1987) reflects that change by recognizing the possibility, although extremely uncommon, of an initial onset after age 45 years. Usually the onset of schizophrenia is seen in the late teens or young adult period, so that 65-year-olds may have a 40- to 50-year history of chronic illness. Most of these patients will have been admitted to a psychiatric hospital long before the mid-1950s' introduction of effective psychotropic drug treatment for their disorders.

There are various groups of psychotic or schizophrenic elderly patients that may be categorized according to their clinical presentations (unfortunately, "psychotic" and "schizophrenic" are often inappropriately used as synonyms). One group of these patients presents with a seemingly first-time, acute onset of a psychotic illness, frequently with paranoid overtones and usually having a clear sensorium, that is, no evidence of cognitive dysfunction, which would indicate a dementing illness. Another large group, the so-called "mixed" population, consists of patients who present with a combination of signs that involve long-standing evidence of both disordered thinking and signs of a dementing illness. A third is a group with a long-standing dementia who may have no observable thought disorder or hallucinations, but who to have enough general cognitive impairment to cause considerable distress to themselves or those around them because of aggressive, belligerent, or otherwise uncontrollable dysfunctional behavior. Patients in any of these groupings, appropriately or not, may carry the label of schizophrenia.

As in early life, although usually not as fulminant, schizophrenia in older patients is characterized by a broad variety of disturbances in thinking (delusional), affect (blunted or inappropriate), and behavior (grossly disorganized). Problems with sense of self, volition, relationships to the external world, and loss of reality testing, such as hallucinations (usually auditory) or illusions, may also be present. These observations fit into the DSM-IIIR symptomatic criteria for schizophrenia (American Psychiatric Association, 1987).

Late-onset schizophrenia has a more frequent incidence in women, it has a better prognosis than the early-onset form, and it will often respond well to neuroleptics. Little data are available on older-onset schizophrenic patients regarding the presence of a familial pattern or on the recurrence of disease episodes often seen in younger schizophrenics. The other two important criteria necessary for diagnosis of schizophrenia are impairment (deterioration from a previous higher level of functioning in work, social functioning, etc.) and duration (continuous signs of the illness for at least 6 months). Similar signs lasting a shorter time, between 2 weeks and 6 months, are considered to be schizophreniform rather than schizophrenic.

Even more than their younger counterparts, elderly schizophrenics have little in the way of effective support systems or a strong family/political lobby. Unfortunately, because of the well-meaning but potentially destructive movement that swept the United States and Canada in the late 1960s and early 1970s, to "deinstitutionalize" patients from state mental hospitals into the community to obtain better "care," many elderly chronic schizophrenics had situations that, for a variety of reasons, went from bad to worse. As a legacy, legions of these pathetic individuals may now be seen on any day in the downtowns of any major city in North America, a constant reminder of the disgracefully inadequate, disorganized, and ineffective mental health care systems currently in place for elderly schizophrenic individuals.

Paraphrenia

Paraphrenia is a concept first described by Kraepelin (Kraepelin, 1912), who described a paranoid psychosis of late onset, characterized by a chronic course, delusions, and hallucinations with minimal effect on intellect. Kraepelin divided paraphrenia into four subtypes: (a) paraphrenia systemica—with a well organized delusional system, (b) paraphrenia expansiva—with predominantly megalomanic delusions, (c) paraphrenia—with confabulation, and (d) paraphrenia phantastica—with massive elaboration of delusions showing no consistency with each other. At present, DSM-IIIR takes the position that paraphrenia does not exist as a separate psychiatric entity. It is thought instead that these symptoms represent a form of late-onset schizophrenia (Kay, 1963).

Late-Occurring Paranoia

Although paranoid thinking may be a part of the symptom complex seen in schizophrenia, it is listed separately because a late-occurring paranoid condition in an elderly patient often represents a first-time presentation of mental illness (Carstensen & Fremouw, 1981). Late-occurring paranoia (also called "delusional disorder"), first described by Kraepelin, is a rare disorder that accounts for a frequency of about 0.1% of hospital admissions (Winokur, 1977). Signs and symptoms include circumscribed and relatively stable delusions accompanied by a clear, orderly sensorium. There is a chronic course without deterioration and, remarkably, an absence of hallucinations. In contrast to late-onset schizophrenia, paranoia affects older men more frequently than women and should be considered as a distinct nosologic entity (Kendler, 1980). Delusional systems in these patients frequently center around conjugal topics, with jealousy as a prominent theme. The onset of paranoia may not occur until age 60 years or later (Manschreck & Petri, 1978). Generally, one can arbitrarily distinguish among four increasing degrees of intensity of paranoid ideation in the elderly: (a) suspiciousness, (b) transitional paranoid reaction, (c) paranoia, and (d) paranoia associated with schizophrenia (Eisdorfer, 1980). This interesting symptomatology may represent an unconscious "face-saving" device by the elderly patient against the gradual loss of self-mastery and control that is being experienced, and the growing fear and helplessness implicit with it (Eisdorfer, 1980). The efficacy of treatment of this disorder with antipsychotics is not well documented, although some patients apparently do improve.

Paranoid symptoms in the elderly frequently have some basis in reality and may require a thorough examination of the patient's psychosocial and family situation, rather than simply initiating treatment with medication. Also, difficulties caused by the normal sensory decline seen in aging should be considered when examining a patient with a late onset of "paranoia." Decreased audition of high-frequency tones and also a decrease in visual acuity and color perception often contribute to a feeling of increased suspiciousness in an already socially isolated elderly individual. There is even some evidence that hearing impairment may be a predisposing factor for paranoid psychosis (Cooper, Garside & Kay, 1976). Sensory decline is an important area in the elderly that must not be overlooked during the assessment process.

Affective Disorders

When discussing affective disorders in the elderly, one usually refers to depression, although mania must also be included (Neshkes & Jarvick, 1987; Shulman & Post, 1980). Affective disorders may be acute or chronic, and may present with or without psychotic features, that is, disorders of thought (Loranger & Levine, 1978).

Depression

Although formal psychiatric depression is significantly overdiagnosed, a predominant psychological disturbance seen in the elderly is dysphoria (Solomon, 1981; Gottfries, 1981; Blazer, 1982). At any age true clinical depression may be viewed as a syndrome lasting at least 2 weeks, interrelating psychological, somatic, and behavioral symptoms and signs. Prominent psychological signs and symptoms include a persistent dysphoric mood (sad, unhappy, "depressed," "blue"), irritability, anhedonia (inability to experience pleasure), guilt feelings, difficulty in concentration, pessimism, loss of interest, somatic concerns or delusions, helplessness, hopelessness, and suicidal thoughts. Some common somatic manifestations include anorexia, insomnia (or hypersomnia), fatigue, reduced sex drive, headache, amenorrhea where applicable, and constipation. Behavioral signs are exemplified by poor grooming, withdrawal, crying, motor retardation (or agitation), self-reproach, and suicide attempts.

In some patients these features may even include a psychosis exemplified by a thinking disorder (e.g., delusions) and/or loss or impairment of reality testing, that is, hallucinations, illusions, or even a depressive stupor. These problems must be observed in the presence of a clear sensorium (assuming the patient can cooperate with testing procedures). The psychotic features may be mood-congruent, that is, the content of the disordered thinking is consistent with depressive themes of inadequacy, guilt, deserved punishment, or death; or they may be mood-incongruent, that is, persecution, grandiosity, thought-insertion, thought-broadcasting, or control. The significance of the mood congruency or incongruency of the psychotic features in affective disorders is currently controversial.

Depression in elderly individuals can be unrecognized when it does not follow the same pattern or have the same aforementioned symptoms and signs as those depressed patients in the younger age group. In the elderly the onset is likely to be more gradual and may even be somatic in its manifestation, although unlike the young, the complaints may focus on generalized pain such as headache, gastrointestinal upset, low-back or other joint problems, and so on. Unfortunately, these complaints may be easily confused with the symptoms and signs of the chronic physical illnesses that are so common in the older patient or the effects of bodily injury suffered in an accident. Importantly, the usual affective symptoms and signs of depression seen in the young, such as guilt and self-deprecation, may be absent in the elderly patient. Also, overt sadness and crying spells are not commonly seen.

Often on examination, depressed elderly patients may demonstrate a considerable impairment of memory, attention, concentration, and comprehension along with psychomotor retardation and loss of initiative. This situation occurs frequently and these congnitive deficits may be so prominent as to confuse a depression with a dementing illness. Depression in the elderly presenting in these unusual ways is sometimes referred to as "atypical" or "masked" depression or, alternatively, as pseudodementia.

It is essential that the differential diagnosis between depression and dementia be clear (Katzman, Lasker, & Bernstein, 1988; Kazniak, 1987) because frequently an elderly patient who is depressed receives a diagnosis of dementia and is then treated accordingly by staff either with medication or institutionalization or both. This treatment, unfortunately, may result in the elderly patient gradually conforming to the situational ambience of his environment, with clear and significant demented activity and behavior eventually following. This is truly unfortunate since depression in the elderly is a treatable problem (Gottfries, 1981).

Mania

Manias are far less frequent in late life than depressions, with first-time onset of mania rarely seen after age 60 years. Frequently, these episodes are part of a bipolar disorder and are usually seen in a patient who had a previous onset of a depressive episode before the age of 50 years. Manic symptoms and signs in these individuals, for example, hyperactivity, pressured speech, flight of ideas, may be mistaken for simple aggressiveness or a personality problem and the correct diagnosis overlooked.

Hostile and/or paranoid behaviors of delusional proportion may also be present in these older patients, which may further complicate the diagnosis of mania. Mania in the elderly has a poorer prognosis than late-onset depression. Nevertheless, treatment with antipsychotics and lithium is indicated in elderly psychiatric patients with a presentation of mania and certainly in elderly patients with a bipolar disorder.

There is a clear association between physiological factors and manic symptoms, the so-called secondary manias (Krauthammer & Klerman, 1978). Numerous agents are known to precipitate a syndrome similar to mania in susceptible individuals. These include a variety of common drugs, metabolic disturbances, hemodialysis, and postoperative states, infections, neoplasms, and epilepsy as etiologic factors. Therefore, secondary mania should be seriously considered in an older patient with a first-time presentation of mania, especially after age 60 years, and treatment should be focused on correcting the underlying physiological problem. If this cannot be done, treatment with lithium has been successful in ameliorating symptoms, even in elderly patients with secondary mania, and it should be used.

Delirium

Delirium (also known as acute confusional state) refers to a fluctuating disorder of awareness, with associated dysfunction in arousal, perception, memory, orientation, thinking, and judgment. There also may be frequent lability of affect, psychomotor disturbances, and a loss of reality testing (manifested by hallucinations and/or illusions). Delirium is rapid in onset and reversible in character and is caused by an acute disruption of brain metabolism. In patients with delirium, the level of awareness varies markedly over time. The hallucinations seen are commonly visual, but also may be auditory. Fear, anger, depression, and sensory misperceptions (greater at night because of a decrease in sensory input, i.e., "sundowning") are also seen in delirium; this syndrome rarely lasts more than 1 month.

At the outset, the only clinical difference observed between dementia and delirium in a patient may be the fluctuating level of awareness, leading to a disordered attention span as the most prominent feature. If the patient is seen for a long enough period and a good history if obtained from a reliable informant, the differentiation of delirium from dementia is rather straightforward. However, if the aged patient is seen in a brief evaluation, as frequently occurs in an emergency room, there may be some early difficulty in deciding on the correct diagnosis. A key point is that in cases of delirium it is important for the patient to have stabilized before any meaningful assessment of their general level of functioning can be made.

There are many known causes of delirium, and many elderly patients diagnosed as demented are found to be delirious instead. By far, the primary cause of delirium in the elderly is drug toxicity. This includes not only prescribed drugs, but off-the-shelf as well as street drugs, social drugs, and drugs shared by family and friends. The drug itself may cause the delirium or side effects of a drug (especially anticholinergic ones), an excess dose, a "normal" dose given to a frail aged patient, and/or drug-drug, drug-diet, or drug-system interactions all may contribute toward causing a delirium in an elderly patient (Vestal & Cusack, 1990).

Other causes of delirium may involve direct or indirect disruption of the CNS, the cardiovascular-pulmonary-renal system, as well as metabolic and endocrine, systemic, and miscellaneous causes. In a frail elderly patient with a normally occurring marked decrease in the ability to maintain appropriate homeostasis in response to stress, such straightforward phenomena as fecal impaction or urinary bladder distention, and even isolation, fatigue, or intensive care unit syndrome may be enough to precipitate a delirium.

Summary

It is clear that the factors leading to cognitive impairment in older adults are many and varied. Although a diagnosis of Alzheimer's or multi-infarct dementia often provides a clear indication that a transfer of power would be appropriate, the individual with chronic obstructive lung disease, or the individual who may have suffered a severe heart attack or who may be receiving large doses of chemotherapy for developing metastases might not be assessed or monitored with respect to alterations in cognitive function. It is unfortunate, however, that the secondary effects of such major assaults on the body can involve the reductions of blood flow to the brain or the destruction of brain tissue to the extent that the person is left with chronic cognitive deficits that may go unmonitored and unaddressed.

Assessment

The nature of the assessment is dictated to some extent by the question that is to be addressed. If the question is one of diagnosis, the patient's neurocognitive ability can often be helpful in adding to the data on which such decisions are based. Diagnostic error in differentiating dementia from depression often can be due to the inadequate assessment of cognitive functioning in older patients by their physicians (McCartney, 1986). It is important to note, however, that a diagnosis on its own does not indicate the degree of disability an individual might be facing when issues of competency arise. Katzman, Lasker and Bernstein (1988) describe the variable course of patients with well established diagnoses of Alzheimer's disease who maintained their mental status for up to 2 years without measurable decline while others have deteriorated completely within 1 year. They also point out the intrasubject variability in the nature of the cognitive decline and the implications of this variability. Some patients have been found who are incapable of giving their own name but who are able to maintain themselves on a day-to-day basis with little assistance. It is clear that a diagnosis, no matter how accurate, does not in itself indicate the individual's current level of competence, which is the issue of primary interest in the legal context. Careful cognitive assessment is still in order.

The most effective approach to determining medical diagnosis or level of competence in an elderly individual is through the use of a multidisciplinary team of professionals with training and experience in geriatrics. The complex interaction between physiological, psychological, and social systems must be carefully considered, particularly in those instances when legal competency questions arise that might seriously affect the rights and freedoms of the individual in question.

Neuropsychologists are often employed to assist in the diagnostic enterprise. The neuropsychologist has come familiarity with the nervous system, is trained to observe and assess behavior, and is able to call on the clinical, psychometric, cognitive, and physiological traditions within psychology to provide the kind of integration such determinations require. A number of excellent sources outline the basic principles of neuropsychological assessment (e.g., Kolb & Whishaw, 1990; Lezak, 1983). There are, however, some issues that arise in the assessment of older adults that need special consideration (e.g., Albert, 1988; Bayles & Kaszniak, 1987, chap. 14; Swihart & Pirozzolo, 1988).

It is commonly acknowledged that the data collected in a neuropsychological evaluation must be analyzed within as full a context as possible. This is true for any assessment but never more so than for the elderly, who have accumulated a lifetime of experiences, physiological, psychological, and social, that will have a bearing on their current level of functioning. Information must be gathered from the individual as well as from family or a close friend with respect to past and current levels of function. Medical, educational, and work history as well as hobbies will all help gauge the expected level of performance.

Special attention must be paid to the existence of chronic conditions such as hypertension, chronic obstructive lung disease, and so forth, because of their possible bearing on the cerebrovascular system. History of head injury is also important to ascertain because the effects of repeated injury can be cumulative and the diffuse damage that we now know can accompany even fairly mild head injury may interact with normative changes in the CNS to exacerbate age-related cognitive decline. As well, drug use and abuse must be determined. For example, the prolonged use of large quantities of alcohol has been shown to affect the level of cognitive function (Ryan & Butters, 1986; Wilson, Kolb, Odland & Whishaw, 1987), as has the toxicity that can develop from inappropriately managed prescription drugs and self-medication (Vestal & Cusade, 1990).

It is important, as in all neuropsychological evaluations, to assess each aspect of information processing in as systematic a manner as is possible. These functions include attention, language, memory, visuospatial ability, constructional ability, conceptualization, and problem solving. Even when cognitive capacities are intact, an individual may be unable to function adequately because of a loss of strength, speed, or fine-motor ability so that measuring performance in these areas should be part of the assessment.

Each assessment should include some well standardized measures such as the appropriate subtests from the Wechsler Adult Intelligence Scale–Revised (Weschler, 1981) if possible. The Vocabulary subtest is one of the best predictors of verbal abilities and the Block Design subtest is the one of the best predictors of overall performance on the nonverbal subtests. There are many long established as well as many new measures of neurocognitive function that are being developed through the ongoing research so that any listing of measures will not likely be complete or timely for long. It is up to neuropsychologists to keep apprised of the growing body of research that concerns the assessment of cognitive functions in the older adult and update their approach accordingly. It is also important to note that no single measuring instrument on its own is sufficient for an adequate analysis of cognitive function in an elderly individual; nor is the unthinking use of an extensive test battery appropriate for most elderly individuals. One needs to plan carefully to get the maximum amount of information while conserving as much as possible the older adults' patience and energy.

Except for the various mental status tests and dementia rating scales, most measurement tools have been developed for use with younger adults. Some include norms for older individuals but rarely do the norms go beyond 65 years, if they exist at all. Lezak (1987) decries the dearth of appropriate age-based norms, claiming that it leaves the assessment of the older individual as much an art as a science.

Age-based norms are essential when one wishes to establish a diagnostic profile or describe patient function relative to others of the same age. The situation becomes more complicated when the goal is to predict to some external criterion such as job performance. Here one wishes to know how well the individual can attend, engage in parallel processing, control fine motor movements, and so on, on some absolute basis. It may be true that a particular patient performs within the normal range for 65-year-olds on some neuropsychological measure but the question remains as to whether the average performance of a normative sample of 65-year-olds would be sufficient for the criterion task.

Another issue to be considered with respect to appropriate normative data is that age-based norms may not be truly representative of the population. A mean test score for a group of older individuals may drop because of the ever-increasing proportion of those with chronic disease in the normative sample. Nonetheless, there remains a substantial number of older adults whose performance on many measures remains exceptional, even by the standards of a 35-year-old. It may be the case that the older the normative sample, the more likely is it that the mean is based on a bimodal distribution and does not really represent most of the individuals in that age group (e.g., Feier & Gerstman, 1980). As well, cohort differences in the amount of education received by most of the population in the early part of the century may make the norms inappropriate for the highly educated individual. In such cases, a highly educated individuals scoring near the mean for the normative sample could indicate a significant loss of function.

As those who have worked in psychogeriatric units know, there is probably no other population for which interface problems so regularly come to the fore during assessment. As well as major hurdles, such as aphasia or visuoperceptual impairments, differences in response speed, the loss of visual and auditory acuity, high levels of stress, fatigueability, and so forth, often complicate the testing situation. Older adults also tend more often to be closely tied to their ethnic background so that many may have difficulty understanding test instructions or they may not share the same cultural history and assumptions as normative samples. In these situations, the neuropsychologist is faced with the task of adapting assessment techniques to the limitations imposed by these interface problems, which in itself adds a further confound to the interpretation of test results.

The adequate assessment of an older adult requires familiarity with normal adult development and a good understanding of the various neurocognitive processes that need to be assessed as well as a comprehensive knowledge of formalized testing strategies. It is often necessary to alter procedures in eliciting the best performance from multiply handicapped individuals. Standardized scores are important and should be obtained whenever possible. It is, nonetheless, the *pattern* of results, combined with medical information, the observations of occupational therapists and other relevant professionals, and the observations of the family that eventually lead to the best diagnostic decisions and the best estimate possible of the patient's current level of function. A quick mental status exam in a physician's office does not constitute an adequate competency assessment. There is no shortcut to an adequate assessment, because there is no shortcut when it comes to describing the deficits and extrapolating to the demands that individuals will have to contend with in their job and/or their daily lives.

Generalizability

Can the clinician predict behavior based on test results? This is probably the poorest documented area in neuropsychology yet the most critical area with respect to legal judgments of competency. Those who have studied the predictive validity of neuropsychological tests (e.g., Chelune & Moehle, 1986; Heaton & Pendleton, 1981; Searight, Dunn, Grisso, Margolis & Gibbons, 1989) have found modest relationships between various global measures of neuropsychological function and various measures of behavioral competency leaving considerable amounts of variance unexplained. This is to be expected given the unbelievably inadequate representations of neuropsychological data on which these correlations are based. In many cases, IQ was used as the primary measure of neuropsychological function. If there is anything that a reader would take away from having read this volume, it is that a competent neuropsychological assessment goes well beyond measures of IQ.

Searight et al. (1989) have attempted to provide a more rigorous test of the predictive validity of neuropsychological measures by examining the relationship between the Halstead-Reitan Neuropsychological Test Battery and measures of daily living in a small sample of mild to moderately demented elderly subjects. They found the usual general relationship between the combined scores on both test batteries but were not able to make impressive predictions between any single H-R subtest and any specific activity of daily living. Again, such results are not surprising given the number of independent variables (25) relative to the size of the population (40), the lack of specific hypotheses to be tested, and the limited range of abilities within the population (subjects were all mildly to moderately demented).

It is clear that further research is needed to determine the predictive validity of neuropsychological assessment. It will, however, be important not to minimize the complexity of the task. First, it is theoretically questionable to attempt to match any single index of information processing skill to a complex behavior. As is the case with most complex tasks, they can be accomplished in a number of ways: they may be overlearned and thus not overly sensitive to alteration in a specific cognitive process, or they may be variably supported by environmental context.

If one wishes to make statements about life skills it may be best to assess them directly. There have been a number of attempts to develop a systematic approach to such an assessment. For example, Wang and Ennis (1986) have developed a competency assessment battery that assesses a patient's orientation to personal matters, social intelligence, memory, reading, management of monetary transactions, safety judgment, and orientation in space. Results can be presented in the form of a competency profile or as a summary index and recommendations are made as to the degree and type of supervision the person is likely to need. It is often the case, however, that the patient's difficulties in everyday life *are* clearly evident and provide the impetus for the referral. When the individual cannot do a task or a subset of tasks, detailed neuropsychological investigation is undertaken to determine why; that is, is the difficulty primarily caused by a deficit in attention, memory, abstract reasoning ability, and so on.

Decisions about competence would most likely involve the ability to engage in higher level problem solving and to show good judgment. These higher level abilities are difficult to assess directly. Such tasks require that an individual perceive the complexities of situations on both a cognitive and emotional level, to organize these perceptions, to envision possible outcomes, and to be able to monitor and control their own impulses and emotions with some degree flexibility. From a neuropsychological perspective this requires the integration of cortically based perceptual and cognitive processes with basic limbic arousal systems. Such integration is considered to take place in the frontal areas of the brain and impairment on tests of frontal lobe function often correspond to poor emotional control and impaired judgment. However, there is evidence (Eslinger & Damasio, 1985) that traditional clinical measures of frontal lobe function are not always sufficient to document severe loss of judgment, especially when the patient was exceptional with respect to premorbid levels of intelligence.

Competence also requires that one have an appreciation of one's weaknesses as well as of one's strengths. Another common consequence of brain damage, whether it be from dementia, stroke, or head injury is a diminished awareness that one has suffered some physiological or cognitive decline or any major personality change. This unawareness is usually referred to as anosognosia and is to be distinguished from the condition whereby an individual seems to be aware of the deficit but does not seem particularly distressed by it. This latter is considered to represent a disorder of affect as opposed to the apparent lack of awareness of a deficit that characterizes anosognosia.

Although clinical reports of anosognosia have existed since the early part of this century (e.g., McGlynn & Schacter, 1989), the phenomenon is not fully understood, nor is an assessment of degree of anosognosia usually part of a standard neuropsychological assessment. There are, however, attempts to devise a systematic approach to assessing the degree of anosognosia in patients (Anderson & Tranell, 1989). The results of their study with 100 brain-injured patients indicated that the unawareness of deficits is quite common, and that it is often associated with unilateral right hemisphere damage. Any extrapolation from laboratory-based test results to the real world would be sorely hampered if this important aspect of competent behavior were not addressed.

Can We Enhance the Accuracy of Behavioral Measures?

Electroencephalogram

The electroencephalogram (EEG) measures the brain's ambient electrical activity. Investigators have documented age-related changes in a number of dimensions of the EEG (see Duffy & McAnulty, 1988, for a review). It was originally thought that aging resulted in an inevitable slowing of EEG activity (a decrease in the frequency and amplitude of alpha activity with a corresponding increase in delta and theta slow waves). However, more recent investigations have indicated that the focal slowing may have been related more to a decline in health than to age per se (e.g., Duffy, Albert & McAnulty, 1984; Katz & Horowitz, 1982; Obrist, 1979). Using spectral analysis, Dustman, LaMarche, Cohen, Shearer, and Talone (1985) have found that even healthy older adults produced a greater correspondence between sites from which EEG is measured, suggesting that there may be less specificity in brain response in old age.

Evoked potentials (EPs) represent a summed EEG response to the repeated presentation of stimuli. Evidence from EP studies is fairly consistent in documenting a slowing in evoked response in older adults (Beck, Swanson & Dustman, 1980). this is consistent with the age-related slowing in reaction time and is most obvious in the frontal and parieto-central regions of the brain (Duffy et al., 1984). Again this is consistent with behavioral data indicating an age-related decline in tasks thought to tap frontal functions (Mittenberg et al., 1989); although when measured concurrently, that is, when one examines the correspondence between P300 latency and behavioral indices of frontal lobe function in the same individuals, these relationships do not hold (Dywan et al., 1990).

EP amplitudes also show age-related changes. Investigators have found that P300 amplitude in older subjects tended to be lower (Mullis, Holcomb, Diner & Dykman, 1985) but they were more reactive to increased intensity of stimuli (Dustman, Shearer & Snyder, 1982). That is, as the intensity of stimuli are increased, older adults produce a disproportionate augmentation in P300 amplitude suggesting that they are less able to dampen or inhibit their response. P300 amplitudes are also found to be more homogeneous across electrode sites (Polich, Howard & Starr, 1985). Together, these changes are considered to be evidence for a general slowing in response time coupled with a reduction in central inhibition and less specificity in brain response in old age.

Abnormality in EEG recordings are generally thought to increase with the development of a dementia so that one eventually may see a slowing or disappearance of the dominant alpha rhythm (Obrist, 1978). However, in the early stages of the disease when confirmatory evidence is most important, EEG changes are less dramatic and can be hard to distinguish from changes in normal aging (Brenner et al., 1986). The later components of EPs are significantly delayed in Alzheimer's disease (Visser et al., 1985) but it is not clear that this slowing is specific to dementia because patients with schizophrenia and depression are similarly affected (Kraiuhin et al., 1986).

Electrophysiological measures can be useful in confirming expected cerebral dysfunction but they cannot, on their own, provide definitive information as to the type or degree of damage. With respect to issues of competence, it is important to note that most studies do not look at behavioral and brain measures concurrently within the same individuals. It would therefore be difficult as yet to extrapolate from EEG records to behavioral competency for any particular individual.

Brain Scans

The ability to peer into the skull without risk to the patient presents incredible new opportunities to learn about the structure and function of the CNS in the living person. The question is, does this technology provide important information with respect to a determination of competence in the elderly?

There are a number of different types of scanning techniques (for example, Metter & Hanson, 1985; Gur & Gur, 1991, chap. 7, in this volume). An important distinction is between those scanning techniques that provide structural as opposed to functional information. Computerized tomography (CT) and magnetic resonance imaging (MRI) techniques provide information about the structure of the brain whereas regional cerebral blood flow (rCBF), positron emission tomography (PET), and single photon emission computed tomography (SPECT) provide information about the efficiency of brain function.

Albert and Stafford (1988) provide a topical review of the major findings relevant to CT scan measures of the aging nervous system. Despite a number of confounds in earlier work, there seems to be some consensus that ventricular size, as indicated by CT scan, remains fairly constant until about the age of 65 years and then begins to expand quite rapidly. CT scan also allows for the measurement of tissue density. In contrast to the exponential change in ventricular size in the later years, it seems that tissue density decreases in a fairly linear fashion (e.g., Stafford et al., 1988). These, along with measures of sulcal size, provide indices of the degree to which the brain has atrophied. As mentioned earlier, some atrophy is expected as part of the normal aging process but if extensive can indicate the presence of pathology.

There has been little work to date that specifically relates normative changes to level of cognitive function. An exception is the work by Albert and Stafford (1986), who have demonstrated that fluid volume, as measured by ventricular size, is significantly correlated with subjects' scores on the Wechsler Memory Scale and the Boston Naming Test as well as with some measures of visuospatial function and abstraction. They also found CT density to be related to measures of mental flexibility and general intelligence. These relationships were evident even after age itself was statistically factored out of the analyses. Such data provide some validity to both behavioral and scanning data and it would be fairly safe to assume that if behavioral indices of cognitive function show normative patterns of decline these are likely indicative of normative changes at the neurological level.

The disease processes involved in the dementias can also alter brain structure over time. Albert and Stafford (1988) report than when ventricular and density measures are taken using reliable computer-assisted techniques and carefully selected subjects, statistically significant differences are found between the brains of Alzheimer patients and normal controls. Longitudinal data indicate that there is a progression of ventricular size correspondent with the progression of the disease (e.g., Brinkman & Largen, 1984), Nonetheless, because of the changes that occur with normal aging, there can be an overlap between CT indices of structural change between normal adults and Alzheimer patients, particularly early in the course of disease.

CT scanning and the more precise MRI have become invaluable in detecting evidence of stroke and tumor and other lesions if they are large enough to be seen themselves or to produce some evident shift in adjacent brain tissue. It is important to appreciate, however, that negative results on CT scans do not rule out the possibility of structural damage. Kuhl, Metter, and Reige (1985) have demonstrated that lesions observable using blood flow studies of glucose metabolism were not observed on CT scans of the same patients. Conversely, some lesions observed on the CT scans were missed by the blood flow studies but these were fewer.

The imaging techniques that supply functional information about the brain indicate the rate of blood flow to various parts of the brain. They are therefore able to indicate areas of the brain that are not adequately supplied with blood as a result of specific or diffuse damage that may not be as apparent as structural lesions. As well, since blood flow to various parts of the brain is commensurate with the amount of activity being carried out by that part of the brain at the time the scan is taken, these measures are well suited to studying regional levels of brain metabolism while the individual is engaged in a particular cognitive task.

The sensitivity of these measures to ongoing cognitive activity result in lower retest reliability than is possible with the structural measures because, even though normative data are collected when subjects are "at rest," subjects' mental state will vary at the time of measurement. Thus, although there have been a number of studies, it is not yet clear that systematic decline in blood flow or metabolism is an integral part of normal aging. It may be that when it is observed, it is simply a manifestation of cerebrovascular disease, which is prevalent in older samples (see Metter, 1988, for a review).

Disease states do, however, affect blood flow and this is seen in the reduced blood flow evident in Alzheimer's patients relative to normal controls and relative to the severity of the disease (Metter, 1988). Blood flow studies may also help differentiate the subtypes of Alzheimer's disease. Foster et al., (1983) have demonstrated that there is a relationship between the primary symptomatology in the early stages of Alzheimer's disease and the reduced metabolism evident in the brain area that is usually considered to subserve the function in question. Blood flow studies have also been quite successful in distinguishing between Alzheimer's disease and multi-infarct dementia. The brains of Alzheimer's patients show a more generalized hypometabolism whereas those of patients suffering from multi-infarct dementia show multiple, focal lesions throughout (Kuhl, Metter & Reige, 1985). In general, researchers are finding that blood flow studies are quite good at reflecting symptomatology. The brains of patients with Pick's disease show marked hypofrontality (Gustafson, Brun, Franck Holmkvist, & Risberg, 1985) and those with slowly progressing aphasia show a severe decrease in blood flow in the left temporal-parietal area (Chawluk et al., 1986). Similar concurrence of hypometabolism and cognitive decline have been demonstrated for the subcortical dementias. As well, longitudinal studies have provided evidence that a continued decrease in blood flow accompanies continued deterioration.

With respect to the issue of competence, it is clear that blood flow studies can provide confirmatory evidence with respect to the existence of impaired function at the level of the CNS; however, such measures cannot replace behavioral data. In fact, Cutler, Haxby, and Duara (1985) followed a patient with Alzheimer's disease and found that changes in cerebral blood flow were not evident until after changes were noted in neuropsychological measures whereas changes in cerebral blood flow have been shown to precede the onset of vascular or multi-infarct dementia (Rogers, Meyer, Mortel, Mahurin & Judd, 1986). Thus, although confirmatory, blood flow data, like other neurophysiological measures, are not more informative with respect to issues of competence than behavioral measures themselves.

Summary and Conclusions

The focus of this chapter has been on the things that can go wrong during the aging process. It is important to note, however, that most people age without suffering serious cognitive decline and even when some form of decline occurs, the relationship between changes in specific functional abilities and general levels of competence in the world is not at all straightforward. Competence can only be considered with respect to what a person wants to do and the demands placed on him—a situation not all that different from any other life stage. One cannot simply ask whether or not an individual is competent without defining what it is that they need to be competent about. While age-related changes can, on their own, lead to some diminution of competencies, the diseases and chronic disorders that so often accompany aging can affect functioning in myriad ways—sometimes insidiously as in the dementias and sometimes more precipitously as in stroke. It is important to appreciate, however, that neither age nor diagnosis, per se, allows one to infer directly an individual's current level of adaptive functioning. Dementias in their early stages do not implicate all aspects of cognitive function and there is a wide range with respect to rate of decline.

The effects of stroke are even more unpredictable. Fields and Lemak (1989) provide some historical examples indicating the range of outcome possible. For example, at the age of 46 years, Louis Pasteur suffered a stroke that resulted in a paralysis of his left side. He recovered motor function over time and went on to complete and publish his research on silkworm diseases and developed healthy moths to revitalize the industry. He also developed the vaccines for chicken-cholera, anthrax, and rabies. Clearly, whatever the sequelae of Pateur's stroke, his creative genius was not diminished.

In contrast, United States President Woodrow Wilson appears to have had his first stroke in April 1919 while in Paris. He was described at the time as having become more irritable and suspicious. He began to think that furniture was being stolen from the house he occupied and became obsessed with the idea that the French servants were all spies. Another stroke in September of 1919 left him severely impaired; he was seen on one occasion doffing his hat and waving to nonexistent crowds in empty streets. However, given his position no one was willing to formally sign the congressional resolution that would have turned power over to the Vice President and the President himself was in no position to decide. As a result, Wilson remained in office until March 3, 1921 for his full term as president of one of the largest and most powerful countries in the world.

When considering issues of competence, there is a tendency to focus on a decline in intelligence or cognitive abilities. These terms represent an amalgam of various processes and skills. Traditional IQ tests, although informative, are inadequate to the task of assessing competence, especially in the older adult. As individuals age, their "intelligence" becomes more intrinsically tied to the domain or domains in which it has been allowed to develop. There are no laboratory-based tests that would be adequate, on their own, to estimate specific competencies in the variety of domains to which people are able to adapt themselves over a long life. In many cases it may be necessary to consult with an expert with respect to the domain in question.

One can, however, attempt to measure some of the more basic neuropsychological processes that underlie these various competencies. This information, along with behavioral, social, and physiological evidence gathered from as many sources as possible, can help in determining the etiology of impaired function and in developing an accurate description of the individual's current level of competence. It is becoming clear, however, that an important part of this assessment would be to examine functions that lie outside of the traditional cognitive domain.

In a recent stroke case, a man had developed acalculia (e.g., he had lost his ability to deal with numbers). He was, however, deemed competent to understand the implications of his signing a power of attorney and so was permitted to do so. His stroke, however, has altered his affective understanding of his world. He had recently become exceedingly suspicious of his wife and signed over the management of his funds, investments, and so forth to his lawyer. His wife of many years has been caring for him and had little choice but to continue caring for him even though she no longer had ready access to their estate. It is clear that linguistic comprehension of the legal document did not fully capture the competence necessary for this decision. The development of systematic ways of determining whether an individual has suffered a decline in metacognitive or executive skills, in the ability to monitor or be aware of acquired deficits, and in the ability to perceive and express emotion accurately continue to provide a serious challenge for those concerned with issues of competency in the geriatric population.

References

Albert, M.S. (1988). Assessment of cognitive dysfunction. In M.S. Albert & M.B. Moss (Eds.), *Geriatric neuropsychology* (pp. 57–81). New York: Guilford Press.

Albert, M.S., Duffy, F.H., & Naeser, M.A. (1987). Nonlinear changes in cognition and their neurophysiologic correlates. *Canadian Journal of Psychology, 41*, 141–157.

Albert, M.S., & Heaton, R.K. (1988). Intelligence testing. In M.S. Albert & M.B. Moss (Eds.), *Geriatric Neuropsychology* (pp. 13–32). New York: Guilford Press.

Albert, M.S., Heller, H.S., & Milberg, W. (1988). Changes in naming ability with age. *Psychology and Aging, 3*, 173–178.

Albert, M.S., & Stafford, J.L. (1986). CT scan and neuropsychological relationships in aging and dementia. In G. Goldstein & R. Tarter (Eds.), *Advances in clinical neuropsychology*, (Vol. 3) (pp. 31–54). New York: Plenum.

Albert, M.S., & Stafford, J.L. (1988). Computed tomography studies. In M.S. Albert & M.B. Moss (Eds.), *Geriatric neuropsychology* (pp. 211–227). New York: Guilford Press.

Albert, M.S., Wolfe, J., & Lafleche, G. (1990). Differences in abstraction ability with age. *Psychology and Aging, 5*, 94–100.

American Psychiatric Association (1980). *Diagnostic and statistical manual of mental disorders* (3rd ed.). Washington, DC: Author.

American Psychiatric Association (1987). *Diagnostics and statistical manual of mental disorders* (3rd ed., rev. ed.). Washington, DC: American Psychiatric Association.

Anderson, S.W., & Tranel, D. (1989). Awareness of disease states following cerebral infarction, dementia, and head trauma: Standardized assessment. *The Clinical Neuropsychologist, 3*, 327–339.

Bayles, K.A., & Kaszniak, A.W. (1987). *Communication and cognition in normal aging and dementia* (pp. 299–323). Boston: Little, Brown.

Beck, E.C., Swanson, C., & Dustman, R.E. (1980). Long latency components of the visually evoked potential in man: Effects of aging. *Experimental Aging Research, 6*, 523–545.

Benton, A.L., Eslinger, P.J., & Damasio, A.R. (1981) Normative observations on neuropsychological test performance in old age. *Journal of Clinical Neuropsychology, 3*, 33–42.

Benton, A.L., Van Allen, M.W., Hamsher, K., & Levin, H.S. (1978). *Test of facial recognition*. Iowa City, IA: University Hospitals.

Blazer, D.G. (1982). *Depression in late life*. St. Louis, MO: CV Mosby.

Boller, F., Mizutani, T., Roessmann, U., & Gambetti, P. (1980). Parkinson disease, dementia, and Alzheimer disease: Clinicopathological correlations. *Annals of Neurology, 7*, 329–335.

Bowen, D.M., Palmer, A.M., Francis, P.T., Procter, A.W., & Lowe, S.L. (1988). "Classical" neurotransmitters in Alzheimer disease. In R.D. Terry (Ed.), *Aging and the brain* (pp. 115–128). New York: Raven Press.

Brenner, R., Ulrich, R., & Spiker, D. (1986). Computerized EEG spectral analysis in elderly normal, demented and depressed subjects. *Electroencephalography and Clinical Neurophysiology, 64*, 483–492.

Brinkman. S.D., & Largen, J.W. (1984). Changes in brain ventricular size with repeated CAT scans in suspected Alzheimer's disease. *American Journal of Psychiatry, 141*, 81–83.

Brizzee, K. (1981). Structural correlates of the aging process in the brain. *Psychopharmacological Bulletin, 17*, 43–52.

Brody, H. (1980). Neuroanatomy and neuropathology of aging. In E. Busse & D. Blazer (Eds.), *Handbook of geriatric psychiatry* (pp. 28–45). New York: Van Nostrand-Reinhold.

Buell, S.J., & Coleman, P.D. (1981). Quantitative evidence for selective dendritic growth in normal human aging but not in senile dementia. *Brain Research, 214*, 23–41.

Carlsson, A. (1985) Neurotransmitter charges in the aging brain. *Danish Medical Bulletin, 32*, 40–43.

Carstensen, L., & Fremouw, W. (1981). The determination of a behavioral intervention for late life paranoia. *Gerontologist, 21*, 329–333.

Cerella, J. (1990). Aging and information processing rate. In J.E. Birren & K.W. Schaie (Eds.), *Handbook of the psychology of aging* (3rd ed.) (pp. 201–221). San Diego: Academic Press.

Cerella, J., Poon, L.W. & Fozard, J.L. (1981). Mental rotation and age reconsidered. *Journal of Gerontology, 36*, 620–624.

Chawluk, J.B., Mesulam, M.M., Hurtig, H., Kushner, M., Weintraub, S., Saykin, A., Rubin, N., Alavi, A., & Reivich, M. (1986). Slowly progressive aphasia without generalized dementia: Studies with positron emission tomography. *Annals of Neurology, 19*, 68–74.

Chelune, G.J., & Moehle, K.A. (1986). Neuropsychological assessment and everyday functioning. In D. Wedding, A. Horton, & J. Webster (Eds.),

The neuropsychology handbook: Behavioural and clinical perspectives (pp. 489–525). New York: Springer.

Cooper, A., Garside, R., & Kay, D. (1976). A comparison of deaf and non-deaf patients with paranoid and affective psychoses. *British Journal of Psychiatry, 129*, 297–302.

Craik, F.I.M., Byrd, M., & Swanson, J.M. (1987). Patterns of memory loss in three elderly samples. *Psychology and Aging, 2*, 79–86.

Crook, T., Bartus, R., Ferris, S., Whitehouse, P, Cohen, G.D., & Gershon, S. (1986). Age-associated memory impairment: Proposed diagnostic criteria and measures of clinical change. *Developmental Neuropsychology, 2*, 261–276.

Cummings, J.L., & Benson, D.F. (1983). *Dementia: A clinical approach*. Boston: Butterworths.

Cutler, N.R., Haxby, J.V., Duara, R. (1985). Brain metabolism as measured with positron emission tomography: Serial assessment in a patient with familial Alzheimer's disease. *Neurology, 35*, 1556–1561.

Dastur, D.K. (1985). CBF and metabolism in normal human aging, pathological aging and senile dementia. *Journal of Cerebral Blood Flow and Metabolism, 5*, 1–9.

Denney, N.W. (1982). Aging and cognitive changes. In B.B. Wolman (Ed.), *Handbook of developmental psychology* (pp. 807–827). Englewood Cliffs, NJ: Prentice-Hall.

Denney, N.W. (1990). Training effects on Raven's Progressive Matrices in young, middle-aged, and elderly adults. *Psychology and Aging, 5*, 144–145.

Duffy, F.H., Albert, M.S., McAnulty, G. (1984). Age-related differences in brain electrical activity of healthy subjects. *Annals of Neurology, 16*, 439–448.

Duffy, F.H., & McAnulty, G. (1988). Electrophysiological studies. In M.S. Albert and M.B. Moss (Eds.), *Geriatric neuropsychology* (pp. 262–289). New York: Guilford Press.

Dustman, R., LaMarche, J., Cohn, N., Shearer, D.E., & Talone, J.M. (1985). Power spectral analysis and cortical coupling of EEG for young and old normal adults. *Neurobiology of Aging, 6*, 193–198.

Dustman, R.E., Shearer, D.W., & Snyder, E.W. (1982). Age differences in augmenting/reducing of occipital visually evoked potentials. *Electroencephalography and Clinical Neurophysiology, 54*, 99–110.

Dywan, J., & Jacoby, L. (1990). Effects of aging on source monitoring: Differences in susceptibility to false fame. *Psychology and Aging, 5*, 379–387.

Dywan, J., Segalowitz, S.J., & Unsal, A. (1990, May). Neuropsychological correlates of health risk in the elderly. *Brain and Cognition, 39*, 600.

Eisdorfer, C. (1980). Paranoia and schizophrenic disorders in later life. In E. Busse & D. Blazer (Eds.), *Handbook of geriatric psychiatry* (pp. 329–337). New York: Van Nostrand-Reinhold.

Eslinger, P.J., & Damasio, A.R. (1985). Severe disturbance of higher cognition after bilateral frontal lobe ablation: Patient EVR. *Neurology, 35*, 1731–1741.

Farver, P.F., & Farver, T.B. (1982). Performance of normal older adults on tests designed to measure parietal lobe functions. *American Journal of Occupational Therapy, 36*, 444–449.

Feier, C.D., & Gerstman, L.J. (1980). Sentence comprehension abilities throughout the adult life span. *Journal of Gerontology, 35*, 722–728.

Fields, W.S., & Lemak, N.A. (1989). *A history of stroke: Its recognition and treatment*. New York: Oxford University Press.

Flood, D.G., Buell, S.J., DeFiore, C.H., Horwitz, G.J., & Coleman, P.D. (1985). Age-related dendritic growth in dentate gyrus of human brain is followed by regression in the "oldest old." *Brain Research*, *345*, 366–368.

Foster, N.L., Chase, T.N., Mansi, L., Brooks, R., Redio, P., Patronas, N.J., & DiChiro, G. (1984). Cortical abnormalities in Alzheimer's disease. *Annals of Neurology*, *16*, 649–654.

Fozard, J.L. (1990). Vision and hearing in aging. In J.E. Birren & K.W. Schaie (Eds.), *Handbook of the psychology of aging*, 3rd. ed. (pp. 150–170). New York: Academic Press.

Gardner, H. (1983). *Frames of mind*. New York: Basic Books.

Gold, D. (1984). Late age of onset schizophrenia: Present but unaccounted for. *Comprehensive Psychiatry*, *25*, 225–237.

Gottfries, C. (1981). Treatment of depression in the elderly: General clinical considerations. *Acta Psychiatrica Scandinavica*, *63*, 401–409.

Gur, R., & Gur, R. (1991). The use of neuroimaging techniques in brain injury. In J. Dywan, R.D. Kaplan & F.J. Pirozzolo (Eds.), *Neuropsychology and the law* (pp. 164–185). New York: Springer-Verlag.

Gustafson, L., Brun, A., & Franck Holmkvist, A. & Risberg, J. (1985). Regional cerebral bloodflow in degenerative frontal lobe dementia of non-Alzheimer type. *Journal of Cerebral Blood Flow and Metabolism*, *5* (Suppl. 1), S141–S142.

Hall, R.C.W. (Ed.) (1980). *Psychiatric presentations of medical illness: Somatopsychic disorders*. New York: SP Medical and Scientific Books.

Hamill, R., & Buell, S. (1982). Dementia: Clinical and basic science aspects. *Journal of the American Geriatrics Society*, *30*, 781–787.

Heaton, R.K. (1981). *A Manual for the Wisconsin Card Sorting Test*. Odessa, FL: Psychological Assessment Resources.

Heaton, R.K., & Pendleton, M.G. (1981). Use of neuropsychological tests to predict adult patients' everyday functioning. *Journal of Consulting and Clinical Psychology*, *49*, 807–821.

Heindel, W.C., Salmon, D.P., Shults, C.W., Walicke, P.A., & Butters, N. (1989). Neuropsychological evidence for multiple implicit memory systems: A comparison of Alzheimer's, Huntington's and Parkinson's disease patients. *Journal of Neuroscience*, *9*, 582–587.

Hertzog, C. (1989). Influences of cognitive slowing on age differences in intelligence. *Developmental Psychology*, *25*, 636–651.

Hochanadel, G., & Kaplan, E. (1984). Neuropsychology of normal aging. In M.L. Albert (Ed.), *Clinical neurology of aging* (pp. 231–244). New York: Oxford University Press.

Horn, J.L., & Cattell, R.B. (1967). Age differences in fluid and crystallized intelligence. *Acta Psychobiologica*, *26*, 107–129.

Jefferson, J.W., & Marshall, J.R. (1981). *Neuropsychiatric features of medical disorders*. New York: Plenum.

Josiassen, R.C., Curry, L., Roemer, R.A., DeBease, C., & Mancall, E.L. (1982). Patterns of intellectual deficit in Huntington's disease. *Journal of Clinical Neuropsychology*, *4*, 173–183.

Kaplan, R.D. (1991). Developing legislation and the concept of disability. In J. Dywan, R.D. Kaplan & F.J. Pirozzolo (Eds.), *Neuropsychology and the law* (pp. 262–273). New York: Springer-Verlag.
Kaszniak, A.W. (1987). Neuropsychological consultation to geriatricians: Issues in the assessment of memory complaints. *The Clinical Neuropsychologist, 1*, 35–46.
Katz, R., & Horowitz, G.R. (1982). Electroencephalogram in the septuagenarian: Studies in a normal geriatric population. *Journal of the American Geriatric Society, 3*, 273–275.
Katzman, R., Lasker, B., & Bernstein, N. (1988). Advances in the diagnosis of dementia: Accuracy of diagnosis and consequences of misdiagnosis of disorders causing dementia. In R.D. Terry (Ed.), *Aging and the brain* (pp 17–62). New York: Raven Press.
Katzman, R., & Terry, R.D. (1983). Normal aging of the nervous system. In R. Katzman & R.D. Terry (Eds.), *The neurology of aging* (pp. 15–50). Philadelphia: F.A. Davis.
Kay, D. (1963). Late paraphrenia and its bearing on the etiology of schizophrenia. *Acta Psychiatrica Scandinavica, 39*, 159–169.
Kemper, T. (1984). Neuroanatomical and neuropathological changes in a normal aging and in dementia. In M.L. Albert (Ed.), *Clinical neurology of aging* (pp. 9–52). New York: Oxford University Press.
Kendler, K. (1980). The nostologic validity of paranoia (simple delusional disorder). *Archives of General Psychiatry, 37*, 699–706.
Kolb, B., & Whishaw, I.Q. (1990). *Fundamentals of human neuropsychology* (3rd. ed.) New York: W.H. Freeman.
Kraepelin, E. (1912). On paranoid diseases. *Zeitschrift fur Gesamte Neurologie und Psychiatrie, 11*, 617–638.
Kraiuhin, C., Gordon, E., Mears, R., & Howson, A. (1986). Psychometrics and event-related potentials in the diagnosis of dementia. *Journal of Gerontology, 41*, 154–162.
Kral, V. (1978). Benign senescent forgetfulness. In R. Katzman, R. Terry, and K. Bick (Eds.), *Alzheimer's disease: Senile dementia and related disorders* (pp. 47–51). New York: Raven Press.
Krauthammer, C., & Klerman, G. (1978). Secondary mania: Manic syndromes associated with antecedent physical illness or drugs. *Archives of General Psychiatry, 21*, 1333–1339.
Kuhl, D.E., Metter, E.J., & Reige, W.H. (1985). Patterns of cerebral glucose utilization in depression, multiple infarct dementia, and Alzheimer's disease. In L. Sokoloff (Ed.), *Brain imaging and brain function* (pp. 211–226). New York: Raven.
Lapidot, M.B. (1983). Is there hemi-aging? In M. Myslobodsky (Ed.), *Hemisyndromes: Psychobiology, neurology, psychiatry* (pp. 193–212). New York: Academic Press.
Larrabee, G.J., & Levin, H.S. (1986). Memory self-ratings and objective test performance in a normal elderly sample. *Journal of Clinical and Experimental Neuropsychology, 8*, 275–284.
Lezak, M.D. (1983). *Neuropsychological assessment* (2nd ed.). New York: Oxford University Press.

Lezak, M. (1987). Norms for growing older. *Developmental Neuropsychology*, *3*, 1–12.
Light, L.L. (1990). Interactions between memory and language in old age. In J.E. Birren & K.W. Schaie (Eds.), *Handbook of the psychology of aging* (3rd. ed.) (pp. 275–290). San Diego: Academic Press.
Light, L.L., & Singh, A. (1987). Implicit and explicit memory in young and older adults. *Journal of Experimental Psychology: Learning, Memory, and Cognition*, *13*, 531–541.
Lons, D. (1985). Aging in the nervous system. *Neurosurgery*, *17*, 348–354.
Loranger, A., & Levine, P. (1978). Age at onset of bipolar affective illness. *Archives of General Psychiatry*, *35*, 1345–1348.
Maletta, G. (1988). Neuropsychiatric problems in the elderly. In S. Gambert (Ed.), *Contemporary geriatric medicine* (Vol. 3). New York: Plenum.
Maletta, G., & Pirozzolo, F. (Eds.). (1980). *The aging nervous system*. New York: Praeger.
Manschreck, T., & Petri, M. (1978). The paranoid syndrome. *Lancet*, *2*, 251–253.
McCartney, J.R. (1986). Physician's assessment of cognitive capacity: Failure to meet the needs of the elderly. *Archives of Internal Medicine*, *146*, 177–178.
McDowd, J.M., & Birren, J.E. (1990). Aging and attentional processes. In J.E. Birren & K.W. Schaie (Eds.), *Handbook of the psychology of aging* (3rd ed.) (pp. 222–233). San Diego: Academic Press.
McDowd, J.M., & Craik, F.I.M. (1988). Effects of aging and task difficulty on divided attention performance. *Journal of Experimental Psychology: Human Perception and Performance*, *14*, 267–280.
McGlynn, S.M., & Schacter, D.L. (1989). Unawareness of deficits in neuropsychological syndromes. *Journal of Clinical and Experimental Neuropsychology*, *11*, 143–205.
Mental Incompetency Act of the Province of Ontario of 1980, Chapter 264.
Metter, E.J. (1988). Positron emission tomography and cerebral blood flow studies. In M.S. Albert & M.B. Moss (Eds.), *Geriatric neuropsychology* (pp. 228–261). New York: Guilford Press.
Metter, E.J., & Hanson, W.R. (1985). Brain imaging as related to speech and language. In Darby, J. (Ed.), *Speech and language evaluation in neurology: Adult disorders* (pp. 123–160). Orlando, FL: Grune & Stratton.
Mittenberg, W., Seidenberg, M., O'Leary, D.S., & DiGiulio, D.V. (1989). Changes in cerebral functioning associated with normal aging. *Journal of Clinical and Experimental Neuropsychology*, *11*, 918–932.
Mullis, R.J., Holcomb, P.H., Diner, B.C., & Dykman, R.A. (1985). The effects of aging on the P300 component of the visual event-related potential. *Electroencephalography and Clinical Neurophysiology*, *62*, 141–149.
Nebes, R.D., & Madden, D.J. (1983). The use of focused attention in visual search by young and old adults. *Experimental Aging Research*, *9*, 139–143.
Neshkes, R., & Jarvick, L. (1987). Affective disorders in the elderly. *Annual Review of Medicine*, *38*, 445–456.
Obrist, W.D. (1975). Cerebral physiology of the aged: Relation to psychological function. In N. Burch & H. Altshuer (Eds.), *Behaviour and brain electrical activity* (pp. 421–430). New York: Plenum.

Obrist, W.D. (1978). Electroencephalography in aging and dementia. In R. Katzman, R. Terry, & K.L. Bick (Eds.), *Alzheimer's disease: Senile dementia and related disorders* (pp. 227–231). New York: Raven Press.

Obrist, W.D. (1979). Electroencephalography in aging and dementia. In R. Katzman, R. Terry, & K.L. Bick (Eds.), *Alzheimer's disease: Senile dementia and related disorders* (pp. 227–231). New York: Raven Press.

Plude, D.J., & Hoyer, W.J. (1985). Attention and performance: Identifying and localizing age deficits. In N. Charness (Ed.), *Aging and performance* (pp. 47–99). New York: John Wiley & Sons.

Polich, J., Howard, L., & Starr, A. (1985). Effect of age on the P300 component of the event-related potential from auditory stimuli: Peak definition, variation, and measurement. *Journal of Gerontology*, *40*, 721–726.

Rabins, P., Panker, S., & Thomas, J. (1984). Can schizophrenia begin after age 44? *Comprehensive Psychiatry*, *25*, 290–294.

Rogers, R.L., Meyer, J.S., Mortel, K.F., Mahurin, R.K., & Judd, B.W. (1986). Decreased cerebral blood flow precedes multi-infarct dementia, but follows senile dementia of the Alzheimer's type. *Neurology*, *36*, 1–6.

Ryan, C., & Butters, N. (1986). The neuropsychology of alcoholism. In D. Wedding, A. MacNiell-Horton, Jr., & J. Webster (Eds.), *The neuropsychological handbook: Behavioural and clinical perspective*. New York: Springer-Verlag.

Salthouse, T.A. (1985a). *A theory of cognitive aging*. Amsterdam: North Holland.

Salthouse, T.A. (1985b). Speed of behaviour and its implications for cognition. In J.E. Birren & K.W. Schaie (Eds.), *Handbook of the psychology of aging* (2nd ed.), (pp. 400–426). New York: VanNostrand Reinhold.

Salthouse, T.A. (1990). Cognitive competence and expertise in aging. In. J.E. Birren & K.W. Schaie (Eds.), *Handbook of the psychology of aging*, (3rd. ed.) (pp. 310–319). San Diego: Academic Press.

Salthouse, T.A., Babcock, R.L., Skovronek, E., Mitchell, D.R.D., & Palmon, R. (1990). Age and experience effects in spatial visualization. *Developmental Psychology*, *26*, 128–136.

Searight, H.R., Dunn, E.J., Grisso, T., Margolis, R.B., & Gibbons, J.L. (1989). The relation of the Halstead-Reitan neuropsychological battery to ratings of everyday functioning in a geriatric sample. *Neuropsychology*, *3*, 135–145.

Segalowitz, S.J., Dywan, J., & Unsal, A. (1990). P300 correlates of memory span in the elderly. *Brain and Cognition*, *39*, 601.

Selkoe, D. (1982). Molecular pathology of the aging human brain. *Trends in Neurosciences*, *5*, 332–336.

Selkoe, D.J. (1988). Protein chemistry of neurofibrillary tangles and amyloid plaques in Alzheimer disease: Relation to the cytoskeleton. In R.D. Terry (Ed.), *Aging and the brain* (pp. 165–182). New York: Raven Press.

Selkoe, D., & Kosik, K, (1984). Neuroclinical changes with aging. In M. Albert, (Ed.), *Clinical neurology of aging* (pp. 53–75). New York: Oxford University Press.

Shulman, K., & Post, F. (1980). Bipolar affective disorder in old age. *British Journal of Psychiatry*, *136*, 26–32.

Solomon, K. (1981). The depressed patient: Social antecedents of psychopathologic changes in the elderly. *Journal of the American Geriatric Society*, *29*, 14–18.

Somberg, B.L., & Salthouse, T.A. (1982). Divided attention abilities in young and old adults. *Journal of Experimental Psychology: Human Perception and Performance*, *8*, 651–663.

Spirduso, W.W., & MacRae, P.G. (1990). Motor performance and aging. In J.E. Birren & K.W. Schaie (Eds.), *Handbook of the psychology of aging*, (3rd ed.) (pp. 183–200). San Diego: Academic Press.

Stafford, J.L., Albert, M.S., Naeser, M.A., Sandor, T. & Garvey, A.J. (1988). Age-related differences in computed tomographic scan measurements. *Archives of Neurology*, *45*, 409–415.

Strub, R.L., & Black, F.W. (1981). Organic brain syndromes: An introduction to neurobehavioural disorders. Philadelphia: F.A. Davis.

Stuss, D.T., & Benson, D.F. (1986). *The frontal lobes*. New York: Raven Press.

Swihart, A.A., & Pirozzolo, F.J. (1988). The neuropsychology of aging and dementia: Clinical issues. In H.A. Whitaker (Ed.), *Neuropsychological studies of nonfocal brain damage, dementia and trauma* (pp. 1–60). New York: Springer-Verlag.

Taylor, A.E., Saint-Cyr, J.A. & Lang, A.E. (1987). Parkinson's disease: Cognitive changes in relation to treatment responses. *Brain*, *110*, 35–51.

Terry, R.D. (1978). Ultrastructural alterations in senile dementia. In R. Katzman & R.D. Terry (Eds.), *Alzheimer's disease: Senile dementia and related disorders* (pp. 375–382). New York: Raven Press.

Terry, R.D. (1988). *Aging and the brain*. New York: Raven Press.

Terry, R., & Davies, P. (1980). Dementia of the Alzheimer type. *Annual Review of Neuroscience*, *3*, 77–95.

Terry, R.D., & Hansen, L.A. (1988). Some morphometric aspects of Alzheimer disease and of normal aging. In R.D. Terry (Ed.), *Aging and the brain* (pp. 109–114). New York: Raven Press.

Timiras, P., & Vernadakis, A. (1972). Structural, biochemical and functional aging of the nervous system. In P. Timiras (Ed.), *Developmental physiology and aging* (pp. 502–526). New York: MacMillan.

Vernadakis, A. (1985). Symposium on the aging process: The aging brain. *Clinics in Geriatric Medicine*, *1*, 61–95.

Vestal, R.E., & Cusack, B.J. (1990). Pharmacology and aging. In E.L. Schneider & J.W. Rowe (Eds.), *Handbook of the biology of aging* (3rd ed.) (pp. 349–383). New York: Academic Press.

Visser, S.L., VanTilburg, W., Hooijer, C. (1985). Visual evoked potentials (VEP's) in senile dementia (Alzheimer type) and in non-organic behavioural disorders in the elderly: Comparison with EEG parameters. *Electroencephalography and Clinical Neurophysiology*, *60*, 115–121.

Volanka, J. (1985). Late-onset schizophrenia: A review. *Comprehensive Psychiatry*, *26*, 148–156.

Wang, P.L., & Ennis, K.E. (1986). Competency assessment in clinical populations: An introduction to the cognitive competency test. In B.P. Uzzell & Y. Gross (Eds.), *The clinical neuropsychology of intervention.* Boston: Martinus Nijhoff.

Wechsler, D. (1981). *WAIS-R manual: Wechsler Adult Intelligence Scale-Revised*. New York: Psychological Corporation.

Wilson, B., Kolb, B., Odland, L., & Whishaw, I.Q. (1987). Alcohol, sex, age, and the hippocampus. *Psychobiology*, *15*, 300–307.

Wingfield, A., Poon, L.W., Lombardi, L., & Lowe, D. (1985). Speed of processing in normal aging: Effects of speech rate, linguistic structure, and processing time. *Journal of Gerontology*, *40*, 579–585.
Winokur, G. (1977). Delusional disorder (paranoia). *Comprehensive Psychiatry*, *18*, 511–521.
Woodward, N.J., & Wallston, B.S. (1987). Age and health care beliefs: Self-efficacy as a mediator of low desire for control. *Psychology and Aging*, *2*, 3–8.
Woodruff-Pak, D.S. (1988). *Psychology and aging* (pp. 189–211). Englewood Cliffs, NJ: Prentice Hall.

6
Legal Applications of Electrophysiological Assessments

DIANA FISHBEIN and ROBERT W. THATCHER

A major obstacle in the evaluation of mental status and civil or criminal liability is the failure to develop adequate assessment tools. Most assessment techniques possess some degree of subjectivity such as the determination of the degree of socialization, personality development, and intellectual development of the individual. However, these traditional tests of development and socialization contain many shortcomings. For example, many psychometric tests of personality and intellect can be culturally biased (Palmer, 1970; Williams, 1971), highly variable (Sattler, 1974), of low predictive value (Megargee, 1976; Monahan, 1981), difficult to administer, and provide only a measure of behavioral product or response and not a measure of the processes giving rise to behavior. Accurate and reliable measures of behavioral variables and their primary constructs are critical for the responsible assessment of mental status and accountability, for evaluation of the efficacy of a remediation program, and for the purposes of early detection and prevention.

Our goal is to augment traditional assessment tools by creating behavioral predictors or classification schemas. One method of improving our measures of behavior is by the application of new techniques in the field of quantitative electrophysiology. Quantitative electrophysiology utilizes computerized analyses of the electroencephalogram and sensory evoked responses to measure brain development objectively. The use of these techniques involves referencing data from an individual to a large normative data base of standardized brain measures. In our labs the data base currently includes data from approximately 4,000 individuals ranging in age from birth to senescence (John et al., 1980; Kaye, John, Ahn & Prichep, 1981; Thatcher, 1978; Thatcher, Lester, McAlaster, Horst & Ignasias, 1983a).

Although psychometric techniques and quantitative electrophysiology share the procedure of referencing individuals to a normative data base, they nonetheless differ in several important features. In contrast to psychometric measures, electrophysiological assessments are minimally culturally biased, do not require verbal or behavioral responses, are not contaminated by repeated testing, require minimal subjective interpretation and personal interaction in test administration, and provide a direct measure of brain processes that underlie behavior (John, 1977; Thatcher & John, 1977). Electrophysiological measures more directly assess the brain, which ultimately provides a template for possible behavioral responses. Nevertheless, we must recognize that, despite precise and systematic methods, a degree of predictability is lost due to numerous external and internal influences on the translation of neural processes into actual behavior.

This chapter describes the quantitative electrophysiological technique, types of data yielded, and their admissibility and utility in legal proceedings. We discuss the advantages in the application of this technique relative to conventional electroencephalographic (EEG) methods. Three examples illustrating the applicability of quantitative electrophysiological techniques in legal proceedings are provided, including the evaluation of: (a) brain damage, (b) effects of toxic elements on brain function, and (c) criminal liability. Finally, we include an overview of several obstacles and precautions in the interpretation and acceptance of electrophysiological findings.

Quantitative Measures of Brain Function

A spectral analysis of the EEG measures is performed to yield three different measures of interest: (a) "total (or absolute) power" reflects the total amount of energy for all frequency bands: delta, theta, alpha, and beta. This measure reveals the amount of these particular activity levels predominant in a given region of the brain; (b) "relative power" is the proportion of total energy of the EEG at particular frequencies. An increase in slow wave activity (delta and theta) in the relative power may reflect either a developmental lag or decreased excitability in the brain area affected. Conversely, an excess in fast wave activity (alpha and beta) may indicate hyperexcitability or the existence of a seizure disorder; (c) "interhemispheric symmetry" refers to the similarity in activity between hemispheres of the brain and can reflect the existence of organic pathology and a general deficiency in neurological functioning. This feature includes two components: amplitude asymmetry and wave shape asymmetry. Amplitude asymmetry indicates that the amount of energy is greater in one hemisphere than the other, indicative of functional strengths and weaknesses. Wave shape asymmetry also consists of two aspects: (a) the similarity of the form of the EEG wave, where excessively high or low values reflect abnormality, and (b) phase information that reflects the time delay in brain responsiveness between two regions. These aspects provide indices of cooperative activity between areas and the intricacy of neural connections on a cellular level; in other words, they assess the degree of coordination between different areas of the brain.

Asymmetries have been found in populations with various psychopathologies, that is, depression, anxiety, schizophrenia, drug abuse, and other affective or emotional states (Tucker, 1983), thus compromising present abilities to precisely predict behavior. Nevertheless, these asymmetries have been observed to occur or remit as a function of the symptomatology that is frequently similar between pathologic conditions even though the behavioral labels may differ. For example, gross organic disorders, such as strokes, tumors, and senile dementia, have been associated with pronounced EEG asymmetries in the clinical literature (Gibbs & Gibbs, 1964; Harmony, 1984; John, Prichep, Fridman & Easton, 1988; Kiloh, McComas & Osselton, 1972). Additional studies have found a relationship between hemispheric asymmetries and cognitive function and intelligence, which suggests that the resting EEG reflects a readiness or capacity to effectively process information (Thatcher, McAlaster, Lester, Horst & Cantor, 1983b).

For diagnostic and predictive purposes there are two aspects of the data that are relevant: (a) features of the EEG that are abnormal, that is, excessive delta activity, excessive similarities in activity between regions (coherence), or deficiency in total power, and (b) the location of the brain where these abnormal features are present. Previous research indicates that the anatomy is the most important aspect of the neurometric diagnosis, although coherence and relative power are particularly important (Ahn et al., 1980; John, 1977; Kaye et al., 1981). These EEG data provide information relating to the functional attributes of brain regions. The frontal lobes are primarily responsible for goal-directed bahavior and complex behavioral sequencing. Temporal lobes are involved in auditory perception, temporal sequencing, memory, and affective state. Central regions are responsible for skilled and gross motor movements and parietal–occipital regions are involved in visual perception, language, and abstract information processing. An abnormal neurometric feature in one of these areas may indicate a corresponding behavioral deficiency (see Thatcher & John, 1977, and John, 1977 for further details).

Another electrophysiological procedure examines cortical evoked potentials (EPs). EPs are characterized by the positive and negative peaks in the EEG waves that occur within a specified time after the presentation of a sensory event (i.e., a flash of light, a tone, or an electrical shock to the skin). In contrast to the EEG, which assesses brain function during relatively inactive states, the evoked potential technique reflects how the brain processes information during a cognitive operation. Examination of these components provides information on the efficiency of strategy, use, memory, and problem-solving abilities. These behaviors are analyzed across task or challenge conditions, across age, or across types of cognitive disorders to determine brain response variabilities. Current research suggests that abnormalities or irregularities in the evoked potential feature may be associated with criminal or aggressive subtypes

(Fishbein et al., 1989; Jutai & Hare, 1983; Syndulko, Parker, Jens, Maltzman & Ziskind, 1985; Raine & Venables, 1987; Syndulko, 1978), learning disabilities (hyperactivity, mental dullness, impulsivity, and short attention span; Donchin & Israel, 1980; Kendall, Moses & Finch, 1980; John et al., 1977; Saletu, Saletu & Itil, 1973), psychosis and schizophrenia (Chouinard, Annable & Dongier, 1977; Dongier, 1973; Roth, Horvath, Pfefferbaum & Kopell 1980; Timsit-Berthier, 1973; Vasconetto, Floris & Morocutti, 1971), drug and alcohol abuse (Begleiter, Porjesz, Rawlings & Eckardt, 1987; Herning, Hickey, Pickworth & Jaffe, 1989; Pfefferbaum, Rosenbloom & Ford, 1987; Porjesz, Begleiter, Bihari & Kissin, 1987), and affective disorders (Perris, 1974; Shagass, Straumanis & Overton, 1975). (See also Johnson, Rohrbaugh & Parasaraman [1988] and Pfefferbaum, Wenegrat, Ford, Roth & Kopell, [1984] for reviews.)

Recent advances in the application of computers and multivariate statistical techniques have made it possible to minimize reliance on the laborious task of visually inspecting EEGs by utilizing pattern recognition algorithms and other quantitative procedures (Courjon, Mauguiere & Revol, 1982; Dolce & Kunkel, 1975; Gotman et al., 1973; John, 1977; John et al., 1988; Kellaway & Petersen, 1973). The conventional EEG, which also records electrical activity in the brain, is subject to numerous sources of artifact; they are read visually and muscle movement may be difficult to distinguish from true electrical output. A number of studies have shown that computerized analysis of the EEG is more accurate in terms of reduced false positives and false negatives, less time is required, and there is greater cost efficiency in the detection of neurodysfunction than conventional or manual EEG methods (Ahn et al., 1980; John, 1977; John et al., 1983, 1988; Matousek, Petersen & Friberg, 1975; Pockberger, Petsche, Rappelsberger, Zidek & Zapotoczky, 1985; Shagass, Roemer, Straumanis & Josiassen, 1984; Volavka et al., 1973).

The goal of computerized analysis of the EEG and sensory evoked potentials is to reduce reliance on the subjective and qualitative judgments of human observers by assessing the EEG and EPs using reliable and replicable quantitative criteria. One of the most successful approaches to this problem is to compare an individual's premorbid baseline EEG and EP to determine whether changes have been incurred from an alleged trauma. This is particularly helpful when the postmorbid EEG/EP remains within normal range but shows substantial alterations from the baseline condition. Unfortunately, the existence of such baseline data is rare. Instead, this procedure permits us to compare statistically EEG and EP measures obtained from an individual to EEG and EP measures observed in a normal population. In this way a metric describing the deviation or distance from normal on a set of measures can be determined for a given individual. This general procedure of quantitatively referencing observed EEG and EP values to a large normative data base, much as psychometrics had done with IQ and other performance measures, forms the basis of these electrophysiological techniques.

An advantage of the EEG technique is that brain activity can be monitored while an active challenge is presented requiring the attention and response of the subject to different tasks. By providing specific information loads, a more meaningful understanding of the components of the neural functions that are challenged as well as a clearer distinction between normal and aberrant functioning can be obtained (see Thatcher & Maisel, 1979). This technique has proved helpful in the assessment of different aspects of cognitive functioning to identify learning disabilities or perceptual impairments that underlie certain behavioral problems. For example, clinical evidence suggests that "stress" plays a major role in the onset of violent bahavior. It is possible that a resting EEG or EP session will not show abnormalities in brain response, but when an "accurate" or "fast" response to a task or some degree of concentration is required, the stress resulting from the challenge may impair the individual's ability to respond appropriately by disrupting normal brain function (Barnes, 1983). The simple active task may use a video display of words or pictures requiring the individual to make a problem-solving decision. Such a dynamic interaction between the subject and his environment cannot be readily simulated using psychometric instuments.

Assessment Needs in Litigation Proceedings

Admissibility of EEG Records and Testimony

Although admissibility of EEG records remains at the discretion of the trial courts, they have been admitted as evidence without difficulty, similar to other medical tests (Woolsey & Goldner, 1975). Two approaches have been used to ensure admissibility. The Uniform Business Records as Evidence Act authorizes, in relevant jurisdictions, the use of EEG records since they qualify as business records. In states without such legislation, EEGs are permitted as evidence as "accurate portrayals of the conditions they purport to represent" (Melford v. Gaus & Brown Const. Co., 1958). Testimony of the treating physician and sometimes the technician further ensure admissibility.

Although the electrophysiological procedure has proven clinical utility for the evaluation of neurological disorders, as described in this section, the technique remains controversial. In particular, the degree to which specific behavioral disorders are associated with specific EEG features is as yet unclear. Similar EEG and EP characteristics have been identified in various behaviors or psychiatric conditions, which makes a ready application of this procedure difficult in a courtroom where precision is required. Also, there is some degree of variation in the types of electrophysiological equipment used by professionals. Consequently, disagreements arise among electroencephalographers as to the rigor of the method used when the court seeks a consensus among experts. The advantage of the quantitative system described herein is the intrinsic objectivity in data interpretation, which is not present when recordings are read visually. Nevertheless, further research is required before precise links can be identified between behavior and electrophysiological features. The following examples illustrate the utility of the EEG technique in evaluating conditions giving rise to neurological impairments that have been associated with deficits in behavior or mental capacity.

Electrophysiological Assessment of Brain Damage

Head trauma resulting in brain damage is generally reflected in the EEG, even in cases where damage is unsuspected. Brain injuries may be either focal (localized) or generalized. A focal injury would be associated with a slow wave abnormality restricted to the damaged area whereas a generalized injury would cause the EEG to be diffusely slow. The EEG can be particularly revealing in cases of mild head injury without obvious cerebral damage as EEG deviations may still appear, indicating the existence of subtle brain damage and the possibility of subtle functional deficits. More severe head injuries, on the other hand, are usually characterized by an association between clinical state and EEG changes. As the clinical condition improves over time, EEG recordings tend to normalize accordingly. Although the EEG may appear to be within normal range, the brain may not have fully recovered and the remaining deficits are more likely to be permanent (Woolsey & Goldner, 1975). There is also the possibility that the trauma has produced a seizure state so that the EEG may appear normal between seizures, and spike and sharp wave activity may occur at times other than recording sessions.

Alterations in the waveform of the auditory evoked potential after closed head injuries have been observed (Cant, Gronwall & Burges, 1974). The severity of the abnormality and return to normal values corresponded with the severity of the head trauma. Head trauma patients were found (Rizzo et al., 1978) to have lower amplitudes in another EP paradigm, the contingent negative variation (CNV). This procedure is considered a measure of "expectancy" or "readiness."

A recent study by Thatcher, Cantor, McAlaster, Geisler, and Krause (in press) of 162 closed-head injured patients admitted to a shock trauma unit provides evidence for the diagnostic and predictive value of quantitative electrophysiological techniques. Each evaluation consisted of: (a) power spectral analyses of EEG recorded from 19 scalp locations referenced to age-matched norms, (b) brain stem auditory evoked potentials, (c) computed tomography (CT) scan, and (d) Glasgow Coma Score at the time of admission and at the time of EEG testing. Functional outcome was assessed using the Rappaport Disability Rating Scale, which includes measures of eye opening, best verbal and motor responses, self-care ability, level of cognitive functioning, and employability. The best overall predictive measures of outcome 1 year postinjury were EEG features reflecting cerebral symmetry (phase, coherence, and amplitude symmetry; see Figure 6.1).

These EEG features are thought to be relatively insensitive to global cerebral phenomena such as swelling and medication and tend to reflect more accurately the magnitude of structural damage, including damage to the white matter. The left and right hemisphere EEG variables were equally represented with most of the significant variables involving the central, temporal, and particularly the frontal leads. Of the brain stem auditory EPs, peak latency of waves, I, III, and V and the interpeak latencies between waves I–III and III–V had the most predictive accuracy, that is, the longer the latency the worse the prognosis. For peak

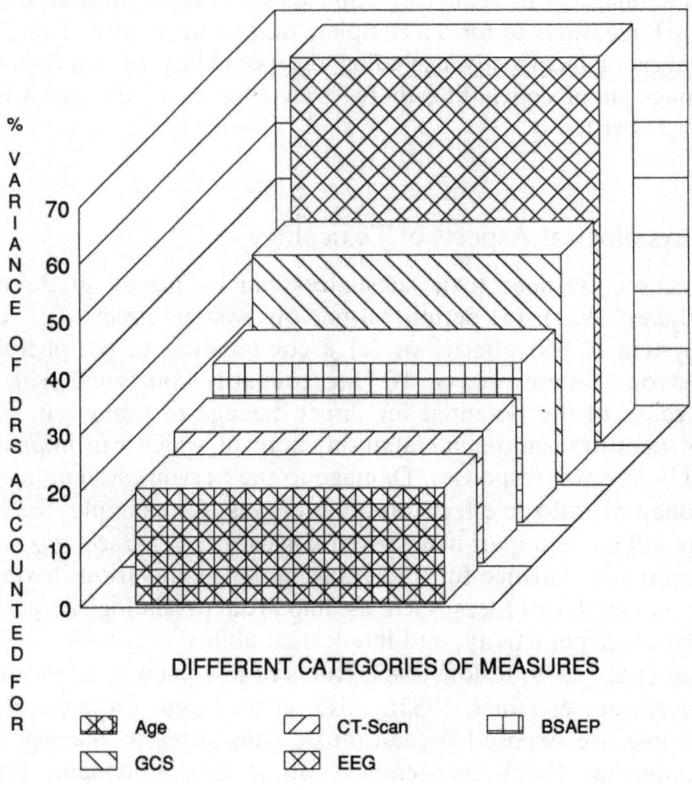

FIGURE 6.1. The percent variance of the Rappaport Disability Rating Scores accounted for by various measures. Measures from each category were obtained in a single multiple regression analysis.

amplitude of the brain stem EPs, the lower the peak amplitude the worse the prognosis. These findings are interpreted as caused by the magnitude of diffuse axonal injury in the cerebral cortex and brain stem.

In a parallel study, Thatcher, Walker, Gerson, and Geisler (1989) obtained measures of EEG power spectral analyses from 608 mild head trauma patients and 108 age-matched normal subjects. A discriminant function was developed and independently cross-validated with different samples of subjects to reduce the possibility of false positives or false negatives. Discriminating EEG power spectral analyses indicated three classes of neurophysiological variables that are attributable to mechanical head injury: (a) increased coherence and decreased phase in frontal and frontal–temporal regions, (b) decreased power differences between anterior and posterior cortical regions, and (c) reduced alpha power in posterior cortical regions.

Although they are important diagnostic aids, electroencephalographic techniques cannot be used in isolation to determine the existence and location of damage or its sequelae. Clinical examination must accompany EEG and EP measures to form a complete diagnostic picture. Thus, there is less chance of incorrectly excluding the possibility of injury-induced brain damage or of concluding there is an absence of damage when it does, in fact, exist.

Electrophysiological Aspects of Toxicology

Damage caused by neurotoxic substances can be placed in three categories (Baker, 1983): (a) peripheral nervous system effects, (b) central nervous system (CNS) effects, or (c) a combination of peripheral and central nervous system effects. We are primarily concerned with CNS effects because of the potential for direct damage to brain cells or disruption of neurotransmitter metabolism, both of which can impair cognitive and behavioral responses. Damage to the nervous system may also occur through neurotoxic effects on other organs, for example, the heart, which may indirectly impair neuropsychological performance.

Studies provide evidence for a relationship between various toxins and various behavioral disorders such as impaired psychological performance, violence, hyperactivity, and intellectual ability (Bryce-Smith, 1972; Needleman et al., 1979; Raloff, 1983; Rimland & Larson, 1983; Thatcher, Lester, McAlaster & Horst, 1982). Also, given recent estimates that 20 million people are exposed to neurotoxic substances in the workplace alone (Anderson, 1982), it becomes critical that individuals are adequately assessed for clinical and subclinical (subtle) impairment. To whatever degree possible, the instrument should be sensitive enough to distinguish between the effects of neurotoxins and other volitional exposures, such as alcohol intake, aging, or other unrelated illnesses.

Clinical evaluation of spontaneous EEG recordings is a relatively insensitive index of neurotoxicity, particularly when exposure levels are light to moderate (Otto, 1983). Computer-based methods of EEG analysis are, however, more appropriate. Relations between behavior/cognition, environmental toxins, and computerized EEG and EP measures have been demonstrated (see Figure 6.2 and 6.3).

For example, a series of studies conducted by Thatcher et al. (1982, 1983a) showed significant inverse relations between hair concentrations of certain toxins, lead and cadmium particularly, and intelligence and school performance among school-aged rural children. The quantitative electrophysiological method enabled investigators to detect impaired neural processes that may be caused by the effects of toxin concentrations, controlling for socioeconomic status, age, and race. Higher concentrations of lead or cadmium were found to be associated with an increase in the amount of slow wave activity in the EEG as well as a decrease in the amplitude of the EEG, thus indicating an abnormality. As the concentration of lead and cadmium increased, the latency of EP components lengthened (indicating a slowed response), and the higher the concen-

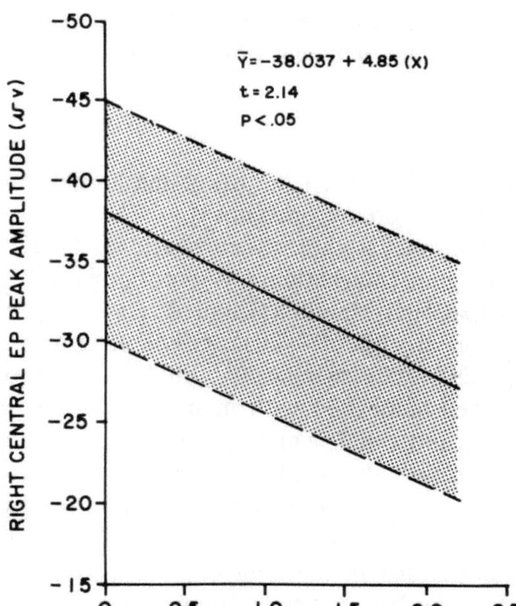

FIGURE 6.2 A regression plot (BMDP5R) of hair lead concentration (independent variable) versus the amplitude of the first negative peal (between 80 and 190 msec) in P3 to the 27 line/inch visual stimulus. Oblique lines represent 1 SE of the mean. $p < .02$, two-tailed.

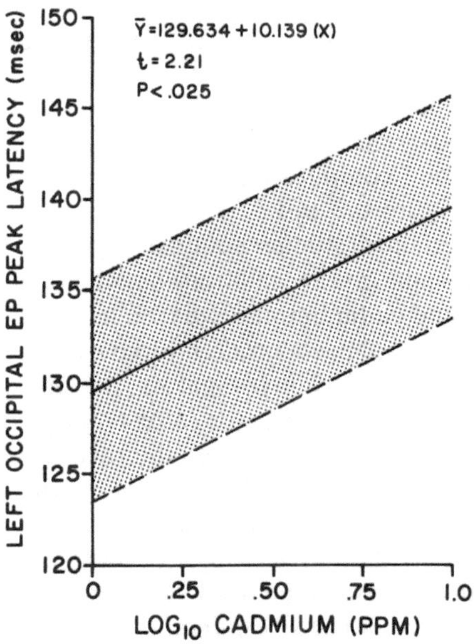

FIGURE 6.3 A regression plot (BMDP5T) of hair cadmium concentration (independent variable) and latency of the first positive peak in O1 to the 7 line/inch visual stimulus. Oblique lines represent 1 SE of the mean. $p < .05$, two-tailed.

tration of cadmium or lead then the lower the amplitude of the evoked response (indicating a decreased response).

A number of additional studies of neurotoxic effects on EP's measures were reported in the International Symposium on Neurobehavioral Methods in Occupational Health (Gilioli & Cassitto, 1983). Otto (pp. 71–78), Franchini et al. (pp. 197–204), Gilioli et al. (pp. 219–229), and Otto et al. (pp. 295–300) specifically noted that neurotoxic chemical exposures have been associated with mental confusion, impaired attention, memory loss, and other symptoms suggestive of cognitive impairment. EP techniques provide excellent, noninvasive measures of cognitive and motor function. Overall, these studies reported positive relationships between toxin levels and slow wave voltage or delayed latencies of the EP, indicating alterations in learning or sensory deficits. Because the information yielded by EP studies is quantifiable, the effects of chronic exposures and early neurobehavioral effects can be evaluated.

Brain stem evoked responses, in particular, appear to be the most promising and sensitive sensory evoked potential feature for evaluating neurotoxicity (Wennberg & Otto, 1985). One study (Holdstein et al., 1986) of 29 adults and children exposed to lead through food, employed auditory brain stem response (ABR) measures. Significant effects of lead on ABRs were observed more frequently among the lead-exposed group than with a normative control group. Most significantly, the interpeak latency differences (between wave I and III and between wave I and V) in lead-exposed subjects were delayed. These measures are thought to reflect myelin impairment and synaptic dysfunction due to lead toxicity. Such delayed latencies of the ABR have been reported in minimal brain dysfunction and mental retardation and may suggest the presence of an organic or functional brain lesion (Sohmer & Student, 1978).

Electrophysiological techniques have detected abnormalities associated with exposures to pesticides, organotins, heavy metals, drugs, and alcohol. The detection of subclinical toxicity, however, has not been adequately demonstrated (Wennberg & Otto, 1985). Like other neuropsychological and medical tests, EEG and EP features are still nonspecific for particular neurotoxic syndromes and indistinguishable from other causes of impairment. Since neurotoxic syndromes are frequently cited in litigation proceedings, it is important to note that there remains much controversy regarding the establishment of links between toxins and behavior/cognition and, in some cases, individual responsibility in their exposure to toxic environments.

Once a neural deficit is noted and the precursor identified, steps may be taken to alleviate the problem, in this case by chelation (the removal of toxins from the body), before complications set in and behavioral disturbances become more permanent. Diagnosis may be confirmed after chelation once the EEG begins to normalize coincident with behavioral or cognitive improvements. Further research is needed to show that recovery of the EEG/EP accompanies recovery of function after chelation reliably enough to be used as an objective method to monitor the recovery process (McCallum, 1988). Consequently, there will be a better understanding of the behavioral disability and treatment of the individual will likely be more appropriate.

Electrophysiological Correlates of Criminality

The offender population is at very high risk for neurological impairment, compared to other populations, because of the frequency with which they incur head injury (Lewis, 1976, 1986; Lewis, Shanok & Balla, 1979; Pincus, 1979), experience parental neglect and abuse, including suboptimal prenatal and postnatal care (Allan, 1978; Eisenberg, Langner & Gersten, 1975; McCord & McCord, 1959; New York State Assembly, 1978; Robins, 1966; Spinetta & Rigler, 1972), and engage in drug and alcohol use (Elliott & Huizinga, 1984; Goldstein, 1985; Kellam, Ensminger & Simon, 1980; Kofoed & MacMillan, 1986; Robins, 1966). Research in the prediction of criminality and dangerousness has repeatedly found evidence for mental abnormality and central nervous system disturbances, such as abnormal EEG, epilepsy, and learning disabilities, as important markers for criminal behavior (Berman, 1972; Blankenship, 1981; Bryant, Scott, Golden & Tori, 1984; Hurwitz, Bibace, Wolff & Rowbotham, 1972; Yeudall, Fedora & Fromm, 1985). Lewis reports in a series of studies (1976, 1981, 1986; Lewis et al., 1979, 1985, 1986, 1988) that juvenile and adult violent offenders manifested significantly more major and minor signs of neurological impairment than their less violent peers. There was also notable evidence of head injury and child abuse that may have contributed to brain dysfunction in these subjects. Despite these findings of neurologic involvement, objective assessment of neurophysiological function among offenders is rarely undertaken.

The diagnostic process in criminal justice agencies is compromised by the lack of available psychological and laboratory tests. Forensic evaluations tend not to be as comprehensive and accurate as community or private mental health evaluations, unless the defendant is wealthy or has committed a sensational crime. It is even difficult to obtain a simple psychological test other than for intelligence in many correctional facilities. More sophisticated tests, such as neuropsychological and electrophysiological batteries are not only unavailable, but personnel are ill-equipped to administer these tests and interpret their results. Although a few facilities have access to equipment in neighboring hospitals, using outside facilities is expensive, requires correctional resources, and may compromise security needs. Accordingly, outside facilities are rarely used even when available. If assessed at all, offenders receive a cursory review of their personal and medical history and a psychological battery of tests that are often unreliable, biased, and of little value with respect to the assessment and prediction of criminal behavior (Monahan, 1981; Shah, 1981).

Incorporating more thorough reviews of medical and psychiatric histories, particularly with respect to neurophysiological damage, may increase our appreciation of how that damage may influence subsequent behavior with respect to such functions as impulse control or judgment. A number of recent studies suggest that neurological distinctions exist between violent and nonviolent juvenile delinquents as revealed by both the conventional and computerized EEG and EP techniques that provide direct measures of brain functioning and impairment (Bender, 1959; Elliott, 1978; Herning et al., 1988; Surwillo, 1980; Yeudall, 1979; Yeudall, Fromm-Auch & Davies, 1982). Quay (1987) convincingly argues that there are four subtypes among delinquent populations, characterized by distinguishable psychological, behavioral, and social features, that elude us when considering delinquents as a homogeneous population. Classifying individuals according to their EEG features may allow investigators to identify significant discriminants of these groups, which may further efforts to describe how they differ from nondelinquents and eventually lead to more appropriate management techniques.

Fishbein et al. (1989) found that overtly aggressive had significant delays in brain stem auditory evoked potentials and more delta activity and less alpha activity in the spontaneous EEG. Relationships among psychiatric diagnoses, paper and pencil measures of aggression, and hostility and electrophysiologic features were examined (Table 6.1). EEG and EP measures did not discriminate between subjects with and without the diagnosis of antisocial personality (ASP) but did show significant differences between those with and without self-reported aggressive behaviors. These findings suggest that certain EEG and EP measures may be markers for an aggressive behavior pattern, not necessarily reflected in a psychiatric diagnosis.

These results have also been observed in "psychopaths" and "criminals" who are described as impulsive, irresponsible, superficial, and unconditionable. There is evidence that 48% to 70% of aggressive psychopaths have abnormal EEGs whereas the incidence in the general population is 10% to 15% (Fedora & Fedora, 1982; Hare & Schalling, 1978; Hill, 1944, 1952; Kligman & Goldberg, 1975; Mawson & Mawson, 1977; Mednick & Volavka, 1980; Mednick, Volavka, Gabrielli & Itil, 1981; Pincus & Tucker, 1974; Raine & Venables, 1987; Sayed, Lewis & Brittain, 1969; Syndulko, 1978; Yeudall, Fedora & Fromm, 1985). Specifically, an abundance of slow wave activity in the EEG and delayed and reduced amplitude of the P300 evoked potential has been reported in psychopathic children and adult offenders (Hare, 1970; Mawson & Mawson, 1977; Mednick et al., 1981; Pincus & Tucker, 1974; Raine & Venables, 1988;

TABLE 6.1. Analysis of covariance for composite measure of aggression[a]: group differences for high versus low scorers (adjusted for age, total drug use, and alcohol use).

	Aggression				
EEG and ERP measures	Low group (n = 31)		High group (n = 23)		F ratio
Relative power	Mean	SD	Mean	SD	
Frontal delta	.33	.15	.47	.16	9.11[c]
Frontal alpha	.43	.17	.30	.15	7.07[c]
Left central delta	.27	.13	.40	.14	11.52[d]
Left central alpha	.49	.15	.34	.15	10.82[d]
Right central delta	.26	.13	.37	.12	9.10[d]
Right central alpha	.49	.16	.37	.15	6.43[c]
Brain stem I	1.80	.14	1.92	.19	6.13[b]

[a] Composite measure of aggression was derived by transforming the Early Experience Questionnaire, Assault scale from the Buss-Durkee, and the Elliott-Huizinga measure of past aggressive/criminal behavior into z scores and summing the result. The mean of this z-score value divided subjects into "low aggressive" (n = 23) and "high aggressive" (n = 31) groups. Analyses of covariance were conducted to assess EEG and brain stem differences between groups, controlling for age, alcohol, and drug use.

[b] $p < .05$.

[c] $p < .01$.

[d] $p < .005$.

Syndulko, 1978). Similar findings have been reported for childhood cohorts; percentages of EEG abnormalities are markedly higher in children with behavior problems, particularly those with aggressive disorders (Assael, Kohen-Raz & Alpeen, 1967; Bender, 1974; Harbin, 1977; Herning et al., 1988; Lewis, Pincus, Shanok & Glaser, 1982; Pincus & Tucker, 1978). Collaborative studies are needed to determine whether these measures differentiate these children from those without problems more effectively than conventional instruments. Most likely, a combined battery of tests will yield a more accurate picture than any one method alone.

In short, research to date has found electrophysiological peculiarities among criminal or antisocial groups that may account for a significant amount of the variation in behavioral response. Such results are indicative of CNS instability, which suggests the presence of maturational lags in CNS development with functional cortical retardation (Surwillo, 1980). According to this view, as the individual ages the impairment may become increasingly manifest as the behavior subserved by damaged or immature neurophysiological structures becomes increasingly necessary for adaptive functioning in society.

It is important to note further that similar features have been found in populations with other behavioral disturbances, such as hyperkinesis and schizophrenia, indicating that EEG and EP findings, thus far, lack a degree of specificity. Possibly, the behavioral outcome of neurophysiological disturbance is a function of developmental and environmental influences. Weinberger (1987) illustrated that the brain pathology thought to be responsible for schizophrenia is also associated with other illnesses. Consequently, he proposed that the pathology itself is a necessary but insufficient explanation for schizophrenia. Instead, Weinberger argued that other factors, for example, age-related aspects of brain physiology or stressors, interact with the primary pathology to contribute specifically to schizophrenia. Similarly, with regard to antisocial behavior, it is possible that internal and external factors interact in a developmental setting with a primary neurological condition to determine the eventual onset of antisocial behavior. Unfortunately, this would suggest that the trauma or other neurological disadvantage may not coincide in time with the clinical manifestation of a disorder, further obscuring cause–effect relationships. Nevertheless, if similar brain pathology can be manifest in a variety of conditions, this could continue to be replicated, to justify testing offenders and delinquents.

Clinical Evaluation of Defendants/Offenders

The issues of potential dangerousness, mental status, and potential for recidivism are considered at four points in the criminal justice process and in the mental health system: (a) determination of competency to stand trial or not guilty by reason of insanity (b) decisions regarding need for restraint or level of security due to possible association between the mental illness and dangerousness, (c) evaluation of mental status for sentencing, and (d) evaluation for release from an indeterminate sentence (Halleck, 1986). Decisions pertaining to the above areas are generally based on observations and psychological examination by legal professionals and clinicians.

In each of these medicolegal cases, the determination of impairment may be facilitated by an electrophysiological clinical evaluation where deviations in brain function are indicated. We now have more accurate scientific evidence of brain state at the time of assessment and we need not depend entirely on self-reports, subjective observations, and psychological questionnaires. The inclusion of electrophysiological measures as admissible scientific evidence may help to overcome the present inability to obtain an objective history among offenders and provide a more comprehensive evaluation of mental state.

We are not currently able to speak of a causal link between specific behavioral disorders such as criminality and electrophysiologic abnormalities. At this stage, we are only able to identify markers or correlates of the behavioral problem using electrophysiological tests. This presents a problem in the courtroom where demands for causal relationships are made. Decisions regarding the granting of bail, release on personal recognizance, sentencing options, guilty pleas, probation, and parole rely heavily on testimony from "expert witnesses." In cases where mental status is at issue, the expert is generally a psychologist, psychiatrist, or other mental health professional. Such experts are expected to present a retrospective evaluation of mental status (at the time the crime was committed) in the determination of guilt, current mental status in the determination of competency to stand trial, and, in some cases, proclivity to recidivate.

Further Applications for Electrophysiological Data

Given the need to integrate behavioral, biological, environmental, and neurological factors in our understanding of normal and aberrant human behavior, the following research strategies are suggested. Any increased understanding eventually may be applied to practical problems in litigation proceedings.

Early Detection

One use of this new technology would be to compare EEG measures from an individual to expected values obtained from a normal population. When deviation from normal is reliably present on a set of measures (e.g., at greater than 2 SD) then an individual could be classified as at risk for abnormal brain development and behavioral maladjustments. It is critical, of course, than an individual not be stigmatized by a label suggesting abnormality or deviance. Instead, information should be used to appropriately identify, manage, and treat the impairment. Careful observation and psychometric testing may ensue to determine whether any behavioral manifestation can be noted. At the earliest indication of the development of behavioral abnormalities (e.g., poor learning, hyperactivity, impulsivity, etc.) that are present in combination with a EEG deviance, remediation strategies should be considered to normalize behavior and EEG. For example, children diagnosed as hyperkinetic with corresponding EEG abnormalities may be remediated with methylphenidate (Ritalin).

If the treatment is appropriately prescribed, EEG deviations should show a tendency toward normalization according to standardized values. Thus, it may be possible to optimize the physiological parameters, for example, through interventions involving medication, diet, minimization of exposure to toxins, environmental enrichment, or education. Once the physiological precursor of a behavioral abnormality is detected, the physiological disturbance can be remediated more easily before the manifestation of a fully developed behavior disorder. When the signs of a potential problem are neglected, disturbances in behavior increase in severity along with numerous developing situational and life-style complications that make it difficult, if not impossible, to separate the physical from the social and psychological contributions. Thus, effective remedial techniques are thwarted.

Intervention Strategies

Studies incorporating quantitative EEG measures promise to facilitate the isolation of significant predictors of inappropriate behavior given the replicability and objectivity of these techniques. As well, electrophysiological assessments may be of value in assessing brain responses to changes in medicinal regimens or other therapeutic trials. For example, a series of baseline EEG measures showing abnormal spiking activity in an area of the brain may be obtained from an individual manifesting aggressive behavior. After administration of an anticonvulsant, successive EEG recordings can be taken and compared to the baseline values. One would expect specific anatomic changes in EEG features. If the direction of change of the EEG measures is toward normal values then this would indicate a corrective effect of the anticonvulsant. Follow-up evaluations could determine whether changes in the EEG are replicable and stable and continue in the direction of normalization. Subsequent adjustments in dosage, amount, or type of treatment application may be contingent on the magnitude and direction of change in EEG measures. Although behaviors influenced by neurological impairment may respond more readily to appropriate treatment after brain function has normalized, maladaptive behavioral patterns are not likely to change easily. Irrespective of the original etiology of the behavioral disturbance, maladaptive patterns usually become well entrenched and reinforced. It is often necessary to establish a course of psychosocial intervention aimed at breaking these unacceptable patterns and at developing a new, more socially appropriate interactive style.

Obstacles and Precautions in the Use of Electrophysiological Data

There are a number of obstacles in the acceptance and application of medical and psychological information in general by the legal system, which may be somewhat alleviated in relevant cases by the inclusion of electrophysiological findings. The first issue involves the role of the expert witness (Black, 1988). Legal professionals commonly believe that expert witnesses have a special ability to identify the nature and source of a mental disorder that may have bearing on the case and to draw inferences about causal relationships. Instead, it is a common reality that courts rely on extraneous factors, such as the expert's credentials or demeanor, rather than evidence that has been scientifically validated. This situation may be a partial result of the inability of the expert witness to identify reliable correlates of behavior that will stand the tests of scientific scrutiny. Thus, expert testimonies frequently contradict one another and, consequently, discredit the mental health profession.

Standards by which we judge the reliability and validity of scientific findings should be applied in the evaluation of expert testimony. The reliance of many expert witnesses on subjective judgments and controversial test results has precluded adherence to true scientific standards and criteria. The use of computerized electrophysiological techniques in court may help validate other measures and render testimony more reliable than that based on traditional measures alone.

Testimony based on an electrophysiological evaluation is intended to indicate whether the degree of abnormality can be plausibly associated with the severity of the alleged insult. To accomplish this, an emphasis in any litigation proceeding is initially placed on establishing the qualifications of the EEG technologist who obtained the tracing and the electroencephalographer who provides the interpretation. It is then necessary to present a description of the injury, evidence of psychological and physical deterioration after the accident, and a medical/psychological history to link the accident with the consequent dysfunction. It is important to note, however, that discrepancies between clinical material and EEG/EP measures do not necessarily disqualify either data source as they are designed in some respects to measure different attributes or levels of impairment. Congruity, however, further strengthens the results of both clinical and electrophysiological procedures.

Another potential problem is that the terminology employed by experts, including electrophysiologists, is not well understood by courtroom players and is prone to misinterpretation. It is therefore important that testimony not be presented in overly technical or field-specific language so that lawyers and jurors are able to determine what bearing such evidence has on the case. It is important, as well, that experts apply the information they have presented to the legal question at hand. An expert is expected to provide a conclusion with "reasonable medical certainty" that some specified condition "caused" the defendant to act in a liable manner.

The potential complexity of including EEG/EPs in legal cases to establish causality is illustrated in the example of an individual who committed theft in a gas station where he was employed. The employers brought criminal charges against the perpetrator who, in turn, claimed insanity at the time of the act because of alleged lead intoxication. In addition, the defendant brought a counter civil suit against the station claiming that the lead poisoning was caused by the station's poor working conditions. In both cases, electrophysiological evaluation was used by the defendant in an attempt to associate lead body burden with EEG and EP abnormality. Should the information gleaned from the assessment allow the defendant to infer causality, thus indicating impairment at the time of crime? The expert witness may be able to establish the level of abnormality with respect to brain function, but can only infer the relationship between lead intoxication, electrophysiological abnormality, and the commission of a crime.

A third issue with respect to the court's use of electrophysiological assessments is that goals of the court are markedly different from the clinical goals for which these procedures were designed. When electrophysiologists testify in court, the same labels are used to rationalize a sentence or plea as used for diagnostic purposes in the clinic. Diagnostic categories lead to appropriate patient management or treatment in the professionals' own territory, but in civil or criminal court they may become inherently condemnatory.

This particular conflict between the goals of the electrophysiologist versus the legal professional can be resolved with the acceptance of two conditions. It is important that the information gleaned from the assessment is used to promote treatment success and not used solely for incarceration or acquittal. If test results are used strictly to label an individual as "imparied" or "abnormal," then such testing is unjustified and possibly counterproductive. Instead, electrophysiological data should be used to develop a complete clinical picture and increase our understanding of behavior by helping to identify the underlying source(s) of a disorder. They can also help to provide criteria for selection of individuals who can benefit from treatment. A determination of whether chelation of toxins, pharmacologic intervention, or simple biofeedback is indicated can be made with more precision than with techniques used in the past. As mentioned earlier, normalizing neurophysiological function may increase the likeihood of successful rehabilitation.

A fourth issue concerning the admissibility of electrophysiological evidence in court is associated with the notion of guilt. A finding of guilt requires that a *mens rea*, or intent, has been established on the part of the defendant. Extenuating circumstances may be admitted as evidence to mitigate an offense or reduce the culpability of the defendant. For example, evidence that the defendant had been coerced or was acting in self-defense is sufficient grounds to reduce the charges or for acquittal. It follows that when evidence is presented to establish the presence of an aggravating or contributory factor, the defendant's accountability for the offense is substantially reduced. Although such conditions are provided for by law, we cannot practice such lines of defense to the letter as it would undermine the entire foundation of the legal system, which requires full intent and accountability in the commission of the crime. We know, for instance that low socioeconomic status (SES) is associated with criminal activity (Hagan, 1985). We do not, however, use SES as an extenuating or mitigating factor or we would have grave difficulty in establishing guilt in a preponderance of cases, according to our present legal system. Thus, the presentation of evidence that the defendant suffers from a neurological or cognitive deficit as reflected in EEG or EP findings, which is possibly related to his alleged criminal activity, should not jeopardize a finding of guilt.

A fifth area of concern is the behavioral scientist's ability to predict future behavior, in particular, criminality. The courts appear to be resistent to the notion that prediction of human behavior is not possible, despite the fact that many mental health professionals and scientists have reached a consensus that there is little reliability in the prediction of future antisocial or libelous behavior (e.g., Monahan, 1981). Predictive techniques currently in use are largely predicated on judgmental and controversial decisions that are prone to predictive inaccuracy and, thus, further compromise our faith in courtroom proceedings. Similarly, electrophysiological testing will provide assessments of neurologic and cognitive status in the present but cannot predict future behavior. It does, however, have the advantage of providing a more objective index of present status that can be applied cautiously to past states and to a determination of the effects and efficacy of treatment over time.

Summary and Conclusions

Despite the strides made in electrophysiological measures, continued research is needed in the area of reliability, validity, and specificity of EEG/EP data. Weaknesses do exist and must be addressed in the assessment of individual and population differences. McCallum (1988) and Pfefferbaum et al. (1984), in their comprehensive reviews of the clinical applicability of EP data, note that electrophysiological measures have yet to discriminate rigorously between neurological, behavioral, and psychological/psychiatric groups. Similar EEG/EP results have been found in various populations, indicating a relative lack of specificity. Moreover, because of the wide range of variability in a normal population, deviations in these measures are not always sufficiently large to be useful; in other words, they may be abnormal for the individual but do not exceed 2 SDs from normative values. This suggests that "normal" findings may not necessarily exclude a diagnosis of pathology. To increase their utility, EEG/EP measures would require clinical specificity and the sensitivity to detect abnormalities even in subclinical syndromes.

The lack of specificity extends to other diagnostic criteria as well. McCallum (1988) argued that diagnostic categories are rarely composed of unequivocal and pure subgroups. Although EEG and EP findings have been shown to be highly reliable, the use of the unreliable or overlapping diagnostic categories frequently encountered in psychiatry reduces the validity and generalizability of EP measures. McCallum emphasized the need for standardized procedures in methodology and classification systems to increase the reliability of findings. It may also be the case (e.g., Surwillo, 1980; Weinberger, 1987) that the underlying dysfunction may be similar in a number of disorders despite their behavioral manifestations. Concentration on areas of impairment as reflected in EPs, irrespective of diagnoses, may enhance their clinical relevance by providing a reliable guide to treatment. In any event, deviations in EEG/EP components are thought to represent in individual's condition and indicate that they may be responsive to intervention.

It is evident, nonetheless, that exposure to environmental abuses and the existence of neurological deficits has a profound impact on the adaptive, cognitive, and emotional abilities of the individual. When the organic assault occurs during developmental stages of childhood, the resultant deficit may be compounded over time and drastically interfere with behavioral functions throughout life. These conditions appear to place an individual at high risk for persistent problematic behavior. Disturbances associated with poor environmental and social conditions coupled with impaired brain function may require medical or psychiatric attention. The unfortunate reality for many of those who come into contact with the courts by virtue of their dysfunction is that the appropriate treatments are unavailable or inaccessible as, indeed, are the most rudimentary facilities for diagnosis. Consequently, the underlying causes of their disorder remain inaccurately evaluated or simply unattended.

Existing physiological or biological abnormalities that are known to impair intellectual development significantly predispose or facilitate the onset of inappropriate behavior. Electrophysiological investigations of the discriminants for behavioral dysfunctions, after adjusting for demographic factors, indicate that the impact of these neurological factors are substantial and, more importantly, amenable to intervention. The electrophysiological capability to identify and predict some of the factors responsible for maladaptive behavior may enable us to employ innovative methods of early detection, prevention, remediation, and evaluation.

The use of these techniques my require a revision of present attitudes toward the use of diagnostic and treatment approaches, especially in criminal proceedings. It is essential that the public recognize the pervasiveness of medical problems among defendants and the need for treatment so that both society and the defendant benefit. Because questionable procedures for diagnoses and treatment have prevailed in the past and have been relatively unsuccessful, the public has grown weary of all approaches dealing with the "rehabilitation" of guilty defendants (Halleck, 1986; Kittrie, 1971; Lipton, Martinson & Wilks, 1975). Many people now feel that we should concentrate on the protection of society by simple incarceration. This trend assures that offenders who are eventually released into the community do so without any improvements in a disturbance that may be present (Menninger, 1968; Shover, 1979; Walker, 1985). Techniques that we have described in this chapter promise to improve our ability to diagnose accurately and perhaps effectively treat neurologically based behavioral disorders. The interests of the community and the offender will be better served by some form of remediation.

Electrophysiological information pertaining to a criminal defendant's mental status may have the most applicability and propriety in the last phase of the judicial proceeding, when a sentencing disposition is accorded. At this stage of such a bifurcated trial system, a determination of guilt has been established without compromising judicial principles. The sentence can more effectively accommodate information from these tests, facilitating an appropriate treatment regimen and reducing the likelihood of recidivism. Thus, electrophysiological information, in relevant cases, becomes an important component of the sentencing disponsition. Further, once the appropriate sentence has been dispensed, it is necessary to evaluate the efficacy of the treatment approach in terms of improvement in brain function and behavior, and to determine the likehood of recidivism. Questions concerning "recovery" from mental disorder and the possibility of persisting dangerousness can be answered more completely when there is access to information on the status of brain function.

In civil cases, electroencephalographic evaluations aid in establishing the degree of neurological impariment that exists so that inference can then be made about the conditions that contributed to an impairment or the degree of disability that may ensue from that impairment. Whether the plaintiff is a manual laborer or a professor, such an evaluation may help to document physical incapacitation or mental impairment that may interfere with normal working activities.

There are many greater benefits to be gleaned by both the defendant and community when objective and sensitive diagnostic batteries, such as computerized electrophysiological measures, are employed. Such procedures are likely to yield more accurate information regarding present condition and treatment efficacy when used in conjunction with conventional examinations. Overall, we may expect the reliability and validity of courtroom testimonies to increase as well as our ability to therapeutically enhance the mental function of a defendant/patient.

The opinions expressed herein are those of the authors and do not necessarily reflect the official position of the National Institute on Drug Abuse or any other part of the U.S. Department of Health or Human Services.

References

Ahn, H., Baird, H., Prichep, L., John, E.R., Kaye, H., & Brown, D. (1980). Developmental equations reflect brain dysfunctions. *Science*, *210*, 1259–1262.

Allan, L.J. (1978). Child abuse: A critical review of the research and the theory. In J.P. Martin, (Ed.), *Violence and the family*. Chichester, England: John Wiley & Sons.

Anderson, A. (1982, July). Neurotoxic follies. *Psychology Today*, 30–42.

Assael, M., Kohen-Raz, R., & Alpeen, S. (1967). Developmental analysis of EEG abnormalities in juvenile delinquents. *Diseases of the Nervous System*, *28*, 49–54.

Baker, E.L. (1983). Neurologic and behavioral disorders. In B.S. Levy and D.H. Wegman (Eds.), *Occupational health: Recognizing and preventing work-related disease* (pp. 317–330). Boston: Little, Brown and Co.

Barnes, A.R. (1983, April). *Evoked potentials and impulsivity in a criminal population*. Unpublished doctoral dissertation, Florida State University.

Begleiter, H., Porjesz, B., Rawlings, R., & Eckardt, M. (1987). Auditory recovery function and P3 in boys at high risk for alcoholism. *Alcohol*, *4*, 315–321.

Bender, L. (1959). Children and adolescents who have killed. *American Journal of Psychiatry*, *116*, 510–513.

Bender, L. (1974). Aggression in children. *Research Publications—Association for Research in Nervous and Mental Disease*, *52*, 201–208.

Berman, A. (1972). Neuropsychological dysfunction in juvenile delinquents: Implications for early intervention. *Child Care Quarterly*, *1*, 264–271.

Black, B. (1988). Evolving legal standards for the admissibility of scientific evidence. *Science*, *239*, 1508–1512.

Blankenship, J. (1981). *Neuropsychological correlates of violent behavior*. Paper presented at the Ninth Annual International Neuropsychology Society Meeting, Atlanta, GA.

Bryant, E.T., Scott, M.L., Golden, C.J., & Tori, D.C. (1984). Neuropsychological deficits, learning disability, and violent behavior. *Journal of Consulting and Clinical Psychology*, *52*, 323–324.

Bryce-Smith, D. (1972). Behavioral effects of lead and other heavy metal pollutants. *Chemistry in Britain*, *8*, 240–243.

Cant, B.R., Gronwell, D., & Burges, R. (1974). Auditory evoked responses after closed head injuries. *Electroencephalography and Clinical Neurophysiology*, *36*, 551–553.

Chouinard, G., Annable, L., & Dongier, M. (1977). Differences in psychopathology with normal and abnormal postimperature negative variation (PINV). *Comprehensive Psychiatry*, *18*, 83–87.

Courjon, J., Mauguiere, F., & Revol. M. (Eds.) (1982). Clinical applications of evoked potentials in neurology. *Advances in Neurology: Vol. 32*. New York: Raven Press.

Dolce, G., & Kunkel, H. (1975). *CEAN: Computerized EEG analysis*. Gustav Fischer Verlag: Stuttgart, Germany.

Donchin, E., & Israel, J.B. (1980). Event-related potentials—approaches to cognitive psychology, In R.E. Snow, P.A. Federico, & W.E. Montague (Eds.), *Aptitude, learning and instruction: Cognitive process analyses*. Hillsdale, NJ: Lawrence Erlbaum Associates.

Dongier, M. (1973). Event related slow potential changes in psychiatry. In S. Bogoch (Ed.), *Biological diagnosis of brain disorders* (pp. 47–59). New York: Spectrum.

Eisenberg, J., Langner, T.S., & Gersten, J.C. (1975). Differences in the behavior of welfare and non-welfare children in relation to parental characteristics. *Journal of Community Psychology*, *3*, 311–340.

Elliott, F.A. (1978). Neurological aspects of antisocial behavior. In W.H. Reid (Ed.), *The Psychopath: A comprehensive study of antisocial disorders and behaviors*. New York: Brunner/Mazel.

Elliott, D.S., & Huizinga, D. (1984). *The relationship between delinquent behavior and ADM problems*. (National Youth Survey. Project Report No. 28), Boulder, Colorado: Behavioral Research Institute.

Fedora, O., & Fedora, S. (1982, April). Some neuropsychological and psychophysiological aspects of psychopathic and nonpsychopathic criminals. In P. Flor-Henry & J. Gruzelier (Eds.), *Laterality and psychopathology: Proceedings of 2nd international conference*, Banff, Canada pp. 41–58.

Fishbein, D.H., Herning, R., Pickworth, W., Haertzen, C.H., Hickey, J., & Jaffe, J.H. (1989). Brainstem evoked response potentials in adult male drug abusers with self-reported histories of aggressive behavior. *Biological Psychiatry*, *26*, 596–611.

Franchini, I., Ferri, F., Lommi, G., & Lotta, S. (1983). Brain evoked potentials in solvent exposure. In R. Gilioli & M.G. Cassitto (Eds.), International symposium on neurobehavioural methods in occupational health (pp. 197–204). New York: Pergamon Press.

Gibbs, F.A., & Gibbs, E.L. (1964). Neurological and psychological disorders. In: *Atlas of Encephalography, Vol. 3*. Reading, MA: Addison-Wesley.

Gilioli, R., & Cassitto, M.G. (1983). *International Symposium on Neurobehavioral methods in Occupational Health* (1st ed.). June 23–26. New York: Pergamon Press.

Goldstein, P.J. (1985). The drugs/violence nexus: A tripartite conceptual framework. *Journal of Drug Isses*, *15*, 493–506.

Gotman, J., Skuce, D.R., Thompson, C.J., Gloor, P., Ives, J.R., & Ray, W.F. (1973). Clinical applications of spectral analysis and extraction of features from the electroencephalograms with slow waves in adult patients. *Electroencephalography and Clinical Neurophysiology*, *35*, 225–235.

Hagan, J. (1985). *Modern criminology: Crime, criminal behavior, and its control*. New York: McGraw-Hill Book Co.

Halleck, S.L. (1986). *The mentally disordered offender*. (DHHS Publication No. ADM 86–1471). Rockville, MD: Department of Health & Human Services. NIMH.

Harbin, H.T. (1977). Episodic dyscontrol and family dynamics. *American Journal of Psychiatry*, *134*, 1113–1116.

Hare, R. (1970). *Psychopathy: Theory and research*. New York: John Wiley & Sons.

Hare, R.D., & Schalling D. (1978). *Psychopathic behavior: Approaches to research*. Chichester, England: John Wiley & Sons.

Harmony, T. (1984). Neurometric assessment of brain dysfunction in neurological patients. In: *Functional Neuroscience: Vol. 3*. Hillsdale, NJ: Lawrence Erlbaum Associates.

Herning, R., Hickey, J., Pickworth, W., & Jaffe, J.H. (1989). Auditory evoked potentials in adolescents at risk for drug abuse. *Biological Psychiatry*, *25*, 598–609.

Hill, D. (1944). Cerebral dysrhythmia: Its significance in aggressive behaviour. *Proceedings of the Royal Society of Medicine*, *37*, 317–330.

Hill, D. (1952). EEG in episodic psychotic and psychopathic behaviour. *Electroencephalography and Clinical Neurophysiology*, *4*, 419–442.

Holdstein, Y., Pratt, H., Goldsher, M., Rosen, G. Shenhav, R., Linn, S., Mor, A., & Barkai, A. (1986). Auditory brainstem evoked potentials in asymptomatic lead-exposed subjects. *Journal of Laryngology and Otology*, *100*, 1031–1036.

Hurwitz, I., Bibace, R.M., Wolff, P.H., & Rowbotham, B.M. (1972). Neuropsychological function of normal boys, delinquent boys, and boys with learning problems. *Perceptual and Motor Skills*, *35*, 387–394.

John, E.R. (1977). Neurometrics: Clinical Applicaltions of Quantitative Electrophysiology. In E.R. John & R.W. Thatcher (Eds.), *Functional neuroscience: Vol. 2*, Hillsdale, NJ: Lawrence Erlbaum Associates.

John, E.R., Ahn, H., Prichep, L., Trepetin, M., Brown, D., & Kaye, H. (1980). Developmental equations for the electroencephalogram. *Science*, *210*, 1255–1258.

John, E.R., Karmel, B.Z., Corning, W.C., Easton, P., Brown, D., Ahn, H., John, M., Harmony, T., Prichep, L., Toro, A., Gerson, I., Bartlett, F., Thatcher, R., Kaye, H., Valdes, P., & Schwartz, E. (1977). Neurometrics. *Science*, *196*, 1393–1410.

John, E.R., Prichep, L, Ahn, H., Easton, P., Fridman, J., & Kaye, H. (1983). Neurometric evaluation of cognitive dysfunctions and neurological disorders in children. *Progress in Neurobiology*, *24*, 239–290.

John, E.R., Prichep, L., Fridman, J., & Easton, P. (1988). Neurometrics: Computer-assisted differential diagnosis of brain dysfunctions. *Science*, *239*, 162–169.

Johnson, R., Rohrbaugh, J., & Parasarman, R. (1988). Current trends in event related potential research. *Electroencephalography and Clinical Neurophysiology, Supplement, 40.*

Jutai, J.W., & Hare, R.D. (1983). Psychopathy and selective attention during performance of a complex perceptual motor task. *Psychophysiology*, *20*, 146–151.

Kaye, H., John, E.R., Ahn, H., & Prichep, L. (1981). Neurometric evaluation of learning disabled children. *International Journal of Neuroscience*, *13*, 15–25.

Kellam, S.G., Ensminger, M.E., & Simon, M.B. (1980). Mental health in first grade and teenage drug, alcohol, and cigarette use. *Drug and Alcohol Dependence*, *5*, 273–304.

Kellaway, P., & Petersen, I. (1973). *Automation of clinical electroencephalography*. New York: Raven Press.

Kendall, P., Moses, J. Jr., & Finch, A., Jr. (1980). Impulsivity and persistence in adult inpatient "impulse" offenders. *Journal of Clinical Psychology*, *36*, 363–365.

Kiloh, L.G., McComas, A.J., & Osselton, J.W. (1972). *Clinical electroencephalography*. London: Butterworth and Co.

Kittrie N. (1971). *The right to be different*. Baltimore: Johns Hopkins University Press.

Kligman, D., & Goldberg, D.A. (1975). Temporal lobe epilepsy and aggression. *Journal of Nervous and Mental Diseases*, *160*, 324–341.

Kofoed, L., & MacMillan, J. (1986). Alcoholism and Antisocial Personality. *Journal of Nervous and Mental Diseases*, *74*, 332–335.

Lewis, D.O. (1976). Diagnostic evaluation of the juvenile offender. *Journal of Child Psychiatry and Human Development*, *6*, 198–213.

Lewis, D.O. (1981). *Vulnerabilities to delinquency*. New York: SP Medical & Scientific Books.

Lewis, D.O. (1986). Psychiatric, neurological, and psychoeducational characteristics of 15 death row inmates in the United States. *American Journal of Psychiatry*, *143*, 838–845.

Lewis, D.O., Moy, E., Jackson, L.D., Aaronson, R., Restifo, N., Serra, S., & Simos, A. (1985). Biopsychosocial characteristics of children who later murder: A prospective study. *American Journal of Psychiatry*, *142*, 1161–1167.

Lewis, D.O., Pincus, J.H., Bard, B., Richardson, E., Prichep, L.S., Feldman, M., & Yeager, C. (1988). Neuropsychiatric, psychoeducational, and family characteristics of 14 juveniles condemned to death in the United States. *American Journal of Psychiatry*, *145*, 584–589.

Lewis, D.O., Pincus, J.H., Feldman, M., Jackson, L., & Bard, B. (1986). Psychiatric, neurological, and psychoeducational characteristics of 15 death row inmates in the United States. *American Journal of Psychiatry*, *143*, 838–845.

Lewis, D.O., Pincus, J.H., Shanok, S.S., & Glaser, G.H. (1982). Psychomotor epilepsy and violence in a group of incarcerated adolescent boys. *American Journal of Psychiatry*, *139*, 882–887.

Lewis, D.O., Shanok, S.S., & Balla, D.A. (1979). Perinatal difficulties, head and face trauma, and child abuse in the medical histories of seriously delinquent children. *American Journal of Psychiatry*, *136*, 419–423.

Lipton, D., Martinson, R., & Wilks, J. (1975). *The effectiveness of correctional treatment: A survey of treatment evaluation studies*. New York: Praeger.

Matousek, M., Petersen, I., & Friberg, S. (1975). Automatic assessment of randomly selected routine EEG records. In G. Dolce & H. Kunkel (Eds.), *Computerized EEG analysis*. Stuttgart: Gustav Fischer Verlag.

Mawson, A.R., & Mawson, C.D. (1977). Psychopathy and arousal: A new interpretation of the psychophysiological literature. *Biological Psychiatry*, *12*, 49–74.

McCallum, W.C. (1988). Potentials related to expectancy, preparation and motor activity. In T.W. Picton (Ed.), *Handbook of electroencephalography and clinical neurophysiology: Rev. Ser. Vol. 3*. Amsterdam: Elsevier.

McCord, W., & McCord, J. (1959). *Origins of crime: A new Evaluation of the Cambridge-Somerville study*. New York: Columbia University Press.

Mednick, S., & Volavka, J. (1980). Biology and crime. In Morris, N. and Tonry, M. (Eds.), *Crime and justice: An annual review of research*: *Vol. 2* (pp. 85–158). Chicago: University of Chicago Press.

Mednick, S.A., Volavka, J., Gabrielli, W.F., and Itil, T.M. (1981). EEG as a predictor of antisocial behavior. *Criminology*, *19*, 212–229.

Megargee, E. (1976). The prediction of dangerous behavior. *Criminal Justice and Behavior*, *3*, 3–221.

Melford v. Gaus & Brown Contruction Co., 17Ill App2d 497, 151 NE2d 128, 66 ALR 2d 528, 1958.

Menninger, K. (1986). *The crime of punishment*. New York: Vintage Press.

Monahan, J. (1981). *Predicting violent behavior*. Beverly Hills: Sage Publications.

Needleman, H.L., Gunnoe, C., Leviton, A., Reed, R., Peresie, H., Maher, C., & Barrett, P. (1979). Deficits in psychologic and classroom performance of children with elevated dentine lead levels. *New England Journal of Medicine*, *300*, 689–695.

New York State Assembly, Select Committee on Child Abuse (1978, March). Summary report on the relationship between child abuse and neglect and later socially deviant behavior.

Otto, D.A. (1983). The application of event-related slow brain potentials in occupational medicine. In R. Gilioli & M.G. Cassitto (Eds.), *International symposium on neurobehavioral methods in occupational health* (pp. 71–77). New York: Pergamon Press.

Otto, D.A., Benignus, V.A., Muller, K.E., & Barton, C.N. (1981). Effects of age and body lead burden on CNS function in young children. I: Slow cortical potentials. *Electroencephalography and Clinical Neurophysiology*, *52*, 229–239.

Palmer, J.O. (1970). *The psychological assessment of children*. New York: John Wiley & Sons. Perris, C. (1974). Averaged evoked responses (AER) in patients with affective disorders. *Acta Psychiatrica Scandinavica, supplement*, 89–98.

Perris, C. (1974) Averaged evoked responses (AER) in patients with affective disorders. Acta Psychiatrica Scandinavica, suppl.: *255*, 89–98.

Pfefferbaum, A., Rosenbloom. M., & Ford, J.M. (1987). Later event-related potential changes in alcoholics. *Alcohol*, *4*, 275–281.

Pfefferbaum, A., Wenegrat, B.G., Ford, J.M., Roth, W.T., & Kopell, B.S. (1984). Clinical application of the P3 component of event-related potentials. II. Dementia, depression and schizophrenia. *Electroencephalography and Clinical Neurophysiology.*, *59*, 104—124.

Pincus, J.H. (1979). There could be a medical link in delinquency. *Medical Post*, 23, 23.

Pincus J., & Tucker G. (1974). *Behavioral neurology*. New York: Oxford University Press.

Pincus, J.H., & Tucker, G.J. (1978). Violence in children and adults: A neurological view. *Journal of the American Academy of Child Psychiatry*, *17*, 277–288.

Pockberger, H., Petsche, H., Rappelsberger, P., Zidek, B., & Zapotoczky, H.G. (1985). On-going EEG in depression: A topographic spectral analytical pilot study. *Electroencephalography and Clinical Neurophysiology*, *61*, 349–358.

Porjesz, B., Begleiter, H., Bihari, B., & Kissin, B. (1987). Event-related brain potentials to high incentive stimuli in abstinent alcoholics. *Alcohol*, *4*, 283–287.

Quay, H.C. (1987). Patterns of delinquent behavior. In H.C. Quay (Ed.), *Handbook of juvenile delinquency*. New York: John Wiley & Sons.

Raine, A., & Venables, P.H. (1987). Contingent negative variation, P3 evoked potentials and antisocial behavior. *Psychophysiology*, *24*, 191–199.

Raine, A., & Venables, P.H. (1988). Enhanced P3 evoked potentials and longer recovery times in psychopaths. *Psychophysiology*, *25*, 30–38.

Raloff, J. (1983). Chemical roots of violent behavior. *Science News*, *124*, 122–125.

Rimland, B., & Larson, G.E. (1983). Hair mineral analysis and behavior: An analysis of 51 studies. *Journal of Learning Disabilities*, *16*, 279–285.

Rizzo, P.A., Amabile, G., Caporali, M. Spadero, M., Zanasi, M., & Morocutti, C. (1978). A CNV study in a group of patients with traumatic head injuries. *Electroencephalography and Clinical Neurophysiology*, *45*, 281–285.

Robins, L.N. (1966). *Deviant children grown up: A sociological and psychiatric study of sociopathic personality*. Baltimore: Williams and Wilkins.

Roth, W.T., Horvath, T.B., Pfefferbaum, A. & Kopell, B.S. (1980) Event-related potentials in schizophrenics. *Electroencephalography and Clinical Neurophysiology*, *48*, 127–139.

Saletu, B., Saletu, M., & Itil, T.M. (1973). The relationships between psychopathology and evoked responses before, during and after psychotropic drug treatment. *Biological Psychiatry*, *6*, 45–74.

Sattler, J.M. (1974). *Assessment of children's intelligence*. Philadelphia: W.B. Saunders Co.

Sayed, Z.A., Lewis, S.A., & Brittain, R.P. (1969). An electroencephalographic and psychiatric study of thirty-two insane murderers. *British Journal of Psychiatry*, *115*, 1115–1124.

Shagass, C., Roemer, R.A., Straumanis, J.J., & Josiassen, R.C. (1984). Psychiatric diagnostic discriminations with combinations of quantitative EEG variables. *British Journal of Psychiatry*, *144*, 381–392.

Shagass, C., Straumanis, J.J., & Overton, D.A. (1975). Psychiatric diagnosis and EEG-evoked response relationships. *Neuropsychobiology*, *1*, 1–15.

Shah, S. (1981). Legal and mental health system interactions. *International Journal of Law and Psychiatry*, *44*, 219–270.

Shover, N. (1979). *A sociology of American corrections*. Illinois: The Dorsey Press.

Sohmer, H., & Student, M. (1978). Auditory nerve and brainstem evoked responses in normal, autistic, minimal brain dysfunction and psychomotor retarded children. *Electroencephalography and Clinical Neurophysiology*, *44*, 380–388.

Spinetta, J.J., & Rigler, D. (1972). The child-abusing parent: A psychological review. *Psychological Bulletin*, *77*, 296–304.

Surwillo, W.W. (1980). The electroencephalogram and childhood aggression. *Aggressive Behavior*, *6*, 9–18.

Syndulko, K. (1978). Electrocortical investigations of sociopathy. In R.D. Hare & D. Schalling (Eds.), *Psychopathic behavior: Approaches to research*. Chichester, England: Wiley.

Syndulko, K., Parker, D., Jens, R., Maltzman, I., & Ziskind, E. (1985). Psychophysiology of sociopathy: Electrocortical measures. *Biological Psychiatry*, *3*, 185.

Thatcher, R.W. (1978). Neuroelectric techniques in clinical neurology. *Proceedings of the 17th Annual San Diego Biomedical Symposium*. New York: Academic Press.

Thatcher, R.W., Cantor, D.S., McAlaster, R., Geisler, F., & Krause, P. (in press). Comprehensive predictions of outcome in closed head injured patients: The development of prognostic equations. *Annals of the New York Academy of Science*.

Thatcher, R.W., & John, E.R. (1977). *Functional neuroscience*: *Vol. 1*: *Foundations of cognitive processes*. Hillsdale, NJ: Lawrence Erlbaum Associates.

Thatcher, R.W., Lester, M.L., McAlaster, R., & Horst, R. (1982). Effects of low levels of cadmium and lead on cognitive functioning in children. *Archives of Environmental Health*, *37*, 159–166.

Thatcher, R.W., Lester, M.L., McAlaster, R., Horst, R., & Ignasias, S.W. (1983a). Intelligence and lead toxins in rural children. *Journal of Learning Disabilities*, *16*, 355–359.

Thatcher, R.W., & Maisel, E.B. (1979). Functional landscapes of the brain: An electrotopographic perspective. In H. Begleiter (Ed.), *Evoked brain potentials and behavior*. New York: Plenum Press.

Thatcher, R.W., McAlaster, R., Lester, M., Horst, D., & Cantor, D. (1983b). Hemispheric EEG asymmetries related to cognitive functioning in children. In E. Perecman (Ed.), *Cognitive processes in the right hemisphere* (pp. 125–145). New York: Academic Press.

Thatcher, R.W., Walker, R.A., Gerson, I., & Geisler, F.H. (1989). EEG discriminant analyses of mild head trauma. *Electroencephalography and Clinical Neurophysiology*, *73*, 94–106.

Timsit-Berthier, M. (1973). CNV, slow potentials and motor potential studies in normal subjects and psychiatric patients. In A. Fessard & G. Lelord (Eds.), *Human neurophysiology, psychology, psychiatry: Average evoked responses and their conditioning in normal subjects and psychiatric patients* (pp. 327–366). Paris: Inserm.

Tucker, D.M. (1983). Asymmetries of activation and arousal in psychopathology. *Advances in Biological Psychiatry, 13*, 9–25.
Vasconetto, C., Floris, V., & Morocutti, C. (1971). Visual evoked responses in normal and psychiatric subjects. *Electroencephalography and Clinical Neurophysiology, 31*, 77–83.
Volavka, J., Matousek, M., Feldstein, S., Roubicek, J., Prior, P., Scott, D.F., Brezinova, V., & Synek, V. (1973). *Die Zuverlassigkeit der EEG-Beurteilung, EEG-EMG* (Stuttgart), *4*, 123–130.
Walker, S. (1985). *Sense and nonsense about crime: A policy guide*. California: Brooks/Cole Publishing Co.
Weinberger, D.R. (1987). Implications of normal brain development for the pathogenesis of schizophrenia. *Archives of General Psychiatry, 44*, 660–669.
Wennberg. A., & Otto, D. (1985). Neurophysiological tests of the central nervous system (CNS). In P. Grandjean (Ed.), *Neurobehavioral methods in occupational and environmental health* (Document 6, pp. 19–22). Copenhagen: World Health Organization.
Williams, R.L. (1971). Abuses and misuses in testing black children. *Counseling Psychology, 2*, 62–73.
Woolsey, R.M., & Goldner, J.A. (1975). Forensic aspects of electroencephalography. *Medical Trial Technique Quarterly, (Winter)*, 333–345.
Yeudall, L.T. (1979, September 26). A neuropsychological perspective of persistent juvenile delinquency and criminal behavior. *Discussion paper: Human nature, crime and society*, New York Academy of Sciences.
Yeudall, L.T., Fedora, O., & Fromm, D. (1985). *A neuropsychosocial theory of persistent criminality: Implications for assessment and treatment*. University of Alberta Hospital, Edmonton, Canada. (Research Bulletin #97).
Yeudall, L.T., Fromm-Auch, D., & Davies, P. (1982). Neuropsychological impairment of persistent delinquency. *Journal of Nervous and Mental Diseases, 170*, 257–265.

7 The Use of Neuroimaging Techniques in Brain Injury

RUBEN C. GUR and RAQUEL E. GUR

A question that may confront the legal handling of brain injured individuals is, "To what extent are behavioral deficits observed after injury related to disturbed brain functioning?". To answer this, it is necessary to understand how behavior is related to the anatomic integrity of brain regions as well as their level of activity. This has been difficult since there were few techniques, until this past decade, for studying the living human brain.

We are currently undergoing a virtual revolution in neuroimaging technology. This has enabled unprecedented advances in the field of neuropsychology, particularly the study of regional brain function in relation to major behavioral dimensions. In this chapter, we will (a) review briefly the main neuroimaging techniques pertinent to evaluation of regional brain anatomy and physiological activity, (b) summarize major findings pertinent to brain–behavior relations, (c) describe a method we have developed for comparing behavioral data with anatomical and physiological findings, (d) list some current limitations and pitfalls in interpreting data from this growing field, and suggest short-term steps required to make these techniques more powerful as clinically applicable tools, and (e) raise possible issues that may face psychologists and other professionals when they introduce imaging measures in court.

Techniques

It is beyond the scope of this chapter to give even a cursory description of the neuroimaging techniques and their clinical applications. Several comprehensive volumes contain such summaries (Reivich & Alavi, 1985; Phelps, Mazziotta & Schelbert, 1986). Here we can mention the main purpose of each technique and describe the kind of information each yields.

Imaging Neuroanatomy

The two major techniques currently available for imaging brain anatomy are x ray computed tomography (CT) and magnetic resonance imaging (MRI). MRI can clearly display with exquisite detail brain structures and many lesions (Fig. 7.1). If behavioral deficits occur after a brain injury and a lesion is detectable on CT or MRI, then it is likely that at least some of the behavioral deficits have been caused by destruction of brain tissue.

In many respects MRI is superior to CT, particularly in brain areas near the skull or other bony tissue, where beam hardening effects of bone distort the CT scans. Some lesions can be missed by CT and detected by MRI. On the other hand, abnormal signal intensity may occur in MRI scans of normal individuals, and the field still lacks standard scanning procedures and normative data (see Zimmerman & Bilaniuk, 1989, for a comparative review). Very small lesions or diffuse neuronal loss such as occurs in Alzheimer's disease can have deleterious effects on behavior and yet be undetectable by routine clinical reading of either CT or MRI. Computerized techniques for quantifying brain atrophy are being pursued, and should prove more sensitive for detection of such tissue loss.

Imaging Neurophysiology

Behavioral deficits can be more severe than would be predicted on the basis of neuronal death in regions showing anatomic destruction. They can be caused by brain cells that are not dead, but are either insufficiently active or too active. Some grave forms of brain dysfunction are caused by abnormalities in regional brain physiological activity. For example, epilepsy has severe behavioral manifestations and there is evidence for interictal deficits in cognitive and emotional functioning (Dodrill & Wilkus, 1976). However, CT or MRI scans are frequently uninformative or even normal (Gastaut, 1970).

In the case of epilepsy, abnormalities in regional brain electric activity measurable by electroencephalography (EEG) have been reliably linked to seizure type and location. However, other brain disorders show abnormalities in electrical activity that are too diffuse or varied to be of diagnostic value. After stroke, for example, slowing of EEG can be seen but the extent of slowing and its precise frequency and topographic distribution is difficult to assess from routine EEG evaluations. There are methods now available such as computerized EEG topography, which can potentially be more helpful in localizing areas of abnormal brain electrical activity. Imaging and quantitative assessment of regional brain physiologic activity is now also feasible with isotopic techniques for measuring regional cerebral blood flow and metabolism.

There are several techniques for generating topographic displays of regional EEG measures. Duffy's brain electrical activity mapping (BEAM) has received much attention (Duffy, 1986), but others such as Bio-Logic's Brain Atlas (Harner, Jackel, Mawhinney-Hee & Sussman, 1987) and those of John (1977) follow similar principles. These quantify

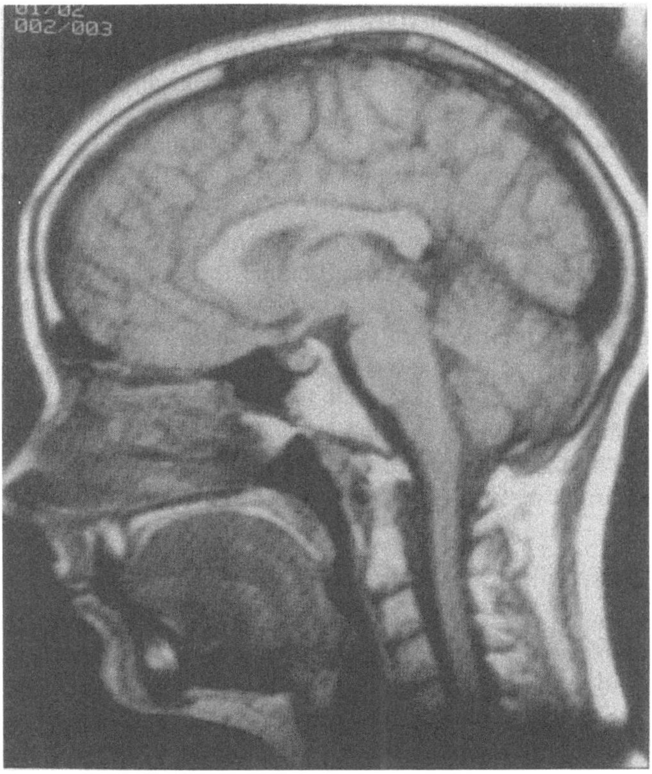

A

FIGURE 7.1. MRI: A: Saggital view of a normal brain; B: axial view of a cerebral infarct.

EEG parameters and produce topographic displays of EEG data as shown in Figure 7.2.

Isotopic techniques for neuroimaging make use of the fact that active neurons have metabolic needs for oxygen and glucose, and that cerebral blood flow rates change in response to these needs. Such measures can help identify regions of abnormal physiological activity associated with behavioral deficits. Furthermore, such measures obtained during the performance of cognitive tasks could help delineate brain regions necessary for regulating cognitive processes.

These isotopic techniques for measuring cerebral metabolism and blood flow can be traced to the pioneering method of Kety and Schmidt (1948) for measuring whole-brain metabolism and blood flow. The technique used intracarotid injection of nitrous oxide, and subsequent measurement of arterivenous concentration differences to yield accurate and reproducible data on brain metabolism and blood flow. However, this technique was limited by providing only whole-brain values and by its invasiveness.

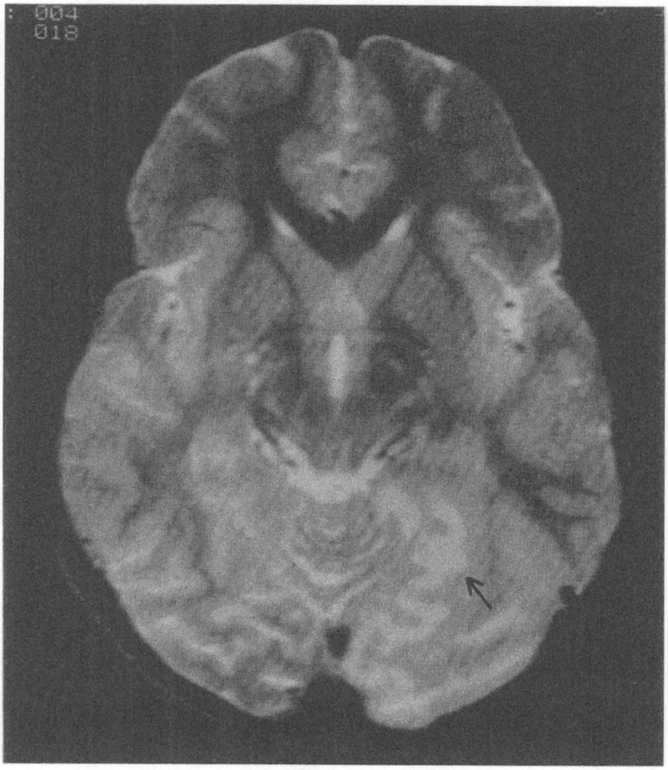

B

FIGURE 7.1. (*continued*).

Safe regional measurements were first made possible by the introduction of the Xenon^{133} (^{133}Xe) clearance techniques for measuring regional cerebral blood flow (rCBF). The highly diffusible ^{133}Xe can be administered as gas mixed in air or in saline. Its clearance from the brain is measurable by stationary scintillation detectors. The rate of clearance enables accurate quantitation of rCBF in the fast clearing gray matter compartment, as well as calculation of mean flow in gray and white matter. Initial applications involved carotid injections (Olesen, Paulson & Lassen, 1971), which were invasive and only enabled measurements in one hemisphere at a time. In 1975 Obrist and colleagues reported the ^{133}Xe inhalation technique (Obrist, Thompson, Wang & Wilkinson, 1975) and presented models for quantifying rCBF with this noninvasive procedure. The technique permits simultaneous measurements from both hemispheres; the number of brain regions that can be measured depends on the number of detectors. Initial studies were performed with up to 16 detectors, 8 over each hemisphere, but there are now commercially available systems with 32 detectors. Recently a system has been introduced that enables the placement of up to 254 detectors. The quantitative data can be displayed topographically as shown in Figure 7.3.

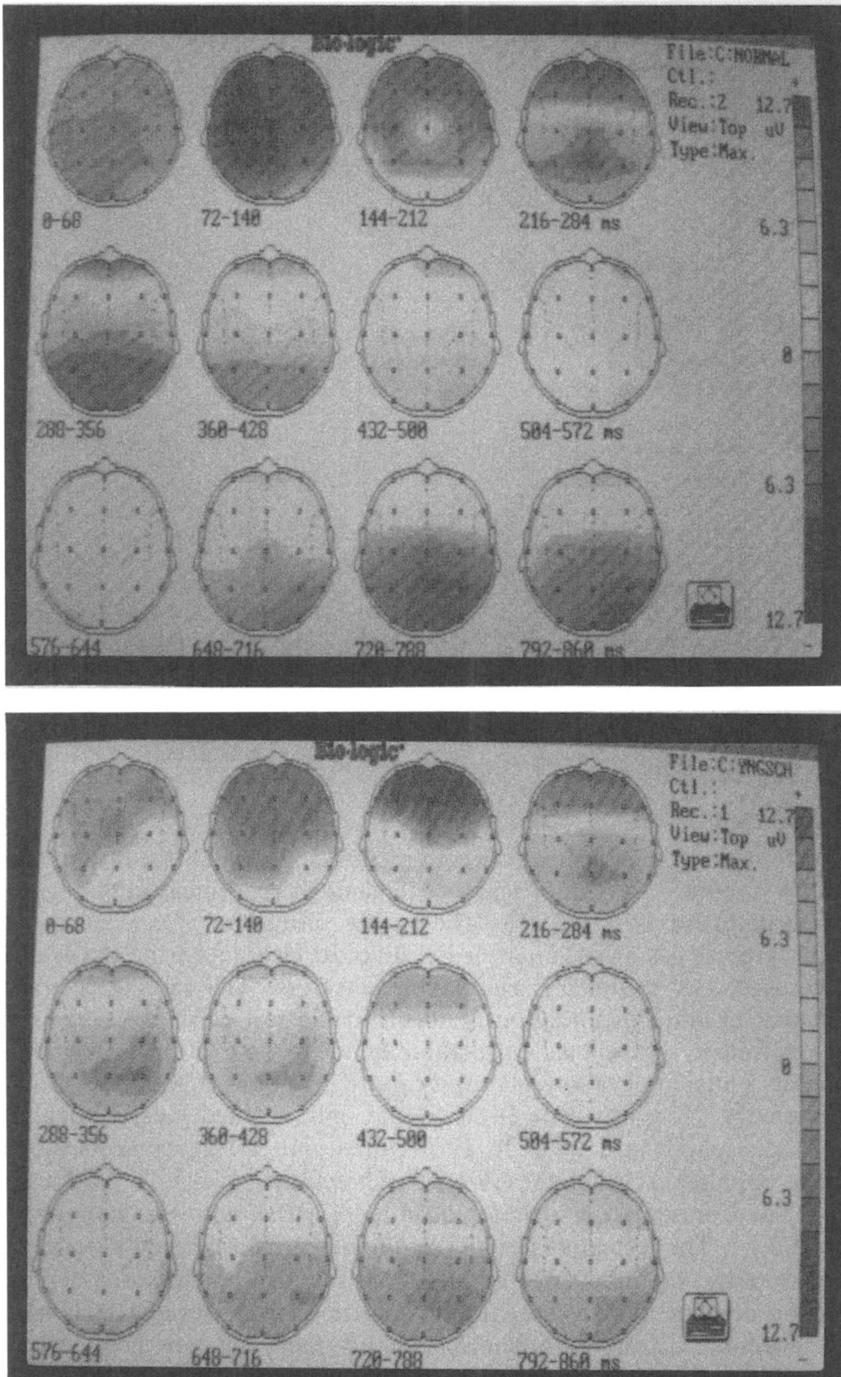

A

B

FIGURE 7.2. Examples of topographic displays of electrophysiological data: A: Integrated voltages of evoked responses for 12 latency windows after stimulus onset are mapped. In this case averaged evoked response amplitudes to a rare

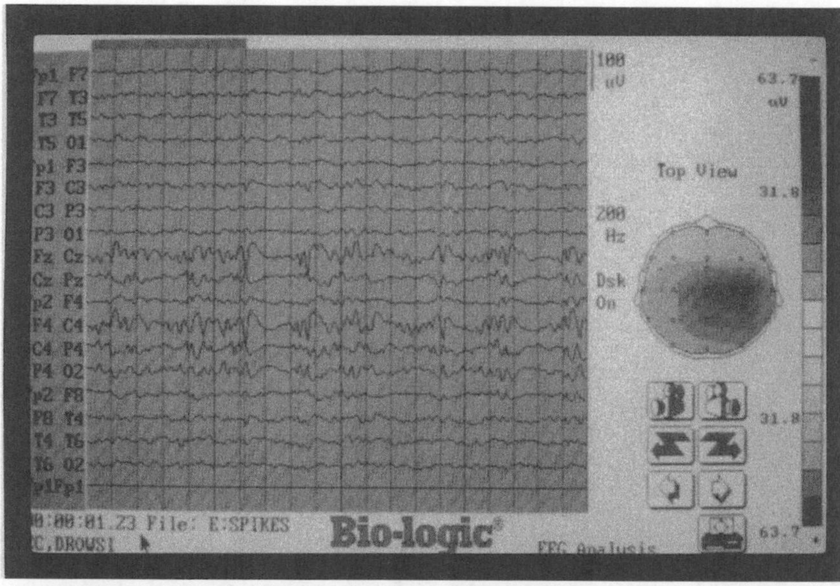

C

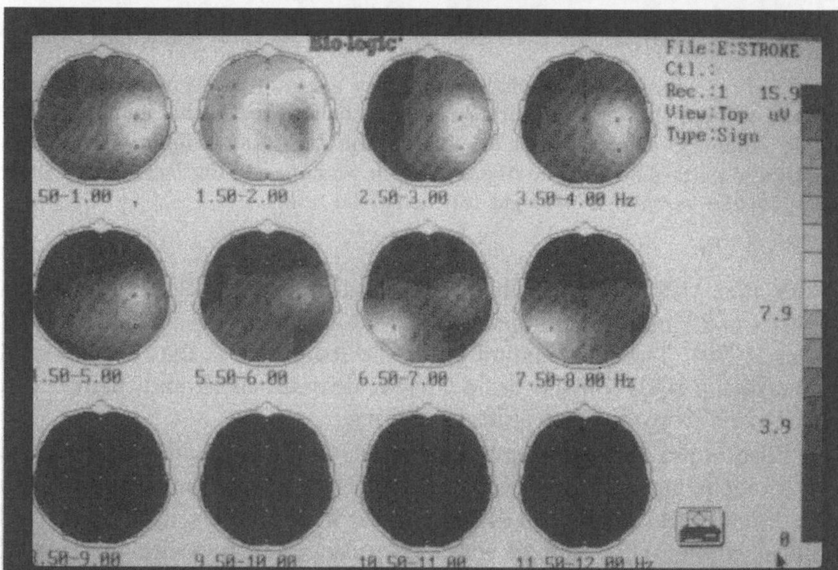

D

stimulus (oddball P300 paradigm) from a normal patient are shown. Note the posterior maxima in the 288–356 msec latency window. B: Similar data to A; but obtained from a schizophrenic patient. When compared with the normal subject, note the overall decreased amplitude as well as the right-sided skew the positive potential has, especially at the 288–356 msec latency window. C: In another example of a voltage map, the map displays the maxima of a spike obtained from an epileptic, which is indicated by the red cursor on the continuous EEG display. D: EEG that has been subjected to frequency analysis and the 12 integrated spectral bands are plotted topographically. In a patient with a right cerebrovascular accident, maximal amplitudes in the delta range (first three maps) are easily appreciated over the right hemisphere.

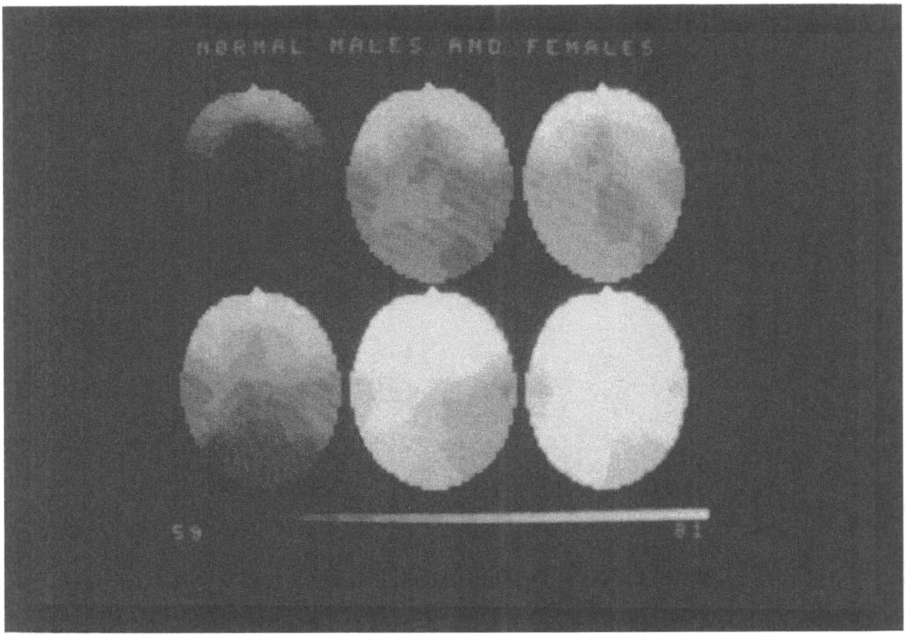

FIGURE 7.3. A topographic display of rCBF in a group of normal men (upper row) and women (lower row) during rest (first column), a verbal analogies task (middle column), and a spatial line-orientation task (last column). Note the hyperfrontal pattern at rest, the higher CBF in women, and the increased CBF in the left for the verbal and the right for the spatial task.

Note that rCBF is typically higher in the front of the brain. This "hyperfrontal" pattern has been observed routinely in normal subjects (Ingvar, 1979). The main limitation of the technique is that it is optimal for measuring rCBF on the brain surface near the skull and, hence, can only be used to study cortical brain regions.

Positron emission tomography (PET) has made it possible to measure in vivo biochemical and physiological processes in the human brain, with three-dimensional resolution. Initial work with animals used selectived chemical compounds, labeled with radioisotopes to measure the rate of biochemical processes. This has been extended to humans by principles of computed tomography (Reivich et al., 1979), and now the technique has been adapted to use several radionuclides that decay through the emission of positrons. Patients are administered radionuclides that are unstable because their nuclei have an excess positive charge. The radionuclides are usually given intravenously and are taken up by tissue. They dissipate their energy through the emission of positrons, each of which undergoes the process of annihilation by interacting with a negatively charged electron. Each annihilation produces two photons that travel in opposite directions and are detected and measured by detector arrays. By CT principles, the coincidental counts are used to generate images reflecting the regional rate of radionuclide uptake. This information enables the calculation, depending on the specific radiolabeled compound, of such varied physiological parameters as oxygen and glucose metabolism, blood flow, or receptor density of neurotransmitters. In order to relate this physiological information to anatomical regions of interest (ROI), an atlas of brain anatomy is required. Such anatomical information can be determined from computerized images of sliced brains, x-ray CT, or MRI Scans, Multiple brain "slices" can be obtained from PET (Figure 7.4).

Another technique recently introduced for three-dimensional imaging of rCBF is single photon emission computed tomography (SPECT). This technique enables three-dimensional imaging of CBF using radionuclides that, unlike positron emitters, do not require the availability of a dedicated cyclotron for their production. However, at present, reliable estimation of rCBF with available radionuclides that can be safely administered is still problematic, and much more work is required to make it applicable in systematic neurobehavioral research.

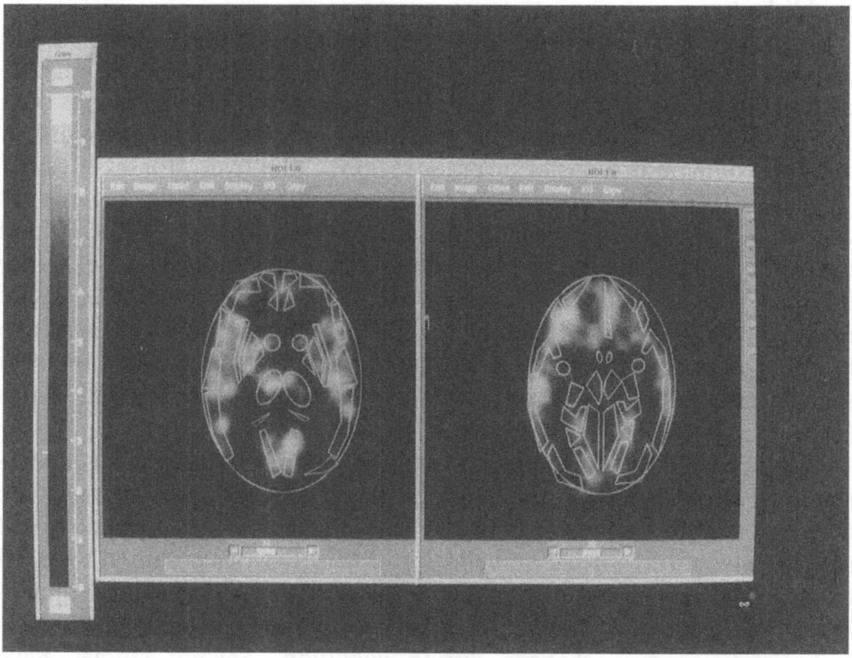

FIGURE 7.4. Placement of regions of interest. From Gur et al., 1987b, with permission. Copyright © 1987 by the AMA.

Regional Brain Function and Behavior

The application of these techniques to the understanding of human behavior is in its infancy. We are still at the stage of identifying the sensitivity and limitation of some of these methods. Moreover, only crude behavioral measures have been examined with respect to the neuroimaging data obtained from these techniques. Here we will describe some of the findings and try to outline where this work could lead.

Several studies have examined the relationship between cognitive dimensions an neuroanatomic data. For example, left hemispheric superiority in language processing corresponds to CT evidence for asymmetry in the size of language-related structures, and performance on cognitive tasks has been correlated with CT measures of atrophy (Naeser, 1985). These seems to be a relationship between the extent and location of anatomical lesions and the severity and pattern of behavioral deficits (Raz, Raz, Yeo, Bigler & Cullum, 1987). However, better normative data on control subjects and more precise quantitation of the CT and MRI results are needed. The most widely used technique for obtaining the neuroanatomical measures is to trace brain regions on the image and to calculate the area using planimetry. A more rigorous method would be to apply segmentation algorithms to the actual data, and such procedures are currently being developed. Their reliability and validity are yet to be established.

Physiological neuroimaging techniques are suitable for dynamic studies of brain–behavior relations. When applied to normal subjects, reliable patterns of physiologic activity have been observed. For example, as seen in Figure 3, the ^{133}Xe technique consistently showed increased rCBF in anterior compared to posterior brain regions, "the hyperfrontal pattern" (Ingvar, 1979). PET shows higher glucose uptake in frontal regions, as well as in the posterior visual (calcarine) cortex (Figure 7.4). Repeated measures in the same normal individuals demonstrate excellent reliability for the ^{133}Xe technique (Warach et al., 1987) and acceptable levels of reliability for PET indices (Gur et al., 1987b). The techniques are sensitive to changes in brain activity produced by sensory stimulation and show specific effects for the visual, auditory, and somatosensory modalities (Reivich, Gur & Alavi, 1983; Gur & Reivich, 1980).

The potential of physiological neuroimaging techniques for understanding brain–behavior relationships is particularly great because the activity of brain regions is dynamic, and changes in neurophysiological activity have direct effects on behavior. To exploit this potential we need to establish links between regional brain activity and behavioral dimensions. We evaluated whether metabolic activity, as measured by these techniques, showed changes during cognition. Several studies have answered this question affirmatively (Risberg & Ingvar, 1973; Leli, Hannay, Falgout, Katholi & Halsey, 1982). In one of the first experiments to test statistically the hypothesis of greater physiological activation in regions that serve specific cognitive functions, we studied a sample of normal right-handed and left-handed men and women (Gur et al., 1982). Measurements of rCBF were performed with the ^{133}Xe inhalation technique at rest and during the performance of a verbal analogies and a spatial line-orientation task. The verbal task was chosen because available evidence suggests that performance of this task is impaired with left hemispheric damage. In contrast, performance on the line-orientation task is impaired with right hemispheric damage (Benton, Hannay & Varney, 1975). Both tasks in our study reliably increased CBF in both hemispheres, but the increase was hemispherically asymmetric. The verbal task produced a greater increase in left hemispheric rCBF, whereas the spatial task produced a greater increase on the right. The reason we examined left-handed and right-handed men and women is that handedness and gender have been shown to influence the direction and degree of hemispheric cognitive specialization (Levy & Reid, 1976). In our rCBF study (Fig. 7.5), women had higher rCBF that men and left-handers differed from right-handers in the pattern of hemispheric activation. This indicated that rCBF measurement is not only sensitive enough to measure regional brain activity in response to certain cognitive tasks, but was also able to detect individual differences known to influence the direction and degree of hemispheric specialization for cognitive function.

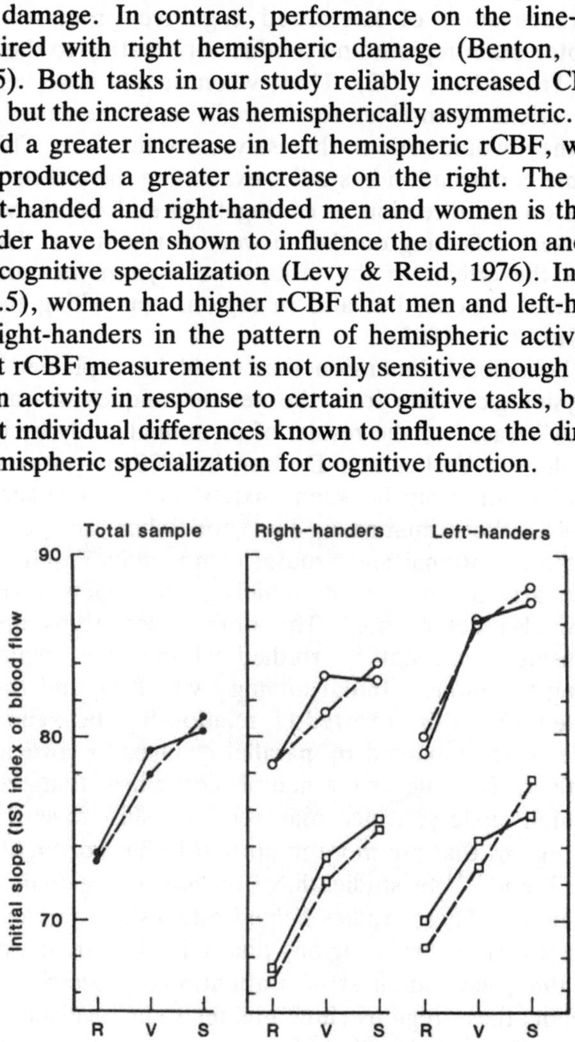

FIGURE 7.5. Initial slope (IS) index of blood flow to the left (——) and right (----) hemispheres for the total sample and for right-handed and left-handed women (○) and right-handed and left-handed men (□) during performance of resting (R), verbal (V), and spatial tasks (S). From Gur et al., 1982, with permission. Copyright © 1982 by the AAAS.

Subsequent studies with rCBF and PET have confirmed and extended these findings. In one PET study with the same verbal analogies and spatial line-orientation tasks described above, asymmetric effects were found in the expected temporoparietal regions that were implicated by the studies on behavioral sequelae of brain damage. However, a less established hypothesis proposed in 1972 by the British neuropsychologist Colwyn Trevarthen was also supported by the data. Trevarthen suggested that neural activation of lateralized cognitive processes could "spill over" to motor brain regions and produce orientation to the contralateral hemispace (Trevarthen, 1972). Thus, when people have verbal thoughts they would orient themselves to the right and when they have spatial cognitions they would orient themselves to the left. This hypothesis received some confirmation in studies examining the effects of verbal and spatial tasks on the direction of conjugate lateral eye movements while individuals were reflecting on the answers to test items. The PET study showed that the effects of the tasks were asymmetric not only in the temporoparietal regions, but also in regions controlling the orientation response (Gur et al., 1983).

Another behavioral dimension that could be explained on the basis of neurophysiological data from the new techniques was anxiety. A behavioral "law" traced to the results of an animal study by the American neuropsychologists Yerkes and Dodson in 1908 proposes a curvilinear, "inverted-U" relationship between anxiety and performance (Yerkes & Dodson, 1908). Performance is not good when anxiety is extremely low, since the attentional and arousal components required for optimal performance are missing. At extremely high anxiety levels, however, performance also deteriorates. The brain mechanisms responsible for this relationship could not be studied without the availability of the neuroimaging techniques. Initial findings with PET and the ^{133}Xe technique showed that this inverted-U relationship between anxiety and performance is accompanied by parallel changes in cortical metabolism and blood flow. This suggests a neural mechanism that reduces cortical activity in high anxiety, which may reflect a shift toward activation of subcortical regions that are more important in fight-or-flight situations.

Other PET and ^{133}Xe studies have examined regional brain involvement in attention. These studies helped establish, for example, the existence of a network of brain regions that animal neuroanatomical studies (Mesulam, 1981) have implicated in attentional processing. It was found that in humans these regions show greater right hemispheric activation. Further elaboration of attentional processes in relation to regional brain activity was elegantly carried out in a series of studies using PET measures of CBF (Posner, Petersen, Fox & Raichle, 1988).

These early and preliminary studies seem to point to the possibility that neuroimaging techniques are sufficiently sensitive to detect the association between regional brain activity and behavior. They encourage more systematic work using the neuroimaging techniques for testing hypotheses and for generating new observations on brain–behavior relationships. This can be done by manipulating behavioral dimensions in normal individuals and examining the effects of such manipulations on regional brain activity.

But how can neuroimaging techniques be used to provide a better understanding of the neural substrates of abnormal behavior? Initial studies have consisted of obtaining neuroanatomical data with CT or MRI (Weinberger, Delisi, Perman, Targum & Wyatt, 1982), and other studies have obtained resting measures of rCBF and glucose metabolism (Buchsbaum et al., 1984; Gur et al., 1987a, 1987b).

The neuroanatomical studies suggested increased ventricular volume in schizophrenics, indicating neuronal loss in mesial brain structures (Andreasen et al., 1986; Weinberger, Torrey, Neophytides & Wyatt, 1979). However, most of these studies used CT, which is not optimal for measuring structural alterations on the brain surface close to the skull (because of beam hardening effects of bone, described earlier). Another limitation of most studies is the use of planimetric measures of surfaces as seen on the scans. As noted above, segmentation of tissue can be done more precisely by algorithms applied to the actual pixel by pixel data. This method was applied by Pfefferbaum et al. (1988), who used a semiautomated computerized approach for volumetric measurements. Diffuse cerebral atrophy distinguished schizophrenics from controls. Sulcal enlargement, more than ventricular enlargement, was implicated.

Andreasen et al. (1990), using MRI measures, also found some confirmation that ventricular enlargement was more evident in schizophrenics relative to controls. However, the results of this study also drew attention to the importance of individual differences within samples and to the marked variability in brain structure that can be found among controls. The group differences in ventricular size could be accounted for by enlarged ventricles in the male, but not the female schizophrenics. As well, it is interesting to note that earlier findings of decreased frontal, cerebral, and cranial size in schizophrenics was not replicated when schizophrenics were compared with education-matched controls. Previous studies had relied for control subjects on the easily obtained university population.

Physiological studies examining regional brain abnormalities in psychiatric populations have usually used resting conditions. Initial reports suggested diffusely reduced CBF and metabolism in schizophrenia (Mathew et al., 1981; Mathew, Duncan, Weinman & Barr, 1982), and evidence for "hypofrontality" (Buchsbaum et al., 1982; Farkas et al., 1984). Few studies have examined both resting and activated conditions. Gur et al. (1983) reported that resting rCBF was normal in medicated schizophrenics, but abnormalities were pronounced in the asymmetry of activation for the verbal analogies and the spatial line-orientation tasks.

Schizophrenics failed to show the normal left hemispheric activation for the verbal task and showed a "paradoxical" left hemispheric activation for the spatial task. This supported Gur's (1979) hypothesis, based on behavioral studies, that schizophrenia is associated with left hemispheric dysfunction due to overactivation of this hemisphere. Further support for the hypothesis was obtained in a sample of unmedicated schizophrenics (Gur et al., 1985a). In this group, resting CBF showed greater left hemispheric values, and abnormal activation of the left hemisphere was associated with increased symptom severity.

There have been other studies in schizophrenia and other psychiatric disorders such as depression, obsessive-compulsive disorders, and anxiety disorders. Such studies could improve diagnostic accuracy and may help identify patterns of abnormal activation in specific forms of psychopathology. A potentially productive strategy for such studies will be to identify the regional abnormalities in brain anatomy and physiological activity associated with focal and nonfocal brain disease, and relate the abnormal pattern to behavioral impairment. It is noteworthy that to date it is not possible to examine a set of MRI, CT, PET, and rCBF data and arrive at a diagnosis of any psychiatric disease. Some neurological diseases can be diagnosed with the help of CT and MRI (e.g., multiple sclerosis, brain tumors, and stroke), but PET and the ^{133}Xe technique have not yet been established as clinical diagnostic procedures.

A Method for Integrating Behavioral and Neuroimaging Data

A key issue for future work centers on the integration of multifaceted data on regional brain function. We can obtain anatomical information on the integrity of brain regions from x-ray CT and from MRI scans, whereas the PET and ^{133}Xe techniques provide information on regional brain physiological activity. Topographic EEG results complement these techniques by providing data on regional brain function with information on electrical activity. Imaging technology provides a means for integrating such multifaceted data in a comprehensible manner, but theory is needed to guide our understanding of how the activity of the brain is related to behavior. Now the challenge is to integrate behavioral theories on regional brain function with the anatomical and physiological neuroimaging data.

Theories on brain regulation of human behavior have been tested in clinical populations by correlating behavioral deficits with clinical signs and post mortem findings. Neuropsychological testing in patients with brain disease provides measures of specific behavioral functions (e.g., memory, learning, praxis). In the process of formulating theories on brain regulation of behavior, the pattern of scores is used to test hypotheses on regional brain involvement for specific behavioral dimensions. The pattern of deficits is used in clinical practice to implicate brain regions putatively affected by a disease (Gur et al., 1985b; Gur, Trivedi, Saykin & Gur, 1988b; Gur, Saykin, Blonder & Gur, 1988).

The process of testing neurobehavioral theories can be aided by quantifying regional brain involvement in the regulation of behavioral dimensions. We have proposed an algorithm that applies such a quantification to standard neuropsychological test scores (Trivedi & Gur, 1987, 1989). The algorithm yields a value for each brain region, which predicts whether it is neurally compromised given the pattern of neuropsychological test scores. These regional values can be examined statistically to test the behavioral hypotheses against clinical data and other neuroimaging data. They can also be presented topographically using standard procedures for translating numbers into a gray scale or a color scale. This can facilitate comprehension of the spatial distribution of implicated regions. Initial testing of the algorithm in clinical cases and populations was encouraging (Gur et al., 1988a, 1988b). There was consistency between the "behavioral images" and the location of lesion in patients with unilateral cerebral infarcts (Figure 6).

The topographic displays corresponded with clinical and CT data, and were consistent with the clinical interpretation of the neuropsychological data. Note that in both cases the behavioral image suggested that regions considerably larger than the CT lesion were behaviorally "hypofunctional," including a contralaterally homotopic region. This was not detected by the clinical evaluation and may reflect inadequacy in the "spatial resolution" of the behavioral images. However, it could also be a true behavioral manifestation of remote physiological effects of focal lesions. As noted above, areas larger than the anatomical lesions have shown metabolic suppression in PET studies of local cerebral glucose metabolism using the 18-F-FDG technique (Kuhl et al., 1980; Kushner et al., 1984) and in studies of regional cerebral blood flow using the ^{133}Xe clearance technique (Gur et al., 1987c). By comparing behavioral images with PET and CT scans it would be possible to evaluate which behavioral effects are accompanied by remote physiologic suppressions.

Present Limitations and Future Steps

The impact of neuroimaging technology is only beginning to be felt. The techniques are still being refined with respect to optimal resolution and scanning procedures. Normative data are lacking, and only rudimentary steps have been taken to identify the neural networks regulating human behavior. Although several brain diseases can be reliably detected by neuroimaging, the diagnostic utility of the techniques for the vast

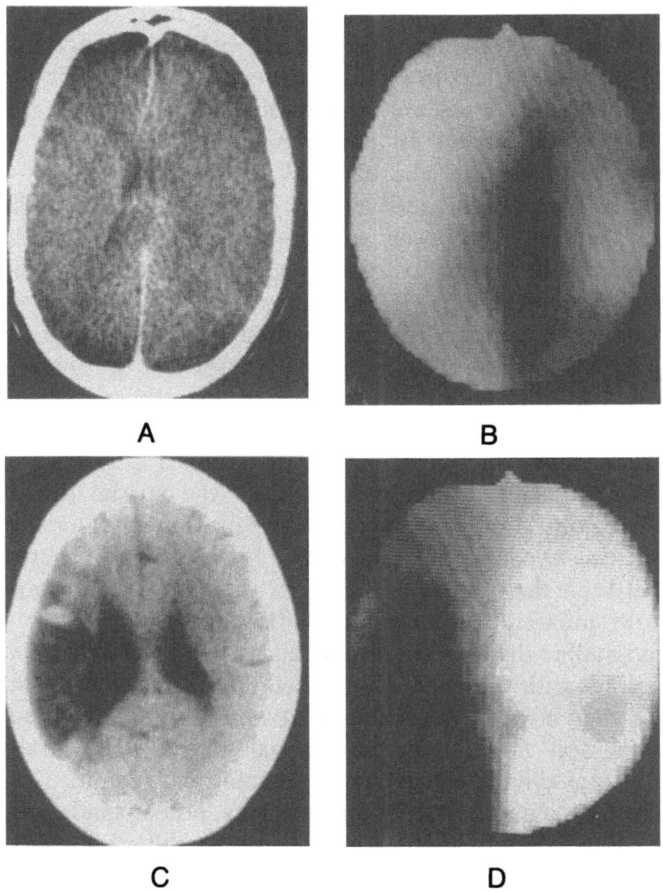

FIGURE 7.6. CT scans and corresponding behavioral images of two patients with cerebral infarcts, one in the right hemisphere (A and B for CT and behavioral image, respectively) and one in the left (C and D). The CT scans were reversed so that the left hemisphere is to the viewer's left. From Gur et al., 1988, with permission.

majority of neurological and for all psychiatric diseases is still unestablished. It is already clear that no one technique will provide all the answers. Each has its relative advantages and limitations and yields data that are complementary but only partially overlapping. What immediate steps can we take to advance our ability to harness this technology for improved diagnosis and treatment?

Populations with behavioral deficits should be studied. Applying these techniques to patients with destructive brain lesions, such as are produced by stroke, head trauma, or brain tumors, could help in determining the extent and topographic distribution of anatomical brain damage and abnormal metabolic activity, either suppressed or increased. There is considerable evidence that metabolism is suppressed even in regions that appear anatomically intact when evaluated by techniques for assessing regional brain anatomy, such as CT scans and MRI. This could explain why so frequently patients show behavioral deficits that are more pervasive than what can be explained by regions of anatomical involvement. For example, when we applied the ^{133}Xe technique to patients with unilateral stroke, we found that the extent of physiological suppression was largest when right hemispheric stroke patients were performing a spatial task and, conversely, when left hemispheric stroke patients were engaged in a verbal task.

Other clinical populations of particular interest include patients suffering from Parkinson's disease and Alzheimer's disease. There is strong evidence that dopamine deficiency is responsible for the symptoms of the former, and some suggestions for the involvement of another neurotransmitter (cholinergic or norepinergic) system in the latter. PET will provide information on the distribution of neurotransmitters, and studying the topographic distribution of metabolic abnormalities in these disorders could help understand how these neurotransmitter systems regulate behavior.

A complementary approach would be to study other behavior disorders where the brain pathology is unclear and use the metabolic studies to help identify regional brain involvement. For example, reading disability and other learning disabilities could be studied, and this could help test hypotheses on regional brain dysfunction that underlie these disorders. Understanding of psychiatric disorders could similarly be enhanced by techniques for measuring regional brain activity. In both psychiatric and neurological populations it would be particularly informative to measure the physiological activity not only at rest, but also while patients are engaged in pertinent behaviors.

However, looking at pathology and patterns of deficits is only one part of the picture. Normal individuals vary considerably both in behavior and abilities, and studying the relationship between this variability and regional brain physiology could shed light on the neural underpinnings of this variability. For example, exceptionally talented individuals in the sciences, arts and humanities could be evaluated. Again, this should be done at rest and during behaviorally "challenged" procedures. How does regional brain activity of a mathematician differ from that of an architect? Which brain regions does a mathematician activate when he is attempting to develop a calculus for a particular problem? Which brain regions does a lawyer activate when preparing or presenting a case? Could we train individuals to activate appropriate brain regions and thereby enhance their abilities? The technology permits us to begin asking such questions.

Thus far the cognitive dimension has received the greatest attention, particularly in the examination of verbal and spatial tasks in relation to hemispheric activation. But emotion and conative or motivational factors could also be studied with these techniques. Such studies could be done not only in normal populations. Its extension to populations representing a large range of human behavior could be informative in understanding regional brain involvement in the regulation of behavior and thus be of considerable relevance to the diagnosis and treatment of dysfunction.

Implications for Legal Practices

In litigation, when there is an issue of whether impairment in behavior is a result of brain injury, evidence can be obtained from experts reviewing neurological, psychiatric, and clinical–psychological observations. CT and MRI scans can now show the area of anatomical destruction, but we know there are severe behavioral aberrations that are not produced by anatomical lesions. These reflect metabolic abnormalities. In epilepsy, for example, seizures may occur in the absence of a lesion detectible by CT. The abnormality often can be seen clearly, however, in EEG and PET studies. Similarly, in the case of closed head injury, the CT lesion may be much smaller than the area of metabolic suppression. Studies with PET or the (much more affordable) ^{133}Xe inhalation technique for measuring rCBF may show the area and extent of metabolic suppression. Regional reduction in brain activity also may be seen in computed EEG topography. The relationship between the behavioral deficits and regional brain function can be established with neuropsychological testing in conjunction with the "behavioral imaging" algorithm described above.

In one court case of a patient who had suffered a closed head injury, the algorithm was helpful in detecting a regional deficit when test scores alone were relatively unrevealing. This was a bright young man, college undergraduate, who complained of loss of concentration and memory. He subsequently dropped out of school. The test scores were all within the normal range, but for many of the tests the norms were not applicable for this highly educated individual. The "behavioral image" revealed a circumscribed area of brain deficit that corresponded to the area implicated by other evidence (Figure 7.7).

The methods may also help evaluate the effectiveness and progress of a rehabilitation program. If a patient's memory deficit can be linked, for example, to suppression of neural activity in the temporal lobe, physiological activation studies could indicate whether improved memory is associated with improved tissue responsiveness to task demands.

The neuroimaging methods can also help in establishing psychiatric diagnosis, for example, in pleas of insanity. Although no specific pattern of physiological disturbance has been established for schizophrenia, some specific patterns are emerging (Gur, 1987). When such diagnostic markers are established, diagnosis of insanity could be made on the basis of more objective data than is possible today.

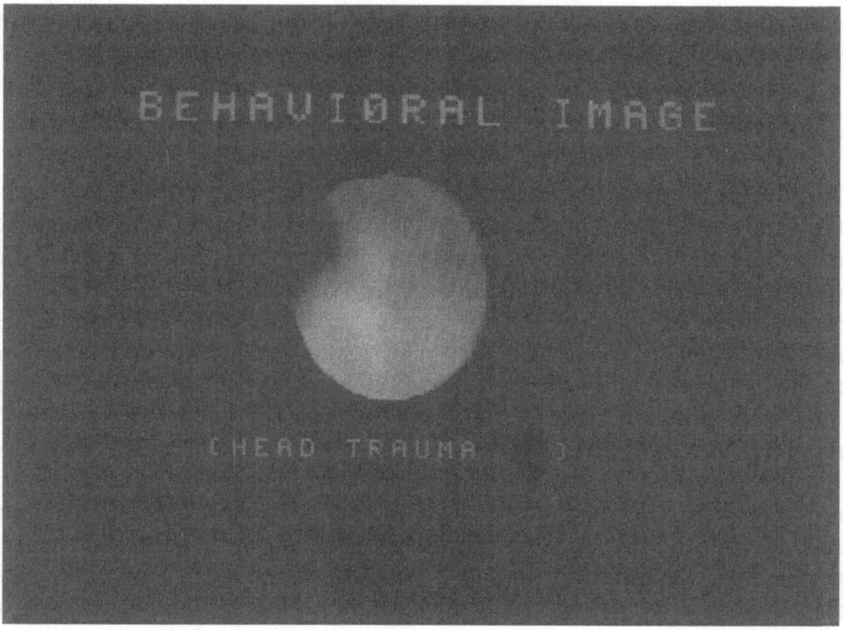

FIGURE 7.7. A behavioral image obtained from a patient with a closed head injury.

In neurobehavioral evaluations, many times individuals undergoing neuropsychological testing or a neuropsychiatric evaluation as part of court proceedings are motivated to "fake bad," or perform poorly. Methods such as the "behavioral imaging" algorithm could help determine whether there is some regional coherence to the pattern of deficits observed. Another advantage of "behavioral imaging" is the reduced need to rely entirely on experts who were hired by one of the parties. Even without willful dishonesty, an expert's opinion can be influenced by the side that called for the testimony. The theoretical weights used in the algorithm are supplied in advance of examining any particular case (they can be obtained from remote and well established experts), and the computer does the rest. Its impartiality could not be questioned.

In dealing with expert testimony based on neuroimaging data, we believe a lawyer would be well advised to rely on experts who do active research in the field. The technology is advancing fast, it is "flashy" and hence appeals to charlatans; level-headed appraisals are more likely to come from someone close to the cutting edge of research, which exposes on a daily basis not only the advantages but also the limitations of the technology. As indicated above, at present there is no established pattern of abnormalities detectible by neuroimaging that is specific for any psychiatric disorder. An "expert" witness may argue that a particular set of scans indicates that an individual is schizophrenic. In this case, issues of reliability and validity of the evidence should be scrutinized carefully.

Conclusions

Despite their current shortcomings and limitations, neuroimaging techniques are already helpful in many clinical situations and their increased use in court is inevitable. We hope this chapter, which in its brevity did not provide much technical detail and did not attempt to cover the range of important studies, has nevertheless helped explain the techniques and what they measure. The preliminary applications for understanding brain–behavior relationships are currently being extended in an increasing number of research centers, and as the technology becomes more available advances are becoming more rapid. There are several specific steps that are needed for establishing the utility of neuroimaging in diagnosis and treatment of brain pathology, and these were outlined. The behavioral side of the equation has been particularly defiant to attempts at objective quantitation, and the "behavioral imaging" algorithm was presented as a step toward addressing this problem. Finally, we gave a limited list of issues that may confront applications of neuroimaging to the court.

References

Andreasen, N.C., Ehrhardt, J.C., Swayze, V.W., Allinger, R.J., Yuh, W.T.C., Cohen, G., & Ziebell, S. (1990). Magnetic resonance imaging of the brain in schizophrenia: The pathophysiological significance of structural abnormalities. *Archives of General Psychiatry*, *47*, 35–44.

Andreasen, N.C., Nasrallah, H.A., Dunn, V., Olson, S.C., Grove, W.M., Ehrhard, J.C., Coffman, J.A., & Crossett, J.H. (1986). Structural abnormalities in the frontal system in schizophrenia: A magnetic resonance imaging study. *Archives of General Psychiatry*, *43*, 136–144.

Benton, A.L., Hannay, H.J., & Varney, N.R. (1975). Visual perception of line direction in patients with unilateral brain disease. *Neurology*, *25*, 907–910.

Buchsbaum, M.S., Delisi, L.E., Holcomb, H.H., Cappelletti, J., King, A.C., Johnson, J., Hazlett, E., Dowling-Zimmerman, S., Post, R.M., Morihisa, J., Carpenter, W., Cohen, R., Pickar, D., Weinberger, D.R., Margolin, R., & Kessler, R.M. (1984). Anteroposterior gradients in cerebral glucose use in schizophrenia and affective disorder. *Archives of General Psychiatry*, *41*, 1159–1166.

Buchsbaum, M.S., Ingvar, D.H., Kessler, R., Waters, R.M., Capelletti, J., van Kammen, D.P., King, A.C., Johnson, J.L., Manning, R.G., Flynn, R.W., Mann, L.S., Bunney, W.E., & Sokoloff, L. (1982). Cerebral glucography with positron tomography. *Archives of General Psychiatry*, *39*, 251–259.

Dodrill, C.B., & Wilkus, R.J. (1976). Relationships between intelligence and electroencephalographic epileptiform activity in adult epileptics. *Neurology*, *26*, 525–531.

Duffy, E.H. (Ed.). (1986). *Topographic mapping of brain electrical activity*. Boston, MA: Butterworths.

Farkas, T., Wolf, A.P., Jaeger, J., Brodie, J.D., Christman, D.R., & Fowler, J.S. (1984). Regional brain glucose metabolism in chronic schizophrenia. *Archives of General Psychiatry, 41*, 293–300.

Gastaut, H. (1970). Clinical and electroencephalographic classification of epileptic seizure. *Epilepsia, 11*, 102–113.

Gur, R.E. (1979). Cognitive concomitants of hemispheric dysfunction in schizophrenia. *Archives of General Psychiatry, 36*, 269–274.

Gur, R.E. (1987). Psychiatric disorders as brain dysfunction. *National Forum, 67*, 29–32.

Gur, R.C., Gur, R.E., Obrist, W.D., Hungerbuhler, J.P., Youngkin, L., Rosen, A.D., Skolnick, E.E., & Reivich, M. (1982). Sex and handedness differences in cerebral blood flow during rest and cognitive activity. *Science, 217*, 659–661.

Gur, R.C., Gur, R.E., Rosen, A.D., Warach, S., Alavi, A., Greenberg, J., & Reivich, M. (1983). A cognitive-motor network demonstrated by positron emission tomography. *Neuropsychologia, 21*, 601–606.

Gur, R.C., Gur, R.E., Silver, F.L., Obrist, W.D., Skolnick, B.E., Kushner, M., Hurtig, H.I., & Reivich, M. (1987c). Regional cerebral blood flow in stroke: Hemispheric effects of cognitive activity. *Stroke, 18*, 776–780.

Gur, R.E., Gur, R.C., Skolnick, B.E., Caroff, S., Obrist, W.D., Resnick, S., & Reivich, M. (1985a). Brain function in psychiatric disorders: III. Regional cerebral blood flow in unmedicated schizophrenics. *Archives of General Psychiatry, 42*, 329–334.

Gur R.C., & Reivich, M. (1980). Cognitive task effects on hemispheric blood flow in humans. *Brain and Language, 9*, 78–93.

Gur, R.E., Resnick, S.M., Alavi, A., Gur, R.C., Caroff, S., Dann, R., Silver, F.L., Saykin, A.J., Chawluk, J.B., Kushner, M., & Reivich, M. (1987a). Regional brain function in schizophrenia. I. A positron emission tomography study. *Archives of General Psychiatry, 44*, 119–125.

Gur, R.E., Resnick, S.M., Gur, R.C., Alavi, A., Caroff, S., Kushner, M., & Reivich, M. (1987b). Regional brain function in schizophrenia. II. Repeated evaluation with positron emission tomography. *Archives of General Psychiatry, 44*, 126–129.

Gur, R.C., Saykin, A.J., Blonder, L.X., & Gur, R.E. (1988a). "Behavioral imaging": II. Application of the quantitative algorithm to hypothesis testing in a population of hemiparkinsonian patients. *Neuropsychiatry, Neuropsychology and Behavioral Neurology, 1*, 87–96.

Gur, R.E., Skolnick, B.E., Gur, R.C., Caroff, S., Rieger, W., Obrist, W.D., Younkin, D., & Reivich, M. (1983). Brain function in psychiatric disorders: I. Regional cerebral blood flow in medicated schizophrenics. *Archives of General Psychiatry, 40*, 1250–1254.

Gur, R.C., Trivedi, S.S., Saykin, A.J., & Gur, R.E. (1988b). "Behavioral imaging"—A procedure for analysis and display of neuropsychological test scores: I. Construction of algorithm and initial clinical evaluation. *Neuropsychiatry, Neuropsychology and Behavioral Neurology, 1*, 53–60.

Gur, R.C., Trivedi, S.S., Saykin, A.J., Resnick, S.M., Malamut, B.L., & Gur, R.E. (1985b). Behavioral imaging. *Journal of Clinical and Experimental Neuropsychology, 7*, 633.

Harner, R.N., Jackel, R.A., Mawhinney-Hee, M.R., & Sussman, N.M. (1987). Computed EEG topography in epilepsy. *Revue Neurologique (Paris)*, *143*, 457–461.

Ingvar, D.H. (1979). "Hyperfrontal" distribution of the cerebral matter flow in resting wakefulness: On the functional anatomy of the conscious state. *Acta Neurologica Scandinavica*, *60*, 12–25.

John, E.R. (1977). *Neurometrics: Clinical applications of quantitative electrophysiology*. Hillsdale, NJ: Lawrence Erlbaum Associates.

Kety, S.S., & Schmidt, C.F. (1948). The nitrous oxide method for the quantitative determination of cerebral blood flow in man: Theory, procedure and normal values. *Journal of Clinical Investigation*, *27*, 476–483.

Kuhl, D.E., Phelps, M.E., Kowell, A.P., Metter, E.J., Selin, C., & Winter, J. (1980). Effects of stroke on local cerebral metabolism and perfusion: Mapping by emission computed tomography of 18 FDG and 13 NH3. *Annals of Neurology*, *8*, 47–60.

Kushner, M., Alavi, A., Reivich, M., Dann, R., Burke, A., & Robinson, G. (1984). Contralateral cerebellar hypometabolism following cerebral insult: A positron emission tomographic study. *Annals of Neurology*, *15*, 425–434.

Leli, D.A., Hannay, H.G., Falgout, J.C., Katholi, C.R., & Halsey, J.H. (1982). Focal changes in cerebral blood flow produced by a test of right-left discrimination. *Brain & Cognition*, *1*, 206–223.

Levy, J., & Reid, M. (1976). Variations in writing posture and cerebral organization. *Science*, *194*, 337.

Mathew, R.J., Duncan, G.C., Weinman, M.L., & Barr, D.L. (1982). Regional cerebral blood flow in schizophrenia. *Archives of General Psychiatry*, *39*, 1121–1124.

Mathew, R.J., Meyer, J.S., Francis, D.J., Schooler, J.C., Weinman, M., & Mortel, K.F. (1981). Regional cerebral blood flow in schizophrenia: A preliminary report. *American Journal of Psychiatry*, *138*, 112–113.

Mesulam, M.M. (1981). A cortical network for directed attention and unilateral neglect. *Annals of Neurology*, *10*, 209–325.

Naeser, M. (1985). Quantitative approaches to computerized tomography in behavioral neurology. In M.M. Mesulam (Ed.), *Principles of behavioral neurology* (pp. 363–383). Philadelphia: F.A. Davis.

Obrist, W.D., Thompson, H.K., Wang, H.S., & Wilkinson, W.E. (1975). Regional cerebral blood flow estimated by ^{133}Xenon inhalation. *Stroke*, *6*, 245–256.

Olesen, J., Paulson, O.B., & Lassen, N.A. (1971). Regional cerebral blood flow in man determined by the initial slope of the clearance of intra-arterially injected ^{133}Xe. *Stroke*, *2*, 519–540.

Pfefferbaum, A., Zipursky, R.B., Lim, K.O., Zatz, L.M., Stahl, S.M., & Jernigan, T.L. (1988). Computed tomographic evidence for generalized sulcal and ventricular enlargement in schizophrenia. *Archives of General Psychiatry*, *45*, 633–640.

Phelps, M., Mazziotta, J.C., & Schelbert, H.R. (Eds.). (1986). *Positron emission tomography and autoradiography: Principles and applications for the brain and heart.* New York: Raven Press.

Posner, M.I., Peterson, S.E., Fox, P.T., & Raichle, M.E. (1988). Localization of cognitive operations in the human brain. *Science*, *240*, 1627–1631.

Raz, N., Raz, S., Yeo, R.A., Bigler, E.D., & Cullum, C.M. (1987). Relationship between cognitive and morphological asymmetries in Alzheimer's dementia: A CT study. *International Journal of Neuroscience*, *35*, 235–243.

Reivich, M., & Alavi, A. (Eds.). (1985). *Positron emission tomography*. New York: Alan R. Liss.

Reivich, M., Gur, R.C., & Alavi, A. (1983). Positron emission tomography studies of sensory stimuli, cognitive processes, and anxiety. *Human Neurobiology*, *2*, 25–33.

Reivich, M., Kuhl, D., Wolf, A.P., Greenberg, J., Phelps, M., Ido, T., Casella, V., Fowler, J., Hoffman, E., Alavi, A., Som, P., & Sokoloff, L. (1979). The 18-F-fluorodeoxyglucose method for the measurement of local cerebral glucose utilization in man. *Circulation Research*, *44*, 127–137.

Risberg, J., & Ingvar, D.H. (1973). Patterns of activation in the grey matter of the dominant hemisphere during memorizing and reasoning. *Brain*, *96*, 737–756.

Trevarthen, C. (1972). Brain bisymmetry and the role of the corpus callosum in behavior and conscious experience. In J. Cernacvek & F. Podivinsky (Eds.). *Cerebral interhemispheric relations* (pp. 319–333). Bratislava: The Publishing House of the Slovak Academy of Sciences.

Trivedi, S.S., & Gur, R.C. (1987). Computer graphics for neuropsychological data. *Proceedings of the National Computer Graphics Association*, *3*, 22–32.

Trivedi, S.S., & Gur, R.C. (1989). Topographic mapping of cerebral blood flow and behavior. *Computers in Biology and Medicine*, *19*, 219–229.

Warach, A., Gur, R.C., Gur, R.E., Skolnick, B.E., Obrist, W.D., & Reivich, M. (1987). The reproducibility of the ^{133}Xe inhalation technique in resting studies: Task order and sex related effects in healthy young adults. *Journal of Cerebral Blood Flow and Metabolism*, *7*, 702–708.

Weinberger, D.R., Delisi, L.E., Perman, G.P., Targum, S., & Wyatt, R.J. (1982). Computed tomography in schizophreniform disorder and other acute psychiatric disorders. *Archives of General Psychiatry*, *39*, 778–783.

Weinberger, D.R., Torrey, E.F., Neophytides, A.N., & Wyatt, R.J. (1979). Structural abnormalities in the cerebral cortex of chronic schizophrenic patients. *Archives of General Psychiatry*, *36*, 935–939.

Yerkes, R.M., & Dodson, J.D., (1908). The relation of strength of stimulus to rapidity of habit-formation. *Journal of Comparative Neurology and Psychology*, *18*, 458–482.

Zimmerman, R.A., & Bilaniuk, L.T. (1989). CT and MR: Diagnosis and evolution of head injury, stroke, and brain tumors. *Neuropsychology*, *3*, 191–230.

8 The Problems of Prognosis

BRYAN D. FANTIE and BRYAN KOLB

This chapter discusses the issues involved when a neuropsychologist undertakes the difficult proposition of predicting the limits of functional recovery in a person who has suffered brain damage. We shall review the major mechanisms through which the central nervous system responds to injury and summarize some of the indicators used to predict outcome. In order to understand better the impact that brain injury has on the lives of the victims and their families, we will discuss the issue of what exactly "recovery" of function after brain damage means and the factors that can affect it. We shall consider also the theoretical and practical concerns that guide neuropsychological research and its clinical application.

As neuropsychologists, we are asked to evaluate to what extent the quality of life, both vocational and personal, has been changed after an individual has suffered a brain injury. We must try to anticipate whether or not the changes are permanent, and, if the changes are deemed temporary, how long they will last. Prediction is one of the fundamental roles of science. Making "educated" guesses about how complex situations with turn out is always difficult since every factor that must be considered increases geometrically the number of potential outcomes. In the clinical setting, one often must make judgments about individual situations without the benefit of the regulated controls provided by a carefully designed scientific experiment. Despite this handicap, it is imperative that prognostic estimations are as accurate as possible because predictions about a patient's potential for recovery can influence the actual outcome.

For example, if the recuperative capacity of a patient is overestimated and the expectations about spontaneous recovery are too optimistic, a therapy program with the potential to effect real benefits might be considered unnecessary and not be adopted. It would be a tragedy also if the patient and family were to bear the emotional and financial demands that long courses of therapy often entail when there is little actual chance for success. Unfortunately, erring on the side of conservative pessimism can also have destructive consequences. If the prognostic picture seems without hope, those involved may just give up without achieving those improvements that may have been possible. In cases where legal liability is concerned, bad predictions about recuperation may cause the responsible party to be forced to assume unjust financial burdens. On the other side of the litigious fence, too narrow a definition of recovery and insufficient understanding of what it means "to recover" could result in the victim being denied appropriate compensation even though the quality of that individual's life has been changed forever.

Epidemiology of Brain Trauma

Although there are many etiologies of neural destruction (e.g., disease, stroke, tumor), we shall try to focus our discussion on brain damage caused by trauma since this is most relevant to the subject matter of this book. In the United States, only vascular disease and cancer kill more people annually than do traumatic injuries. For Americans between the ages of 1 and 38 years old, however, the period that includes the majority of people's most productive work years, accidental and intentional injuries are the leading cause of death (Trunkey, 1983). More than half the cases of fatalities resulting from trauma are caused by head injury. For example, in fatal road accidents, injury to the brain occurs in nearly 75% of the cases (Gissane, 1963). In patients with multiple injuries, the head is the part of the body most commonly damaged. Head injury exceeds stroke as a cause of death in men aged 45 to 64 years (U.S. Department of Health, Education, and Welfare, 1974).

Recent advances in lifesaving technology, particularly in the area of emergency treatment of the trauma victim, have created a population of people whom, if they had suffered their injuries before such advances were made, would most likely be dead. Riger (1988) reported that the mortality rate associated with severe head injury has dropped from 87% to 9% in the past 10 years. Unfortunately, knowledge about long-term recovery from wounds of this nature and severity lags behind. Annually, as many as 30,000 people suffer serious head traumata in Canada (Ivan, 1984) and, in the United States, approximately 400,000 patients with new injuries of the head are admitted to hospitals (National Institutes of Health, 1984). These figures probably represent a conservative measure of the actual number of people affected since there is clear neuropathological and neuropsychological evidence that significant damage to the central nervous system can also result from minor head injury or concussion (Jane, Steward & Gennarelli, 1985; Levin & Eisenberg, 1979; Nevin, 1967; Oppenheimer, 1968; Rimel, Giordani, Barth, Boll & Jane, 1981; Rubens, Geschwind, Mahowald & Mastri, 1977; Stuss et al., 1985). It now seems undeniable that brain damage sufficient to alter the level of consciousness, even momentarily, or to produce what appears to be transient impairment of sensory, motor, or cognitive functions, probably leaves some residual deficits (Binder, 1986; Lezak, 1983). There are, therefore, two large populations of head-injured people about whom we have very little information. Part of this group consists of those whose physical condition would have proved fatal in the past; the other part comprises individuals with injuries about which the full impact may have been underestimated. This second group might, in fact, be experiencing real, lasting changes in the way they function from day to day as a result of their "minor" injury.

The Relevance of the Animal Literature

Reliable scientific information about human brain trauma upon which confident behavioral prognostication can be made is scarce. There is so much variability in the nature of naturally occurring lesions that the relationships between causative and resultant variables are often obscured. The fundamental question posed by the discipline of neuropsychology asks how brain structure and function relate to behavior. We need to know if damage to specific neural areas results in predictable behavioral deficits. Obviously, we cannot expect to run carefully controlled experimental studies in humans. Either a patient's clinical needs, in the case of surgical excision, or chance, in the case of trauma, determine the location and extent of cerebral damage. In both cases, hopefully, the availability of histological material is limited to a small portion of the patient population so it is extremely difficult to delineate the exact degree and location of the damaged brain tissue involved in producing posttraumatic abnormal behavioral manifestations. Thus, we must use animal models to study systematically the effects of specific brain lesions and we find it useful to turn to the animal literature to get some idea of what we might expect to happen to behavior after neural damage.

Reitan and Wolfson (1986) have questioned the value of information obtained from studies of experimental injuries using animals as subjects and raise a number of objections. The emotional issue of whether or not any animal research is justified on ethical grounds is beyond the scope of this chapter and is a topic much too serious and important to be treated by mere sweeping statements and self-righteous generalities from either side of the ideological fence. They go on, however, to claim that:

> Statistics have documented the fact that there is no shortage of human beings who have damaged their brains by striking their heads against a fixed object. Neurosurgeons who specialize in the evaluation and treatment of craniocerebral trauma have gained extensive information about the types of damage and clinical consequences of brain trauma from the thousands of patients who survive such injuries as well as from the thousands of victims in whom autopsies are performed. There is therefore no lack of human material from whom the biological consequences, pathological changes, or clinical manifestations of head injuries can be learned. (Reitan & Wolfson, 1986, p. 5)

We feel compelled to disagree with this sentiment. At best, they seem to suggest that all we need to know about brain trauma is already known. At worst, these authors appear to have a surprisingly naive understanding of the scientific method and the need to control as many variables as possible in order to sort out and understand complex phenomena. Admittedly, animal research is not a perfect simulation of what occurs in instances of human head injury. Of course, the variables that relate to anatomy (shape of head, thickness of skull, characteristics of brain structure) are different. Nevertheless, there is much valuable information that can be and has been gathered from these studies when the experiments have been well planned and the aforementioned differences are used to temper rather than cripple the interpretation.

The objection to the appropriateness of animal research in neuropsychology has been made on the behavioral and/or cognitive level as well.

> ... neuropsychological consequences of traumatic brain damage in primates—especially in terms of higher level cognitive functions and their potential for recovery—are of almost no relevance to man because of the tremendous gap that exists between the higher level brain functions of primates and human beings. (Reitan & Wolfson, 1986, p. 5)

Evidence continues to accumulate that the aforementioned "tremendous gap" is shrinking rapidly and that a class of mammals shares many more behaviorally relevant neural mechanisms than was believed just a few years ago (Warren & Kolb, 1978). Albeit, if a behavior or mechanism can be proved to be unequivocally unique to humans, this process can be studied in its entirety only in humans. Nevertheless, it certainly does not follow that because you cannot study everything using animal models that you cannot study anything. In fact, if our main interest is in recovery after brain damage, it has been consistently demonstrated quite clearly that restitution of behavioral function follows an orderly progression regardless of what behavior is being observed. Therefore, one need not be restricted to the study of specific functions in order to learn anything that is meaningfully related to behavioral recovery or rehabilitation.

Rosenzweig (1980) has summarized four criteria for guiding the selection of appropriate models in the exploration of the effects of brain lesions and rehabilitation. First, for pragmatic and ecological reasons, the species selected as a model should be abundant, inexpensive, easy to handle, and should breed well in captivity. Second, the model should enable the process of interest to be studied as directly and simply as possible. Third, the functional properties of the model's behavior must be similar to those of concern in the human being. Fourth, the model and the human must be presumed to be employing the same causal mechanisms when performing the function in question. Although the differences in behavior and brain structure among mammalian species cannot be neglected, there are still generalities in brain–behavior relationships that can prove useful to our understanding of many human neuropsychological functions.

The overwhelming majority of what we know about neural reaction to injury has come from animal research. At the cellular level, there is little doubt that a neuron is a neuron (at least if they are both mammalian) and that there are factors that exert a greater influence on the reaction to trauma (e.g., the victim's premorbid status, age, and the etiology of the damage) than does species of origin. We will now review some of the cellular events that take place after brain damage and discuss how these phenomena can influence the processes of interpretation and prediction.

Neural Responses to Injury

One of the problems with prognosis is the fact that the locus of brain damage, especially that after trauma, is never simple. Lesions are rarely discrete and significant additional cell death usually occurs at points distant to the primary site of injury through a variety of processes. Trauma produces short, intermediate, and long-term changes in brain tissue in addition to the actual loss of neurons caused by the initial insult. Precisely what changes occur depends on the type of brain damage. All of these factors make it difficult to establish brain–behavior relationships clearly from the results of brain trauma. Despite these difficulties, significant contributions have been made in the understanding of functional brain organization from the study of penetrating wounds (e.g., Luria, 1965; Teuber, 1962) and from surgical excisions (Taylor, 1969, 1979).

When trauma includes the violent removal of part of the brain's substance (e.g., penetrating wounds), a cavity lined with dead tissue results. Surrounding this border of necrosis is an area consisting of injured, dead, and normal cells. The cavity may continue to expand for about a week while fluid accumulates inside it and the surrounding, critically damaged tissue degenerates and shrinks. Within 24 hours phagocytes (astrocytes and microglia) infiltrate the area to remove debris. The accumulation of glial cells and the disruption of the extracellular matrix eventually form a scar in the area, which may hamper or block any functional regeneration of remaining live neural cells. After a week or two, the cavity begins to constrict and, with time, it may disappear completely and thus may not be directly visible on computed tomography CT scans. The shrinkage of the cavity is almost invariably accompanied by distortions of the surrounding tissue. The ventricles are able to expand in reaction to the loss in encompassing cortical volume. Abnormally enlarged ventricles are usually visible on CT scans and provide a clue that there has been a loss in total brain mass.

When an area of brain is ablated, the cell bodies of the neurons at the local site are removed or destroyed. Fibers of passage, coursing through the damaged area but originating from neural cell bodies distant from the site of injury, are interrupted. If the cell body of a neuron is destroyed the whole cell dies. When a nerve is severed, the portion distal to the cut (on the side opposite the cell body) always degenerates. This process is called anterograde degeneration. If the remaining proximal portion of the axon (that portion still connected to the cell body) is sufficiently robust, it and the cell body will not degenerate. If, on the other hand, the damage has been quite extensive a process called retrograde degeneration will take place and the axon will die. For the axons of some neurons (e.g., motor neurons) retrograde degeneration is reversible, whereas in others (e.g., thalamic neurons) it is not.

Neurons that project to or receive input from a destroyed or degenerated neuron also may die. This phenomenon is called transneuronal degeneration. An example of this is observed in the visual system after the optic nerve is cut and degenerating neurons are found in the lateral geniculate nucleus. There are two hypotheses as to why the lateral geniculate cells degenerate: either they require a minimal level of stimulation to survive and they no longer receive any input from the severed optic nerve or they have lost the supply of some vital trophic substance supplied by the ends of the fibers composing the optic nerve. Transneuronal degeneration may occur across more than one synapse; for example, cells in the visual cortex may also begin to die after the lateral geniculate body degenerates. If the cells that have lost their input degenerate, the process is referred to as anterograde transneuronal degeneration. If cells degenerate after they lose the targets of their output, the process is called retrograde transneuronal degeneration. Transneuronal degeneration may also be associated with accumulating deposits of calcium, a process called calcification. For example, in response to neocortex damage, calcification may occur in degenerating thalamic neurons (also a site of retrograde degeneration) and in the basal ganglia (a possible site of secondary transneuronal degeneration). These deposits can be so pronounced that they are easily seen in CT scans and can be taken as an indication of certain kinds of cortical or subcortical damage (Beresford, 1965; Kolb & Whishaw, 1985b; Schoenfeld & Hamilton, 1977).

In addition to the death of neurons, there may be large changes in the structure of the remaining neurons. For example, if neurons lose significant numbers of their inputs in adulthood the dendritic fields may retract, reflecting the loss of synaptic inputs, or in some cases the dendritic arbor may actually expand, reflecting active synaptogenesis.

These different degenerative processes suggest a number of issues that neuropsychologists need to consider. First, the fact that the degenerative processes are so varied and exert their effects in such a widespread manner makes it impossible to believe that even the most refined lesion can be precisely localized. For example, although damage to the frontal cortex may be small and easily visualized, retrograde degeneration and calcification will occur in the thalamus, secondary transneuronal degeneration and calcification will appear in the basal ganglia, and anterograde and terminal degeneration will appear throughout the neocortex, brainstem, and spinal cord. Second, many of these degenerative changes are known to continue for years. Consequently, the functional boundaries of a brain lesion are not static in spatial or temporal dimensions. Hence, the timing of the neuropsychological evaluation is crucial and one should remember that often only a transitory stage of the patient's condition is measured rather than an enduring state.

Mechanisms Associated with Neurological Recovery

Overlapping with the time course of the aforementioned degenerative processes are the effects of four major neural mechanisms thought to be important in mediating the nervous system's ability to compensate for damage. These include: (a) regeneration, (b) sprouting, (c) denervation supersensitivity, and (d) disinhibition.

Perhaps the simplest form of naturally occurring healing consists of the regrowth of new tissue to replace that which was lost. Although this is the way our skin, bone, and muscle recover from injury, under most circumstances the adult mammalian central nervous system does not have the capacity to generate new neurons when existing ones are destroyed. In some cases, if an individual nerve cell is not too badly damaged, it is possible that portions of that cell can regrow. Regeneration refers to a process by which damaged tissue regrows connections to the area it previously innervated. Regeneration is a well-known and common occurrence in the peripheral nervous system, where both sensory and motor neurons send forth new fibers to reinnervate their previous targets. It is believed that Schwann cells, the cells that provide myelin on peripheral fibers, multiply and provide a tube or tunnel that guides the regenerating fibers to their appropriate destination. Unfortunately, the capacity of the human brain and spinal cord to repair themselves after injury in a like manner is restricted.

Another reactive process, known as sprouting, can take two forms. In one, the remaining intact processes of a partially damaged nerve increase their efficacy by growing new branches on their undamaged limbs. Collateral sprouting, the second variation, has occurred when it is neighboring neurons that grow the new processes to occupy the sites vacated by other dead or degenerated neurons. Sprouting is a likely outcome of damage in the peripheral nervous system (Edds, 1953; Lund, 1978) and there is a good possibility that similar sprouting takes place in the central nervous system (Björklund & Stenevi, 1979; Goldberger & Murray, 1974; Goodman & Horel, 1966; Liu & Chambers, 1958; Moore, Björklund &

Stenevi, 1974; Murray & Goldberger, 1974). Even though there have been demonstrations that these newly formed connections can be functional (e.g., neurochemically, electrophysiological, etc.), it has yet to be determined whether they are behaviorally relevant and, if they are, whether they actually help or hinder recovery. Sprouted connections could cause the target neuron to function abnormally and may compete with regenerating fibers and block them from reconnecting to the appropriate sites.

Denervation supersensitivity is another process that, at least on the surface, appears to compensate for a loss by making more of what is left intact. Cannon and Rosenblueth (1949) found that when some of the fibers innervating a muscle were cut, after a period of time that muscle became hyperresponsive to the application of the neurotransmitter normally supplied to it by the partially severed nerve bundle. Since a given amount of chemical input produced a greater effect after injury, the hypersensitivity is thought to result from a proliferation of receptors on the target tissue. This means that there are more receptors in a unit area available to be stimulated. Similar receptor proliferation is thought to occur in the brain. As with sprouting, the question remains about whether denervation supersensitivity is a mechanism with some adaptive or compensatory value.

After mapping the regions of the thalamus and cerebral cortex from which an evoked potential could be recorded when a rat's forelimb or hindlimb was stimulated (electrophysiological evidence that the areas are connected), Wall and Egger (1971) cut the pathway from the lower spinal cord to the brain to sever the connections with the hindlimb. Immediately after the surgery, stimulation of the limbs produced, as expected, the usual reaction of the forelimb region but no response in the hindlimb area. After 3 days, however, the region that had previously exhibited evoked potentials on stimulation of the hindlimb now showed these potentials on stimulation of the forelimb.The evoked response looked normal, as if this region had always been wired up to the forelimb. Since it generally takes between 7 and 10 days for pathways formed by sprouting to be able to transmit evoked potentials, sprouting could not account easily for this effect. It does not seem unlikely, therefore, that fibers from the forelimb were always connected to the hindlimb area but were under some form of inhibition. Once fibers from the hindlimb area were severed, the suppressing input was lost, and the area became disinhibited.

There is evidence to suggest that the disinhibited area can potentially become involved in controlling overt behavioral responses. For example, if one eye of a kitten is patched closed at birth, the cortical cells that it should normally drive are taken over by the nonoccluded eye. Later, after a critical period has elapsed and the patch removed, the cat appears completely blind in the eye that was covered. If the good eye is removed, however, the previously blind eye becomes functional. This suggests that the good eye inhibited pathways that were capable of mediating sight in the previously occluded eye (Kratz, Spear & Smith, 1976).

Findings of this nature suggest that the connections laid down in the developing nervous system are more diffuse than those actually used by the normal, intact adult. Although there is considerable overlap in innervation of various parts of the brain, specificity is maintained through inhibition. Removal of inhibition allows some takeover by the previously inhibited area. Wall (1980) has presented a strong case supporting the idea that this process of unmasking is largely responsible for much of the late recovery of function after brain injury. The release of suppressed connections is not always a good thing, however, and often can be maladaptive. Further impairment could result if the newly released activity provides a disorganizing influence by introducing surplus information the recovering nervous system is unable to handle.

The Problem of Localization

A colleague once naively stated that neuropsychologists would soon be "out of business" since the new computer-assisted imaging technology (e.g., CT, MRI) could reveal "just about any existing neural abnormality." There are several flaws in the fundamental understanding of both neuropsychology and brain–behavior relationships revealed by this statement that are directly relevant to the problems of prognosis. Many focal lesions can be visualized using one of the modern imaging techniques but the precise delineation of the complete extent of white matter damage, however, may be attainable only through post mortem microscopic examination. Alterations in the dynamic neurochemical relationships between communicating neurons can be disturbed without visible anatomical correlates. Such a view presupposes that all dysfunction is associated with visually detectable anatomical abnormalities. Cortical dysfunction, particularly widespread dysfunction, does not automatically require an identifiable cortical lesion and neuropsychologists assess function, not anatomy. Nevertheless, neuropsychological assessment often can be used to make predictions about where a lesion may be present.

Localization of the lesion, in the cases where one does indeed exist, is only one part of the neuropsychologist's problem. The aforementioned posture also assumes that determining the site of pathology yields an unambiguous revelation of its complete neurological and psychological expression. This, unfortunately, is just not the case. Often both the patient's behavior and pattern of neuropsychological test performance do not conform to textbook descriptions for a lesion of that particular area. Although the site of damage usually does determine many features of the attendant modifications of behavior, the degree, intransigence, and troublesomeness of these changes depends on a wide range of other variables. It is virtually impossible, therefore, to make much more than a rough sketch of the basic behavioral symptoms one should expect merely from knowledge of the lesion's location (Geschwind, 1974; Lezak, 1983; Smith, 1975, 1979).

Perhaps the most insidious presumption implicitly expressed by this underestimation of the discipline of neuropsychology is the notion that *all* behavioral functions can be localized in discrete areas of the brain. Undoubtedly, behavioral neuroscience holds that all behavior is, indeed, reducible to the actions of the neural substrate; but this is not the same thing. Stating that the identification of focal lesions is all one needs to know in order to predict complex behavioral manifestations seeks to raise the worst of the fallacy-ridden spirits of phrenology from a well-deserved grave. The brain is an integrated organ and many of the psychological and behavioral phenomena it produces are the result of the dynamic actions and interactions of subsets of its substance. The question of exactly what functional units of behavior can be reduced to anatomically distinct areas has not been completely answered. It is clear that many behaviors are the result of a more "diffuse" action of several connected but anatomically separate neural areas. When considering the type of test one would use appropriately to assess the condition of a function, one must try to distinguish between those functions that are localized to some discrete brain area and those that are more diffusely represented (see section on Type of Tests). Additionally, the potential for recovery is different if damage occurs to discrete brain areas performing unique functions compared to a portion of brain tissue with a role that is much less specialized and idiomorphic (see section on Location of the Lesion).

Focal Versus Diffuse Effects

Traditionally, head injury has been broadly classified as either "open" or "closed" (Adams & Victor, 1981; Haymaker, 1969). Open head injuries refer to cases wherein the vault of the skull and dural coverings are perforated. In addition to the damage caused by direct contact with the penetrating object, bone fragments from the broken skull can be driven into the brain. If the injury is caused by a high-velocity missile like a bullet, which dynamically compresses and then decompresses almost anything in its path, surrounding tissue can be disrupted by the resulting shock waves and vacuum (Adams & Victor, 1981; Grubb & Coxe, 1974; Gurdjian & Webster, 1958; Haymaker, 1969).

Closed head injury results from one or a combination of mechanical forces impinging on the brain. These include impact deceleration (the moving head strikes a fixed or solid object), linear acceleration (the head is relatively motionless and is struck by a more rapidly moving object), rotational or angular acceleration (twisting), and shearing stress. Damage usually occurs at the site of impact (coup) and at the opposite side of the brain (countercoup). The poles of the frontal and temporal lobes appear particularly vulnerable to injury during blunt head trauma because of the shape of the inner vault of the skull (Grubb & Coxe, 1974; Lampert & Hardman, 1984; Ommaya & Gennarelli, 1974; Reitan & Wolfson, 1986).

In addition to the sites of relatively localized damage, there is some degree of widespread destruction of nerve fibers (Adams, Graham, Murray & Scott, 1982; Jane, Steward & Gennarelli, 1985; Povlishock, Becker, Cheng & Vaughan, 1983; Strich, 1956, 1961). These diffuse injuries do not affect all brain structures equally and several factors determine where damage will be most concentrated. It should be noted that even the most focal injury usually entails some diffuse repercussions (Smith, 1975; Teuber, 1969). Further complicating matters is the neural destruction caused by the indirect effects of the trauma. Physiological processes like hemorrhage, edema, and infection may cause as much, if not more, destruction of brain tissue than the immediate effects of the impact (Grubb & Coxe, 1974; Jennett & Teasdale, 1981; Lezak, 1983; Plum & Posner, 1980).

At least four kinds of behavioral effects can result from head injuries. First, there is usually discrete impairment of those functions mediated by the cortex at the site(s) of the focal damage. Focal neural injury is not always restricted to the brain tissue that is located directly under the wound on the surface of the head. Often in cases where there was a great deal of momentum on impact, typical of motor vehicle accidents, deficits associated with damage at the primary site of impingement may be observed along with other deficits symptomatic of focal lesions elsewhere in the brain. As a result of coup and countercoup damage, one can expect victims of trauma situations involving significant momentum to give a pattern of test results consistent with multifocal or bilateral damage. It is not unusual for there to be no distinguishable signs of lateralization regardless of what side of the head suffered the insult (Brooks & Aughton, 1979; Bigler, 1982; Levin, Benton & Grossman, 1982).

A second pattern of specific impairments can be attributed to the fairly localized lesions of the poles of the frontal and temporal lobes which, as stated above, are particularly vulnerable to injury during trauma. Generally speaking, frontal lobe damage can result in the faulty regulation and control of activity as well as defective conceptual and problem-solving behavior. Temporal lobe involvement typically produces deficits in various aspects of memory and learning. These dysfunctions are distinguished by their relative ubiquity from the symptoms of other accident-related focal lesions that tend to be more idiosyncratic in character and depend on the particular circumstances of the accident to determine their location and form. Almost all head injuries produce some degree of frontal and temporal lobe dysfunction.

Third, as a consequence of the minute lesions scattered throughout the brain, there manifest less clearly defined disorders characterized by a general decline in complex cognitive functions including mental speed, attention, cognitive efficiency, and the ability to concentrate (Alexander, 1982; Auerbach, 1983, Lezak, 1983; Teuber, 1969, 1975). When this kind of damage is severe, high-level concept formation and complex reasoning abilities also suffer (Gronwall & Sampson, 1974; Lezak, 1983; Van Zomeren & Deelman, 1978). All of these behavioral difficulties are common among closed head injury victims (Hécaen & Albert, 1975; Lezak, 1979, 1983; Luria, 1966; Schachter & Crovitz, 1977). A person who has suffered anything more than an extremely minor traumatic brain injury rarely presents with only one of these patterns of impairment. Although it is not surprising of the most severely injured, many people with moderate damage also produce symptoms of both focal and diffuse neural dysfunction accompanied by some characteristically temporal and frontal deficits (Lezak, 1983).

Also most likely associated with damage to multiple neural foci is a fourth category of behavioral complaints that can be described as "psychiatric symptoms." Reports of disabilities in coping and in social interaction, for example, are common after head injury, but are difficult to characterize objectively or to quantify. Typically, patients are described as having either a "frontal syndrome," which seems to imply a lack of foresight and concern, irresponsibility, and a loss of insight, or a "temporal lobe syndrome," which supposedly implies irritability and hostility. (In view of the complexity of the effects of frontal and temporal lobe lesions, the use of such terms is neither recommended nor encouraged!) In addition, there appear to be two types of psychiatric syndromes known as "post-concussion syndrome" and "posttraumatic psychosis."

The post-concussional syndrome is defined by Levin, Benton, and Grossman (1982) as a constellation of somatic and psychological symptoms including headache, dizziness, fatigue, diminished concentration, memory deficit, irritability, anxiety, insomnia, hypochondriacal concern, hypersensitivity to noise, and photophobia. Most consussion victims suffer some of these symptoms immediately after the injury and it appears that more than 50% of people with mild head trauma still suffer at least one of these symptoms 6 weeks after the injury. These symptoms are more likely to be prolonged in people who have been described as "neurotic" or "anxious" before the injury. Further, the presence of such symptoms in the absence of any obvious physical symptoms is often associated with social difficulties with close relatives, who may become frustrated with the complaints.

Posttraumatic psychosis is a broad term that usually refers to depressive or manic reactions, or to any other forms of psychotic behavior. The psychotic reactions, including hallucinations or disordered thought, may result from temporal lobe seizures or from neurochemical abnormalities, either of which could result from the head trauma. Posttraumatic depression has not been well studied but it may be an appropriate reaction to serious neurologic injury, especially if there are obvious deficits such as sensory loss, dysphasia, weakness, and so forth. Further, there are likely to be feelings of helplessness in people who awaken in neurological units and who have a retrograde amnesia for the events surrounding their admission to the hospital. And, again, neurochemical changes resulting from the injury could lead to depression as well. Most postconcussional and psychotic reactions appear to subside over time, but the preinjury personality and other social factors almost certainly interact with the length and severity of the symptoms.

Because of their likelihood to affect just about every aspect of a patient's behavior, the widespread effects associated with diffuse damage often overshadow those from all but the most debilitating focal lesions (Grimm & Blighbugg, 1986). Patients frequently complain about an inability to concentrate or to perform complex mental operations. They find themselves regularly confused and frustrated by what they feel to be is their failure to do things as well as before the accident. They are more irritable and much more prone to fatigue than they remember themselves to be (Lezak, 1983). From a clinical perspective, the diffuse lesions typically resulting from closed head injury appear to be responsible for much of the prolonged disability that is associated with poor outcome.

Variables Affecting Recovery

Factors Related to the Lesion

We now return to the central problem of prognosis: What predictive value does each of the variables associated with the circumstances and dynamics of a trauma have for eventual outcome? We will first review factors relating directly to the lesion.

Severity of Lesions

Perhaps the most obvious predictor of outcome directly related to the lesion itself is the severity of the injury. It probably goes without saying that one can expect better recovery after injuries that are less severe—the more severe the injury, the less the likelihood of good recovery. The question of the best method to evaluate the severity of an injury has, by no means, received unanimous support. There are several methods for evaluating severity, however, which have received some degree of consensus.

Length of Unconsciousness

The length of time a head trauma victim remains unconscious appears inversely related to good prognosis (Gilchrist & Wilkinson, 1979; Najenson et al., 1974; Timming, Orrison & Mikula, 1982). Increased duration of loss of consciousness correlates directly with mortality (Heiskanen & Sipponen, 1970), psychosocial dependency (Gilchrist & Wilkinson, 1979; Najenson et al., 1974), and intellectual impairment (Kløve & Cleeland, 1972; Levin, Benton & Grossman, 1982; Levin, Grossman, Rose & Teasdale, 1979). Unfortunately, consciousness is not an "all or nothing" phenomenon and clinicians need a fairly regular way to estimate both the degree of impairment as well as the interval that a patient's sensibilities have been compromised.

Glasgow Coma Scale

Teasdale and Jennett (1974) have developed the Glasgow Coma Scale, a tool now widely accepted as the standard means to describe all posttraumatic conditions of altered consciousness from the mildest confusional state to deep coma. This relatively simple and brief assessment technique can be used effectively in situations even when vision or speech are impaired by factors other than altered consciousness. Furthermore, the nature of this test allows for it to be used repeatedly to monitor successive changes in a patient's status from the earliest posttrauma period of testing. The Glasgow Coma Scale comprises three response dimensions and enables the calculation of a coma score, ranging from 3 to 13. Scores of 8 or higher in the first few days after injury are considered to be predictive of good outcome (Jennett, Teasdale & Knill-Jones, 1975; Lezak, 1983). The Glasgow Coma Scale has proven also to be a good predictor of outcome in cases of coma resulting from other nontrauma-related medical conditions (Levin, et al., 1979; Plum & Caronna, 1975). One difficulty of this scale as a measure of the severity of brain injury is that up to 50% of hospital admissions who have scores indicating no coma still show significant neuropsychological sequelae of the head injury.

Duration of Posttraumatic Amnesia

Another standard means of evaluating the severity of a head injury is based on the degree of memory disturbance that results from the trauma. Specifically, an estimation is made of the length of posttraumatic amnesia (PTA). PTA is said to occur during the interval beginning when the trauma took place and ending at that point when the victim is able to consolidate new memories. If the patient was unavailable for testing while still suffering from PTA, the rough limits of this period can be approximated by estimating the time passed from the injury to the first event they can recall. If PTA is prolonged, on the other hand, one can administer standardized memory tests at regular intervals until the patient shows the ability to form new memories. Two tests that are particularly appropriate for this use are the Wechsler Memory Scale—Revised and a test with less language dependency like the picture and face recognition task designed by Artioli i Fortuny, Briggs, Newcombe, Ratcliff, and Thomas (1980) specifically to monitor PTA. Duration of PTA has a relatively long history as a measure of the general severity of head injury (Ruesch & Moore, 1943; Russell, 1932; Russell, 1971; Russell & Nathan, 1946; Smith, 1961), has been shown to correlate with length of coma (Evans, 1975), and has demonstrated its utility as a prognostic measure regarding mental, social, and vocational outcome (Jennett, Snoek, Bond & Brooks, 1981; Jennett & Teasdale, 1981; Lishman, 1968). In fact, PTA was found to be more closely associated with cognitive status 2 years after head injury than was length of coma (Brooks, Aughton, Bond, Jones & Rizvi, 1980). Interestingly, when Brooks (1974) used a recognition task to assess memory deficits after head injury, PTA was more highly correlated to performance in older (30 years or older) than in younger (16–30) patients (see section on Age).

Galveston Orientation and Amnesia Test

The Galveston Orientation and Amnesia Test (GOAT) is an assessment tool that evaluates head injury severity by incorporating measures of disrupted memory with an index of the degree of confusion produced by the trauma that is suffered by the patient. Levin, O'Donnell, and Grossman (1979) have devised this brief mental status exam by combining a series of questions relating to orientation for time, place, and person with requests for the first event the patient can remember "after injury" and the last event "before the accident." Like the Glasgow Coma Scale, this test can be used appropriately as a repeated measure to monitor progress throughout any desired time span. An early return of orientation is usually a predictive sign for good outcome, the expectation of which diminishes as the interval of disorientation becomes more prolonged (Lezak, 1983).

Skull Fracture

Surprisingly, a skull fracture can have a positive relation to good outcome (Timming et al., 1982). Although Timming and colleagues did not characterize what types of skull fracture they were examining, common sense would dictate that this sort of complication would prove beneficial only when it somehow decreases the compression damage to the brain that would normally occur in a nonyielding skull. Presumably the fracture could serve also as an outlet for relieving the increased intracranial pressure produced by edema and hemorrhage. Consistent with this hypothesis is the finding that depressed skull fracture, a condition wherein the deformity of bone would be expected to reduce practical skull volume and increase intracranial pressure, is a negative prognostic factor (Jennett et al., 1979).

Computer-Assisted Tomography

Even though CT scan abnormalities (e.g., hypodensities, hyperdensities, enlarged ventricles, etc.) have been reported to be related to poor recovery (Levin & Grossman, 1978; Timming et al., 1982), Snoek, Jennett, Adams, Graham, and Doyle (1979) found that more than a third of their patients with severe head injuries displaying marked behavioral impairment had normal CT scans. It is probable that the proportion of undetected pathology will decrease as imaging techniques become more sensitive and recent studies with magnetic resonance imaging (MRI) confirm this hypothesis. For example, Wilberger, Deeb, and Rothfus (1987) reported that, in a series of 24 patients without any evident lesion on repeated CT scans, all demonstrated lesions on MRI scans. Similarly, a parallel study by Levin et al. (1987) reported that, of 16 consecutive admissions with "minor or moderate" closed head injury, one had an abnormal CT scan whereas 14 had abnormal MRI scans. In sum, the conclusion appears inescapable that even mild head trauma may be associated with some pathology.

Focal Neurologic Symptoms

Immediate behavioral effects of trauma that can be detected by a comprehensive neurological exam are also useful for forming a prognosis. The presence of various focal neurologic symptoms, such as hemiparesis, aphasia, hemianopsia, and occulovestibular deficits is more likely to occur when the injury is severe and is related to poorer outcome than what can be expected in cases when these signs are not present (Gilchrist & Wilkinson, 1979; Levin et al., 1979; Najenson et al., 1974).

Location of the Lesion

The location of the lesion is predictive of recovery insofar as the site of the damage is a major determinant of the type of deficit one can anticipate. As we discussed, the behavioral manifestations of brain injury can take both focal and diffuse forms. There are significant differences in how much eventual reduction of overt impairment can be expected even when the injury is relatively localized and the resulting behavioral deficit is what would be considered focal. Since the extent of direct neurological recovery is limited, the possibilities of adaptation are restricted largely by the nature of the function disrupted.

First-order modality-specific defects, like scotomata or achromatopsia, can result from lesions in primary sensory or unimodel association cortex.

In these cases one cannot count on much more restitution of function after the first year after the injury. Little, if anything, can be done to compensate directly for the experienced loss of sensation. An additional, but by no means less important, dimension of the impact a deficit of this type has on the patient's life is measured by the level of frustration produced from dealing with reduced sensory input. For example, the annoying and distracting presence of a new scotoma or blindspot in one's visual field can interfere with the facility and desire to read. The magnitude of the defect is related directly to how likely and quickly a person will habituate to their loss. Also important to compensation, but far more difficult to measure, is the amount of determination available in the character of the affected person that can be dedicated to the effort to get used to and overcome the impediment. Generally speaking, however, defects that limit but do not devastate a person's ability to function in a particular sensory domain are related to better overall outcome than those with a widespread debilitating influence on other behaviors.

When higher order processing is disrupted or processing components are disconnected, often the consequence of damage to unimodal and/or heteromodal association cortex, the resulting deficits are usually complex and much more idiosyncratic. Patients with this type of disorder may develop a modality-specific amnesia or an agnosia. On one hand, disturbances of this nature are much more suited to behavioral compensation (see below) than are pure sensory deficits because people are able to use alternate strategies for problem solving. The deficit remains but the affected person learns new ways to work around their particular impediment and achieve the same ultimate goals. Even though the overt manifestation of this particular type of brain damage eventually may appear minimal, the real, lasting impact on day-to-day functioning should not be underestimated. Recuperation is not based on habituation but depends on reeducation and the persistent effort to make the new way of doing things as automatic as possible. Unfortunately, the prosthetic processes are rarely, if ever, as efficient or easy as the original, undisrupted manner of performing a task.

Etiology of the Lesion

Recovery and prognosis depend to some degree on how the damage to the brain is caused. As a broad rule of thumb, the tissue loss associated with most survivable head trauma is usually less extensive than that affected in strokes. Since the more expansive damage is, the poorer the prognosis, adults who have had a head injury generally show better recovery than those with a cerebrovascular accident. For example, patients with posttraumatic aphasia recover better than patients with aphasia after stroke (Butfield & Zangwill, 1946; Godfrey & Douglass, 1959; Luria,

1970; Marks, Taylor & Rusk, 1957; Wepman, 1951). More than half of the posttraumatic cases of aphasia showed complete recovery.

There is a caveat, however, to this generalization: In some studies age and the magnitude of lesion were confounding variables (Kertesz, 1985; Kertesz & McCabe, 1977). Although the scatter was considerable, the mean age of the patients with traumatic aphasia was younger. In addition, the extent and severity of lesions in the trauma group were more variable than those of the stroke victims. Even in cases where there was an equivalent degree of initial impairment, however, instances of dramatic spontaneous recovery, such as the amelioration of a global aphasia to a mild anomic state, took place after closed head injury but not after cerebrovascular accidents.

It is likely that entire functional systems are removed by strokes because they damage large areas of the brain, both cortically and subcortically, that are anatomically related and subserved by a common branch of the blood supply. Damage from traumatic injuries, on the other hand, are usually more random, diffuse, and less complete and are apt to spare some parts of many areas. In many cases a small residual part of a system is capable of mediating substantial recovery. For example, a patient has been described in whom only 17% of the pyramidal tract was sufficient to allow nearly normal reestablishment of motor ability (Kolb & Whishaw, 1985b).

Surgical excisions and penetrating head wounds caused by low velocity objects can be expected to be associated with better prognosis than closed head injury and stroke because the potential for rehabilitation is greater if the lesions are clean, complete, and result primarily from the simple removal of neural matter. Injuries that leave little or no diseased tissue behind are less conducive to repercussions on other, anatomically unrelated functions (Lezak, 1983; Newcombe, 1969; Teuber, 1969). Many behavioral neuroscientists have espoused the tenet that "no brain is better than a bad brain" and it seems clear that the functional impairments associated with the residual, active-but-malfunctioning, diseased or damaged tissue, such as that ensuing from strokes or closed head injuries, tend to result in behavioral aberrations involving other functions. These repercussions can extend to high level cognitive processes and frequently also affect personality (Deutsch, 1960; Diller, 1973; Weiskrantz, 1968). Furthermore, "bad brain" frequently forms the focus of epileptic seizures, which have both social and cognitive repercussions.

Factors Relating to the Victim

Age

Another widely held maxim, generally referred to as the Kennard principle (Kennard, 1936, 1940), states that the younger an organism is when an injury takes place, the more likely and complete the potential recovery. There is no doubt that many studies have illustrated how age can exacerbate the impact of a brain injury. For instance, at 1 year posttrauma, Najenson and colleagues discovered just more than half of their patients 45 years of age or older were still classified as significantly dependent compared to 12% of younger patients (Najenson et al., 1974; Najenson, Groswasser, Mendelson & Hackett, 1980). In a like manner, Timming et al. (1982) reported that 69% of their patients aged 16 to 20 years were able to achieve functional independence compared to 43% of patients aged 21 to 40 years and 33% of patients aged 41 to 55 years. Miller et al. (1981) found a similar increase in mortality and decrease in "good recovery" with older patients, although the frequency of vegetative outcome was not found to be related to age.

Is the poorer prognosis ascribed to older trauma victims merely a direct result of a reduced capacity for resilience? Or, are there processes involved that tend to obscure the full expression of actual recovery? It should be remembered that the incidence of spontaneously occurring brain lesions (e.g., those resulting from stroke, tumors, etc.) increases with the age of the population observed. The presence of any such abnormality is more than likely to have a detrimental effect on potential recovery. In addition, those in the older age groups may be exhibiting natural declines in motor and cognitive function due to the normal processes of aging. Thus, when one uses improvements in performance measures to define recovery in an aged population, true progress may tend to be masked.

Increased age is often thought to be associated with a greater probability of cognitive deficits, psychiatric sequelæ, and the impairment of various other capacities (Adler, 1945; Brooks, 1972, 1974; Jennett et al., 1975; Russell, 1932; Teuber 1975). Confoundingly, youthfulness, defined as being under 25 years old, has also been associated with greater cognitive impairment resulting from head trauma (Jurko, 1979). This and other pieces of a growing body of evidence suggest that the Kennard principle does not always hold true (Kolb & Fantie, 1989; Kolb & Whishaw, 1985a). Knowing how old a person is at the time of their injury does not really give the neuropsychologist anything but the broadest index for making a prognosis. For example, when severity is not taken into account, it is difficult to make any sort of consistent differentiation using age as a predictor of outcome for traumatically injured patients classified as young to middle-age adults (Gilchrist & Wilkinson, 1979; Lezak, 1979, 1983). Evidence is now accumulating to suggest that even in young children there are marked differences in outcome of early head injuries that are related to precise age and extent of injury. In particular, it appears that prenatal damage or damage in the first year of life may be associated with poor brain development and severe behavioral loss. In contrast, damage later in early childhood (2–5 years) may allow significant reorganization of function and does not disturb brain development as younger injuries do (e.g., Kolb & Fantie, 1989). A complicating factor in prognosis is that many symptoms of early injuries do not appear until well into adolescence, making it difficult to make predictions in children.

Relocation of Function—Costs

At the other end of the chronological continuum, the applicability of the Kennard principle depends on the breadth of one's vision. When one looks at how one particular function survives disruption of its putative neural substrate, the prevailing evidence seems compelling; in both animals and humans, infants show more rapid and more complete recovery of a particular function than when sustaining comparable damage later in life (Kennard, 1936, 1940). This functional revivescence has been attributed to the greater plasticity of the immature nervous system. Plasticity, in this case, is operationally defined as the ability to transfer the function subserved by a destroyed or incapacitated site to some other location.

Despite the preponderance of experimental literature and case studies citing enhanced functional recovery in infants, the general statement that injuries in infancy are less disruptive is shortsighted. There is a major flaw in the way this conclusion is reached. Almost invariably the location of the lesion is known, either because it is created by the experimenter in the case of the animal research or it has been diagnosed by some other means in the human clinical setting. This bit of knowledge focuses attention on the specific function associated with that neural site. Further reinforcing this tunnel vision, in many cases, is the fact that this is usually the only behavior in which there are immediate and dramatic changes caused by the injury. The faulty assumption is then made that all other functions are normal and unaffected, and will remain so, because either they are not subserved by the damaged tissue or they appear relatively normal immediately after the insult.

So, for example, if a baby has a left hemisphere lesion, it is not unlikely that the development and performance of behaviors typically ascribed to the left hemisphere, particularly language because of its significance to vocational, social, and academic achievement, will be scrupulously monitored to the almost complete exclusion of other forms of left hemisphere function as well as those correlated with the undamaged right hemisphere. We are thus encouraged by reports supporting the fairly accurate but unqualified prediction that the recovery from acquired aphasia will be excellent in children who are injured before the age of 12 years (e.g., Basser, 1962; Hécaen, 1976). This is based on the observation that their language deficits are usually short-lived and there is almost total restoration of conversational speech. When Milner (1974) tested patients who had damaged left frontal lobes from childhood injuries, she often observed that there had been a shift in language representation to the right hemisphere. Nevertheless, she found these people to be impaired at the performance of other tests of frontal lobe function such as the Wisconsin Card Sorting Test. We have seen similar results in a small sample of patients who suffered unilateral frontal lobe injuries in childhood (largely head trauma and birth injury) when we used the Chicago Word Fluency Test and a test of copying facial movement sequences (see Kolb & Milner, 1981, for details of this test).

Still using the recovery of language as a focus, we propose the following generalizations from the studies of children who have suffered unilateral brain damage. Language commonly survives a left hemisphere injury incurred during infancy. If the child is 5 years of age or younger and the damage involves both the left frontal and temporal language areas, there is a good possibility that language function will shift to the right hemisphere. If, however, the lesion is restricted to either the anterior or posterior speech zone, only the language function subserved by the affected area is likely to shift, thus leading to bilateral speech representation. Most importantly, when language shifts to the right hemisphere it is not without a price. The most common consequence of the relocation of language function to the right hemisphere is an impairment of visuospatial ability. It should be noted that these functions are not usually adversly affected when the damage occurs later in life. Similar injuries that occur after 5 years of age rarely alter speech representation and it is assumed that any observed recovery is mediated by some sort of intrahemispheric reorganization.

There is growing evidence that brain damage during the first year of life, a period when tremendous changes in brain morphology take place, may actually have more severe consequences than similar damage later. When an injury takes place before the child's first birthday, their Verbal and Performance IQ scores are consistently below the mean of their uninjured age peers. In contrast, the effects of lesions after the first birthday depend on which side of the brain is damaged. Left-hemisphere lesions are associated with lower Verbal and Performance IQ scores whereas right-hemisphere lesions appear to affect adversely only the Performance IQ score. Thus, even when recuperation from injuries in infancy or early childhood may appear complete for many specific verbal skills, more global assessments of cognitive status suggest that the recovery is often accompanied by new deficits that affect other functions. When one adopts a more comprehensive approach to behavioral examination, there is little doubt that this apparent sparing of function is not without some cost (Fletcher, Levin & Landry, 1984; Kolb & Fantie, 1989; Milner, 1974; Rasmussen & Milner, 1975, 1977; St. James-Roberts, 1981; Taylor, 1984; Teuber, 1975; Woods, 1980; Woods & Teuber, 1973).

Gender

Anatomical evidence is accumulating to demonstrate that sex hormones have an organizing effect on brain development leading to significant differences in the anatomical organization of the male and female brain. Obviously, the way in which a function is localized in the neural substrate will determine to a large extent how the behavior mediated by that area will be affected by an injury. Evidence from neuropsychological research with normal individuals suggests that the neural structure of the two sexes is not functionally homologous (Bryden, 1979; Buffery & Gray, 1972; Hannay, 1976; Harris, 1978; Witelson, 1976). There are sex differences in the patterns of cerebral organization, particularly the degree of lateralization of verbal and visuospatial functions to the left and right hemispheres, respectively. This hemispheric specialization tends to be more pronounced for males. A lesion of some given size would be less likely to destroy a specific functional unit completely if that unit was represented diffusely, especially if the representation extended into both hemispheres. One would predict, therefore, a woman should be less profoundly affected than a man by a similar brain lesion. This appears to be the case. For example, after unilateral brain damage, men tend to show deficits in functions associated with the side of lesion that are more concentrated and conspicuous than those of women with similar lesions (Harris, 1978; Lezak, 1983; McGlone, 1976; Piazza, 1980). Similarly, there is recent evidence that the pattern of intrahemispheric organization may differ in men's and women's brains (Kimura, 1987), a difference that would also influence the prognosis for recovery.

Handedness

Variations in degree of cerebral lateralization are also associated with handedness. So, for much the same reason as gender, handedness may influence the outcome of brain damage. Familial left-handers are thought to be less lateralized in function than right-handers and are more likely to have language function in both hemispheres. Consequently, it is more likely that brain injury will result in some form of aphasias in left-handers but these disturbances are typically less severe and more likely to improve than aphasias in right-handers (Geschwind, 1974; Gloning, Gloning, Haub & Quatember, 1969; Kertesz, 1985; Piazza, 1980). In addition, Kertesz (1985) reported better recovery in global aphasics who had atypical occipital-frontal torques and width: anatomical correlates of a more bilateral or reverse distribution of language function than is typical of normal right-handers.

Premorbid Level of Function

Intellect

Perhaps one of the best (and certainly one of the most often quoted) rules of thumb for the neuropsychologist who must assess traumatic brain damage is that "it is not only the kind of injury that matters, but the kind of head" (Symonds, 1937). Weinstein and Teuber (1957a, 1957b), who had one of the rare benefits of wartime, being able to test soldiers at induction, before trauma, and retest subsequent to injury, found that on the Army General Classification Test the more intelligent or the more educated people were, the larger the demonstrable loss in their scores after brain damage. Even with this apparent difference in degree of decrement, the achievement in intellectual pursuits after brain damage still tends to be directly related to the prior intellectual capacity of the victim (Chapman, Thetford, Berlin, Guthrie & Wolff, 1958; Dresser et al., 1973; Hillbom, 1960). Obviously a person is much more likely to function adequately in day-to-day situations if their posttraumatic, residual capacity is within the "normal" range, a condition much more likely, despite larger apparent losses, in those with a higher starting status. For both groups, however, not being able to do things as quickly and easily as before the injury and the loss of the potential to actualize premorbid goals and ambitions can be expected to have direct significance on psychological well-being and rehabilitative efforts.

Self-report may be helpful as a sign that there has been an alteration in a patient's ability to do things. This method is by no means perfect. One must exercise caution in weighing the testimony of those whose sensitivity has been altered by the circumstances of having been directly involved in a traumatic injury or being closely connected to someone who has suffered one. Unfortunately, one of the consequences in the aftermath of a tragedy of this type is often a decrease in the threshold of deciding what is considered an abnormality. This produces an increase in the tendency to interpret the troughs in the normal variance of performance as a new problem originating from the injury. Seeking confirmation of altered performance from those who have considerable personal contact with the patient can provide a moderate check against which the patient's self-report may be measured; but, as we have said, their perceptions may also be altered by the experience. In contrast, there are patients whose severe injuries have limited their capacity for self-awareness and self-evaluation, a possible complication of extensive frontal lobe damage. They can appear quite untroubled by their radically compromised performance and still express intentions to return to work, fly airplanes, or enter a high-skill profession despite the most conspicuous cognitive or motor impairment. (Lezak, 1983). Ideally, premorbid performance on the neuropsychological measures would provide the best unambiguous baseline against which to gauge change. Since this is rarely available, the neuropsychologist can use academic and vocational achievements to estimate premorbid aptitude.

Lack of information about the premorbid level of functioning is less a problem for prognsosis than it is for providing insight into how patients have been affected by their loss. The neuropsychologist may underestimate the impact of an injury when faced with a patient who produces scores on standardized tests that are within the normal limits of the victim's age peers. Although useful when making a prediction of the potential for future accomplishment, these scores must be considered relative to the premorbid status when an estimation of the magnitude of the deficit is attempted both for diagnosis and compensation purposes. Without a measure of the premorbid level of performance, the neuropsychologist may erroneously conclude that the seemingly "normal" test scores are an indication that only extremely minor or, possibly, no posttraumatic consequences have occurred. Similarly, if the patient's development in different abilities is grossly skewed and the brain injury affects primarily their area of strength, the neuropsychologist may underrate or miss altogether the patient's deficit based on a profile of average-looking test results with little intertest variability (Adams, Boake & Crain, 1982; Lezak, 1983). Clearly, a normal set of test scores does not confirm that no change has taken place and anyone arriving at such a conclusion would be making a fundamental logical error in confusing absence of evidence with evidence of absence. Furthermore, factors other than brain damage can produce significant test score scatter. Differential performance can result from situations where the patient's background provided large discrepancies in the occasions for learning various skills and their subsequent practice (Lezak, 1983).

Socioeconomic Status

One of the most influential factors in determining the number and quality of people's opportunities is the socioeconomic stratum in which they are situated. Developmental and other childhood disorders are much more common in persons who have been raised in deprived conditions. Deprivation can be defined as the lack of sufficient medical care, an inadequate diet, or a paucity of environmental stimulation. Any of these situations can adversely affect brain function (Amante, VanHouten, Grieve, Bader & Margules, 1977; Winick, 1976). Early impoverishment seems to have long-lasting consequences and people with histories of this type tend to be less resilient to brain damage even if the injury is incurred in adulthood (Jennett et al., 1975).

Culture

Prevailing attitude and the capacity to understand fully the implications of one's condition are a direct function of not only the patient's educational background but of social and cultural influences as well. Errors of both overinclusion (false positives) and overexclusion (false negatives) can befall examining neuropsychologists who fail to consider that these factors can alter a patient's test performance (Adams et al., 1982; Anastasi, 1982; Loehlin, Lindzey & Spuhler, 1975; Vernon, 1979). For example, some subcultures may place so much emphasis on academic accomplishment that their members often defer opportunities to become involved in physical activities and, by so doing, will likely fail to develop their motor skills to a level anywhere comparable to that of their scholastic expertise. This potential deficiency in hand-eye coordination and manual dexterity may prove detrimental to the successful execution of tasks involving hand skills and may produce a large disparity between verbal and visuoconstructional test scores (Backman, 1972). From our experience with some native North American patients in southern Alberta, we have learned that a seemingly dismal failure on any task requiring verbal or writing skills may be more a reflection of differences in cultural values and pedagogical experience than a true indication of language difficulty after brain injury. Furthermore, for many natives English remains a second language and since our verbal tests are in English (and most native languages are exclusively oral) one must interpret apparent language difficulties with considerable caution.

Personality

At the individual level, a person's premorbid personal and social adjustment can guide predictions about the rate and degree of progress after brain damage as well as the quality of the ultimate adjustment (Gloning, Gloning & Hoff, 1968; Symonds & Russell, 1943; Walker & Jablon, 1959). Rather than radically change personality, although instances of drastic alteration have been reported, brain injury seems more often to exaggerate the existing premorbid features of the victim's character (Andersen, 1950; Lishman, 1973). One can easily see how the amplification of certain peculiarities or peccadilloes could prove maladaptive to rehabilitation. If the premorbid personality is not handicapped by tendencies to dependent behavior, hypochondriasis, passivity, perfectionism, irresponsibility, or other behavioral aberrations, a much better prognosis can be offered (Lezak, 1983). On the other side of the coin, patients with a history of psychiatric disturbance before head injury have an increased risk of persistent or chronic disability (Hillbom, 1960; Symonds & Russell, 1943). The victim's premorbid personality and social adjustment typically determine the depth and breadth of the reservoir of reliable, emotionally stable, and mature allies usually composed of family members and friends, from whom the handicapped patient can receive emotional and moral reinforcement (Lezak, 1983). One of the best predictors of outcome after a debilitating injury is the quality of the social support system the victim has outside of the institutional setting.

Pending Litigation

One aspect of a patient's posttraumatic situation, treated with more than a respectable degree of cynicism by many clinicians, unfortunately, is whether or not the circumstances of the injury have produced a court action. It is sometimes presumed when there are no visible signs of significant tissue damage that persisting complaints and other symptoms dependent on a subjective report represent a psychogenic reaction to the trauma or an exacerbation of a previous neurotic condition (Guttman, 1946; Levin et al., 1982; Lishman, 1973; Miller, 1961). The popular mythology has come to view this behavior as directly or indirectly motivated to aid in the attempt to recover monetary damages when litigation is pending and that the symptoms mysteriously vanish when the case is settled. Significantly, there is a great deal of correspondence across patients in the type and nature of their complaints. Symptoms typically include frequent headaches, dizzy spells, greater susceptibility to fatigue, memory trouble, decreased ability to concentrate, increased irritability, anxiety, insomnia, undue concern about bodily functions, and hypersensitivity to both light and noise (Lewin, 1968; Lishman, 1978; Reitan & Wolfson, 1986).

In addition to the similarity in complaints, there are other points that should be considered before yielding to the tendency to trivialize information with a direct bearing on the patient's well-being and rehabilitative progress. As we discussed earlier, clinical neurological examination, including imaging techniques, do not always reveal objective evidence of tissue damage, particularly in cases of concussion. Contrary to the beliefs of many, not being able to find something does not actually prove that nothing is there. Various studies have questioned the notion that pending litigation results in increased complaints. Merskey and Woodforde (1972) divided a series of postconcussion patients into two groups: one composed of people who had either no claims or claims that had already been settled and the other group made up of those whose cases were still before the court. The quality and quantity of subjective symptoms reported by both groups were comparable. Rimel et al., (1981) reported that pending litigation had a negligible effect, if any, on the level of adjustment achieved by head injury patients, thereby contradicting any suggestion that litigants are delaying their progress by fraudulently producing additional complications. One interesting observation leads us to our final point concerning the putative side effect of legal complications. Brooks (unpublished, cited in Lezak, 1983) stated that, rather than presenting more symptoms or deficits than similar patients who do not have compensation claims, those seeking compensation for their injuries tend to complain more than other patients. We have always been struck by the assumption that the litigation is responsible for the persistence of complaints; is it not just as likely to expect that those people whose discomfort and deficits are, in fact, persistent will be more likely to adopt legal recourse when available and less likely to be deterred or discouraged by the effort and time investment required to win a court battle?

Factors Related to the Relevant Behavior

Neuropsychologists need to consider the nature of the behavior they are examining and the way it has been affected by brain damage in order to optimize diagnosis, prognosis, and therapy. From what we know about the costs of the relocation of function that sometimes occurs in traumatized developing nervous systems, it is crucial to not take too narrow a view of an injury's behavioral sphere of influence (see section on Type of Tests). For many reasons, some obvious and others unknown, the expectancy of recovery differs with different behaviors. One must also define what exactly is meant by "recovery of function." Since full restitution of function to its original intact level after brain injury is highly unlikely, how much improvement from the immediate postmorbid state must take place in order to be considered recovery? Again, this will depend to a large extent on the particular behavior in question and the way it is measured.

Behavioral Compensation

Behavioral compensation explains recovery from a functional perspective. In contrast to physiological processes that might effect restitution of function by rerouting connections or replacing lost tissue, the impaired organism actually bypasses its deficits by developing alternate ways to accomplish goals that rely on processes mediated by the residual structures. Sperry (1947) has described some examples of tricks and alternate maneuvers employed by brain-damaged humans to compensate for difficulties arising from their defects. As we stated earlier, the adult human brain does not have the capacity for complete functional regeneration at the neuronal level. Therefore, the general rule is that restitution is unlikely for highly specific functions mediated by localized brain areas if that entire area is destroyed. When the measure of recovery is a complex skill, however, comprised of many components, the apparent improvements in performance may be extensive because there are many strategies available for obtaining the same end. Thus, it is commonly expected that impaired general performance will improve over time while more specific, localizable deficits will persist (Kolb & Whishaw, 1985b; Newcombe, 1969). Language and constructional disorders are good candidates to show significant improvement from behavioral compensation. Visual blind spots or reduced tactile sensitivity, however, will persist unchanged indefinitely (Teuber, 1975).

We shall now look at some of the variables predictive of outcome associated with three major complex behaviors, executive function, memory, and language, of particular interest to the clinician and relevant to the patient's everyday life. More accurately, these behaviors should be thought of as functional categories since they comprise many dissociable behavioral elements. The relative capacity for compensation after brain injury for each component or group of components forming a functional unit is directly related to the uniqueness of that unit's specific contribution to the manifest behavior. It is not our intent to describe the full range of behavioral deficits associated with brain injury, a task obviously beyond the scope of this chapter (the interested reader should refer to Kolb & Whishaw, 1985b for a review). Instead, we will use these important functions to organize some clues available to the neuropsychologist that may help predict the probability of recovery of that specific behavior and, in some cases, other functions as well.

Executive Functions

The term "executive functions" has been adopted to designate a group of processes that enable people to act independently and in a purposeful manner guided by their own self-interest (Lezak, 1983). To date, little is understood about the underlying mechanisms that mediate this group of behaviors. They sometimes are referred to, however, as "frontal" functions because damage to the frontal lobes often produces a cluster of deficits that seems to reflect a diminished capacity to control and direct behavior even though cognitive processes (language, memory, mathematical ability, etc.) are left relatively intact. Although the frontal lobes clearly play a special role in generating these behaviors, the neural substrate of executive function is likely distributed diffusely since it is also often the case that deficits of this nature can arise from brain damage occurring just about anywhere and the magnitude of the impairment is usually directly proportional to the amount of brain tissue destroyed.

Intact executive functions are especially important to behavioral recovery. No matter how well preserved the faculties of higher cognition are, people with impaired self-control or self-direction will have difficulties taking care of themselves on a daily basis. Characteristic behavioral manifestations can take either of two extremes: the patient may be recklessly impulsive or have a drastically reduced capacity to initiate or modify activity. Compounding the problem, these people display behavior that has been attributed to profoundly lowered or absent motivation (abulia) as well as show defects in planning and executing behavioral sequences (Hécaen & Albert, 1975; Lezak, 1984; Luria, 1966; Walsh, 1978a). Frequently these patients will fail to maintain normal social relationships in light of the accompanying flattening of affect, emotional lability, and increased irritability. On the other hand, despite a severe cognitive incapacitation, individuals with intact executive functions still have the ability to act in their best interest by being self-motivated and constructively productive (Lezak, 1983). Because of their propensity to retard the rehabilitative process, deficits in executive functions are associated with a poorer prognosis.

Memory

Memory difficulties are probably the most frequently reported consequence of traumatic brain injury. One can attribute this to the fact that the ability to remember things is such a pervasive part of everyday life. In fact, because the difficulties they encounter in this area seem so conspicuous, many patients may feel that their memory problems are their major impairment. Memory deficits, unless unusually severe as in the case of global amnesia, are rarely as debilitating as compromised executive functions (Brooks & Aughton, 1979; Lezak, 1983; Oddy, Humphrey & Uttley, 1978b). Because the term "memory" really refers to a wide range of behavioral entities subserved by different combinations of separate and interacting neural processes, memory difficulties resulting from brain injury can take many forms (Gronwall & Wrightson, 1981; Schachter & Crovitz, 1977). Not only will the exact nature of how mnemonic ability is altered be largely idiosyncratic, but the time course of recovery will also differ from individual to individual (Lezak, 1983).

When memory is affected by unilateral damage, deficits in either the ability to retrieve memories or the ability to create and store them usually affect one modality more than another. In other words, one person will have trouble learning new words or other verbal material while retaining the ability to remember visuospatial stimuli such as pictures. Another person, with the injury in the opposite hemisphere, may have it the other way around. Amelioration of these types of memory deficits is usually tied to the potential for recovery of the patient's general verbal or visuospatial functioning and one should expect them to improve in parallel. Improvement in these complex processes can be expected to be quite slow. Putative memory problems also can stem from a chronic posttraumatic attentional dysfunction associated with extensive frontal or subcortical damage. The resulting inability to concentrate on the task at hand or the apathetic reluctance to initiate retrieval, in actuality an executive function deficit, should not be confused with a true memory impairment since therapeutic and rehabilitative strategies will have to be different. Improvements in these cases can be quite small and, if they are to occur, will do so fairly soon after the patient regains consciousness (Gronwall & Sampson, 1974; Lezak, 1978, 1983). True memory disorders may, to some extent, be more receptive to behavioral compensation depending on the propensity for developing effective alternative mnemonic devices. For example, a patient whose difficulty lies with verbal material may use visual associations, in effect, storing and retrieving the words in pictorial form.

Although in most cases retrograde amnesias associated with the period before the trauma are very short (i.e., durations that can be measured in seconds), when significantly longer they generally resolve in a progressive manner in reverse chronological order with more recent memories returning first. For example, Barbizet (1970) reported that, in the case of a 40-year-old man who had suffered a head trauma and had been comatose for 7 weeks, the envelope for amnesia, extending back in time from when the trauma took place, shrank from 2 years to 1 year to 2 weeks over successive examinations that took place at 5, 8 and 16 months, respectively. This temporal pattern is not always rigidly adhered to, especially in cases of less severe injury (Whitty & Zangwill, 1966). In other cases, islands of memory exist throughout the sea of mnemonic void that eventually expand or multiply and connect until they form larger masses that fill the gap of lost experience.

Language

In the usual course of events, residual language deficits tend to reflect the severity of the injury, particularly the extent of damage to the dominant hemisphere, which, in most cases, is the left. Some language components appear to be more resistant to brain damage than others. In cases where the language centers are not directly damaged and the acute symptoms have resolved, it is not unusual for even the severely injured head trauma patient to have little difficulty with overpracticed behaviors such as reading, writing, and speech and perform at normal levels on verbal tests that involve overlearned material. The ability to name people and objects, repeat words orally, comprehend nouns, and respond appropriately to a yes-or-no type question usually remains relatively intact. This functional immunity apparently afforded to such fundamental features of language is probably because of the great amount of practice a person has performing behaviors of this type or, as others have suggested, because the underlying processes are mediated bilaterally with the nondominant, usually right, hemisphere also playing some sort of role in their execution (Kertesz, 1979). Conversely, one of the most common symptoms of brain damage manifesting in language is a difficulty with word retrieval (dysnomia). Much to the consternation of the patient, these problems frequently persist after other verbal behaviors have been fully restored or have reached near normal levels (Levin, Grossman, Sarwar & Meyers, 1981; Lezak, 1983).

There have been reports stating that some types of aphasia improve more quickly than others but problems emerging from inconsistency of classification between studies have produced conflicting conclusions (Head, 1926; Kertesz, 1985). For example, researchers have suggested that expressive (Broca's) aphasias are associated with both the most improvement (Butfield & Zangwill, 1946; Kertesz & McCabe, 1977; Messerli, Tissot & Rodriguez, 1976; Weisenburg & McBride, 1935) and the least (Vignolo, 1964). Still others have failed to detect any difference between the recovery rates of fluent and nonfluent aphasic patients (Basso, Faglioni & Vignolo, 1975). Perhaps a great part of the difficulty in producing an opposite dichotomization of the aphasias ensues from the fact that there is an expressive component in many of the different kinds of aphasias including those typically categorized as receptive (Kertesz, 1985).

As the patient recovers, the characteristics of the aphasic disorder generally change in stages after a fairly predictable course ranging from global aphasia to anomic aphasia. Patients whose aphasia is predominantly fluent (Wernicke's), however, do not turn into pure nonfluent (Broca's) aphasics (Basso, Capitani & Zanobio, 1982). This is not surprising considering the distinct differences in the location of the anatomical substrate associated with these two types of language dysfunction. During the first 3 months after the injury, the patient will show the greatest degree of improvement. Progress should continue at a diminished rate over the next 6 months and reach asymptote during the next 6 months, after which little recovery can be expected. Restitution of function is generally faster and typically more complete in posttraumatic head injury victims compared to stroke patients. Younger people sometimes show better recovery and there is a slight possibility intelligence, occupation, and sex will have a modest effect on outcome (Kertesz, 1979, 1985). There is excellent prognosis for recovery from aphasias produced by anterior lesions that present either without accompanying hemiparesis or, if present, a paralysis that proves transient (Benson &Geschwind, 1985).

Psychosocial Outcome

Virtually any alteration of central nervous system activity can change an individual's personality. Impairments of movement, language, or perception not only determine to a large extent how an individual behaves, but how they are perceived by others and, in turn, how they see themselves. Head trauma frequently causes a change in disposition or personality, especially when there is damage to the frontal or temporal lobes (Blumer & Benson, 1975; Gulbrandsen, 1984; Levin & Eisenberg, 1979; Tabaddor, Mattis & Zazula, 1984; van Zomeren & van den Burg, 1985). Abnormal personality and affect frequently result in difficult patients, both with regard to medical and psychological treatments as well as rehabilitative efforts. In the long run, even subtle personality disturbances will hamper the patient's ability to reestablish psychological and social independence more than will a cognitive impairment or physical disability (Bond, 1975; Jennett, 1975b; Jennett et al., 1981; Oddy et al., 1978a, 1978b).

The presence or absence of depression can serve indirectly as a useful prognostic indicator. Most adults who suffer sufficient brain damage to produce symptoms become depressed, usually within the first year after their injury (Brooks & Aughton, 1979; Lezak, 1978; Lezak, Cosgrove, O'Brien, & Wooster, 1980; Lishman, 1978). The depth of the depressive reaction and how long it is likely to last varies a great deal between patients. A spectrum of factors interact ranging from the neurological details of the brain damage to the patient's social and personal resources (Merskey & Woodforde, 1972; Ross & Rush, 1981). Although some people remain chronically depressed and, in extreme cases, may become suicidal (Buck, 1968), over time most find that the depression resolves or drastically reduces in intensity (Dikmen & Reitan, 1977). Inversely, when a person has sustained a profound, permanent disability yet claims not to be experiencing any depression at all, the probability of a good rehabilitative outcome is significantly diminished. The absence of some sort of depressive reaction is a clear indication that the patient has a reduced capacity for self-appreciation and reality-testing, or has maladaptively adopted denial as a way of dealing with the situation (Reitan & Wolfson, 1985). Successful rehabilitation programs rely on the patient's ability to cooperate; a process necessarily guided by the fairly realistic comprehension of strengths and limitations.

Different major criteria define a successful social outcome for people from different age brackets of the general population. Scholastic achievement serves as the prime measure of psychosocial recovery for children. For younger adults, who compose the vast majority of head trauma patients, it is the return to gainful employment. For those beyond the traditional optimal years of productivity, the relevant dimension along which to judge psychosocial outcome is the degree of independence and self-care the individual is capable of since this will ultimately determine whether or not the patient can return home or must be restricted to a chronic care facility (Lezak, 1983).

Scholastic Achievement

We have found that performance on the Wechsler Intelligence Scale (WISC–R or WAIS–R, depending on the age of the child), particularly Verbal IQ, is usually a good correlate of success in school. Klonoff, Crockett, and Clark (1984) examined children annually for 5 years and reported that IQ was significantly lower in those who had suffered a head injury compared to matched controls. The difference between groups was greatest during the initial posttraumatic assessment and the 1-year follow-up. Using *post hoc* methods to determine which of the measures they employed were related to the existence of neurological sequelae in children 5 years after traumatic brain damage, this group found Full Scale IQ to be by far the best predictor, followed by the period of unconsciousness and duration of posttraumatic amnesia. Posttraumatic IQ, therefore, cannot be used to match subjects in studies comparing performance on other neuropsychological measures without fear of reducing the sensitivity of the instrument and artificially diminishing the apparent impact of the injury on the proband group.

Employment and Recreation

Overall, there are two general trends in the number of people who return to full-time employment after head injury. The proportion of those employed increases as time elapses after the injury and persons with penetrating wounds are more likely to be working as opposed to those who have suffered blunt head trauma (Grimm & Blighbugg, 1986). The ability to hold a job, however, is not a sensitive index of recovery and employment rates (some as high as 80–90%) can be misleading (Dresser et al., 1973; Oddy & Humphrey, 1980). When most moderate to severely-injured victims of head trauma reenter the work force, they must settle for lower status jobs with demands necessarily set below those of their premorbid work capacity (Lezak, et al., 1980; Weddell, Oddy & Jenkins, 1980). Notably, in a domain with less latitude for alternative levels of existence, few students who have sustained severe head injuries ever resume their studies (Bond, 1975; Lezak, 1983).

Although these aforementioned limitations may, in some cases, be related to cognitive and physical restrictions (Najenson et al., 1974; Stambrook, Peters, Moore, Deviaene & Hawryluk, 1988), people whose personalities show alterations after head injury are less likely to return to their former line of work. This holds true even when their cognitive abilities have been relatively unaffected (Weddell et al., 1980). Many of the common posttraumatic changes in disposition (e.g., apathy, impaired initiative, inability to plan and carry out behavioral sequences, low tolerance to frustration, etc.) are incompatible with success in the workplace.

Other common, personality-related sequelae such as defective social judgment, childishness, egocentricity, and irritability not only affect potential employability but have a tendency to disrupt other aspects of the victim's social life as well. In addition to the downgrade in vocational status, many people do not resume their leisure activities or reestablish their social contacts to the same extent as before their injury. Rehabilitation programs and therapy should not be directed solely toward returning the patient to work but also must consider helping to restore leisure activities and social relations (Oddy & Humphrey, 1980). One should not underestimate the serious implications that lost or diminished recreational and leisure activities have for the quality of life. For example, Dywan (personal communication) told us of a patient she had seen who had lost the capacity to gain pleasure from listening to music even though this had been one of the major sources of joy in his life.

Personal Relationships

As we stated earlier, one of the most important factors determining the success or failure of the recovery process is the quality of the support provided by the patient's personal affiliations. Although in the past there was a tendency to concentrate only on the individual who had been injured, the importance of family therapy and the involvement of everyone in the patient's home environment in the readjustment process has become increasingly clear. Numerous reports have confirmed that the relatives of head-injured patients experience increased stress (Fahy, Irving & Millac, 1967; Klonoff, Costa & Snow, 1986; Klonoff, Snow & Costa, 1986; McKinlay, Brooks, Bond, Martinage & Marshall, 1981; Panting & Merry, 1972; Rosenbaum & Najenson, 1976; Thomsen, 1974). Marital relationships are particularly vulnerable to disruption when head injury affects one of the partners. Understandably, marital maladjustment varies directly with the severity of the injury, the amount of psychopathology, and the degree of financial strain (Peters, Stambrook, Moore & Esses, 1988).

Changes in personality further compromise domestic situations and are associated with greater family friction (Weddell et al., 1980). Just one of the aforementioned character aberrations is likely to interfere to some degree with any relationship, let alone, in the worst scenario, a cluster of changes accompanied by a physical disability. Unfortunately for all involved, a person who has suffered moderate to severe head injuries is often perceived by those with whom they live as an annoyance, in the milder cases, or, when the symptoms are particularly intense, as a torment (McKinlay et al., 1981; Panting & Merry, 1972; Weddell et al., 1980). It is not unusual for the value of the victim's residual capacities to be overlooked and unexploited in lieu of their overriding character flaws. It comes as no surprise that these people are rarely able to form or maintain close relationships (Weddell et al., 1980), and those who can still fully appreciate the situation are often lonely and depressed as well (Lezak, 1983; Lezak et al., 1980; Oddy & Humphrey, 1980).

Patient Self-Reports

The definition of recovery cannot be limited to the realms of employment and domestic harmony; indicators that may, on the surface, prematurely announce that recovery is complete. Just as many features of the external environment with which they interact need to be altered, brain-injured people must adjust aspects of their internal environments as well. To appreciate fully the impact of brain damage we need to know what changes each person has had to make in order to cope not only in respect to pragmatic function but how their individual, subjective experience of the world has been transformed. One way to tap this dimension is to provide patients with an opportunity to report their feelings. Generally, because of the difficulties with objective quantification, scientists have paid little attention to these reports. To the intrepid scientist, whose curiosity about psychological function is greater than the fear of the intellectual challenge associated with using an imperfect tool, and to the clinician, who must deal directly with problems arising from subjective experience, patients' self-reports can provide valuable insight into factors directly related to function. An assessment of recovery is incomplete if this aspect of the brain-damaged person has not been addressed.

For example, over a 5-year period a group of men who had suffered traumatic brain damage submitted an evaluation of their personal situation at 1-year intervals (Lezak et al., 1980). With the exception of aphasia, overall emotional well-being and social adjustment did not seem to be correlated significantly to physical disability. Although prevalent at high frequencies during the first year or two after the injury, the number of reported problems with depression, initiative, and significant relationships eventually began to decrease. Troubles persisting at elevated levels even after 5 years fell within the domains of anger (irritability to aggression), social contact, work/school, and leisure.

Situations in which Further Deterioration can be Expected

Posttraumatic Epilepsy

The presence of seizures at any time during hospitalization is related significantly to poorer outcome (Timming et al., 1982) and a greater possibility of developing posttraumatic epilepsy (Jennett & Teasdale, 1981). Although the incidence of a subsequent chronic epileptic disorder appears low when one considers all types of head injuries (only about 5% of victims are affected by recurring seizures [Gabor, 1982]), a number of factors are associated with a drastic increase in the probability of occurrence. For instance, whereas closed head injury patients rarely develop epilepsy, the same cannot be said for victims of penetrating wounds, particularly if the dura has been broached (Caveness, 1976). Missile injuries, in general, are followed by epilepsy in 20% to 60% of cases (Caveness, 1976; Salazar et al., 1985). When depressed skull fracture lacerates the substance of the brain, epilepsy appears in about 60% of cases. Although only 10% of cases with epidural bleeding are associated with epilepsy, the rate increases fourfold when the hemorrhages are intracerebral or subdural (Gabor, 1982; Ommaya, 1972).

Both the size and location of the lesion appear to be important factors in determining the likelihood of posttraumatic epilepsy. Not surprisingly, the larger the lesion the greater the chance of epilepsy (Salazar et al., 1985). More than half the patients with damage involving the motor strip of the central sulcus develop seizures; a rate that is almost twice as great as that associated with lesions of a similar size located near the frontal or occipital poles (Russell & Whitty, 1952). Patients who present with focal neurological signs, hemiplegia, or hemiparesis are at increased risk to have seizures (Russell & Whitty, 1952; Salazar et al., 1985).

Fortunately, about half of those who experience a small number of seizures in the period immediately after their injury never have them again. The earlier the seizures occur, however, the greater the chance that they will persist (Jennett, 1969, 1975a). Approximately one quarter of the patients who had a seizure during the first week went on to develop persistent epilepsy in contrast to only 3% of the patients whose first week was seizure-free. The frequency of attacks during the first year is also important. Ten or more seizures usually indicate that the patient will have a long-term problem (Caveness, 1963). Age is also a useful prognostic clue. Children younger than 16 years of age develop late seizures about half as often as those who are older even though those under 5 years old are more likely to have a seizure during the first week postinjury (Hendrick, Harwood-Hash & Hudson, 1964). The latency between the time of the trauma and the initial episode of epilepsy can extend to an amazingly long period of time. Only about half of those patients eventually troubled by seizures had their first attack during the year after their injury. Significantly, approximately one quarter were seizure-free for 4 years or longer and about 10% went at least 10 years before the first epileptic incident (Jennett, 1965, 1975a; Jennett & Teasdale, 1981; Rasmussen, 1969).

Unmasking of Previously Silent Neurological Disorders

There are times when a patient's condition is considerably worse than one would expect in light of the injury sustained. One possible explanation for this anomaly concerns the situation when the victim has a previously undiagnosed and symptomatically silent neurological disease process such as a brain tumor, berry aneurysm, arteriovenous malformation, or brain abscess. If the circumstances are correct, even an extremely minor head injury may unmask the functionally dormant pathology and trigger a full array of complications (Wallis & Wilson, 1983). The degree of impairment and further deterioration will depend largely on the interaction among the severity of the injury, the extent of neurological and behavioral consequences arising from it, and the nature of the pathological process unmasked.

Prognostic Strategy

When is the Best Time to Test?

It is futile to try to perform a comprehensive neuropsychological battery on individuals who are so disoriented from their injury that they cannot respond. Therefore, formal testing is not recommended before the patient is capable of achieving a score in the "normal" range of the GOAT (i.e., 75 or better). The neuropsychologist should note that, even though the patient appears alert and oriented and is capable of responding sufficiently well to cooperate in an assessment, the patient may still be under the influence of posttraumatic amnesia and may fail to recall any of the procedures when quizzed at a later date (Lezak, 1983). In the period immediately after a trauma, it is more than likely that the most common behavioral sequelae of an acute brain disorder will completely dominate performance. At this stage most patients will seem to be more or less the same: they will have difficulty paying attention and concentrating; memory will be impaired; they will fatigue easily and will be plagued by emotional lability.

The only distinguishing characteristics will likely be the manifestations of the specific functional deficits associated with damage at the site of the lesion. Whether or not these are noticeable or are masked by the gross behavioral disruptions will be determined largely by the severity of the damage and the conspicuousness of the type of deficit produced. The patient's neurobehavioral status will be more a function of the time elapsed since the damage occurred than any other factor in cases of single-event, nonprogressive insults such as stroke or trauma (Gronwall & Sampson, 1974; Gronwall & Wrightson, 1974; Kertesz & McCabe, 1977; Lezak, 1983; Lezak et al., 1980; Ruesch & Moore, 1943; Sarno, 1976). Although there is considerable individual variation in the degree of spontaneous recovery that can be expected in higher level brain function (Dikmen & Reitan, 1976), the overwhelming influence of diffuse symptoms should subside within 3 to 6 months when injuries are relatively mild or within the first year or, in some severe cases, 2 years when the lesion is predominantly focal (Gronwall & Sampson, 1974).

Recovery is seldom, if ever, a sudden total restitution of function. The full process usualy stretches over years and may, in fact, never reach completion. Functional improvements follow a relatively predictable sequence conforming to the well-recognized rostral-caudal and proximal-distal ontological development of the body and of behavior. Rather than a gradual, steady accumulation of progress, advances occur in stages and different functions improve at different rates (Kertesz, 1979; O'Brien & Lezak, 1984). Within the limitations set by the location and severity of the lesion and the patient's premorbid level of functioning, the general trend is for old memories to return before recent memory and well-practiced skills to be restored before the patient has the ability to learn new ones (Lezak, 1983).

When one looks at recovery within a particular behavior, the stages of recovery in many ways parallel the same developmental pattern of the behavior as it originally emerged during infancy. This recapitulation of development can be seen in a wide variety of species. It is typical of the recovery of feeding and walking in the rat after experimental brain lesions (Teitelbaum & Epstein, 1962; Teitelbaum & Stellar, 1954) and, in humans, most obvious with restitution of motor function after spinal shock or motor cortex damage. There is evidence that the restoration of cognitive functions shows a similar orderliness. For example, impaired speech often recovers in stages from global to anomic aphasia. From a clinical perspective, rich behavioral descriptions that identify relative progressive behavioral epochs allow the rate and degree of recovery to be monitored. If the process ceases before completion, residual abilities can be understood within the context of the particular stage of recovery that was reached.

Most of what restoration of cognitive skills will ultimately take place generally occurs within the first 6 months to a year after the injury (Bond, 1979; Eson, Yen & Bourke, 1978; Gronwall & Sampson, 1974; Kertesz & McCabe, 1977; Newcombe & Artiola i Fortuny, 1979; Reitan & Wolfson, 1986; Seron, 1979; Walker & Jablon, 1959, 1961). The pattern of recovery follows a typical profile. Although the patient's age and the type, location, and severity of the lesion influence the rate, it is usual for improvement to be swift in the beginning (Newcombe et al., 1975; Seron, 1979). Advances can be so pronounced that day-to-day changes are obvious (Lishman, 1978). Because of these rapid gains, assessments made during the initial posttraumatic period may be obsolete within weeks or even days (Lezak, 1983). Gradually, the pace of advancement decreases until, ultimately, it reaches asymptote and little further progress can be expected in the patient's condition (Newcombe et al., 1975; Seron, 1979; Walker & Jablon, 1959, 1961). In cases of single-event brain injury (e.g., trauma or stroke) recovery may continue to take place, albeit at an extremely slow rate, for as long as a decade and more (Eson et al., 1978; Newcombe & Artiola i Fortuny, 1979; Seron, 1979). Many of these slowly occurring improvements are likely the product of behavioral compensation or learned accommodations rather than restitution of function (see section on Behavioral Compensation).

Unfortunately, as one might suspect, all change subsequent to brain damage is not for the better. After improvements or the initial appearance of being intact, some functions may suffer a decline (Dikmen & Reitan, 1976; Reitan & Wolfson, 1987; Smith, 1961). Reitan & Wolfson (1987) suggest that during the 12 to 18 months interval after head injury a patient's cognitive status may be especially sensitive to deterioration. Other studies of traumatically injured patients have reported that the latency for this retrogression may be several years or more (Anttinen, 1960; Daghighian, 1973; Hillbom, 1960).

Lezak (1983) has cautioned against making premature conclusions concerning a patient's ultimate level of recovery during the period when a great deal of irregular fluctuation is expected in performance. Because of these large variations over time and between specific functions, it is wise to wait at least 2 years after the injury before attempting to make a confident prediction unless, of course, the severity of the damage makes it obvious that the ensuing disabilities are permanent and totally disabling. Arrangements concerning legal settlements, long-term vocational status, and financial compensation need to be flexible for the initial period and allow for the contingency that a patient's condition may change.

There are at least three good reasons to necessitate repeated testing. As we have stated above, rapid changes during the acute phase of recovery require updating in order to reflect accurately the patient's current status. Repeated testing is also a means for assessing the present rate of improvement and, thereby, the degree of further potential progress. If advances are still being made dynamically, one can assume that restorative processes are still operating full force and significant further progress can be anticipated. Finally, even when a patient's performance appears to have reached a plateau, the possibility for both negative and positive alterations almost always will exist.

Global Versus Specific Tests

Two basic types of assessment tool exist distinguished principally by the breadth of function they claim to measure. One group of tests, which we refer to as global (e.g., Wechsler Adult Intelligence Scale—Revised, Wechsler Memory Scale—Revised, Halstead-Reitan Neuropsychological Battery, etc.), attempts to quantify the patient's overall intellectual ability, usually as an operational definition of some hypothetical construct such as intelligence, memory, or general brain dysfunction. These tests traditionally come in the form of a standardized package or battery. The individual components of the battery, the subtests, generally arise from commonsense or abstract theoretical subdivisions of the major construct targeted by the full battery. Scores from the subtests are pooled to form a collective measure or cumulative index for each subject. This score is compared to a table of standardized norms in order to categorize the patient's performance according to percentile-based cutoff limits.

In contrast, individual tests exist that are associated with the specific deficits arising from focal brain dysfunction. These tests, used primarily for diagnostic purposes, were obtained from studies of patients with atrophic lesions. Although a number of these tests can be combined to form a fairly routine battery, such as the ones used at the Boston VA or the Montreal Neurological Institute, the results are not pooled into any sort of cumulative index. The individual tests are less dependent on norms than are global tests and the decision of whether or not performance is abnormal is usually based on a clinical decision that considers additional relevant factors, particularly the patient's performance on other tests. Specific dysfunctions often can be isolated even when diffuse effects depress overall function because it is the relative strength or weakness of each behavior that is important.

Another feature of behavioral specificity that differentiates these two categories of tests concerns the relative sensitivity of the measure to distinguish actual recovery of function from functional compensation. The broader the behavior assessed, the more difficult to detect when alternate strategies are being used (see section on Behavioral Compensation). Perhaps this point is best illustrated with an example. The Wisconsin Card-Sorting Task is particularly susceptible to dorsolateral frontal cortex dysfunction just as the ability to recall successfully the Rey Complex Figure depends on an intact, operational right temporal lobe. Even 20 years after lesions were made in either of these cortical sites, there was no recovery in the respective, associated function (Kolb & Whishaw, 1985b). Conversely, when paired-associate learning (part of the WMS–R) was assessed periodically after temporal lobectomy, Blakemore and Falconer (1967) found that, provided the patients were young, this ability, which had been devastated immediately after surgery, showed substantial recovery within 2 or 3 years. This improvement in performance is almost certainly the result of alternate mnemonic strategies. For instance, temporal lobectomy patients can improve their performance on the paired-associate task by using imagery (Jones, 1974). So, to help learn the word pair "dog-candle," they picture a dog jumping over a candle.

Theoretically, tests that fractionate behavior and relate them to neural function are important to our understanding of brain–behavior relationships. Our goal is to dissociate behavioral components into functional elements that can be related in a meaningful way to anatomical substrate. In this way, we will not only learn more about the physiological mechanism underlying behavioral function but will learn useful things about the behavior itself. Behavior can be used to unlock the secrets of the brain just as the brain can be used to teach us more about the organization of behavior. There are many fruitful avenues for this type of cross-correlative investigation. We can study the development of specific functions as they relate to the developing nervous system (Kolb & Fantie, 1989) or, as is particularly relevant to this book, we can delineate as clearly as possible both the alteration of behavior by brain damage and any capacity for subsequent recovery.

Some specific deficits can be devastating but do not appear significant on global tests if, indeed, they are detected at all (Gronwall & Sampson, 1974; Lezak, 1983; Walsh, 1978b). Many of the traditional global batteries that generate indices of intelligence and general brain dysfunction rely on tests of perception and constructional ability, functions mediated chiefly by posterior cortical areas. Patients may produce adequate performances on tasks of this type because these areas are less likely to be damaged in the typical head injury. It is not unusual for patients with significant brain damage to perform within the "normal" range on conventional psychological examinations or one of the prepackaged neuropsychological test batteries (Lezak, 1983). For example, despite the existence of a major behavioral deficit such as apathy, impaired memory, profoundly slowed cognitive processes, or defective mental tracking, disabilities sufficient to prevent employment or, in some cases, to assume any social responsibility whatsoever, traumatically brain injured adults were able to produce test patterns on the Wechsler Adult Intelligence Scale "that tended to approximate the average" (Lezak, 1983; McFie, 1975, 1976).

Ultimately, the question one asks will determine what type of test is appropriate. If the goal is to obtain a rough index of general functioning in order to make a general prediction about rehabilitative success then the global tests may be adequate. Our preference is for getting a clear descriptive picture of the patient's behavioral strengths and weaknesses in as specific a form as possible. The better we understand the exact nature of a patient's deficit, the easier it is to create and direct appropriate therapeutic and rehabilitative efforts. Global tests may be useful for measuring net functional recovery, a legitimate and important concern. Insight into how patient's lives have changed and what they need to do to function day to day can be obtained only when we understand the nature of the changes and all they entail, not just a vague summary of the adequacy of their behavior to make due. The neuropsychological assessment should treat each patient as an individual and be so designed to meet the needs of the situation as it presents itself.

References

Adams, J.H., Graham, D.I., Murray, L.S., & Scott, G. (1982). Diffuse axonal injury due to nonmissile head-injury in humans: An analysis of 45 cases. *Annals of Neurology*, *12*, 557–563.

Adams, R.D., & Victor, M. (1981). *Principles of neurology* (2nd Ed.). New York: McGraw-Hill.

Adams, R.L., Boake, C., & Crain, C. (1982). Bias in a neuropsychological test classification related to education, age, and ethnicity. *Journal of Consulting and Clinical Psychology*, *50*, 143–145.

Adler, A. (1945). Mental symptoms following head injury. A statistical analysis of two hundred cases. *Archives of Neurology and Psychiatry*, *53*, 34–43.

Alexander, M.P. (1982). Traumatic brain injury. In P.F. Benson & D. Blumer (Eds.), *Psychiatric aspects of neurologic disease* (Vol. 2, pp. 219–249). New York: Grune & Stratton.

Amante, D., VanHouten, V.W., Grieve, J.H., Bader, C.A., & Margules, P.H. (1977). Neuropsychological deficit, ethnicity, and socioeconomic status. *Journal of Consulting and Clinical Psychology*, *45*, 524–535.

Anastasi, A. (1982). *Psychological testing* (5th Ed.). New York: Macmillan.

Andersen, A.L. (1950). The effect of laterality localization of brain damage on Wechsler-Bellevue indices of deterioration. *Journal of Clinical Psychology*, *6*, 191–194.

Anttinen, E.E. (1960). On the apoplectic conditions occurring among brain injured veterans. *Acta Psychiatrica et Neurologica Scandinavica*, *35*(Suppl. 143), 1–150.

Artiola i Fortuny, L., Briggs, M., Newcombe, F., Ratcliff, G., & Thomas, C. (1980). Measuring the duration of post traumatic amnesia. *Journal of Neurology, Neurosurgery, and Psychiatry*, *43*, 377–379.

Auerbach, S.H. (1983). Cognitive rehabilitation in the head injured: A neurobehavioral approach. *Seminars in Neurology*, *3*, 152–162.

Backman, M.E. (1972). Patterns of mental abilities: Ethnic, socioeconomic, and sex differences. *American Educational Research Journal*, *9*, 1–12.

Barbizet, J. (1970). *Human memory and its pathology*, San Francisco: Freeman.

Basser, L.S. (1962). Hemiplegia of early onset and the faculty of speech with special reference to the effects of hemispherectomy. *Brain*, *85*, 427–460.

Basso, A., Capitani, E., & Zanobio, E. (1982). Pattern of recovery of oral and written expression and comprehension in aphasic patients. *Behavioral Brain Research*, *6*, 115–128.

Basso, A., Faglioni, P., & Vignolo, L.A. (1975). Etude controlée de la rééducation du langage dans l'aphasie: Comparaison entre aphasiques traités et nontraités. *Revue Neurologique*, *131*, 607–614.

Benson, D.F., & Geschwind, N. (1985). Aphasia and related disorders: A clinical approach. In M-M. Mesulam (Ed.), *Principles of behavioral neurology* (pp. 193–238). Philadelphia: F.A. Davis.

Beresford, W.A. (1965). A discussion on retrograde changes in nerve fibres. *Progress in Brain Research*, *14*, 33–56.

Bigler, E.D. (1982). Clinical assessment of cognitive deficit in traumatic and degenerative disorders: Brain scan and neuropsychologic findings. In R.N. Malatesha & L.C. Hartlage (Eds.), *Neuropsychology and cognition* (Vol. II, pp. 165–182). The Hague: Martinus Nijhoff.

Binder, L.M. (1986). Persisting symptoms after mild head injury: A review of the postconcussive syndrome. *Journal of Clinical and Experimental Neuropsychology*, *8*, 323–346.

Björklund, A., & Stenevi, U. (1979). Regeneration of monoaminergic and cholinergic neurons in the mammalian central nervous system. *Physiological Reviews*, *59*, 62–100.

Blakemore, C.B., & Falconer, M.A. (1967) Long-term effects of anterior temporal lobectomy on certain cognitive functions. *Journal of Neurology, Neurosurgery and Psychiatry*, *30*, 364–367.

Blumer, D., & Benson, D.F. (1975). Personality changes with frontal and temporal lobe lesions. In D.F. Benson & D. Blumer (Eds.), *Psychiatric aspects of neurologic disease* (pp. 151–169). New York: Grune & Stratton.

Bond, M.R. (1975). Assessment of the psychosocial outcome after severe head injury. In Ciba Foundation Symposium 34 (New Series). *Outcome of severe*

damage to the central nervous system (pp. 141–157). Amsterdam: Elsevier–Excerpta Medica–North-Holland.
Bond, M.R. (1979). The stages of recovery from severe head injury with special reference to late outcome. *International Rehabilitation Medicine, 1*, 155–159.
Brooks, D.N. (1972). Memory and head injury. *Journal of Nervous and Mental Disease, 155*, 350–355.
Brooks, D.N. (1974). Recognition memory, and head injury. *Journal of Neurology, Neruosurgery, and Psychiatry, 37*, 794–801.
Brooks, D.N., & Aughton, M.E. (1979). Psychological consequences of blunt head injury. *International Rehabilitation Medicine, 1*, 160–165.
Brooks, D.N., Aughton, M.E., Bond, M.R., Jones, P., & Rizvi, S. (1980). Cognitive sequelae in relationship to early indices of severity of brain damage after severe blunt head injury. *Journal of Neurology, Neurosurgery, and Psychiatry, 43*, 529–534.
Bryden, M.P. (1979). Evidence for sex-related differences in cerebral organization. In M.A. Witting & A.C. Petersen (Eds.), *Sex-related differences in cognitive functioning* (pp. 121–143). New York: Academic Press.
Buck, M. (1968). *Dysphasia: professional guidance for family and patient.* Englewood Cliffs, NJ: Prentice-Hall.
Buffery, A.W.H. & Gray, J.A. (1972). Sex differences in the development of spatial and linguistic skills. In C. Ounsted & D.C. Taylor (Eds.), *Gender differences: Their ontogeny and significance* (pp. 123–157). Edinburgh/London: Churchill Livingstone.
Butfield, E., & Zangwill, O.L. (1946). Re-education in aphasia: Review of 70 cases. *Journal of Neurology, Neurosurgery, and Psychiatry, 9*, 75–79.
Cannon, W.B. & Rosenblueth, A. (1949). *The supersensitivity of denervated structures*. New York: Macmillan.
Caveness, W.F. (1963). Onset and cessation of fits following craniocerebral trauma. *Journal of Neurosurgery, 20*, 570–583.
Caveness, W.F. (1976). Epilepsy, a product of trauma in our time. *Epilepsia, 17*, 207–215.
Chapman, L.F., Thetford, W.N., Berlin, L., Guthrie, T.C., & Wolff, H.G. (1958). Highest integrative functions in man during stress. In H.C. Solomon, S. Cobb, & W. Penfield (Eds.), *The brain and human behavior: Research publication of the association of nervous and mental disease. 36*, 491–534.
Daghighian, I. (1973). Le vieillissement des anciens traumatisés du crâne. (Etude catamnestique de 88 cas hospitalisés en millieu psychiatrique.). *Schweizer Archiv fur Neurologie, Neurochirurgie und Psychiatrie (Zurich), 112*, 399–447.
Deutsch, J.A. (1960). *The structural basis of behavior.* Chicago: University of Chicago Press.
Dikmen, S., & Reitan, R.M. (1976). Psychological deficits and recovery of functions after head injury. *Transactions of the American Neurological Association, 101*, 72–77.
Dikmen, S., & Reitan, R.M. (1977). Emotional sequelae of head injury. *Annals of Neurology, 2*, 492–494.
Diller, L. (1973). Hemiplegia. In J.F. Garrett & E.S. Levine (Eds.), *Rehabilitation practices with the physically disabled* (pp. 294–328). New York: Columbia University Press.

Dresser, A.C., Meirowsky, A.M., Weiss, G.H., McNeel, M.L., Simon, G.A., & Caveness, W.F. (1973). Gainful employment following head injury: Prognostic Factors. *Archives of Neurology*, *29*, 111–116.

Edds, M.V., Jr. (1953). Collateral nerve regeneration. *Quarterly Review of Biology*, *28*, 260–276.

Eson, M.E., Yen, J.K., & Bourke, R.S. (1978). Assessment of recovery from serious head injury. *Journal of Neurology, Neurosurgery, and Psychiatry*, *41*, 1036–1042.

Evans, C.D. (1975). Discussion of *scale, scope and philosophy: the clinical problem*. In Ciba Foundation Symposium 34 (New Series). *Outcome of severe damage to the central nervous system* (pp. 12–18). Amsterdam: Elsevier–Excerpta Medica–North-Holland.

Fahy, T.J., Irving, M.H., & Millac, P. (1967). Severe head injuries. A 6-year follow-up. *Lancet*, *2*, 475–479.

Fletcher, J.M., Levin, H.S., & Landry, S.H. (1984). Behavioral consequences of cerebral insult in infancy. In C.R. Almli & S. Finger (Eds.), *Early brain damage, Vol. 1: Research orientations and clinical observations* (pp. 189–213). New York: Academic Press.

Gabor, A.J. (1982). Post-traumatic epilepsy. In J.R. Youmans (Ed.), *Neurological surgery* (Vol. 4, 2nd ed. pp. 2188–2194). Philadelphia: W.B. Saunders Co.

Geschwind, N. (1974). Late changes in the nervous system: An overview. In D.G. Stein, J.J. Rosen, & N. Butters (Eds.), *Plasticity and recovery of function in the central nervous system* (pp. 467–508). New York: Academic Press.

Gilchrist, E., & Wilkinson, M. (1979). Some factors determining prognosis in young people with severe head injuries. *Archives of Neurology*, *36*, 355–359.

Gissane, W. (1963). The nature and causation of road injuries. *Lancet*, *2*, 695–698.

Gloning, I., Gloning, K., Haub, G., & Quatember, R. (1969). Comparison of verbal behavior in right-handed and non right-handed patients with anatomically verified lesion of one hemisphere. *Cortex*, *5*, 43–52.

Gloning, I., Gloning, K., & Hoff, H. (1968). *Neuropsychological symptoms and syndromes in lesions of the occipital lobe and the adjacent areas.* Paris: Gauthier-Villars.

Godfrey, C.M., & Douglass, E. (1959). The recovery process in aphasia. *The Canadian Medical Association Journal*, *80*, 618–624.

Goldberger, M.E., & Murray, M. (1974). Restitution of function and collateral sprouting in the cat spinal cord: The deafferented animal. *Journal of Comparative Neurology*, *158*, 37–54.

Goodman, D.C., & Horel, J.A. (1966). Sprouting of optic tract projections in the brain stem of the rat. *Journal of Comparative Neurology*, *127*, 71–88.

Grimm, B.H., & Blighbugg, J. (1986). Psychological rehabilitation in traumatic brain injury. In S.B. Filskov & T.J. Boll (Eds.), *Handbook of clinical neuropsychology* (Vol. 2, pp. 495–560). New York: Wiley & Sons.

Gronwall, D., & Wrightson, P. (1974). Delayed recovery of intellectual function after minor head injury. *Lancet*, *2*, 605–609.

Gronwall, D., & Wrightson, P. (1981). Memory and information processing capacity after closed head injury. *Journal of Neurology, Neurosurgery, and Psychiatry*, *44*, 889–895.

Gronwall, D.M.A. & Sampson, H. (1974). *The psychological effects of concussion.* Auckland, N.Z.: Auckland University Press/Oxford University Press.

Grubb, R.L., & Coxe, W.S. (1974). Central neurvous system trauma: Cranial. In S.G. Eliasson, A.L. Prensky, & W.B. Hardin, Jr. (Eds.), *Neurological pathophysiology* (pp. 292–309). New York: Oxford University Press.

Gulbrandsen, G.G. (1984). Neuropsychological sequelae of light head injuries in older children 6 months after trauma. *Journal of Clinical Neuropsychology, 6,* 257–268.

Gurdjian, E.S., & Webster, J.E. (1958). *Head injuries: Mechanisms, diagnosis and management.* Boston: Little, Brown, & Co.

Guttman, E. (1946). Late effects of closed head injuries: Psychiatric observations. *Journal of Mental Science, 92,* 1–18.

Hannay, H.J. (1976). Real or imagined incomplete lateralization of function in females? *Perception and Psychophysics, 19,* 349–352.

Harris, L.J. (1978). Sex differences in spatial ability: Possible environmental, genetic, and neurological factors. In M. Kinsbourne (Ed.), *Asymmetrical function of the brain* (pp. 405–522). Cambridge: Cambridge University Press.

Haymaker, W. (1969). *Bing's local diagnosis in neurological disease*, St. Louis: C.V. Mosby.

Head, H. (1926). *Aphasia and kindred disorders of speech.* Cambridge: The University Press.

Heiskanen, O., & Sipponen, P. (1970). Prognosis of severe brain injury. *Acta Neurologica Scandinavica, 46,* 343–348.

Hendrick, E.B., Harwood-Hash, D.C.F. & Hudson, A.R. (1964). Head injuries in children: A survey of 4465 consecutive cases at the Hospital for Sick Children, Toronto, Canada. *Clinical Neurosurgery, 11,* 46–65.

Hécaen, H. (1976). Acquired aphasia in children and the ontogenesis of hemispheric functional specialization. *Brain and Language, 3,* 114–134.

Hécaen, H., & Albert, M.L. (1975). Disorders of mental functioning related to frontal lobe pathology. In D.F. Benson & D. Blumer (Eds.), *Psychiatric aspects of neurologic disease* (pp. 137–149). New York: Grune & Stratton.

Hillbom, E. (1960). After-effects of brain-injuries. *Acta Psychiatrica et Neurologica Scandinavica, 35*(Suppl. 142), 1–195.

Ivan, L.P. (1984). The impact of head trauma on society. *Canadian Journal of Neurological Sciences, 11,* 417–420.

Jane, J.A., Steward, O., & Gennarelli, T. (1985). Axonal degeneration induced by experimental noninvasive minor head injury. *Journal of Neurosurgery, 62,* 96–100.

Jennett, B. (1975a). *Epilepsy after non-missle head injuries* (2nd edn). London: Heinemann Medical Books.

Jennett, B. (1975b). Scale, scope and philosophy of the clinical problem. In Ciba Foundation Symposium 34 (New Series). *Outcome of severe damage to the central neurvous system* (pp. 3–9). Amsterdam: Elsevier–Excerpta Medica–North-Holland.

Jennett, B., Snoek, J., Bond, M.R., & Brooks, N. (1981). Disability after severe head injury: Observations on the use of the Glasgow Outcome Scale. *Journal of Neurology, Neurosurgery, and Psychiatry, 44,* 285–293.

Jennett, B., & Teasdale, G. (1981). *Management of head injuries.* Philadelphia: F.A. Davis Co.

Jennett, B., Teasdale, G., Braakman, R., Minderhoud, J., Heiden, J., & Kurze, T. (1979). Prognosis of patients with severe head injury. *Neurosurgery, 4*, 283–289.

Jennett, B., Teasdale, G., & Knill-Jones, R. (1975). Prognosis after severe head injury. In Ciba Foundation Symposium 34 (New Series). *Outcome of severe damage to the central nervous system* (pp. 309–319). Amsterdam: Elsevier–Excerpta Medica–North-Holland.

Jennett, W.B. (1965). Predicting epilepsy after blunt head injury. *British Medical Journal, 1*, 1215–1216.

Jennett, W.B. (1969). Early traumatic epilepsy: Definition and identity. *Lancet, 1*, 1023–1025.

Jones, M.K. (1974). Imagery as a mnemonic aid after left temporal lobectomy: Contrast between material-specific and generalized memory disorders. *Neuropsychologia, 12*, 21–30.

Jurko, M.F. (1979). The mechanics of head injury and some behavioral, psychological, and EEG test findings. Paper presented at the *Seventh Annual Meeting of the International Neuropsychological Society*, New York City.

Kennard, M,A. (1936). Age and other factors in motor recovery from precentral lesions in monkeys. *American Journal of Physiology, 115*, 138–146.

Kennard, M.A. (1940). Relation of age to motor impairment in man and in subhuman primates. *Archives of Neurology and Psychiatry, 44*, 377–397.

Kertesz, A. (1979). *Aphasia and associated disorders: Taxonomy, localization, and recovery*. Orlando: Grune & Stratton.

Kertesz, A. (1985). Recovery and treatment. In K.M. Heilman & E. Valenstein (Eds.), *Clinical neuropsychology* (2nd ed., pp. 481–505) New York: Oxford University Press.

Kertesz, A., & McCabe, P. (1977). Recovery patterns and prognosis in aphasia. *Brain, 100*, 1–18.

Kimura, D. (1987). Are men's and women's brains really different? *Canadian Psychology, 28*, 133–147.

Klonoff, H., Crockett, D.D., & Clark, C. (1984). Head injuries in children: A model for predicting course of recovery and prognosis. In R.E. Tarter & G. Goldstein (Eds.). *Advances in clinical neuropsychology* (pp. 139–157). New York: Plenum Press.

Klonoff, P.S., Costa, L.D., & Snow, W.G. (1986). Predictors and indicators of quality of life in patients with closed-head injury. *Journal of Clinical and Experimental Neuropsychology, 8*, 469–485.

Klonoff, P.S., Snow, W.G., & Costa, L.D. (1986). Quality of life in patients 2 to 4 years after closed head injury. *Neurosurgery, 19*, 735–743.

Kløve, H., & Cleeland, C.S. (1972). The relationship of neuropsychological impairment to other indices of severity of head injury. *Scandinavian Journal of Rehabilitation Medicine, 4*, 55–60.

Kolb, B., & Fantie, B. (1989). Development of the Child's Brain and Behavior. In C.E. Reynolds & E. Fletcher-Janzen (Eds.), *Handbood of clinical child neuropsychology* (pp. 17–39). New York: Plenum Press.

Kolb, B., & Milner, B. (1981). Performance of complex arm and facial movements after focal brain lesions. *Neuropsychologia, 19*, 491–503.

Kolb, B., & Whishaw, I.Q. (1985a). Earlier is not always better: Behavioral dysfunction and abnormal cerebral morphogenesis following neonatal cortical lesions in the rat. *Behavioural Brain Research, 17*, 25–43.

Kolb, B., & Whishaw, I.Q. (1985b). *Fundamentals of human neuropsychology*, (2nd ed.). New York: W.H. Freeman & Company.

Kratz, K.E., Spear, P.D., & Smith, C.D. (1976). Postcritical-period reversal of effects of monocular deprivation on striate cortex cells in the cat. *Journal of Neurophysiology*, *39*, 501–511.

Lampert, P.W., & Hardman, J.M. (1984). Morphological changes in brains of boxers. *Journal of the American Medical Association*, *251*, 2676–2679.

Levin, H.S. Benton, A.L., & Grossman, R.G. (1982). *Neurobehavioral consequences of closed head injury*. New York: Oxford University Press.

Levin, H.S., & Eisenberg, H.M. (1979). Neuropsychological outcome of closed head injury in children and adolescents. *Child's Brain*, *5*, 281–292.

Levin, H.S., Gary, H.E. Jr., High, W.M. Jr., Mattis, S., Ruff, R.M., Eisenberg, H.M., Marshall, L.F., & Tabaddor, K. (1987). Minor head injury and the postconcussional syndrome: Methodological issues in outcome studies. In H.S. Levin, J. Grafman, & H.M. Eisenberg (Eds.), *Neurobehavioral recovery from head injury* (pp. 262–275). New York: Oxford University Press.

Levin, H.S., & Grossman, R.G. (1978). Behavioral sequelae of closed head injury: A quantitative study. *Archives of Neurology*, *35*, 720–727.

Levin, H.S., Grossman, R.G., Rose, J.E., & Teasdale, G. (1979). Long-term neuropsychological outcome of closed head injury. *Journal of Neurosurgery*. *50*, 412–422.

Levin, H.S., Grossman, R.G., Sarwar, M., & Meyers, C.A. (1981). Linguistic recovery after closed head injury. *Brain and Language*, *12*, 360–374.

Levin, H.S., O'Donnell, V.M., & Grossman, R.G. (1979). The Galveston Orientation and Amnesia Test: A practical scale to assess cognition after head injury. *Journal of Nervous and Mental Diseases*, *167*, 675–684.

Lewin, W. (1968). Rehabilitation after head injury. *British Medical Journal*, *1*, 465–470.

Lezak, M.D. (1978). Subtle sequlae of brain damage. Perplexity, distractibility, and fatigue. *American Journal of Physical Medicine*, *57*, 9–15.

Lezak, M.D. (1979). Recovery of memory and learning functions following traumatic brain injury. *Cortex,* 15, 63–72.

Lezak, M.D. (1983). *Neuropsychological assessment* (2nd ed.). New York: Oxford University Press.

Lezak, M.D. (1984). An individualized approach to neuropsychological assessment. In P.E. Logue & J.M. Schear (Eds.), *Clinical neuropsychology: A multidisciplinary approach* (pp. 29–49). Springfield, IL: C.C. Thomas.

Lezak, M.D., Cosgrove, J.N., O'Brien, K., & Wooster, N. (1980). Relationship between personality disorders, social disturbance, and physical disability following traumatic brain injury. Paper presented at the *Eighth Annual Meeting of the International Neuropsychological Society*, San Francisco.

Lishman, W.A. (1968). Brain damage in relation to psychiatric disability after head injury. *British Journal of Psychiatry*, *114*, 373–410.

Lishman, W.A. (1973). The psychiatric sequelae of head injury: A review. *Psychological Medicine*, *3*, 304–318.

Lishman, W.A. (1978). *Organic psychiatry*. Oxford: Blackwell Scientific Publications.

Liu, C.-N., & Chambers, W.W. (1958). Intraspinal sprouting of dorsal root axons. *Archives of Neurology and Psychiatry*, *79*, 46–61.

Loehlin, J.C., Lindzey, G., & Spuhler, J.N. (1975). *Race differences in intel-*
Wolman (Ed.), *Handbook of clinical psychology*, (pp. 689–754). New York:
Lund, R.D. (1978). *Development and plasticity of the brain: An introduction*. New York: Oxford University Press.

Luria, A.R. (1965). Neuropsychological analysis of focal brain lesions. In B.B. Wolman (Ed.), *Handbook of clinical psychology* (pp. 689–754). New York: McGraw-Hill.

Luria, A.R. (1966). *Higher cortical functions in man*. (B. Haigh, Trans.) New York: Basic Books.

Luria, A.R. (1970). *Traumatic aphasia*. Hague: Mouton.

Marks, M., Taylor, M., & Rusk, H.A. (1957). Rehabilitation of the aphasic patient: A survey of three years' experience in a rehabilitation setting. *Neurology*, *7*, 837–843.

McFie, J. (1975). *Assessment of organic intellectual impairment*. London: Academic Press.

McFie, J. (1976). In M. Piercy (Director), Restitution of function following cerebral lesions. Presented at the Eighteenth International Symposium of Neuropsychology (Summary). *Neuropsychologia*, *14*, 265–268.

McGlone, J. (1976). Sex differences in functional brain asymmetry. Psychology Department Research Bulletin 378, London, Ontario: Universit of Western Ontario.

McKinlay, W.W., Brooks, D.N., Bone, M.R., Martinage, D.P., & Marshall, M.M. (1981). The short-term outcome of severe blunt head injury as reported by relatives of the injured persons. *Journal of Neurology, Neurosurgery, and Psychiatry*, *44*, 527–533.

Merskey, H., & Woodforde, J.M. (1972). Psychiatric sequelae of minor head injury. *Brain*, *95*, 521–528.

Messerli, P., Tissot, A., & Rodriguez, J. (1976). Recovery from aphasia: Some factors of prognosis. In Y. Lebrun & R. Hoops (Eds.), *Neurolinguistics 4: Recovery in aphasics* (pp. 124–135). Amsterdam: Swets & Zeitlinger, B.V.

Miller, H. (1961). Accident neurosis. *British Medical Journal*, *1*, 919–925.

Miller, J.D., Butterworth, J.F., Gudeman, S.K., Faulkner, J.E., Choi, S.C., Selhorst, J.B., Harbison, J.W., Lutz, H.A., Young, H.F., & Becker, D.P. (1981). Further experience in the management of severe head injury. *Journal of Neurosurgery*, *54*, 289–299.

Milner, B. (1974). Sparing of language functions after early unilateral brain damage. *Neurosciences Research Progress Bulletin*, *12*, 213–217.

Moore, R.Y., Björklund, A., & Stenevi, U. (1974). Growth and plasticity of adrenergic neurons. In F.O. Schmitt & F.G. Worden (Eds.), *The neurosciences: Third study program* (pp. 961–977). Cambridge, MA: MIT Press.

Murray, M., & Goldberger, M.E. (1974). Restitution of function and collateral sprouting in the cat spinal cord: The partially hemisected animal. *Journal of Comparative Neurology*, *158*, 19–36.

Najenson, T., Groswasser, Z., Mendelson, L., & Hackett, P. (1980). Rehabilitation outcome of brain damaged patients after severe head injury. *International Rehabilitation Medicine*, *2*, 17–22.

Najenson, T., Mendelson, L., Schechter, I., David, C., Mintz, N., & Groswasser, Z. (1974). Rehabilitation after severe head injury. *Scandinavian Journal of Rehabilitation Medicine*, *6*, 5–14.

National Institutes of Health. (1984). *Head injury: Hope through research*. NIH Publication No. 84–2478.

Nevin, N.C. (1967). Neuropathological changes in the white matter following head injury. *Journal of Neuropathology and Experimental Neurology*, *26*, 77–84.

Newcombe, F. (1969). *Missile wounds of the brain: A study of psychological deficits*. London: Oxford University Press.

Newcombe, F., & Artiola i Fortuny, L. (1979). Problems and perspectives in the evaluation of psychological deficits after cerebral lesions. *International Rehabilitation Medicine*, *1*, 182–192.

Newcombe, F., Marshall, J.C., Carrivick, P.J., & Hiorns, R.W. (1975). Recovery curves in acquired dyslexia. *Journal of Neurological Sciences*, *24*, 127–133.

O'Brien, M.T., & Lezak, M.D. (1981). Long-term improvements in intellectual function following brain injury. Paper presented at the *Fourth European Conference of the International Neuropsychological Society*, Bergen, Norway.

Oddy, M., & Humphrey, M. (1980). Social recovery during the year following severe head injury. *Journal of Neurology, Neurosurgery, and Psychiatry*, *43*, 798–802.

Oddy, M., Humphrey, M., & Uttley, D. (1978a). Stresses upon the relatives of head-injured patients. *British Journal of Psychiatry*, *133*, 507–513.

Oddy, M., Humphrey, M., & Uttley, D. (1978b). Subjective impairment and social recovery after closed head injury. *Journal of Neurology, Neurosurgery, and Psychiatry*, *41*, 611–616.

Ommaya, A.K. (1972). Head injuries in adults. In H.F. Conn (Ed.), *Current therapy* (pp. 692–697). Philadelphia: W.B. Saunders Co.

Ommaya, A.K., & Gennarelli, T.A. (1974). Cerebral concussion and traumatic unconsciousness: Correlation of experimental and clinical observations on blunt head injuries. *Brain*, *97*, 633–654.

Oppenheimer, D.R. (1968). Microscopic lesions in the brain following head injury. *Journal of Neurology, Neurosurgery, and Psychiatry*, *31*, 299–306.

Panting, A., & Merry, P.H. (1972). The long term rehabilitation of severe head injuries with particular reference to the need for social and medical support for the patient's family. *Rehabilitation (Bonn)*, *38*, 33–37.

Peters, L., Stambrook, M.G., Moore, A.D., & Esses, L. (1988). The psychosocial impact of head injury on the marital relationship. *Canadian Psychology*, *29*, 610.

Piazza, D.M. (1980). The influence of sex and handedness in the hemispheric specialization of verbel and nonverbal tasks. *Neuropsychologia*, *18*, 163–176.

Plum, F., & Caronna, J.J. (1975). Can one predict outcome of medical coma? In Ciba Foundation Symposium 34 (New Series). *Outcome of severe damage to the central nervous system* (pp. 121–136). Amsterdam: Elsevier–Excerpta Medica–North-Holland.

Plum, F., & Posner, J. (1980). *Diagnosis of stupor and coma* (3rd Ed.). Philadelphia: F.A. Davis.

Povlishock, J.T., Becker, D.P., Cheng, C.L.Y., & Vaughan, G.W. (1983). Axonal change in minor head injury. *Journal of Neuropathology and Experimental Neurology*, *42*, 225–242.

Rasmussen, T. (1969). Surgical therapy of posttraumatic epilepsy. In A.E. Walker, W.F. Caveness, & M. Critchley (Eds.), *The late effects of head injury* (pp. 277–305). Springfield: Charles C. Thomas.

Rasmussen, T., & Milner, B. (1975). Clinical and surgical studies of the cerebral speech areas in man. In K.J. Zülch, O. Creutzfeldt, & G.C. Galbraith (Eds.), *Cerebral localization* (pp. 238–257). New York: Springer-Verlag.

Rasmussen, T., & Milner, B. (1977). The role of early left-brain injury in determining lateralization of cerebral speech functions. *Annals of the New York Academy of Sciences, 299*, 355–369.

Reitan, R.M., & Wolfson, D. (1985). *Neuroanatomy and neuropathology: A clinical guide for neuropsychologists*. Tucson: Neuropsychology Press.

Reitan, R.M., & Wolfson, D. (1986). *Traumatic brain injury, Vol. 1: Pathophysiology and neuropsychological evaluation*. Tucson, AZ: Neuropsychology Press.

Reitan, R.M., & Wolfson, D. (1987). *Traumatic Brain Injury, Vol. 2: Recovery and Rehabilitation*. Tucson, AZ: Neuropsychology Press.

Riger, J. (1988). *Health (The Washington Post Supplement), 4*, 4.

Rimel, R.W., Giordani, B., Barth, J.T., Boll, T.J., & Jane, J.A. (1981). Disability caused by minor head injury. *Neurosurgery, 9*, 221–228.

Rosenbaum, M., & Najenson, T. (1976). Changes in life patterns and symptoms of low mood as reported by wives of severely brain-injured soldiers. *Journal of Consulting and Clinical Psychology, 44*, 881–888.

Rosenzweig, M.R. (1980). Animal models for effects of brain lesions and for rehabilitation. In P. Bach-y-Rita (Ed.), *Recovery of function: Theoretical considerations for brain injury rehabilitation* (pp. 127–172). Bern: Hans Huber.

Ross, E.D., & Rush, A.J. (1981). Diagnosis and neuroanatomical correlates of depression in brain-damaged patients. *Archives of General Psychiatry, 38*, 1344–1354.

Rubens, A.B., Geshwind, N., Mahowald, M.W., & Mastri, A. (1977). Post-traumatic cerebral hemispheric disconnection syndrome. *Archives of Neurology, 34*, 750–755.

Ruesch, J., & Moore, B.E. (1943). Measurement of intellectual functions in the acute stage of head injury. *Archives of Neurology and Psychiatry, 50*, 165–170.

Russell, W.R. (1932). Cerebral involvement in head injury: Study based on examination of 200 cases. *Brain, 55*, 549–603.

Russell, W.R. (1971). *The traumatic amnesias*. New York: Oxford University Press.

Russell, W.R., & Nathan, P.W. (1946). Traumatic amnesia. *Brain, 69*, 280–300.

Russell, W.R., & Whitty, C.W.M. (1952). Studies in traumatic epilepsy: 1. Factors influencing the incidence of epilepsy after brain wounds. *Journal of Neurology, Neurosurgery, and Psychiatry, 15*, 93–98.

Salazar, A.M., Jabbari, B., Vance, S.C., Grafman, J., Amin, D., & Dillon, J.D. (1985). Epilepsy after penetrating head injury. I. Clinical correlates: A report of the Vietnam Head Injury Study. *Neurology, 35*, 1406–1414.

Sarno, M.T. (1976). The status of research in recovery from aphasia. In Y. Lebrun & R. Hoops (Eds.), *Neurolinguistics 4: Recovery in aphasics* (pp 13–30). Amsterdam: Swets & Zeitlinger B.V.

Schacter, D.L., & Crovitz, H.F. (1977). Memory function after closed head injury: A review of the quantitative research. *Cortex, 13*, 150–176.

Schoenfeld, T.A., & Hamilton, L.W. (1977). Secondary brain changes following lesions: A new paradigm for lesion experimentation. *Physiology and Behavior, 18*, 951–967.

Seron, X. (1979). *Aphasie et neuropsychologie*. Bruxelles: Pierre Mardaga.

Smith, A. (1961). Duration of impaired consciousness as an index of severity in closed head injuries: A review. *Diseases of the Nervous System*, *22*, 69–74.
Smith, A. (1975). Neuropsychological testing in neurological disorders. In W.J. Friedlander (Ed.), *Advances in neurology, Vol. 7*. New York: Raven Press.
Smith, A. (1979). Practices and principles of clinical neuropsychology: Focusing on the hole rather than the doughnut. *International Journal of Neuroscience*, *9*, 233–238.
Snoek, J., Jennett, B., Adams, J.H., Graham, D.I., & Doyle, D. (1979). Computerized tomography after recent severe head injury in patients without acute intracranial haematoma. *Journal of Neurology, Neurosurgery, and Psychiatry*, *42*, 215–225.
Sperry, R.W. (1947). Effect of crossing nerves to antagonistic limb muscles in the monkey. *Archives of Neurology and Psychiatry*, *58*, 452–473.
St. James-Roberts, I. (1981). A reinterpretation of hemispherectomy data without functional plasticity of the brain: 1. Intellectual function. *Brain and Language*, *13*, 31–53.
Stambrook, M., Peters, L.C., Moore, A.D., & Hawryluck, G.A. (1988). Return to employment following moderate and severe closed head injury: Social dependency in long term survival. *Canadian Psychology*, *29*, 746.
Strich, S.J. (1956). Diffuse degeneration of the cerebral white matter in severe dementia following head injury. *Journal of Neurology, Neurosurgery, and Psychiatry*, *19*, 163–185.
Strich, S.J. (1961). Shearing of nerve fibres as a cause of brain damage due to head injury. A pathological study of twenty cases. *Lancet*, *2*, 443–448.
Stuss, D.T., Ely, P., Hugenholtz, H., Richard, M.T., La Rochelle, S., Poirier, C.A., & Bell, I. (1985). Subtle neuropsychological deficits in patients with good recovery after closed head injury. *Neurosurgery*, *17*, 41–47.
Symonds, C.P. (1937). Mental disorder following head injury. *Proceedings of the Royal Society of Medicine*, *30*, 1081–1094.
Symonds, C.P., & Russell, W.R. (1943). Accidental head injuries. Prognosis in service patients. *Lancet*, *1*, 7–10.
Tabaddor, K., Mattis, S., & Zazula, T. (1984). Cognitive sequelae and recovery course after moderate and severe head injury. *Neurosurgery*, *14*, 701–708.
Taylor, H.G. (1984). Early brain injury and cognitive development. In C.R. Almli & S. Finger (Eds.), *Early brain damage, Vol. 1: Research orientations and clinical observations* (pp 325–345). New York: Academic Press.
Taylor, L.B. (1969). Localization of cerebral lesions by psychological testing. *Clinical Neurosurgery*, *16*, 269–287.
Taylor, L.B. (1979). Psychological assessment of neurosurgical patients. In T. Rasmussen & R. Marino, Jr. (Eds.), *Functional neurosurgery* (pp 165–180). New York: Raven Press.
Teasdale, G., & Jennett, B. (1974). Assessment of coma and impaired consciousness: A practical scale. *Lancet*, *2*, 81–84.
Teitelbaum, P., & Epstein, A.N. (1962). The lateral hypothalamic syndrome: Recovery of feeding and drinking after lateral hypothalamic lesions. *Psychological Review*, *69*, 74–90.
Teitelbaum, P., & Stellar, E. (1954). Recovery from the failure to eat produced by hypothalamic lesions. *Science*, *120*, 894–895.
Teuber, H.-L. (1962). Effects of brain wounds implicating right or left hemisphere in man: Hemisphere differences and hemisphere interaction in vision,

audition, and somesthesis. In V.B. Mountcastle (Ed.), *Interhemispheric relations and cerebral dominance* (pp 131–157). Baltimore: The Johns Hopkins Press.

Teuber, H.-L. (1969). Neglected aspects of the posttraumatic syndrome. In A.E. Walker, W.F. Caveness, & M. Critchley (Eds.), *The late effects of head injury* (pp 13–34). Springfield: Charles C. Thomas.

Teuber, H.-L. (1975). Recovery of function after brain injury in man. In Ciba Foundation Symposium 34 (New Series). *Outcome of severe damage to the central nervous system* (pp 159–186). Amsterdam: Elsevier–Excerpta Medica–North-Holland.

Thomsen, I.V. (1974). The patient with severe head injury and his family. *Scandinavian Journal of Rehabilitation Medicine*, *6*, 180–183.

Timming, R., Orrison, W.W., & Mikula, J.A. (1982). Computerized tomography and rehabilitation outcome after severe head trauma. *Archives of Physical Medicine and Rehabilitation*, *63*, 154–159.

Trunkey, D.D. (1983). Trauma. *Scientific American*, *249*, 28–35.

United States Department of Health, Education, and Welfare (1974). *Facts of life and death*. DHEW Publication Number (HRA 74–1222), Rockville:National Center for Health Statistics.

van Zomeren, A.H., & Deelman, B.G. (1978). Long-term recovery of visual reaction time after closed head injury. *Journal of Neurology, Neurosurgery, and Psychiatry*, *41*, 452–457.

van Zomeren, A.H., & van den Burg, W. (1985). Residual complaints of patients two years after severe head injury. *Journal of Neurology, Neurosurgery, and Psychiatry*, *48*, 21–28.

Vernon, P.E. (1979). *Intelligence: Heredity and environment*. San Francisco: W.H. Freeman.

Vignolo, L.A. (1964). Evolution of aphasia and language rehabilitation: A retrospective exploratory study. *Cortex*, *1*, 344–367.

Walker, A.E., & Jablon, S. (1959). A follow-up of head-injured men of World War II. *Journal of Neurosurgery*, *16*, 600–610.

Walker, A.E., & Jablon, S. (1961). *A follow-up study of head wounds in World War II*. Washington, D.C.: *Veterans Administration Medical Monograph*.

Wall, P.D. (1980). Mechanisms of plasticity of connection following damage in adult mammalian nervous systems. In P. Bach-y-Rita (Ed.), *Recovery of function: Theoretical considerations for brain injury rehabilitation* (pp 91–105). Bern: Hans Huber.

Wall, P.D., & Egger, M.D. (1971). Formation of new connexions in adult rat brains after partial deafferentation. *Nature*, *232*, 542–545.

Wallis, W.E., & Wilson, J. (1983). Head injury unmasking other brain diseases. *Acta Neurochirugica*, (Suppl. 32), 125–127.

Walsh, K.W. (1978a). Frontal lobe problems. In G.V. Stanley & K.W. Walsh (Eds.), *Brain impairment: Proceedings of the 1976 brain impairment workshop*. Parkville, Victoria, Australia: Neuropsychology Group, Department of Psychology, University of Melbourne.

Walsh, K.W. (1978b). *Neuropsychology: A clinical approach*. New York: Churchill Livingstone/Longman.

Warren, J.M., & Kolb, B. (1978). Generalizations in neuropsychology. In S. Finger (Ed.), *Recovery from brain damage* (pp 35–48). New York: Plenum Press.

Weddell, R., Oddy, M., & Jenkins, D. (1980). Social adjustment after rehabilitation: A two year follow-up of patients with severe head injury. *Psychological Medicine*, *10*, 257–263.

Weinstein, S., & Teuber, H.-L. (1957a). Effects of penetrating brain injury on intelligence test scores. *Science*, *125*, 1036–1037.

Weinstein, S., & Teuber, H.-L. (1957b). The role of preinjury education and intelligence level in intellectual loss after brain injury. *Journal of Comparative and Physiological Psychology*, *50*, 535–539.

Weisenburg, T., & McBride, K.E. (1935). *Aphasia: A clinical and psychological study*. New York: Commonwealth Fund.

Weiskrantz, L. (1968). Treatments, inferences, and brain function. In L. Weiskrantz (Ed.), *Analysis of behavioral change* (pp 400–414). New York: Harper & Row.

Wepman, J.M. (1951). *Recovery from aphasia*. New York: Ronald Press.

Whitty, C.W.M. & Zangwill, O.L. (1977). Traumatic amnesia. In C.W.M. Whitty & O.L. Zangwill (Eds.), *Amnesia* (2nd ed., pp 118–135). London: Butterworths.

Wilberger, J.E., Deeb, Z., & Rothfus, W. (1987). Magnetic resonance imaging in cases of severe head injury. *Neurosurgery*, *20*, 571–576.

Winick, M. (1976). *Malnutrition and brain development*. New York: Oxford University Press.

Witelson, S.F. (1976). Sex and the single hemisphere: Specialization of the right hemisphere for spatial processing. *Science*, *193*, 425–427.

Woods, B.T. (1980). The restricted effects of right-hemisphere lesions after age one; Weschler test data. *Neuropsychologia*, *18*, 65–70.

Woods, B.T., & Teuber, H.-L. (1973). Early onset of complementary specialization of cerebral hemispheres in man. *Transactions of the American Neurological Association*, *98*, 113–117.

9
Can Competencies be Retrained? A Critical Appraisal of Cognitive Rehabilitation

CATHERINE A. MATEER and ALISON MARY WEBER

Cognitive Competency

Competency can refer to both basic underlying mental abilities and to the application of these abilities to particular tasks or activities. Neuropsychologists view as basic abilities such cognitive processes as attention, memory, executive function, receptive and expressive language, visuoperceptual skills, problem solving, reasoning, and judgment. Assessment of these areas is usually based on an individual's performance on objective standardized measures or tests. Both these underlying cognitive functions and the ability to apply them are critical for successful, independent functioning and both need to be considered in evaluating the retraining of cognitive competency.

Cognitive Incompetency and Rehabilitation

Brain injury often disturbs basic cognitive functions. Such impairment often causes considerable reduction of competency and has widespread impact on the person's emotional and social functioning. Brain-injured persons vary with respect to site and severity of damage and thus differ in their patterns of deficit and the severity of their impairment. They also vary in regard to the competency demands of their life situations. Age may also be a factor both with respect to impact of injury and environmental competency demands. Furthermore, the same individual may show changes in pattern and degree of cognitive impairment at different stages of recovery. To be effective, cognitive rehabilitation must therefore be adapted to these various factors as they pertain to each individual.

The ultimate goal in rehabilitation is improving the individual's quality of life. For the most part this is reflected, in our society, in achieving the highest possible capacity for independence in living and for productive work. That is, quality of life depends heavily on competency. Rehabilitation typically involves at least three components: *restoration* of functions to as near as possible their preinjury level, *compensation* for or accommodation to deficits that cannot be restored, and *adjustment* to changes in ability or in life style.

Cognitive rehabilitation refers to the therapeutic process of increasing or improving an individual's capacity to process and use incoming information so as to allow increased functioning in everyday living. This includes methods to restore cognitive function, compensatory techniques that allow an individual to use alternative means to compensate for decreased cognitive ability, and adjustment to ability and life style changes so as to optimize use of residual capacity. Goldstein and Ruthven (1983) describe an approach to management of brain damaged patients that they term "rational rehabilitation." Rational rehabilitation is that rehabilitation based on solid, scientific knowledge of brain–behavior relationships and that is designed to meet specifically defined treatment goals. These two components, theoretically motivated cognitive rehabilitation programs and identification of well-prescribed treatment goals, are important facets of cognitive rehabilitation.

Contextual Considerations

Cognitive rehabilitation for traumatically brain-injured people usually occurs within a broader rehabilitative context. An understanding of this broader context is useful in evaluating cognitive rehabilitation. First, the stages of recovery and rehabilitation determine the goals of cognitive retraining efforts and, second, these cognitive treatment endeavors need to be understood within the broader perspective of whole rehabilitative process.

Treatment of brain injury and its consequences usually involves care over a series of distinct periods, each with its own goals. These periods are: (a) emergency care aimed at keeping the patient alive and preventing as much permanent neurological damage as possible, (b) coma care during which continuing efforts at medical stabilization occur, (c) inpatient rehabilitation aimed at redeveloping basic communication, mobility, and self-care skills (dressing, eating, grooming, etc.), (d) outpatient rehabilitation aimed at maintenance and extension of stage c skills when the patient returns home, and (e) community reintegration. The first four stages, both by tradition and necessity are medically oriented and conducted within the "medical model." The fifth stage of community reintegration is often conducted in a nonmedical setting and aims at assisting patients to achieve independence with respect to vocational, educational, domestic, transportation, and social/leisure functioning.

Not all patients require the entire spectrum of rehabilitation, but for many individuals with severe to moderate head injuries, such a continuum is ideal. Some patients, however, never regain full consciousness or sustain injuries too severe to allow them to benefit from the later stages of service. Others, who are mildly injured, may not require the earlier stages of service or only to a minimal extent.

Cognitive rehabilitation can begin as early as the second stage, that is, coma care, and can play an increasingly significant role across the subsequent stages of rehabilitation. During coma care, controlled sensory stimulation activities such as visual tracking exercises, auditory stimulation, and tactile stimulation can form an important part of early rehabilitation. As the patient becomes more able to respond to the environment, orientation, attention, memory, visuospatial, language, reasoning, and executive function exercises can be introduced according to individual patterns and levels of deficit as the patient goes through inpatient and outpatient phases of rehabilitation. By the fifth stage, community reintegration, cognitive factors often are the most crucial determinants of the patient's level of independence. Follow-up studies 2, 3, 4, and even 15 years postinjury have revealed that the major problems or limitations of patients at this stage are cognitive in nature and often involve significant psychosocial consequences; that is, inability to achieve independent functioning is the result of underlying problems in concentration, memory, executive function, visuospatial skills, communication, and so on.

Cognitive rehabilitation is a newcomer to the rehabilitation scene. It has a unique and vital contribution to make but also needs to be integrated with the traditional therapies (occupational, physical, speech), nursing concerns with basic safety and self-care, vocational, and recreational training, and counseling. There needs to be a two-way interaction between these programs and cognitive training: (a) patients often have difficulty understanding how cognitive training exercises relate to their general rehabilitation goals and efforts unless the connections and appropriate generalizations are fostered both by cognitive therapists and others, and (b) cognitive factors often impede progress in other therapy or treatment areas unless these factors are understood and dealt with as they impact on these other areas. For example, a patient with attention problems may not see the relevance of and be reluctant to engage in reaction time tasks during cognitive therapy sessions because they do not seem related to the patient's primary concern with regaining walking ability. Yet when receiving ambulatory instruction in physical therapy, this same patient's progress may be retarded by poor attention to instruction, kinesthetic sensations, and environmental cues. If the patient's cognitive therapy addresses the importance of focusing and sustaining attention, the cognitive therapist needs to talk about how this aspect of attention affects walking. The physical therapists also need to remind the patient about focusing and maintaining attention as needed during ambulation classes. At a more advanced stage of rehabilitation, cognitive training needs to be integrated in a similar fashion and for similar reasons but with more sophisticated activities such as performance in work stations or financial planning.

Evaluating Cognitive Rehabilitation: General Issues

Efficacy studies in the area of cognitive rehabilitation are at an embryonic stage at best. There are several reasons for such the dearth of evaluative studies. Perhaps the most fundamental obstacle to assessing treatment efficacy arises from individual differences in spontaneous recovery from brain injury. The individual differences most relevant to recovery include: location of lesion, extent or magnitude of neurological damage, time postonset, age at injury, rate of improvement immediately after injury, and premorbid level of functioning (e.g., socioemotional factors, presence of drug or alcohol abuse, and external factors, such as type of job, family support, community resources, and financial status). Such differences related to spontaneous recovery are easily confounded with treatment effects, thus making it difficult to evaluate treatment outcomes.

An additional reason for limited research on treatment efficacy arises from the fact that most treatment is done by clinicians in clinical (usually fee-for-service) settings. Thus, there may not be the research experience, resources, and incentives to undertake carefully controlled studies. There are also ethical dilemmas inherent in conducting traditional clinical experimental studies that present further obstacles to efficacy research. The bulk of experimental work is conducted using group designs, which require use of a control or notreatment group. Since withholding treatment is not a reasonable clinical practice, many have been discouraged from carrying out efficacy treatment studies. One solution to this problem has been the use of single-subject designs to examine the outcomes of various cognitive rehabilitation methods (e.g., Gianutsos & Gianutsos, 1979; Sohlberg & Mateer, 1987). Single-subject methodology has gained increasing respect as an approach to evaluate treatment efficacy and allows the investigator to evaluate changes longitudinally. A second solution that has been proposed is the use of persons on rehabilitation program waiting lists as the matched head injury control group. Results from this study model are yet to appear in the literature.

In the past 5 years there has been an increase in the number of studies examining treatment effects. The field has begun to evolve from a purely descriptive discipline to one whose practices are starting to be data-based and grounded in sound theoretical underpinnings derived from the cognitive sciences.

Can Cognitive Competencies be Retrained?

There are many aspects of cognitive function that may be affected by neurological insult. Those deficits resulting from focal injury secondary to stroke have been the focus of attention in rehabilitation over the longest period. Thus, there are well established techniques for evaluating and providing treatment for speech and language deficits and for visuospatial or perceptual impairments (Johns, 1978; Weinberg, et al., 1977, 1979). While still the subject of some controversy, the effectiveness of these interventions by speech/language pathologists, psychologists, and occupational therapists in rehabilitation settings is generally acknowledged. In contrast, there are few, if any, well developed or standardized approaches to the most common deficits that accompany traumatic brain injury (i.e., attention, memory, executive function, and psychosocial/behavioral deficits). The literature relative to each of these will be discussed in the following sections.

Rehabilitation of Attention Deficits

Attention is the basis of all mental functions. The mind is a limited capacity system that cannot possibly deal with every sight, sound, smell, thought, memory, and action impinging on it at a given moment. To function competently, it has to select some of these stimuli for processing while neglecting or ignoring others. As Geschwind (1982) points out, normal mental functioning requires that the person select a limited number of stimuli to be processed at any given instant and that the basis for this selection be maintained over sufficient time to give coherence to thought and action. Although the person should not be distracted by irrelevant stimuli, they should be monitoring a wide range of "unattended" stimuli so that possibly relevant stimuli can be detected and brought into focus. Any shift of attention to include new or different stimuli must be made on the basis of appropriate need and relevance of those stimuli in the person's life. Brain impairment can result in deficits in the amount of information a person can attend to within a given time and in the person's ability to control and direct the attentional capacity they have.

Damage to the brain stem reticular formation areas can result in generally lowered mental arousal or alertness that limits both capacity and control. When people emerge from coma, arousal levels are generally still low and they are disorganized and vague in their attention to their surroundings and in their ability to follow a train of thought. At this stage, appropriate remediation involves providing stimulation that is simple and that captures interest easily and readily. Even while the person is still in coma, stimulation with favorite music, familiar voices, etc., has been considered beneficial in improving alertness (Frazier, 1980; LeWinn & Dimancescu, 1978; Lynch, 1978). Wood (1989) argues, however, that any such stimulation be provided in a structured and controlled fashion because overstimulation or poorly organized input may have deleterious effects.

The diffuse damage that typically occurs in closed head injury results in reduced attentional capacity, even when the patient is fully alert (see van Zomeren, Brouwer & Deelman, 1984, for review). Limited attentional capacity results in stress from the feeling of "overload" and from the continual mental effort and concentration necessary to perform tasks that were once relatively easy. As well as diffuse damage, head trauma patients often sustain frontal lobe damage, which causes deficits in the ability to control, direct, organize, and monitor their activity, both motor and mental. Such a control deficit diminishes their ability to utilize whatever attentional capacity they do have. They may be able to attend fairly well if someone else gets them started on a particular task and reminds them to stay on the task until it is completed. When left to their own initiative, however, they easily lose track of what they are doing, saying, or thinking, and are easily distracted but also have difficulty moving their focus of attention from one task to another in a controlled but appropriately flexible way. Attention thus underlies many daily activities and mental capacities, including memory, communication, and problem solving.

A variety of approaches to dealing with attentional deficits have been proposed, including behavioral, pharmacological and electrophysiological approaches. Wood (1986) reported increases in attentive behavior during therapy sessions in some severely head injured patients with use of a token economy program. Klove (1987) described beneficial effects of stimulant medication in three of four patients with chronic arousal deficits (but reported no formal assessment). Birbaumer, Elbert, Rockstron & Lutzenberger (1986) provided two sessions of electroencephalography (EEG) biofeedback training to 10 head-injured patients in an attempt to teach them to voluntarily regulate slow-potential shifts known to correlate with response latency and vigilance. Head-injured patients were unable to alter such EEG shifts without consistent feedback of the EEG signal.

Most attention studies have focused on attempts to retrain underlying attentional skills. The assumption behind attention training is that it is more efficient to focus on cognitive functions underlying daily activities than it is to focus on the training of such activities directly, that is, to focus on causes rather than symptoms. In this way cognitive rehabilitation differs from a purely functional approach to treatment. Since the ultimate goal of rehabilitation is the improvement of skills that would allow the individual to regain independence or employment, improvement in cognitive function based on training activities must be shown to generalize.

To date, 13 studies addressing the treatment of attentional disorders have appeared in the literature. Eight of these used exposure to and repetition of specific laboratory-based activities or tasks that provided opportunity to exercise attentional skills. The remaining studies looked at the effectiveness of a behavioral token economy, EEG biofeedback, and pharmacological intervention.

Ben-Yishay and Diller (1983, 1978–1983) developed five training tasks (one auditory, four visual) that were hierarchically ordered in terms of the number of subfunctions involved and the relative difficulty level. The five tasks were related loosely to existing cognitive models of attention but included reference to Posner's (1975) model of effortful processing. Goals included improved self-monitoring and efficient utilization of feedback about performance. Eleven head-injured patients were evaluated in a multiple baseline design to determine improvement on training tasks and generalization to independent untrained tests. Task-specific training effects were reported as well as improvements in reaction time, attention to visual deficit, and visuomotor speed.

Sohlberg and Mateer (1987) reported on the effectiveness of a cognitive rehabilitation program specifically designed to address a broad range of attentional deficits (Attention Process Training) combined with selective computer programs. The authors based the administration of hierarchically organized treatment tasks on a five-level model of attention: focused, sustained, selective, alternating, and divided attention. More than 60 exercises corresponding to the specific components of attention were used to provide repeated exercise of attention in a gradual and progressively more demanding sequence. Treatment was individualized and varied from 4 to 8 weeks with each patient receiving seven to nine sessions per week. Attention Training and Visual Process Training were used in a multiple baseline design replicated across four patients. Gains in attention were seen during and after attention training and gains on a visual task were seen during and after visual process training. Results were interpreted to indicate domain-specific cognitive improvement. Mateer and Sohlberg (1988) went on to report positive effects on memory performance after attention training in a series of five additional patients. In this way attention training was demonstrated to have a beneficial effect on another measured cognitive process area dependent on attention. Wood (1986), using visual and auditory training tasks, also reported changes on measures of both verbal memory and attentive behavior in other therapeutic environments.

Niemann (1989) evaluated the effects of attention training versus memory training in two groups of head-injured patients. Attention training tasks were similar to those described by Sohlberg and Mateer (1987). Memory training consisted of training on a variety of mnemonic strategies. Results indicated gains on specific measures of attention and of memory function in the group receiving attention training. Similar gains were not seen in the group receiving memory training. Neither group, however, demonstrated gains in an independent set of neuropsychological measures administered pretreatment and posttreatment.

Sturm, Dahmen, Hartje, and Willmes (1983) evaluated the effect of attention training on two groups of patients (15 each in a full-time inpatient rehabilitation setting and two groups of normal controls). Patient and control subjects in the experimental group received 7 hours of training on tasks involving visual and auditory stimuli that were manipulated for complexity and speed. Improvement in the experimental groups was seen on a number of independent measures taken from common German intelligence and vocational tests. Results of the study are somewhat confounded, however, by the relatively early stage of recovery (10 months mean chronicity) and the high percentage of cerebrovascular as opposed to head trauma patients.

Kewman et al. (1985) evaluated the efficacy of attention training in a group of head-injured patients (n = 13, average chronicity 3.7 years) and a head-injured and normal control group. The experimental training required the subjects to maneuver a modified battery powered wheelchair along courses of increasing difficulty while they responded to auditory and visual stimuli. The head-injured control group attended a classroom driving course but had no exposure to the attention tasks. Normal control subjects participated in advanced parts of the experimental training. All groups underwent on-the-road evaluation before and after training. Both experimental groups improved significantly on the training tasks as well as in on-the-road driving skills as compared to the head-injured control group. The study demonstrated effects of cognitive training on a functional skill.

Weber (1990) describes an approach to the treatment of two patients, one with an attentional capacity deficit and one with an attentional control deficit. Although the same basic tasks were used to treat both types of deficits, the way in which they were used was varied according to the relative proportions of capacity and control difficulties. Weber argues that an individual whose main problem is limited capacity will primarily make errors of omission on monitoring tasks whereas the person with control problems makes frequent commission or false positive errors in addition to omissions. The patient with limited-capacity benefits from repetition of the task, increasing familiarity, and knowing where the "danger spots" are so that he can increase attentional effort at these particular places. He also benefit from learning relaxation and self-pacing techniques to reduce/prevent "overload". The patient with a control deficit may respond to repetition and feedback about errors by becoming more entrenched in his error pattern and the retraining procedure needs to include ways of preventing or disrupting such inappropriate response sets and teaching the person how to do this himself, such as through role reversal strategies, goal-setting, and task structuring techniques.

In contrast to these studies, several negative reports regarding the efficacy of attention training have appeared (Wood & Fussey, 1987; Malec, Jones, Rao & Stubbs, 1984; Ponsford & Kinsella, 1988). Wood and Fussey (1987) did not report significant improvement on psychomotor or vigilance tasks or on two behavioral measures of time-on-task in head-injured patients who were at least 1 year postinjury. Training, however, may have been too limited or narrow in that only one computerized visual attention task was used in treatment.

Malec et al. (1984) evaluated the effects of a 2-week visual attention training program in 10 patients with severe head injury within 6 months after the trauma. Improvements were found but were independent of training. Problems may have emerged here because of the interaction with spontaneous recovery, the short training period, and the use of a single visual attention task. In addition, the authors used a withdrawal treatment design. Subjects were assigned to an ABAB or a BABA protocol where a week of training (A) was altered with a week of nontraining (B). It may be that treatment effects on a cognitive function cannot be withdrawn as can intervention for more behaviorally controlled variables.

Ponsford and Kinsella (1988) trained 10 patients with an average chronicity of 9 months on five visual attention tasks (e.g., simple and choice reaction time, visual search) in a staggered baseline design. Total time on treatment tasks was 15 hours. One of two treatment phases was associated with reinforcement and feedback while the other was not. Attention tests, an attention rating scale, and a video evaluation of attentive behaviors were used as independent measures. None of the measures revealed treatment related effects although 3 of the 10 patients were reported to respond favorably to feedback and reinforcement. The nature and amount of feedback given to patients about their training task performance may well be significant factors in determining outcome of treatment and explain some of the discrepant findings between studies.

Despite these somewhat conflicting studies of attention training efficacy, reasons for optimism remain and further investigation is clearly warranted. Several factors emerge from these investigations that may be critical to treatment success. All three of the attention training studies with negative effects used only visually based training tasks and a limited number of relatively unmodifiable tasks. Studies reporting greater success tended to use a much broader range and number of training tasks. Retraining of underlying cognitive skills is likely to require not only sufficient repetitive practice but exposure to tasks of a sufficiently broad and demanding attentional load. Issues of what training tasks are beneficial, for what patients, at what time postinjury, and with what effects have only just begun to be critically addressed.

The direction in neuropsychological assessment has increasingly been toward development of task measures that more adequately reveal the way in which a cognitive process is disrupted. Similarly, process-oriented cognitive rehabilitation must increasingly move toward applying specific treatments to specific patients based on the individual nature of their deficits. Sohlberg and Mateer's (1987) model of treatment provides for the application of specific attentional training exercises (i.e., sustained, selective, alternating, and divided attention) based on the particular profile of deficits a patient demonstrates. In a similar vein, Weber's (1990) approach argues for matching the attention treatment plan to the individual's specific attentional deficits (capacity and control).

In summary, the targeted treatment of attention appears to be an appropriate and promising focus for rehabilitation efforts. In order for the field to progress, clinicians will need to incorporate current models of attentional functioning into treatment efforts. Training tasks must not only emerge from such models but must reflect and incorporate everyday aspects of attentional functioning.

Rehabilitation of Memory Functions

Disturbances of memory are among the most frequently voiced complaints and most commonly demonstrated impairments of individuals with head trauma. Damage to many areas of the brain can disrupt different aspects of memory functioning (see Sohlberg & Mateer, 1989a, for review). Specific approaches to the rehabilitation of memory have only recently been the subject of development and study. These include approaches that attempt to restore or improve memory function per se and approaches that might help the individual with a memory deficit cope with the effects of memory impairment. Restorative approaches would include pharmacological therapies, surgical interventions, or the use of behavioral exercises or drills that would restore memory to a level closer to premorbid function. Compensation approaches would include the development and training of internal or external strategies that might help the individual to improve his ability to access information.

Pharmacological or drug therapies have included the administration of cholinergic agents (Goldberg, Gerstmann & Mathis, 1982) and oral physostigmine (McLean, Stanton & Cardenas, 1987). Neurosurgical approaches have included techniques such as stereotaxic electrical brain stimulation. Recently, interest has turned to the possibility of using transplants of fetal or other brain tissue to improve aspects of brain functioning. Although of interest, such interventions are as yet in an embryonic stage of development and may not be beneficial or accessible to the vast majority of individuals with acquired memory deficits secondary to brain injury.

Restorative approaches of a more behavioral nature have focused on repetitive practice, drill, or recall tasks. List learning or paragraph recall tasks are commonly included in this approach, as exemplified by many workbook activities and computer programs for memory. Published studies have, however, quite consistently documented the failure of such approaches to improve scores on untrained memory tasks or to impact functional memory outside the clinic (Crovitz, 1979; Godfrey & Knight, 1985; Prigatano et al., 1984, Schacter, Rich & Stamp, 1985).

An alternative approach to memory restoration proposed by Mateer and Sohlberg (1988) is the development of prospective memory capacity. Prospective memory refers to the capacity to carry out future intended actions—in a sense to remember to remember. This kind of memory, which involves such common everyday activities as remembering to take medications, remembering to return a phone call, or remembering to pick up items at the store has been proposed to be an ecologically important component of memory. These authors report preliminary findings that suggest that the length of prospective memory, that is, the duration of time over which actions can be recalled and independently carried out, can be increased and that such increases are related to improved scores on independent measures of memory function.

Finally, as discussed in the previous section, several authors (Mateer & Sohlberg, 1988; Niemann, 1989) have reported gains in memory function after targeted training of attentional skills. Since attention is critical to the receipt and registration of information, improvement in this first stage of the information processing system for memory might be expected to have positive effects in memory for those individuals in whom memory deficits are secondary to attentional deficits.

Internally based compensatory memory techniques are strategies that the individual applies from within to enhance the ability to encode, store, or retrieve information to be recalled. These techniques focus on increasing organization of information to be recalled, rehearsing information to be remembered, or training of specific mnemonic devices such as peg words or visual imagery (Wilson & Moffat, 1984). Several studies have suggested that recall performance in memory disordered patients can be improved through training of such internal mnemonic learning schemes (Cermak, 1975; Crovitz, Harvey & Horn, 1979; Gianutsos & Gianutsos, 1979; Gasparrini & Satz, 1979; Lewinsohn, Danaher & Kikel, 1977; Parente & Anderson, 1983; Wilson, 1981, 1982).

Results are somewhat conflicting, and none of these studies has demonstrated that use of these strategies is maintained or that such schemes generalize to naturalistic settings. There is some indication that use of such internally generated strategies may be beneficial in patients with mild head injuries who have considerable residual memory ability (Wilson, 1987). Patients with moderate to severe memory deficits have been found to have difficulty generating and applying mnemonic strategies spontaneously (Crovitz et al., 1979). Since these techniques place heavy demands on already compromised cognitive systems, they are generally inappropriate for persons with severely compromised intellectual or memory functions. Similar criticisms, in terms of a need for high level abstraction skills, can be leveled against verbal mediation techniques such as chaining or linking, alphabetical cuing, and semantic or phonetic elaboration. Overall results of these studies suggest that for most head injury patients gains are likely to be short-lived and positive results may not generalize to everyday tasks.

In addition, few everyday situations lend themselves to imagery or to other forms of mnemonic association so that such training is not easily generalized. These strategies require considerable memory resources to learn and there is little evidence that normal individuals, much less memory impaired patients, can use such techniques effectively for the recall of the myriad of facts, people, and intentions for action necessary in daily life.

Another set of procedures has been proposed to use with memory impaired individuals that might be considered under the rubric of self-instructional techniques. One such study technique is known as PQRST (Preview, Question, Read, State, Test). Glasgow, Zeiss, Barrera, and Lewinsohn (1977) reported success in teaching a head-injured patient to recall and understand newspaper articles using this method. Wilson (1987) reported a similar favorable outcome, using this technique in two head-injured patients with severe memory disorder and a group of patients with less severe memory problems. Generalization and maintenance of these techniques have not, however, been reported and again success may be restricted to patients with milder impairments or relative sparing of general intellectual skills.

Recent experimental research in amnesic patients has revealed the presence of certain categories or types of preserved memory in even severely memory disordered patients. These sorts of preserved memory vary with respect to content (e.g., motor, perceptual) but have in common the improvement of performance across trials despite the patient having no recollection of these previous trials. Two techniques for memory rehabilitation have been based on these potentially preserved abilities. Glisky, Schacter, and Tulving (1986) developed a technique known as the "method of vanishing cues" in which apparent fading of cues was used to teach memory disordered patients a computer vocabulary. After a long course of intensive training, four patients were able to use this technique to learn a small "domain-specific" body of knowledge involving a computer vocabulary.

A second approach to treatment of compensatory approaches in individuals with memory impairment involves training in the use of external memory aids. External memory aids include organizational devices, prospective memory devices, and environmental modification. Organizational devices include such tools as electronic memories, memory notebook systems, and computers that allow an individual to organize, store, and retrieve significant amounts of information. Prospective memory devices include tools to remind a memory impaired person to perform a particular action at a specific future time. These would include alarms, calendars, buzzers, and watches. Environmental modifications involve any restructuring or alteration of the environment to decrease the impact of memory deficits or everyday functions. These would include posted checklists, labeled shelves, alphabetized cupboards, and special structured work environments.

Clinicians often report difficulty in getting patients to learn and use external aids. Effective use of such systems often involves a fairly complex set of activities. Given the inherent problems with new learning as well as with initiation, planning, and insight into the need for use of such devices, training in such techniques has often been frustrating to clinicians. Sohlberg and Mateer (1989b) have described the use of a three-stage behaviorally based training technique for memory notebook use in a severely memory disordered patient. The technique is based on principles of learning and involves use of acquisition, adaptation, and application phases. These begin with teaching of basic facts about the system and its structures, move on to providing structured opportunities for notebook use through role play activities, and finally incorporate notebook training into community-based activities. The training is data-based and works on building skills with notebook use in a progressive hierarchy. While no claim is made for any benefit to underlying memory capacity, effective use of such a system can support a memory impaired individual in a living and work environment.

In a case described by Sohlberg and Mateer (1989b), a severely head-injured 19-year-old man with severe attention deficits and a profound amnesia began memory notebook training 12 months after his injury. It took him 17 program days to achieve 100% accuracy in response to questions about his book, 23 days to consistently write in his log in the clinic, 32 days to write in his log at home, and 38 days before he could appropriately use the book in three role play situations on 2 consecutive days. Three additional months of training were needed before he could use the book in real-life situations on a regular basis. After treatment, his scores on memory tests did not change, but he was able to live in an apartment with only weekly assistance and work in an electronic assembly position. The memory book use was instrumental in achieving these levels of independence.

Rehabilitation of Executive Function Deficits

"Executive function" is a relatively new term that refers to people's ability to set goals, plan how to achieve such goals, organize their behavior in accord with such plans, and check, monitor, and adapt their behavior along the way. They also need to be able to modify their goals and plans in light of changing circumstances. Without such ability, an otherwise highly intelligent person can be unemployable, have significant problems managing their daily affairs, and be a constant source of irritation and concern to their family and friends. This executive ability is also crucial to the person's rehabilitative potential with respect to other sorts of deficits. That is, executive function includes the ability to generate compensatory strategies and implement such strategies in a purposeful way (Stuss & Benson, 1986).

Although there are neuropsychological tests that have been designed to detect the presence of executive function problems, it is possible for a person to have mild but significant problems in this area and still score normally on such tests. This test insensitivity occurs because standardized testing typically involves the tester setting the task goal, ensuring that the person stays on task, and perhaps providing general prompts encouraging the person to think about the task and how to solve it. Thus, the tester provides the necessary executive functions and the patient's difficulty in so doing does not become apparent. In less structured, naturalistic settings at home and work however, the patient may fail to initiate task-oriented behavior, fail to complete tasks, and generally show disorganized behavior (Lezak, 1983). Diagnosis, in such cases, may depend on anecdotal and observational data.

Treatment programs designed to restore or compensate for executive function deficits are still in the early stages of development. The only published program at this time is that of Sohlberg and Mateer (1989a) and it includes tasks designed to train the selection and execution of cognitive plans, time management, and self-regulation. These three broad areas of treatment are broken down into a number of more concrete components such as planning, initiation, speed of response, time scheduling, awareness, impulse control, and so on.

At this time, there are no studies evaluating the effectiveness of executive function training programs. However, the treatment of executive function deficits is often crucial to the successful community reentry of head-injured people and may also influence their ability to benefit from other more traditional therapies such as physical, occupational, and speech therapies.

Rehabilitation and Psychosocial Problems

Psychosocial and behavioral problems commonly occur in brain-impaired individuals and usually constitute a significant focus of postacute rehabilitation efforts. Such problems may occur as the direct result of brain damage (e.g., behavioral disinhibition, social insensitivity) or reflect emotional reactions to the experience of impairment and the resulting changes in the person's life (e.g., depression, anxiety, social withdrawal).

During the acute phase of the person's recovery, agitation, fear, and suspiciousness may occur as part of general mental confusion. Structuring of the environment with simple and familiar objects, repeated simple explanations of their situation, and other efforts to facilitate their orientation to time, place, and person are all useful at this time.

Individuals with frontal lobe damage often show impulsive, disinhibited, emotionally labile behavior and their socially inappropriate, insensitive, and sometimes crude or aggressive conduct can seriously jeopardize their social relationships at home, work, or in society at large. It is also possible for damage in certain frontal areas of the brain to cause a personality change in which the person shows little motivation to do anything at all, becomes very passive and inert, and is unable to engage actively in activities without continuous prompting and urging from others (Lezak, 1987). Treatment of such organically based problems often comprises a major part of the rehabilitation program. Behavior modification techniques are generally more effective than insight-oriented psychodynamic therapies because such patients often have difficulty monitoring and being aware of their own behavior and its effects on others. Sohlberg and Mateer (1989a) report on the use of an external cuing technique with a patient with severe frontal injury. This technique increased the frequency of initiating conversation and of responding to others' comments in a group setting. Wood (1987) in his book describing behavioral intervention techniques provides the greatest single source for use of behavioral interventions with brain-injured patients. These techniques can be used to shape or increase desirable behaviors and decrease undesirable or disruptive behaviors.

A common result of the diffuse damage that often occurs in cases of closed head injury is slowed mental processing. Although people may still be able to do the same tasks as before their injury, they now find that they are slower and have to put forth maximum mental effort and concentration to do things that were formerly routine. The continual effort and stress often result in feelings of frustration, anxiety, irritation, inadequacy, and depression. Patients usually benefit from being helped to understand the nature of the problem and from learning to deal with it through realistic goalsetting and stress-management techniques. Such insight-oriented approaches have been well described and discussed by several investigators/clinicians (Ben-Yishay et al. 1987a, 1987b; Diller & Weinberg, 1977; Prigatano, 1986; Weber, 1990).

Right hemisphere damage sometimes results in impaired ability to perceive and/or express emotion by means of intonation, facial expression, and other nonverbal means. This sort of deficit can result in inappropriate perception of and response to the emotional communications of others. It can also result in a rather flat, neutral style of expression that fails to communicate appropriately the person's own feelings. Appropriate remedial procedures for such difficulties have not yet been well established but attempts are beginning to be made to find effective treatment techniques (Sohlberg & Mateer, 1990). Social skills training will need to take into account the individual's specific pattern of cognitive strengths and deficits.

Any cognitive deficit is likely to evoke grief, anxiety, depression, and frustration because of the loss of function itself and because of the impact of this deficit on the person's everyday life. Deficits in memory, attention, and executive function can have a major impact on most areas of life: the ability to engage meaningfully in conversation, to empathize with others, to enjoy films, television, or reading, to get household chores done, to live safely with respect to turning off electrical appliances, to navigate safely when driving, to care for and discipline children, to do things on schedule such as keeping appointments, taking medication, and doing homework assignments, to budget, balance checkbooks, write letters, or to engage in work at some former level of competency and salary. In addition to the distress of not being able to do things as they used to, patients also often lose their vocational, social, and family roles and income. This can be very distressing for the family too. Both patients and their families (or other close associates) can benefit from information and counseling about the nature of the deficits. They also often benefit emotionally from the process of cognitive retraining with its opportunities for understanding the deficits at an experiential level and for gaining hope and self-esteem from progress in learning how to compensate for their difficulties (Ben-Yishay & Diller, 1983; Prigatano, 1986; Sohlberg & Mateer, 1989a; Weber, 1990).

Emotional reactions of the patient and family are likely to vary at different stages of recovery. Effective treatment of psychosocial problems requires appropriate versatility in this respect. Often one of the basic issues in the early stages of rehabilitation is that of denial or lack of awareness by the patient (and sometimes family) of the cognitive and psychosocial deficits. Confrontation with concrete experiences of failure or error often need to be incorporated into the rehabilitation program at this stage, although this needs to be combined with support and the hope of overcoming such problems through retraining. Group work is often helpful in facilitating such awareness and in providing moral support from people who are going through the same experiences.

Later, as the patient and family face the reality of the permanent changes, despair is a more common reaction than denial. The distribution of responsibility within the family may alter radically, the family income may be severely depleted, and the patient may no longer be the person he used to be. Even in welladjusted families, these changes can cause major emotional and psychological upheaval, loss, and grief. Family counseling and support groups can play an important role in helping both the patient and family to deal with these issues and prevent further exacerbation of psychosocial problems (Lezak, 1978, 1987).

In summary, the treatment of psychosocial problems is usually a key focus of rehabilitative efforts to optimize the person's competency. The techniques used should be appropriate to the particular nature of the problem if intervention is to be effective.

Overall Effectiveness of Cognitive Rehabilitation

The degree of competence and independence achieved by brain-injured patients varies not only in response to the effectiveness of cognitive treatment but also as a function of the nature and severity of damage. Thus, defining successful outcome of treatment is a complex matter.

Depending on the particular circumstances, successful outcome might include anything from satisfactory behavioral adjustment to institutionalization through to total independence. Some of the intermediary levels of competence include attendant care, group home placement, selective monitoring (i.e., intermittent supervision), sheltered workshop, supported work (i.e., the disabled person is assisted as needed on the job by another employee who is paid to do so), and modified work setting.

There are a number of ways to measure treatment outcomes. The Disability Rating Scale (Rappaport, Hall, Hopkins & Bolleza, 1982), which includes the Glasgow Coma Scale, a four-point scale rating cognitive ability for feeding, toileting, and grooming; an overall rating of cognitive independence scaled on a six-point continuum; and a four-point scale of employability ranging from "not restricted" to "not employable." Surveys and structured interviews offer alternative means to rating scales for gathering information about a patient's level of functioning (Jacobs, 1988).

Articles reporting outcomes for postacute rehabilitation programs have only recently begun to be published. Findings in such articles suggest that increases in cognitive and psychosocial functioning have yielded better community reintegration for many brain-injured patients (Ben-Yishay et al., 1987b; Fryer & Haffey, 1987; Kreutzer, Wehman & Morton, 1988; Prigatano et al., 1984; Sohlberg & Mateer, 1989a). It is important to identify, however, whether employment outcomes are measured according to an individual's *capability* to return to work or to their actually *being employed*. In other words, a patient might be judged to be capable of competitive employment by treatment staff but not be placed in a job and thus remain unemployed. The employability status of such individuals is not at all clear.

Mateer and Sohlberg (1989) reported outcome statistics for 43 program graduates of a postacute day treatment program. Of those, 26 had sustained moderate to severe injury and were involved in a full-day treatment program and a transitional living situation. Their average age was 34.5 years (range 20–58 years), they averaged 25.2 months postinjury at time of program entry (range 2–108 months), and they spent an average of 6.8 months in program (range 4–9 months). The program provided a full complement of cognitive therapy, speech/language therapy, occupational therapy, physical conditioning, individual, family, and group counseling, recreational therapy, and vocational rehabilitation and placement.

When followed up 3 months postdischarge, 15 were competitively employed, 2 were in supported work, 1 was in a sheltered workshop, 3 were in vocational training, and 1 was a homemaker (see Table 9.1). Only 4 of the 26 were unemployed or nonproductive. Fifteen of the 26 participants were at least 1 year postdischarge at the time of the report; of these, 60% remained fully employed. Those individuals who lost jobs did

TABLE 9.1. Vocational competency of moderately to severely brain-injured graduates of the center for cognitive rehabilitation.

Scale	Status on entry (n = 26)	Status at 3 months (n = 26)	Status at 12 months (n = 15)[a]
1 Competitive	0	15	7
2 Supported	1	2	2
3 Sheltered	0	1	0
4 Training	0	3	1
5 Unreimbursed	0	1	0
6 Nonproductive	25	4	4 (1 deceased)

[a] Reflects number of graduates who were out of program for 12 months at the time of this report.

so because of substance abuse or financial disincentives. Most of the individuals served in this program could not return to former positions or had little preinjury work experience. Most but not all of the jobs obtained after program participation were entry-level positions.

Seventeen of the 43 graduates had suffered mild head injuries and were independent for self-care and transportation. They were, however, having difficulty returning to work because of residual cognitive limitations, and were experiencing emotional response to loss. These individuals average 36.8 years of age (range 21–54 years) and were an average 30.5 months postinjury (range 9–102 months). They were in the program an average of 7.3 months (range 3–10) and received cognitive therapy, psychosocial counseling, and vocational rehabilitation in a 12-hour per week program. Five of the 17 were employed (2 part-time) at the time they entered the program. Three months after the program, all but two of the individuals were employed (see Table 9.2). One left the job and one was severely reinjured in a fall. Of the 10 individuals who had been followed for 1 year at the time of the report, 9 were employed (80%), and all on a full-time basis. Many of these individuals were able to return to former positions in the same firm or to similar positions in another company. These outcomes suggest that a comprehensive, multidisciplinary postacute program can be effective not only in returning individuals to work but in facilitating long-term maintenance of productive employment.

Recent literature is also building a case for cost effectiveness of cognitive rehabilitation programs. A study by Aronow (1987) examining the benefits to society of such programs showed that hospitalized patients who were provided with rehabilitation were returned to productive or nonburdensome levels of functioning at the same rate as a less severe nontreatment group. Among patients with similar severity of disabilities, those receiving rehabilitation cost less on average than a comparison nontreatment group. Aronow suggests that once the resources are com-

TABLE 9.2. Vocational competency of mildly head-injured graduates of the center for cognitive rehabilitation.

Scale	Status on entry (n = 17)	Status at 3 months (n = 17)	Status at 12 months (n = 10)[a]
1 Competitive	4 (2 part-time)	15 (2 part-time)	9
2 Supported	1	0	0
3 Sheltered	0	0	0
4 Training	0	0	0
5 Unreimbursed	0	0	0
6 Nonproductive	12	2 (1 reinjured)	1 (1 left job)

[a] Reflects number of graduates who were out of program for 12 months at the time of this report.

mitted to save the life of a severely injured traumatic brain-injured victim in the emergency room, the most cost effective measure is to provide rehabilitation services and prevent or reduce long-term disability payments by government or private disability funds.

Similar findings regarding the cost effectiveness of rehabilitation were found in a study by Sohlberg and Brock (1985), who performed a hypothetical cost comparison of postacute rehabilitation services with long-term disability/welfare payments (assuming only a 40% success rate for returning head-injured patients to productive work and independent living). Results showed that substantial savings, on the order of millions of dollars, would be achieved by financing postmedical cognitive rehabilitation as opposed to disability and social welfare payments.

Conclusions

There is emerging evidence that cognitive rehabilitation can effectively increase the competency of brain-injured individuals and that such cognitive treatment is cost effective. Clarification of the degree to which competency can be retrained requires further research that examines the relationship of particular treatment techniques to particular cognitive deficits in a process-specific fashion. Broad mental functions such as attention, memory, and executive function need to be broken down into their subcomponents and underlying dimensions and treated according to the particular deficit patterns. Treatment approaches need to be defined not only in terms of tasks and amount of practice, but also with respect to the nature of feedback given, the way the patient is taught the task, the focus on developing awareness of deficit and successful compensation strategies, and the attention given to facilitating generalization of what is learned on cognitive training tasks to activities of daily living and other treatment goals.

References

Aronow, H.U. (1987). Rehabilitation effectiveness with severe brain injury: Translating research into policy. *Journal of Head Trauma Rehabilitation*, *2*, 24–36.

Ben-Yishay, Y., & Diller, L. (1983). Cognitive deficits. In M. Rosenthal (Ed.), *Rehabilitation of the head injured adult*. Philadelphia: F.A. Davis.

Ben-Yishay, Y., & Diller, L. (1978–1983). Working approaches to remediation of cognitive deficits in brain damaged persons. New York, New York University Medical Center. *Rehabilitation Monographs Nos. 59–62*, 64, 66.

Ben-Yishay, Y., Piasetsky, E.B., & Rattock, J. (1987a). A systematic method for ameliorating disorders in basic attention. In M.J. Meier, A.L. Benton, & L. Diller (Eds.), *Neuropsychological rehabilitation* (pp. 165–181). New York: Guilford Press.

Ben-Yishay, Y., Silver, S., & Piasetsky, E. (1987b). Relationship between employability and vocational outcome after intensive holistic cognitive rehabilitation. *Journal of Head Trauma Rehabilitation*, *2*, 35–48.

Birbaumer, N., Elbert, T., Rockstroh, B., & Lutzenberger, W. (1986). Biofeedback of slow cortical potentials in attentional disorders. In W.C. McCallum, R. Zapolli, & F. Denoth (Eds.), Cerebral psychophysiology: Studies in event-related potentials. *Electroencephalography and Clinical Neurophysiology*, *38*(Suppl.), 440–442.

Cermak, L.S. (1975). Imagery as an aid to retrieval for Korsakoff patients. *Cortex*, *11*, 163–169.

Crovitz, H.F. (1979). Memory retraining in brain-damaged patients: The airplane list. *Cortex*, *15*, 131–134.

Crovitz, H.F., Harvey, M.T., & Horn, R.W. (1979). Problems in the acquisition of imagery mnemonics: Three brain-damaged cases. *Cortex*, *15*, 225–234.

Diller, L., & Weinberg, J. (1977). Hemi-inattention in rehabilitation: The evolution of a rational remediation program. In E.A. Weinstein & R.P. Friedland (Eds.), *Advances in Neurology*, *18*, 63–82.

Frazier, L.M. (1980). Biofeedback in coma rehabilitation: Case study. *American Journal of Clinical Biofeedback*, *3*, 148–154.

Fryer, L.J., & Haffey, W.J. (1987). Cognitive rehabilitation and community reintegration: Outcomes from two program models. *Journal of Head Trauma Rehabilitation*, *2*, 51–63.

Gasparrini, B., & Satz, P. (1979). A treatment for memory problems in left hemisphere CVA patients. *Journal of Clinical Neuropsychology*, *91*, 66–73.

Gianutsos, R., & Gianutsos, J. (1979). Rehabilitating the verbal recall of brain-injured patients by mnemonic training: An experimental demonstration using single-case methodology. *Journal of Clinical Neuropsychology*, *2*, 117–135.

Glasgow, R.E., Zeiss, R.A., Barrera, M. Jr., & Lewinsohn, P. (1977). Case study on remediating memory deficits in brain-damaged individuals. *Journal of Clinical Psychology*, *33*, 1049–1054.

Glisky, E., Schacter, D., & Tulving, E. (1986). Learning and retention of computer related vocabulary in memory-impaired patients: Method of vanishing cues. *Journal of Clinical and Experimental Neuropsychology*, *8*, 292–312.

Godfrey, H., & Knight R. (1985). Cognitive rehabilitation of memory functioning in amnesiac alcoholics. *Journal of Consulting and Clinical Psychology*, *43*, 555–557.

Goldberg, K., Gerstmann, L. J., & Mathis, S. (1982). Selective effects of cholinergic treatment on verbal memory in post-traumatic amnesia. *Journal of Clinical Neuropsychology*, *4*, 219–234.

Goldstein G., & Ruthven, L. (1983). *Rehabilitation of the brain-damaged adult.* New York: Plenum.

Jacobs, H. (1988). The Los Angeles head injury survey: Procedures and initial findings. *Archives of Physical Medicine and Rehabilitation*, *69*, 425–431.

Johns, D.F. (1978). *Clinical management of neurogenic communication disorders.* Boston: Little, Brown & Co.

Kewman, D.G., Seigerman, C., Kintner, H., Chu, S., Henson, D., & Reeder, C. (1985). Simulation training of psychomotor skills: Teaching the brain-injured to drive. *Rehabilitation Psychology*, *30*, 11–27.

Klöve, H. (1987). Activation, arousal and neuropsychological rehabilitation. *Journal of Clinical and Experimental Neuropsychology*, *9*, 297–309.

Kreutzer, J., Wehman, P., & Morton, M. (1988). Supported employment and compensatory strategies for enhancing vocational outcome following traumatic brain injury. *Brain Injury*, *2*, 205–223.

LeWinn, E.B., & Dimancescu, M.D. (1978). Environmental deprivation and enrichment in coma. *The Lancet*, *2*, 156–157.

Lewinsohn, P.M., Danaher, B.G., & Kikel, D. (1977). Visual imagery as a mnemonic aid for brain-injured persons. *Journal of Consulting and Clinical Psychology*, *45*, 717–723.

Lezak, M.D. (1978). Living with the characterologically altered brain-injured patient. *Journal of Clinical Psychiatry*, *39*, 592–598.

Lezak, M.D. (1983). *Neuropsychological assessment.* New York: Oxford University Press.

Lezak, M.D. (1987). Relationships between personality disorders, social disturbances, and physical disability following traumatic brain injury. *Journal of Head Trauma Rehabilitation*, *2*, 57–59.

Lynch, J.J. (1978). The simple act of touching. *Nursing*, *8*, 32.

Malec, J., Jones, R., Rao, N., & Stubbs, K. (1984). Video game practice effects on sustained attention in patients with craniocerebral trauma. *Cognitive Rehabilitation*, *2*, 18–23.

Mateer, C.A., & Sohlberg, M.M. (1988). A paradigm shift in memory rehabilitation. In H. Whitaker (Ed.), *Neuropsychological studies of nonfocal brain damage: Dementia and trauma.* New York: Springer-Verlag.

Mateer, C.A., & Sohlberg, M.M. (1989). Vocational outcomes following post-acute rehabilitation. Bulletin of the Center for Cognitive Rehabilitation. Puyallup, Washington: Good Samaritan Hospital.

McLean, A. Jr., Stanton, K.M., & Cardenas, D.D. (1987). Memory training combined with the use of and physostigmine. *Brain Injury*, *1*, 145–159.

Niemann, H. (1989). *Retraining of attention in head injured individuals.* Unpublished doctoral dissertation, University of Victoria, Victoria, British Columbia, Canada.

Parente, R., & Anderson, J.K. (1983). Techniques for improving cognitive rehabilitation: Teaching organizational and encoding skills. *Cognitive Rehabilitation*, *1*, 20–22.

Ponsford, J.L., & Kinsella, G. (1988). *Journal of Clinical and Experimental Neuropsychology*, *10*, 693–708.

Posner, M.I. (1975). Psychobiology of attention. In M.S. Gazzeniga & C. Blakemore (Eds.), *Handbook of psychology* (pp. 441–480). New York, London: Academic Press.

Prigatano, G. (1986). *Neuropsychological rehabilitation after brain injury*. Baltimore: Johns Hopkins University Press.

Prigatano, G., Fordyce, D., Zeiner, H., Roueche, J., Pepping, M., & Wood, B. (1984). Neuropsychological rehabilitation after closed head injury in young adults. *Journal of Neurology, Neurosurgery, and Neuropsychiatry*, *47*, 505–513.

Rappaport, M., Hall, K.M., Hopkins, K., & Belleza, T. (1982). Disability rating scale for severe head trauma: Coma to community. *Archives of Physical Medicine and Rehabilitation*, *63*, 118–123.

Schacter, D., Rich, S., & Stamp, A. (1985). Remediation of memory disorders: Experimental evaluation of the spaced-retrieval technique. *Journal of Clinical and Experimental Neuropsychology*, *7*, 79–96.

Sohlberg, M.M., & Brock, M. (1985). Taking the final step: The importance of post-medical cognitive rehabilitation. *Cognitive Rehabilitation*, *3*, 10–14.

Sohlberg, M.M., & Mateer, C.A. (1987). Effectiveness of an attention-training program. *Journal of Clinical and Experimental Neuropsychology*, *9*, 117–130.

Sohlberg, M.M., & Mateer, C.A. (1989a). *Introduction to cognitive rehabilitation: Theory and practice*. New York: Guilford Press.

Sohlberg, M.M., & Mateer, C.A. (1989b). Training use of compensatory memory books: A three stage behavioral approach. *Journal of Clinical and Experimental Neuropsychology*, *11*, 871–891.

Sohlberg, M.M., & Mateer, C.A. (1990). Evaluation and treatment of communication skills. In J.S. Kreutzer & P. Lehman (Eds.), *Community integration following traumatic brain injury* (pp. 67–83). Baltimore: Paul H. Brookes Publishing Co.

Sturm, W., Dahmen, W., Hartje, W., & Willmes, K. (1983). Ergebnisse eines trainingsprogramms zur verbesserung der visuellen auffassungsschnelligkeit und konzentrationsfahigkeit bei hirngeschadigten [Results of a program for the training of perceptual speed and attention in brain damaged patients]. *Archiv fur Psychiatrie und Nervenkrankheiten* [Archives of Psychiatry and Neurological Sciences], *233*, 9–22.

Stuss, D.T., & Benson, D.F. (1986). *The frontal lobes*. New York: Raven Press.

van Zomeren, A.H., Brouwer, W.H., & Deelman, B.G. (1984). Attentional deficits: The riddles of selectivity, speed, and alertness. In N. Brooks (Ed.), *Closed head injury. Psychological, social, and family consequences* (pp. 74–107). New York: Oxford University Press.

Weber (1990). A practical clinical approach to understanding and treating attentional problems. *Journal of Head Trauma Rehabilitation*, *5*, 73–85.

Weinberg, J., Diller, L., Gordon, W.A., Gerstman, L.J., Liebermann, A., Lakin, P., Hodges, G., & Ezrachi, O. (1977). Visual scanning training effect on reading-related tasks in acquired right-brain damage. *Archives of Physical Medicine and Rehabilitation*, *58*, 479–486.

Weinberg, J., Diller, L., Gordon, W.A., Gerstman, L.J., Liebermann, A., Lakin, P., Hodges, G., & Esrachi, O. (1979). Training sensory awareness and spatial organization in people with right brain damage. *Archives of Physical Medicine and Rehabilitation*, *60*, 491–496.

Wilson, B. (1981). Teaching a patient to remember people's names after removal of a left temporal tumor. *Behavioral Psychotherapy*, *9*, 338–344.

Wilson, B. (1982). Success and failure in memory training following a cerebral vascular accident. *Cortex*, *18*, 581–594.

Wilson, B. (1987). *Rehabilitation of memory*. London: Guilford Press.

Wilson, B., & Moffat, N. (Eds.) (1984). *Clinical management of memory problems*. Rockville, MD: Aspen.

Wood, R.L. (1986). Rehabilitation of patients with disorders of attention. *Journal of Head Trauma Rehabilitation*, *1*, 43–53.

Wood, R.L. (1987). *Brain injury rehabilitation: A neurobehavioral approach*. Rockville, MD: Aspen.

Wood, R.L. (1989). *Clinical model for sensory stimulation for patients in coma and PVS*. Paper presented at the Santa Clara Valley Medical Center Twelfth Annual Conference, San Jose, CA.

Wood, R.L.I., & Fussey, I. (1987). Computer-based cognitive retraining: A controlled study. *International Disability Studies*, *9*, 149–153.

10
Developing Legislation and the Concept of Disability

RONALD D. KAPLAN

In the preceding chapters, both the strengths and weaknesses of neuropsychological methods and the limits of our current knowledge have been explicated. Our approach to the field has been selective rather than inclusive, issue-oriented rather than a practical how-to approach. This chapter provides a case illustration of the consequences when legislation that governs the area of personal injury compensation does not use up-to-date concepts and proposes a disability assessment model that encompasses neuropsychological and other approaches.

Outdated Concepts and Their Implications: The Case of No Fault Automobile Insurance in Ontario

Neuropsychological and other knowledge can be of maximum use only if the model of deficit and disability held by members of the legal and health professions is shared. When new legislation is being developed, close cooperation between legal and health professions is essential so that the legislative effort is informed by developments in the health and psychological sciences. Recent developments in Automobile Insurance in Ontario (Ontario Motorists, Protection Plan, 1990) will be cited to illustrate the underlying conceptual framework that informed the new law and the role of health professions in the development of the legislation.

The Tort System with No Fault Add On in Ontario

Automobile accident injury compensation was dispensed in Ontario until June 22, 1990 by the tort system with a No Fault Add On. All individuals had access to the courts to sue for pecuniary (financial) and nonpecuniary or general damages such as pain and suffering and loss of enjoyment of life, and family members could be recompensed for both pecuniary losses and general damages. In 1972 a No Fault weekly income and rehabilitation benefits component was added to automobile insurance providing as of 1978 $140.00 (Canadian) per week for total disability for individuals who were employed at the time of the accident, and up to $25,000 (Canadian) for necessary rehabilitation as recommended by a physician. There were no limitations on the right to a lawsuit and all types of injuries and disabilities were treated equally before the law.

History of the Debate on Automobile Insurance in Ontario

In recent years the Ontario government has been under pressure to make fundamental changes the system in part because of the costs of the system and perceived inadequacy of rates.

I will briefly outline the recent history of automobile insurance studies in Ontario to illustrate the underlying concepts of injury and disability. The Select Committee on Company Law (SCCL) in 1978 recommended a *threshold no fault system*. A threshold usually is a set of statements describing the type of injury that must be demonstrated before access to the courts is allowed. The SCCL threshold proposal based access to courts on suffering (a) "serious and permanent injury resulting in substantial and medically demonstrable impairment affecting the resumption of customary activities, (b) permanent loss of important bodily functions, or (c) significant permanent scarring or disfigurement." A number of phrases in this statement were later brought forward in the Ontario Motorist Protection Plan, the law in Ontario as of June 22, 1990. Some of the key concepts are "serious," "permanent," "injury," "medically demonstrable," "impairment," and "important bodily functions."

A perceived world-wide crisis in liability insurance in 1985–1986 probably triggered the Ontario government's latest series of actions. A task force appointed by the Ministry of Community and Commercial Relations in Ontario proposed a *pure No Fault* plan providing no access to third-party fault-based relief (i.e., the courts) but also suggested the possibility of an alternative threshold No Fault plan such as the one in Michigan. The Michigan threshold No Fault Plan has been a pivotal model in the recent Ontario debates. It requires *serious impairment of bodily function* before an injured person can sue on a fault basis for noneconomic loss, pain, suffering, loss of enjoyment of life, and so on. Under a threshold plan first-party No Fault benefits are provided to all accident victims, while tort actions are only allowed above the threshold.

As one step in the process, an Inquiry into Motor Vehicle Accident Compensation in Ontario was commissioned under an experienced jurist, Mr. Justice Coulter Osborne of the Supreme Court of Ontario, and a lengthy two-volume report was prepared in 1988 (Osborne, 1988). There was an extensive process of consultation and research, resulting in a recommendation to preserve the full right of access to the courts but with enhanced (no fault) weekly income and rehabilitation benefits.

Justice Osborne extensively examined methods of limiting lawsuits, particularly threshold systems. The Commission rejected this approach as relatively inefficient and unnecessarily arbitrary. Justice Osborne argued, "Apart from costs, thresholds seem to be designed to keep less serious cases out of court or to allow more serious cases into court . . . aside from reduced transaction costs, what is saved is that general damages are not paid in those cases which fail to meet the threshold."

In the late 1960s to mid-1970s, eighteen U.S. states opted for Threshold No Fault plans to compensate automobile accident victims. However, no new plans have been put in place in the last decades. Two states, Pennsylvania and Nevada, have abolished their threshold system and returned to unrestricted access to the court system. One state has a monetary threshold, 4 states have exclusively verbal thresholds, and 11 states have a combination of monetary and verbal thresholds.

Verbal thresholds have the advantage of better defining and establishing the kind of injury for which a victim might be able to sue for loss. But the general language that a verbal threshold must inevitably be couched in contains its own seeds of difficulty. Words such as "serious," "significant," or "permanent" are not always easy to apply individually and even more difficult to apply in combination.

The Ontario government was not satisfied with Judge Osborne's rejection of a Threshold No Fault Plan and in March 1989 required the Ontario Automobile Insurance Board (AIB) (1989) to examine two alternative verbal thresholds and a choice system.[1]

The AIB concluded that proposed enhanced No Fault benefits: particularly the disability income benefits, rehabilitation, and long-term care benefits represented a substantial improvement over current Ontario No Fault benefit levels ($140 vs. $600 weekly income, $25,000 vs. $500,000 for rehabilitation). However, any insurance premium savings to drivers would occur only by a reduction in the benefit levels available under the current compensation system, which combines recovery in tort with add on No Fault benefits. The AIB concluded that the threshold options presented for study (based on New York and Michigan) "are capable of denying recovery in respect of serious injuries" (p. 2–3). The AIB asserted that "nonpecuniary losses represent real losses. No evidence was presented to the Board that would establish such losses are unworthy of compensation" (p. 3).

---

[1] The author of this chapter communicated extensively with Mr. Justice Osborne regarding the impact of verbal thresholds on brain-injured and other accident victims and presented an extensive brief to the Automobile Insurance Board regarding these same issues.

The AIB's conclusion is of great relevance to neuropsychologists. "Threshold systems affect in a disproportionate manner moderately injured persons with soft tissue injuries, minor to moderate head injuries, emotional trauma, and other injuries that are not permanent or objectively verifiable. Thresholds that specifically require injuries be objectively manifested or permanent require very serious analysis as their only merit is that they save costs" (p. 3).

In the body of their report, the AIB presented evidence by health professionals including neuropsychologists. The Board noted that the Michigan threshold is the most restrictive threshold in the United States applying the phrase "serious impairment of bodily function." "The Michigan threshold precludes recovery not only from minor and transient injuries but also serious injuries requiring hospitalization, operations, chronic pain, several months absence from work and restrictions of an individual's previous employment, household and recreational activities. Witnesses confirmed that soft tissue injuries, psychological injuries, and other injuries, not objectively manifested tend to cause difficulties" (p. 50). The author of this chapter is quoted as rejecting a "biomechanical or lesion approach to injury which attempts to measure tissue damage rather than dysfunction or disability" (p. 54).

The next stage in the process of development of new automobile legislation in Ontario was the tabling in the legislature on September 19, 1989 of Bill 68, the Ontario Motorist Protection Plan (OMPP). Bill 68 is essentially a threshold No Fault plan with an extremely steep or high threshold, tougher than the Michigan Threshold. Other than death and permanent serious disfigurement, an individual can have access to the courts for both financial and general damages only if they "sustained permanent serious impairment of an important bodily function caused by continuing injury of a physical nature." A package of weekly income benefits, rehabilitation, and long-term care benefits was included. The regulations specifying the No Fault benefits provided comprehensive access to psychologists as disability determiners, prescribers of services, and health care providers. The lobbying around Bill 68 by health and mental health professions, unions, and disability organizations was intensive. This lobbying exercise was aimed in large part toward educating those in positions of authority about the implications of this bill for brain-injured and psychologically dysfunctional individuals.

A major overriding principle that has been articulated is that the tort system (with all its costs and inefficiencies) is a system that allows individualized compensation through the integrated evaluation of the individual with the most modern methods and approaches in medicine, psychology, and the rehabilitation sciences. It has been argued that the court system is the best we have for the evolution of values and for the full application of new concepts regarding loss, injury, and disability.

Unfettered access to the courts allows new ideas and empirical knowledge to be applied to every type of injury.

The most fundamental argument we have made as members of the Ontario Psychological Association[2] and as one of several organizational members of a Mental Health Coalition is that the verbal threshold in the Ontario law would selectively exclude from the courts individuals with serious suffering and disability who could not demonstrate a continuing detectable physical cause. Psychological disorders, including neuropsychological disorders, are more likely to fail to meet the verbal threshold as they often are not accompanied by continually detectable physical lesions. The nature of injury to the brain and its various behavioral rather than physical markers has been explained to legislators. The distinction between injuries that are objectively manifested on x rays and those injuries that are not have been fundamental concepts determining the direction of automobile legislation. It has become clear that the ability of lay people such as legislators to understand the importance of behavioral observations and behavioral disorders is crucial in order that brain-injured individuals will not have their rights removed. What has been achieved, on a case by case basis, through education and legal rulings painstakeningly through the years, can be lost with the stroke of a pen. Unfortunately, what judges and lawyers have learned through interaction with behavioral scientists such as neuropsychologists is difficult to present to the citizens, bureaucrats, and members of the legislator in a brief time without close case study, especially when there are strong political/fiscal pressures and a belief that psychological disorders are not as real as physical disorders.

One point of view is that the requirement that an impaired bodily function be shown to derive from a physical injury is a cynical response by the insurance industry against the successes of the last decades in compensating a wide variety of psychological and neuropsychological disorders produced by accidents. The stigma attached to the "mentally ill," the belief that these disorders are not real or are less deserving than injuries that involve broken bones or lacerated organs, is widely held. Regressive attitudes are given legitimacy in Ontario's new legislation. The high likelihood the OMPP will remove rights selectively from the "psychologically injured" is tied closely to its use of an outdated conceptual framework. The legislation may yet founder in the courts because of its discriminatory nature and use of scientifically unacceptable language. The legislation rests on mind/body dualism or the functional/organic distinction. As stated by the DSM IV Organic Disorders Working group of the American Psychiatric Association (Tucker, Papkin, Caine,

---

[2] The author is a member of the Ontario Psychological Association Task Force on No Fault Insurance.

Folstein & Grant, 1990), "... accumulating knowledge about the numerous biological and physiological factors that contribute to a wide variety of traditionally 'nonorganic' mental disorders has now made the organic-nonorganic dichotomy obsolete." (p. 722) (DSM IV will replace part of the organic category with "cognitive impairment disorders.")

This breakdown of an older way to categorize behavioral disorders is understood in neuropsychology. However, a more telling example of the anachronistic nature of the functional versus organic distinction derives from a disorder traditionally viewed as "purely psychological"—post-traumatic stress syndrome. Van der Kolk (1988) summarizes a wide variety of biological findings in this common sequela of accidents. He finds that "physiological changes in fact account for most posttraumatic symptomatology: (a) the tendency to react to relatively minor stimuli as if there were a recurrence of the trauma: startle reactions and irritability, which interfere with an adequate cognitive assessment of current events and result in fight/flight/freeze reactions, (b) visual and motoric reliving experiences: nightmares, flashbacks, and behavioral reenactments generally are preceded by physiological arousal which activates long-term potentiated memory pathways, (c) persistent hyperarousal also can account for the avoidance and escape behavior characteristic of people with post traumatic stress disorder (PTSD), psychologically as a defense, physiologically as downregulation of receptors in response to over stimulation, and (d) compulsive reexposure to circumstances reminiscent of the trauma may be related to both the neophobia seen in previously traumatized animals under stress and to the conditioned endogenous opioid release seen in traumatized animals and humans." (p. 275).

The OMPP, with its verbal threshold restricting the right to sue, and thus limiting comprehensive compensation only to those with severe permanent impairment of an important bodily function caused by continuing injury of a physical nature, attempts to make an end run around the current openness of the courts to individuals with a wide variety of dysfunctional syndromes. A law that enshrines an obsolete conceptual model results in unfairness to people with certain types of problems and rules out the application of certain scientific disciplines. However, if clinicians and scientists are up to date in their reports and testimony, the law must ultimately yield to the findings and the concepts of the health and behavioral sciences.

The verbal threshold in the OMPP potentially limits the role of neuropsychologists by restricting access to the courts of a large percentage of their patients. Pressure is placed to detect brain lesions rather than to describe dysfunction. This is the converse of the situation many neuropsychologists now face in court when their expertise is scrutinized and they are restricted to testify about behavior, not about the brain basis of altered behavior. The OMPP would make it extremely unlikely that one could present psychological syndromes unless they can be related to a physically detectable lesion in some part of the body or they are a psychological reaction to other physical injuries.

This lobbying experience demonstrates that for the future of our profession and our patients it is not sufficient to argue the validity of our professional expertise in individual cases but that we must remain ever attentive to developments in legislation that might prevent our own expertise from being considered and our patients from being treated equally before the courts.

The Disability Assessment Model

Juse as the law must keep up with the sciences, neuropsychological/legal assessments must meet the demands of the courts for relevance and comprehensiveness. We have argued that the traditional critique of clinical prediction is based on attacking a strawman. Most studies critical of neuropsychology present only test scores for interpretation (see chapter 1). Our actual approach to clients is neither so narrow as the critics suggest nor as comprehensive as they should become.

While a neuropsychological evaluation provides a far more rigorous and objective perspective on a patient's level of functioning that either a standard clinical interview or mental status examination, real world tasks provide an opportunity for more ecologically valid assessment of disability. However, when patients have problems performing real world tasks, it is not always easy to discern the nature of the underlying deficit. The challenge is to marry neuropsychological tests, which allow dissection of attention, input and recall, and recognition, monitoring abilities, and so on, with patient and other reports and real world performance.

Neuropsychological findings are not considered by the courts in isolation. These findings must necessarily be interpreted in the life context of the person who is seeking compensation for brain dysfunction or for the individual whose competence is being evaluated with respect to an important life role. In question might be the individual's ability to administer funds, instruct counsel, and/or care for themselves. Following from the comments above, this chapter will propose a model wherein neuropsychological assessment is viewed as one component of an overall disability assessment process.

Disability Model

Neuropsychological practitioners frame their role narrowly or broadly depending on their training, philosophical orientation, and the context in which they work; but the legal system requires inference that is broad and detailed, possibly beyond the neuropsychologist's comfort level with their own methodology. This situation may lead to neuropsychologists widening their areas, adopting new methods and expertise, or alternatively working closely with other disciplines that have unique methods and knowledge base.

The *disability assessment model*[3] is one of several possible ways of conceptualizing the many different issues that arise in a personal injury/competency case. This model is applicable across disciplines, types of injuries, or dysfunctions. The thrust of the model is to emphasize both the sequence of events and the complexity and level of analysis of the problems that follow from injury. It is a departure from a strictly biomechanical, lesion, or physical injury approach to medicolegal assessment and incorporates the application of a wide variety of assessment methods, disciplines, and approaches.

According to Dr. Norman White (1988) "between the initial accident event and the eventual disability there is a regular causal sequence, the logic of which is crucial to the understanding of how to manage these problems. There are four steps in the sequence of events: *cause*, *lesion*, *syndrome* and *disability*. The causal factor, usually a collision, interacts with the physical characteristics of the person to produce damage which is referred to as a 'lesion.' The lesion interacts with the person's emotional/behavioural characteristics to produce a 'syndrome.' A syndrome consists of deficits, dysfunctions, distresses and symptoms. A syndrome interacts with a person's environment to produce the actual disability" (p. 460).

Neuropsychology attempts primarily but not exclusively to assess, describe, and analyze the syndrome: a constellation of cognitive, motor, and emotional deficits. Based on test findings and other information the neuropsychologist makes inferences about the types of disabilities with which a person will present in various environments. However, the question arises whether the tools and methods that we use for characterizing a syndrome, analyzing stages of information processing, or localizing a lesion are also applicable for assessing a disability. We may be good at naming syndromes and inferring the lesions that underlie them. We do this on the basis of history, interview, neuropsychological studies, and the results of other investigations that are carried out in a clinical setting. When we are asked to comment on someone's disability we often make the best guess about their home/work environment.

White and others are critical of this process of inferring disability from clinical investigations alone. "In the overwhelming majority of less obvious cases, however, neither the guess nor extrapolation is of much value if the intention is to arrive at a precise assessment for either rehabilitation or compensation reasons. Physicians seldom possess the conceptual and technical tools because they are not trained to conduct

---

[3] The work of Professor Norman White of McMaster University is cited heavily in this section.

this kind of assessment properly. The data necessary for it are different from clinical data and they must be interpreted using a different kind of logic. The data gathering must be done largely in the person's real world and involves technical procedures which are quite unfamiliar in most clinics" (White, 1988, p. 461).

The thrust of White's criticism of medical assessment and diagnosis is that the tools are rather indirect or inappropriate for making precise statements about function in work, social, and avocational settings. Are neuropsychological tools more relevant for precise disability statements? In an era when inference about lesions is less important in professional neuropsychology, conclusions about disability have become more important and there is a growing concern about the validity of neuropsychological measures for day-to-day functioning of the patient. The disability model raises the possibility that neuropsychological assessment has built-in limitations. In the clinical setting, it may be wrong in principle to make precise statements about real world disability! Recent neuropsychological/rehabilitation literature has also argued for a more broad-based conceptual model of assessment and rehabilitation. Diller and Gordon (1981) propose the concept of *rehabilitation diagnosis*. They distinguish between *impairment*, which is a structural modification of a person that alters function and a *disability*, a limitation or inability to perform expected roles or tasks in the social environment.

"The clinical neuropsychologist is concerned with the diagnosis and description of cognitive impairments and their relationship to parameters of brain damage while rehabilitation poses the issue of how descriptions of impairments impact the person's skills, environment, activity patterns, and statuses. To achieve maximum effectiveness in a rehabilitation setting the clinical neuropsychologist must relate their findings to these aspects of functioning" (p. 708).

They also make the point that the rehabilitation environment is a real life laboratory for assessment of the patient. In our own work we conceptualize the rehabilitation trial as a component of the assessment process. Using this model, the initial assessment information describes a number of impairments and probable disabilities. The rehabilitation trial attempts to modify the patient's impairments and or environment, and concludes with a more precise evaluation regarding which disabilities will persist and affect the person in important life spheres.

Hart and Hayden (1986) suggest the need for test results that can predict the effects of dysfunction in activities of daily living, educational, and vocational arenas. They criticize neuropsychological tests and test batteries for lack of "ecological validity," a concept developed by Brunswick. Brunswick used the concept to refer to the validity of generalizing from the results of one or a set of experiments to other experiments. Ecological validity derives from a scientific literature where a performance/behavior is measured in a highly controlled situation. Hart and Hayden (1986) use the concept more broadly to apply to success or failure of intervention in enhancing everyday function. Their goal is to enhance the "ecological validity" of both evaluation and rehabilitation procedures. What is central to their argument are notions of predictability from the laboratory to specific real world situations.

This position leads to a critique of particular aspects of the testing situation that have historically been its strengths: standardization of procedures and high level of control of stimulus and response. Brain-injured patients have underlying deficits in information processing such that in a highly structured one-to-one testing situation their performance may not reflect performance in a naturalistic environment where the information load, time pressures, and stressors are uncontrolled. Structured one-to-one testing tends to minimize or exclude distraction and time-sharing demands. Many jobs, however, provide uncontrolled pressure and high information processing demands. Testing may at times provide relatively low information processing demands.

On the other hand, the strategies that patients have developed to deal with their impairments in the real world may not be applied in the testing situation and thus testing many underestimate real life performance. Prigatano, Pepping, and Klonoff (1986) reiterated that the nature of testing, which minimizes distraction and emphasizes routine, orderliness, structure, and direction, may minimize the impact of many brain-related deficits. "Problems with attention and concentration may not be as evident in their scope or severity when viewed through the filter of a quiet testing room set of questions" (p. 137). "Test procedures do not adequately evaluate a series of cognitive behaviors that become more pronounced in a low structured environment. These include disorders of communication (e.g., tangentiality, talkativeness, and disinhibition) and disorders of judgment and perception (e.g., misinterpretation of the actions or intentions of others, unrealistic self-appraisal" (Prigatano et al., p. 163). Also, some forms of intelligence are not tapped in the testing situation: social and work abilities, motivation, and susceptibility to fatigue may be more difficult to monitor (p. 137). There is also a tendency in neuropsychology to isolate cognitive and affective domains that are integrated in real world behavior. A simlar critique has also been made by a number of authors who refer to the particular difficulties neuropsychologists have in assessing frontal lobe deficits. Testing may minimize the demand for initiative, spontaneity, planning, and self-monitoring.

From the Rehab Setting to the Neuropsychological/ Legal Evaluation

The rehabilitation setting, especially inpatient, day programs, and vocational rehabilitation centers, provide an opportunity to integrate fully clinical neuropsychological findings in overall disability and rehabilitation diagnosis. However, neuropsychological/legal assessments often take place in outpatient settings, typically a private office without access to the full interdisciplinary resources of a rehabilitation center. How than can a neuropsychologist best contribute to the overall disability assessment? Probably the most useful model is the interdisciplinary team, whether institutionally or independently based, with one health professional usually coordinating the various assessment components and treatment or rehabilitation trials.

There are both positive and negative aspects to working with such an interdisciplinary team. On the positive side the neuropsychologist has available a range of other assessment skills and knowledge and can answer questions beyond the neuropsychological assessment alone. On the negative side, working with interdisciplinary tesms is time consuming and expensive, requires that tesm members have a common language and appreciate each other's methods and conceptual frameworks, and requires the development of more objective quantifiable rather than anecdotal observational methods. A number of neuropsychologists have suggested the use of some of the commonly available behavioral rating scales that can be completed in work or training settings, schools, in the home, or in artificially designed environments. The complex cognitive challenges that are provided in rehabilitation or vocational settings can be used in the overall disability assessment.

One real life testing situation (see Reed, 1987) is a simulated shopping environment.[4] We have applied this approach in the community. In their home the client makes up a grocery list of about 20 items and then drives/is taken to a grocery store with which they are not familiar (they may have a compensatory pattern in their normal store). At the store the observer adds items to the list. They are given specific tasks such as to evaluate the relative cost per pound of boneless chicken versus chicken parts. Most stores are high stimulus environments that require the capacity for careful visual search. Patients have to organizre or reorganize their list and develop an approach to find the items on the list. The observer ascertains whether patients have judgment about the nutritional value of food, if they can find items on their own, and if can they handle crowds. We observe the degree of emotional arousal, distress, or confusion. Completion of the list and time are noted.

This task was developed by Reed (1987) for dementing elderly but can be applied by a neuropsychologist or other health professional for brain injury patients in a naturalistic environment. The method provides information about a number of impairments: sensory problems, scanning and perceptual difficulty, motor or gait problems, planning and sequencing abilities, information processing limits, and judgment and calculation

[4] The suggestions regarding the application of this approach by Mr. Terry Pearce, M.S.W., are appreciated.

abilities. One can also observe emotional reactivity, which is often seen by others as the primary problem of patients whose neuropsychological syndromes are not well understood. Some patients have also developed phobic responses to such high stress environments and are reluctant to leave their homes to shop.

The application of neuropsychological concepts and methods to resolution of competency and disability issues in the courts is one of the major growth areas in the health/legal interface. The legal arena should motivate us to be critical and reflective and to improve on knowledge and approaches. We are optimistic for the positive impact on neuropsychology. We hope, as well, that advances in neuropsychology will have a positive influence on the development of legislation and the enlightened disposition of those cases in which compentency comes into question.

References

Diller, L., & Gordon W. (1981). Rehabilitation and clinical neuropsychology. In S. Filskov & T. Boll (Eds.), *Handbook of clinical neuropsychology* (Vol. I, pp. 702–733). Toronto: John Wiley and Sons, Inc.

Hart, T., & Hayden, M.D. (1986). The ecological validity of neuropsychological assessment and remediation. In B. Uzzel & Y. Gross (Eds.), *Clinical neuropsychology of intervention* (pp. 21–50). Boston: Martinus Nijhoff Publishing.

Honourable Mr. Justice Coulter A. Osborne: Supreme Court of Ontario, Commissioner (1988). *Report of inquiry into motor vehicle accident compensation in Ontario* (Vols. I and II). Toronto: Queen's Printer for Ontario.

Ontario Automobile Insurance Board (1989). An examination of threshold no fault and choice no fault systems of privately delivered authomobile insurance: *Report to the Lieutenant Governor in Council.* Toronto: Queens Printer for Ontario.

Ontario Motorist Protection Plan (1990). Toronto: Queens Printer for Ontario.

Prigatano, G., Pepping, M., & Klonoff, P. (1986). Cognitive, personality, and psychosocial factors in the neuropsychological assessment of brain-injured patients. In B. Uzzell & Y. Gross (Eds.), *Clinical neuropsychology of intervention* (pp. 135–166). Boston: Martinus Nijhoff Publishing.

Reed, D.E. (1987) Neuropsychological assessment of memory in the elderly. *Canadian Journal of Psychology*, *41*, 158–174.

Tucker, G., Papkin M., Caine, E., Folstein, M., & Grant, I. (1990). Reorganizing the "organic" disorders. *Hospital and Community Psychiatry*, *41*, 722–724.

Van der Kolk, B.A. (1988). The trauma spectrum: The interaction of biological and social events in the genesis of the trauma response. *Journal of Traumatic Stress*, *1*, 273–290.

White, N.F. (1988). The function of determine in motor vehicle accident compensation schemes. In C. Osborne (Ed.), *Report of inquiry into motor vehicle accident compensation in Ontario* (pp. 436–463). Toronto: Queen's Printer for Ontario.

Author Index

C

N

O

P

Subject Index

MIX
Papier aus verantwortungsvollen Quellen
Paper from responsible sources
FSC® C105338
FSC
www.fsc.org

If you have any concerns about our products,
you can contact us on
ProductSafety@springernature.com

In case Publisher is established outside the EU,
the EU authorized representative is:
Springer Nature Customer Service Center GmbH
Europaplatz 3, 69115 Heidelberg, Germany

Printed by Libri Plureos GmbH
in Hamburg, Germany